Armies and Societies in Southeast Asia

ARMIES AND SOCIETIES IN SOUTHEAST ASIA

Edited by

Volker Grabowsky and Frederik Rettig

Hamburgische Wissenschaftliche Stiftung

Silkworm Books

ISBN 978-616-215-154-5

First edition published in 2019 by
Silkworm Books
430/58 M. 7, T. Mae Hia, Chiang Mai 50100, Thailand
info@silkwormbooks.com
http://www.silkwormbooks.com

Typeset in Garamond Premier Pro 11.5 pt. by Silk Type

Printed and bound in Thailand by O. S. Printing House, Bangkok

5 4 3 2 1

Contents

Figures

Maps

Tables

Abbreviations and Acronyms

ISDV	Indische Sociaal-Democratische Vereeniging (Indies Social Democratic Association)
ABRI	Angkatan Bersenjata Republik Indonesia (Republic of Indonesia Armed Forces)
AFP	Armed Forces of the Philippines
AFPFL	Anti-Fascist People's Freedom League
APRIS	Angkatan Perang Republik Indonesia Serikat (Federal army)
ASEAN	Association of Southeast Asian Nations
BAYAN	Bagong Alyansang Makabayan (New Nationalist Alliance)
BDA	Burma Defence Army
BIA	Burma Independence Army
BMP	Bukluran ng Manggagawang Pilipino
BNA	Burma National Army (Bama Tatmadaw)
CAFGU	Civilian Armed Forces Geographical Unit
CAOM	Centre des Archives d'Outre-Mer

CATI	Comité d'Assistance aux Travailleurs Indochinois (Assistance Committee for Indochinese Workers)
CAZ	Commissariaat van Ambonezenzorg (Directorate of Ambonese Care)
CGT	Confédération Générale du Travail (General Confederation of Labour)
CIA	Central Intelligence Agency
CPP	Communist Party of the Philippines
CPP-NPA	Communist Party of the Philippines-New People's Army
CS	Chunlasakkarat (Cūḷasakarāja)
CSIS	Center for Strategic and International Studies
CVO	Civilian Voluntary Organization
DALO	Democratic Alliance of Labor Organizations
DIWA	Democratic and Independent Workers Association
DPR	Dewan Perwakilan Rakyat (People's Representative Council)
F-ABRI	Fraksi ABRI (ABRI faction), see: ABRI
GDDI	General Directorate for Defense Industry
GDP	Gross Domestic Product
GG	Governor-General
GGI	Governement Général de l'Indochine (General Government of Indochina)
ICG	International Crisis Group
ICMI	Indonesian Association of Muslim Intellectuals
ICP	Indochina Communist Party
INA	Indian National Army
KL	Koninklijke Landmacht (Royal Army)
KMCM	Khlong Rüang Mangthra Rop Chiang Mai (Mangthra's War against Chiang Mai)
KMT	Kuomintang Army
KNIL	Koninklijk Nederlands-Indisch Leger (Royal Netherlands East-Indies Army)
LPA	Lao People's Army
LPDR	Lao People's Democratic Republic

LPRP	Lao People's Revolutionary Party
MADC	Mountain Area Development Corporation
MOI	Main d'Oeuvre Indochinoise (Indochinese Labor Force)
MPR	Majelis Permusyawaratan Rakyat (People's Consultative Assembly)
MTA	Mong Tai Army
NCO	Non-commissioned officer
NDF	National Democratic Front
NFSW	National Federation of Sugar Workers
NGO	Non-governmental Organization
NIT	Negara Indonesia Timur (Republik East-Indonesia)
NPA	New People's Army
PDI	Partai Demokrasi Indonesia (Indonesian Democratic Party)
PETA	Sukarela Tentera Pembela Tanah Air (Volunteer Army of Defenders of the Homeland)
PIM	Partai Indonesia Merdeka (Free Indonesia Party).
PKI	Partai Komunis Indonesia (Indonesian Communist Party)
PLA	People's Liberation Army (of China)
PPP	Partai Persatuan Pembangunan (United Development Party)
PR	Public Relations
RI	Republic Indonesia (Republic Indonesia)
RIS	Republic Indonesia Serikat (United States of Indonesia)
RLA	Royal Lao Army
RLG	Royal Lao Government
RMS	Republik Maluku Selatan (Republic of the South Moluccas)
RPA-ABB	Revolutionary Proletarian Army-Alex Boncayao Brigade
RPM-P	Rebolusyonaryong Partidong Manggagawa-Pilipinas
RS	Resident Superior
RTC	Ronde Tafel Conferentie (Round Table Conference)
SDAP	Sociaal-Democratische Arbeiderspartij (Social Democratic Workers' Party)
SHAN	Shan Herald Agency for News
SHRF	Shan Human Rights Foundation

SI	Sarekat Islam (Islamic Union)
SSA	Shan State Army
SSA-N	SSA-North, *see*: SSA
SSA-S	SSA-South, *see*: SSA
SSNA	Shan State National Army
SUA	Shan United Army
SURA	Shan United Revolution Army
SWAN	Shan Woman's Action Network
TGPF	Tim Gabungan Pencari Fakta
TNI	Tentara Nasional Indonesia (National Army of Indonesia)
UN	United Nations
US	United States
UWSA	United Wa State Army
VCP	Vietnam Communist Party
VNQDD	Viet Nam Quoc Dan Dang (Vietnamese Nationalist Party)
VPA	Vietnam People's Army
YM	Yunit milisya (militia unit)

Preface and Acknowledgments

The twelve chapters brought together in this volume eschew traditional military history's tendency of 'one bloody battle after bloody battle' in favor of a more multi-faceted and multi-layered approach, which is also distinct from the modern scientific approach to isolate variables at the nation-state level for comparative purposes. The volume's introduction and the two main sections of six chapters each hence aim to offer an original approach to the study of military-society relations in Southeast Asia over wide stretches of time and considerable ranges of terrain.

This longitudinal, comparative, and often highly contextualized approach invites Southeast Asianists and military historians to think about the social and political history of the region's armed forces differently from earlier attempts.[1] Historically grounded studies thus far have focused on particular eras, notably on ancient and early modern Southeast Asia, or on particular types of armies, such as Western and Asian colonial armies. Studies with a political science perspective have dealt with particular themes and the more immediate past, such as civil-military relations in post-independence Southeast Asia and Asia. In contrast, this volume provides a multi-disciplinary approach, with a multi-national team of authors bringing in their 'disciplinary' backgrounds, including history, sociology, social anthropology, political science, and philology. The introduction highlights the historical continuities and changes, but also seeks to identify points of comparison between countries, while not neglecting contingencies and context.

No book is without its challenges. The intellectual seeds for this volume were planted during and after a panel on 'Colonial Armies in Southeast

Asia' (organized by Professor Ian Brown and Tobias Rettig, then his doctoral student) that was held in July 2001 at the third conference of the European Association for Southeast Asian Studies (EuroSEAS) in London, at the School of Oriental and African Studies (SOAS). While the panel would lead to two major collective publications,[2] conversations with one of the conference contributors, Marie-Eve Blanc, led to the realization that a world beyond colonial armies remained to be explored. Marie-Eve roped in Gilles de Gantès, both of them at the time very closely tied to the research community and networks centered around (what was until 2012) the Institut de Recherche sur le Sud-Est Asiatique (IRSEA), which was backed by France's Centre National de la Recherche Scientifique (CNRS) and the University of Provence, and the Maison Asie-Pacifique in Marseilles, southern France. They managed to mobilize an amazingly creative number of scholars and also found a then new publisher, Les Indes savantes, who was willing to take on a volume with contributions in French and in English.

Regrettably, despite much effort and a lot of heartbreak and loss of face, the bilingual version of the book never made it from the proof stage (2008) to the printing press. When we tried for a relaunch of the project, now with Volker Grabowsky as co-editor, it became clear that a bilingual publication was not feasible and translations into English too expensive. We cannot express how grateful we are to the following for their contribution to the initial French-English project and the grace with which they handled the disappointment of not seeing their efforts rewarded:[3] Gilles de Gantès (lead author of the introduction, coordination, co-editor), Pheuiphanh Ngaosrivathana (Laos), Grégory Mikaelian (Cambodia), George Dutton (Vietnam), Roger Kershaw (Brunei), Guy Lubeigt (Burma), Pierre Le Roux (southern Thailand), Haude Le Guen (southern Philippines), Marie-Eve Blanc (Vietnam, coordination, co-editor), Xavier Huetz de Lemps (Philippines), Jean Baffie (Thailand), Jean Deuve (Laos), Jean-Louis Margolin (Singapore), and Tim Huxley (Singapore).

The contours of the new book began to take shape with an expression of interest by Silkworm Books and eventually twelve chapters, with Felice Noelle Rodriguez and Amporn Jirattikorn joining the project, and the following contributors from the initial project giving us more than the benefit of the doubt: Volker Grabowsky, Kees Van Dijk, Marie-Eve Blanc, Frederik Rettig, Joyce Lebra, Jun Honna, Henk Smeets, Carl Thayer, Geoffrey Gunn, and Rosanne Rutten. We are grateful for their continued support and trust.

Many persons and institutions have finally contributed to the difficult birth of this volume. We are in particular indebted to the Hamburgische Wissenschaftliche Stiftung (Hamburg Scientific Foundation), which has contributed a substantial subsidy to enable the publication of our volume.

We are grateful to Adrian Cheng Sai Pong for his help with the bibliographies in the earlier effort, and to Singapore Management University for providing funding for his research assistance. We thank our colleagues Gilles de Gantès and Marie-Eve Blanc for the admirable energy they put into the bilingual version of the first project, and the IRSEA's then director Bernard Sellato for his support.

Special thanks go to Lara Wolters who helped in the formatting of the volume, to Natthaly Natschke who skillfully made the index, and to Neil Huggett for the English proofreading of several chapters. Finally, we thank Joel Akins, our copy-editor, and Trasvin Jiittidecharak, our experienced publisher, for the patience and confidence they have shown to us.

Hamburg and Singapore, August 2019

Notes

1. Two very recent publications on warfare and armies in Southeast Asia reached us unfortunately too late to be acknowledged in our volume: Paul Chambers and Napisa Waitoolkiat (eds.), *Khaki Capital: The Political Economy of the Military in Southeast Asia* (Copenhagen: NIAS Press, 2017), and Michael W. Charney and Kathryn Wellen (eds.), *Warring Societies of Pre-colonial Southeast Asia: Local Cultures of Conflict Within a Regional Context* (Copenhagen: NIAS Press, 2018).

2. A special issue of *South East Asia Resarch* (Vol. 10, No. 3, November 2002) with five of the conference papers, and *Colonial Armies in Southeast Asia* (London: Routledge, 2006), edited by Karl A. Hack and Tobias Rettig.

3. Names follow the sequence of the chapters.

Introduction

Volker Grabowsky and Frederik Rettig

When twelve teenage boys of the Wild Boars (*mu pa*) football team and their young coach disappeared on June 23, 2018, in the Tham Luang Nang Non (Great Cave of the Sleeping Lady), a little-known cave in a remote corner of northernmost Thailand, few observers would have expected the unfolding of an exceptionally massive, and ultimately successful, rescue mission involving up to 10,000 people, 2,000 soldiers, 200 divers, and 100 government agencies, as well as vital contributions by individuals and countries from all over the world.[1] Prime Minister Prayuth Chan-ocha, the former commander-in-chief of the Royal Thai Army, who seized power in 2014, made two field visits. King Vajiralongkorn, who accended to the throne in 2016, also contributed materially to the relief effort. The real heroes, however, were the Thai Navy SEALs,[2] of whom a retired volunteer died tragically, and foreign cave diving experts.

The rescue mission not only drew attention to the karstic porosity of Doi Nang Non and the sponge-like quality of the Tham Luang (cave) system within its bowels, but also the permeability of this frontier region, which had become an integral part of Siam (known as Thailand since June 1939) with the full integration of Chiang Mai and other northern Thai (Lan Na) vassal states into an increasingly centralized Siamese kingdom since the 1880s.[3] Its recorded history, however, goes back to at least 1262 when King Mangrai, the founder of Lan Na, established his capital at Chiang Rai (Royal City of [Mang]rai).[4] Indeed, almost one-third of the Wild Boars—four of the teenage players and their assistant coach—were stateless and thus were living witnesses of cross-border dynamics.[5] Ekapol Chanthawong, the Wild Boars' assistant coach, who belongs to the Shan ethnic group, was orphaned at the age of ten but at the age of twelve found refuge in a Buddhist monastery. In contrast, fourteen-year-old Adul Sam-On, the team's multilingual interpreter, was sent to a local Baptist church school in Mae Sai by his ethnic Wa parents who regarded this as the best way out of a region in which guerrilla warfare, including dragooning into guerrilla forces, opium cultivation, and the trafficking of methamphetamines, can make for a deadly mix. The four boys and their coach were finally offered Thai citizenship.

These recent events illustrate what we intend to achieve in putting together this volume—to deal with topics relating to "armies" and "societies" while eschewing temptations to focus on one bloody battle after another or the potential conceptual straitjacket driven by sociological and political methodologies of comparing civil-military relations by utilizing states as the main unit of analysis.

What many observers probably did not realize about the cave rescue mission, apart from the use of twenty-first century technology like live coverage, is that many of the dynamics of the rescue have been established practice in the region for centuries. Hence, joining a monastery for a parentless orphan and seeking refuge from potential conscription and dragooning by crossing the border to join a church-led educational institution were natural moves.[6] That the Thai state took advantage of the situation to offer citizenship to the four non-Thai boys and coach was also in line with time-honored policies such as "Put vegetables into baskets, put people into towns" discussed in Grabowsky's chapter below (although in the past the saying may have entailed enslavement and enforced relocation).

In addition to this introduction, the volume brings together twelve chapters, all dealing with a broad definition of "armies" and "societies," and with each author adopting a different approach. Thus, the term *armies* in this book refers to a wide range of fighting forces, such as "armed forces" in the contemporary sense,[7] including the Armed Forces of the Republic of Indonesia, Southeast Asia's most populous country (Honna);[8] and former revolutionary armies that succeeded in winning independence, such as the Lao People's Armed Forces (Gunn) and the Vietnam People's Army (Thayer).

We also include "armies" in the classical sense, which may include naval forces vital for river and coastal warfare and for longer expeditions, but in this volume mostly referring to polities prior to the coming of the modern state,[9] such as the mandala-like states and principalities[10] that left their imprint on the early modern polity of Lan Na (Grabowsky).[11] These polities could usually not muster big standing armies, so instead they were usually centered around a core of palace forces that could draw on additional servicemen.[12] Also included are small-scale conquering forces like those of the "Hernan Cortez of the Philippines," Juan de Salcedo, who from an indigenous perspective probably would have been regarded as a late sixteenth-century newcomer to the native game of raiding (Rodriguez).

Our definition of "armies" also encompasses the armed wings of revolutionary movements such as the Communist Party of the Philippines-New People's Army (Rutten); Japanese-initiated armies including the Indian National Army, the Burma Independence Force, and the Defenders of the Homeland, and auxiliary and self-defense units such as the Japanese-organized *giyuugun* and *giyuutai* in Japanese-occupied Southeast Asia (Lebra), and even *romusha* (forced labor). Our broad definition does not neglect colonial troops and labor forces specifically conscripted for overseas service, such as the Vietnamese soldiers who served in France during World Wars I and II (Blanc); French-led but predominantly indigenous colonial troops such as the Tirailleurs Tonkinois or Tonkinese Riflemen in interwar French Indochina (Rettig); a wide range of European and indigenous land and naval forces in the Netherlands East Indies (van Dijk); and soldiers and their families from the Moluccas in the Royal Netherlands East-Indies Army, who in 1951 found themselves evacuated and stranded in the Netherlands (Smeets). Likewise, propaganda units such as those of the Shan Army Musical Band are included (Amporn), even though this unit, most strongly associated with war and drug lord Khun Sa's army, never represented an internationally recognized state.

The term "societies" in the context of this volume is also used in a broad sense. It can range from head-hunting societies and other small-scale societies and tribes,[13] their numerical strength varying from perhaps several dozen or several thousand human beings to larger polities such as the united Tai confederation of Lan Na under the suzerainty of Chiang Mai studied here by Grabowsky; armies recruited from a particular ethnic group such as the Shan (Amporn); more centralized states such as the Burmese and Siamese kingdoms that vied for Lan Na's population resources;[14] imperial entities such as the Americans, British, French, Portuguese, and Dutch, and also the Japanese, who could create colonial troops to conquer, pacify, and dominate foreign territories and populations. The most powerful of these empires were capable of shuffling troops around between imperial possessions and sometimes to metropolitan battle grounds (Blanc). In more recent times, armies in Southeast Asia also include United Nations-sanctioned peacekeeping forces within the region, such as UNTAC in Cambodia after 1991 and UNAMET in Timor Leste in 1999;[15] the participation of Southeast Asian military and police forces in UN missions beyond Southeast Asia; and the military forces of postcolonial states, state-nations, and nation-states emerging after independence in Southeast Asia.

Apart from a framework of a society encompassing an entire polity, we also understand the term more narrowly pertaining to smaller groups and organizations within a society. This may include epistemic (knowledge) communities such as the Spanish friars and their local interlocutors and counterparts who put together Tagalog-Spanish and Spanish-Tagalog dictionaries (Rodriguez). It could refer also to cohorts and military elites formed in military academies such as the Chulachomklao Royal Military Academy established by King Rama V in 1887, and to the masculinist cultures created in these military academies, such as the Philippine Military Academy. It ought to be stressed that different cohorts were socialized differently and hence made different choices when acting against coups or getting involved in them, as in the case of the Philippine Military Academy (McCoy 1999 and 2000).

"Southeast Asia" refers to the ethnically, linguistically, religiously, politically, and geographically diverse socio-geographical space between the Indian subcontinent and southern China, and broadly covers the combined territories of the ten member states of the Association of Southeast Asian

Nations (ASEAN), namely the five founding members of Indonesia, Malaysia, the Philippines, Singapore, and Thailand (all in 1967), and the five later additions, namely Brunei (1984), Vietnam (1995), Laos (1997), Myanmar (1997), and Cambodia (1999), with Timor-Leste as a potential new member state. ASEAN's westernmost state, Myanmar, borders Bangladesh, India, and China, while Laos and Vietnam also share land borders with China. To the far east, Indonesia's province of West Papua (formerly Irian Jaya) borders Papua New Guinea, while most other parts of the region are bordering each other or are demarcated by the Indian Ocean and the Pacific Ocean, with Australia the nearest land mass in the southeast.

For the purposes of this volume, we also note the distinction between the lowlands and the highlands, with the former allowing for the emergence of large-scale and sometimes quite homogeneous polities, and also rivers and seas that could connect countries commercially and serve as natural boundaries, but could also be used for attacking each other.

As two of our chapters cover extended overseas sojourns of Vietnamese soldiers and workers during World War I and II (Blanc) and the temporary and eventually permanent relocation of Moluccan soldiers and their families to the Netherlands in 1951 (Smeets), we also consider these groups as extensions of "Southeast Asia" into Europe.

Having defined key terms such as "armies," "societies," and "Southeast Asia," and suggested the wide range of armies and societies touched upon in this volume, we would like to highlight the sources that have been applied by the contributors in their respective case studies.

The twelve chapters use a variety of disciplinary approaches—historical, philological, sociological, and ethnographic—to cover a wide range of historical, socio-military, and geographical ground in terms of past military practices, such as abducting populations for strategic resettlement; the military's involvement in the economy in the form of army-linked firms (soldiers as entrepreneurs); policies and discourses centering on the military; and how cadres and armies had to reinvent themselves following important domestic and international political changes. They are worthy of being explored on their own terms and do not necessarily have to be molded into theory-driven attempts at establishing the relationship between soldiers and politics, armies and civil society, militaries and societies.

The rich socio-historical ground researched in this volume, combined with many different disciplinary perspectives, is also reflected in the sources. These range from royal chronicles to colonial archival records for the earlier historical periods to field research, interviews, newspaper reports, official sources, and even audio-visual materials. Grabowsky's sources on Lan Na, for instance, include northern Thai and Siamese archival sources in Lan Na and Thai languages, whereas Rodriguez draws on sixteenth-century Spanish chronicles and a very rich Tagalog vocabulary relating to warfare recorded by Spanish friars in early seventeenth-century Spanish-Tagalog and Tagalog-Spanish dictionaries. Writing on Dutch anxieties prior to and during World War I about the capability of European and indigenous soldiers and sailors to resist a foreign enemy, van Dijk makes not only good use of Dutch archival records from the National Archives and the Colonial Office, mail reports and parliamentary proceedings, but also Dutch newspapers, such as the progressive daily *De Locomotief*, which was printed in the important coastal city of Semarang, central Java. Blanc's chapter on Vietnamese soldiers and soldier-workers in metropolitan France during World Wars I and II, and that of Rettig on the causes of the 1930 mutiny against the French at the garrison of Yen Bay in northern Vietnam, both largely draw on French archival sources, most notably materials held at the French Overseas Archives in Aix-en-Provence. In contrast, Lebra's chapter summarizes her path-breaking book, which drew heavily on contemporary Japanese and other sources on the Japanese-trained armies in the Japanese-occupied parts of Southeast Asia during 1942–45.

The next four chapters generally rely on newspaper articles, academic sources, and other contemporary sources. This is the case in Honna's chapter on the politics of the Indonesian Army during the Suharto regime and in the wake of his fall; Smeets' contribution on Moluccan soldiers stranded in the Netherlands (because these loyal "Black Dutchmen" were considered "Dogs of the Dutch" in the wake of the failed attempt to establish a republic of the South Moluccas); Thayer's study on the expanding economic roles of the Vietnam People's Army; and Gunn's account of the transition of victorious Lao communist guerrillas to military guardians of the Lao People's Democratic Republic.

In contrast to these mostly nation-wide studies with their top–down focus, Rutten and Amporn tackle regional and transnational phenomena. Rutten examines the varied post-movement careers of former Communist guerrilla fighters in the Philippine province of Negros Occidental, the country's "sugar bowl," in the late 1990s until 2001, whereas Amporn investigates the trans-border careers of leading members of the Shan Army Musical Band in the Burmese-Thai borderlands from the mid-1980s to about 2006. Both scholars rely on locally gained insights, sometimes obtained through repeated research stays, and Amporn also conducts an audio-visual study of cassette tapes and VCDs.

As is evident from the above examples, the time periods studied vary considerably. Grabowsky's chapter on Lan Na covers more than five centuries, from La Na's time as a Tai confederation under the leadership of Chiang Mai (since the late thirteenth century), to more than two hundred years under Burmese rule or dominance (1558–1775), to roughly seven decades under the reign of King Kawila of Chiang Mai and his successors (1782–c. 1850). In contrast, Rettig's chapter on the anti-French mutiny, linked to a wider but failed insurrection of the Vietnamese Nationalist Party, by Vietnamese soldiers of the Tirailleurs Tonkinois Regiment at Yen Bay in northern French Indochina, is largely limited to the late 1920s and the year 1930. Compared to the timeframe of these two studies—one encompassing a lengthy period, the other focused on an event compressed in time—the remaining contributions roughly cover periods ranging from a few years to half a century.

This introduction not only plays a key role in illuminating historical continuities and changes but also identifies points of comparison between countries. The twelve chapters are organized into two main sections: Chapters 1–6 in the section titled "Southeast Asian Armed Forces in the Precolonial and Colonial Periods" and Chapters 7–12 in the section "Southeast Asian Armed Forces after Independence." On their own and together as an edited volume, the twelve chapters offer an original approach to the study of military-society relations in Southeast Asia. How did societies or groups within a society or within a polity shape the military (armed forces)? How did armed forces reflect and impact societies and polities as well as economies? Precolonial Southeast Asian polities could not maintain large standing armies which were subject to the seasonal ebbs and flows of weather, especially the monsoons, and agricultural cycles.

The unique longitudinal and comparative approach of this volume invites Southeast Asian scholars and military historians to think differently about the social and political history of the region's armed forces because we have cast our net wider and occasionally deeper than earlier attempts. As such, we expect to contribute to a relatively new and neglected field of study and open it up even further to new approaches in order to develop a critical mass of studies that will, in the future, allow for more syncretic overview studies.

How does the present volume compare and relate to earlier and contemporary literature on similar topics? We believe that it partially straddles earlier historically grounded studies on Southeast Asian warfare as well as political science-based studies on more contemporary armies and civilian-military relations. We want to build on these earlier studies and, because of our long-range perspective and slightly different focus, namely on "armies" and "society" rather than on "warfare" or "civilian-military relations," offer fresh and original perspectives. We acknowledge and embrace the diversity of the region and the diversities within—between centers and peripheries, high politics and low politics, the past and the present, insiders and outsiders, sojourners and migrants, imperialism and independence movements—as well as the considerable differences in terms of expertise of our contributors, by bringing together a wider range of topics and themes than could be accommodated in more conceptual- and theory-driven approaches.

Historically grounded book-length studies on Southeast Asia have generally focused on "warfare," written by scholars who started out as specialists of one or more of mainland Southeast Asia's polities. For example, Horace Geoffrey Quaritch-Wales (1900–81) began his future academic career as an adviser to the courts of Rama VI and VII of Siam in the 1920s before earning one of the first PhD degrees at the budding School of Oriental Studies, whereas Michael W. Charney, like his supervisor Victor G. Lieberman, initially focused on early modern Burmese polities. Although separated by more than fifty years, the titles of Quaritch-Wales' (1952) and Charney's (2004) seminal studies signaled their focus on "warfare," with the former's temporal reach restricted to "ancient Southeast Asian warfare," roughly the precolonial period, whereas Charney's timeframe extending from 1300 to 1900, into the early modern and modern periods.

Of the two monographs, Charney's one deals with a far wider range of topics than Quaritch-Wales' study. The topics are organized into ten chapters starting with "culture and warfare," then "personal weaponry" and "firearms," and the importance and variants of "sea and river warfare." The book then emphasizes the importance of beasts of burden, namely "elephants" and "horses and cavalry," and the crucial importance of "supply and transport" in a region in which the seasonal winds and the monsoons could facilitate campaigns or condemn them to failure. It is only in the penultimate chapter that the focus turns to "soldiers," including the challenges for states to mobilize them and human strategies to avoid military service, before analyzing eventually doomed attempts in the nineteenth century to keep up, through imitation or purchases, with more aggressive and concerted Western powers and their rapidly increasing military technologies.

Thus, in terms of range and the period covered, Charney's study not only substantially adds to Quaritch-Wales' pioneering work but also to one of the most important and relatively accessible reference sources for those seeking an overview of the region's military traditions, namely Anthony Reid's treatment of the military revolution in the second volume of his magisterial *Southeast Asia in the Age of Commerce, 1450–1680: Expansion and Crisis* (1993). Although the term "warfare" is not contained in the subsection "military revolution" of Reid's book, it is nevertheless acknowledged as a most important phenomenon, and Reid deals with Southeast Asian rulers' adoption of firearms, including for ceremonial purposes, well before the arrival of Europeans in the region.

"Warfare" also promises to cover more ground than "armies" or "societies," especially as many earlier polities and societies had few, if any, specialized armed forces, let alone standing armies in the modern sense. Hence, Charney does not have a single chapter on "armies," although mention of them can be found throughout the book, and not a single index entry for "army." However, his chapter on "soldiers" is an excellent account of the difficulties in forming an army in early modern Southeast Asia, which he sees as "[l]he challenge of mobilizing human resources [that] presented a chronic and serious problem for indigenous rulers." He notes, moreover, that Southeast Asian royal absolutism was limited by societal complexities "in which labor and land, the bases of power, were internally divided among competing elites, . . . among whom the ruler was often simply the *primus inter pares*" (2004, 213).[16] As a result, rulers might be able to draw on a mix of palace forces or royal guards, mobilize additional men through other dependent lords or vassals or some kind of territorial quotas, or engage the services of mercenaries (for example, Portuguese or Japanese). Even today, most ASEAN states are far from having a system of universal conscription, whereas Singapore and Brunei still engage the services of foreign elite troops, the Gurkhas.

In contrast to a focus on a particular historical era and on warfare (Quaritch-Wales and Charney) or on the military revolution (Reid), other authors have made "armies" the principal subject of their book-length studies. These include Lebra's pioneering *Japanese-trained Armies in Southeast Asia* (1977), of which the author generously summarized the key content specially for this volume, and Bayly and Harper's *Forgotten Armies: The Fall of British Asia, 1941–1945* (2005), with its great narrative thrust and eye for telling detail.[17] In both volumes, one discovers a plethora of armies against the backdrop of a fast-changing and often mercurial international, regional, and local context during a relatively short but crucial period in Southeast Asia's history, which left an indelible mark on those who experienced it and nurtured a desire to become their own masters.

In contrast to these two books, which largely focus on the impact of the Japanese conquest and occupation of Southeast Asia, the volume edited by Karl Hack and Tobias Rettig on *Colonial Armies in Southeast Asia*

(2006) covers a far longer historical period, one that stretches more than six centuries.

Unlike Quaritch-Wales, Charney, or Reid, Hack and Rettig opted for an edited volume with a more typological approach, with "colonial armies" as the key unit of analysis rather than "warfare" proper. This allowed them to build a bridge between the aforementioned studies of earlier armies and those after independence. Among the colonial armies covered are a wide range of distinct forces, including not only the Western colonial forces in the region but also the Ming Chinese forces that occupied Vietnam in the early 1400s and Admiral Zheng Ho's forces that got involved roughly at the same time in what today would likely be called "peacekeeping" engagements, not to mention the various forces created by Japanese officers during the brief but crucial Japanese occupation of the region, or the Indonesian-sponsored militias terrorizing East Timorese keen on gaining independence.

Hack and Rettig's volume is also a useful resource because of its coverage of different types of military units, such as the Dutch-raised *maréchaussée* and mixed units in the Netherlands East Indies (Teitler); the differing fates of the Chasseurs Annamites and Tirailleurs Tonkinois in French-controlled Annam and Tonkin (Eckert); the Philippine Scouts in the American Philippines (Meixsel); and the British-raised Malay Regiment in 1930s Malaya (Blackburn). It also discusses various types of lightly armed policing forces employed in rural areas,[18] such as the French-created Garde *indigène* operating in the various territories of French Indochina (Eckert; Womack); the French-armed partisans in the restive *territoires militaires* bordering China (Eckert); the Dutch-engineered *maréchaussée* in the Netherlands East Indies (Teitler); the pro-Indonesian and Indonesian-sponsored militias in East Timor (Robinson); and the private units (*tat*) linked to indigenous politicians that mushroomed in 1930s Burma (Taylor).

While the Japanese hand in raising various independence armies and auxiliary units during Japan's occupation of Southeast Asia is discussed (Abu Talib), contributions to the volume also articulate a wide range of themes, extending from debates about the ideal ethnic proportion in Dutch colonial forces (Teitler); official, popular, and personal post-colonial memories of the

Malay Regiment in Malaysia and Singapore (Blackburn); accounts of violence by Indonesian or Indonesian-sponsored militias that failed to break the desire of most East Timorese for independence from an Indonesian Republic perceived to be a colonial power (Robinson); and analysis of the impact of Southeast Asia's decolonization on British colonial forces and world power (Hack).

In contrast to studies covering either several hundred years or more narrow periods of history, such as the Japanese occupation of Southeast Asia, scholarly works that focus more on the present and more recent past tend to be more theory-inspired and written from a sociological or political science perspective.[19] For them, the standard of reference was no longer "warfare" (Quaritch-Wales; Charney) or "military revolution" (Reid), nor the empire-periphery relationships articulated by reference to and institutionalized within "Japanese-trained armies" (Lebra), "colonial armies" (Hack and Rettig), or even "forgotten armies" (Bayly and Harper), but rather the "military," "soldiers," the "armed forces" in relation to the post-independence state as best articulated by the term "civil-military relations."

Most of these studies contain the term "military" in the title, usually in relation to one or more key themes or explanatory variables. Just a few years after Samuel Huntington (1957), Morris Janowitz (1960), and Samuel Finer (1962) had laid the foundation of a new field of study, John J. Johnson (1962) and contributors tried to apply these ideas to the "role of the military in underdeveloped countries," including, among places in other parts of the developing world, three of today's ASEAN countries—Burma, Indonesia, and Thailand. Although these three countries arguably were still largely underdeveloped in 1970, the next major study, edited by James F. Guyot and Ann Ruth Willner in the *Journal of Comparative Administration* (1970), zoomed in, more flatteringly, on the "military as political elites in Asia."

It is worth remembering that the region in the early 1960s was in the throes of decolonization and state- if not nation-building, including, at times, civil war. Who would replace the colonial masters or the old royal regime; what should the relation between state, soldiers, and society be; what kind of outside interference was acceptable; and in what direction they should develop was not yet clear. Even Thailand, the central state in the Indochinese peninsula, which had never been formally colonized, threatened to be pulled into the conflicts of its neighbors, but its astute diplomacy helped it to largely maintain domestic stability and develop economically even though it meant the occasional coup and sometimes lengthy phases of military dictatorship. In contrast, its large neighbor to the west, Burma, had been granted independence in early 1948 almost as an afterthought to India's independence, which was soon threatened by disagreements about the interpretation and implementation of the Panglong Agreement and the unhappiness about a parliamentary political system that was increasingly perceived to be dysfunctional.

By 1975 the process of decolonization had settled with the end of the Second Indochina War. In fact, events had progressed so rapidly that the identity of two of the political entities, Cambodia and South Vietnam, had irreversibly changed and their armed forces destroyed. Unlike earlier publications, J. Stephen Hoadley's *Soldiers and Politics in Southeast Asia* (1975) was the first to feature five case studies from the region and the first to carry "civil-military" in the title. In addition to Burma, Indonesia, and Thailand, Hoadley added two more country chapters—"Marshal Lon Nol's Khmer Republic" and "South Vietnam: A Militarized Polity"—and further comparative chapters on military interventions in politics. He also evaluated the role of the military in development.[20]

In April 1975, however, events on the ground violently escalated, abruptly ending Lon Nol's Khmer Republic and the Republic of South Vietnam. Pol Pot's Khmer Rouge marched into Phnom Penh and seized state power in Cambodia to create the radical agrarian-communist state of Democratic Kampuchea. Laos was also taken over by revolutionary forces, and Hanoi's troops took control of the Republic of South Vietnam, with north and south formally reunified as the Socialist Republic of Vietnam in 1976. The Hanoi-backed Pathet Lao proclaimed the Lao People's Democratic Republic in December 1975. In the meantime, the Republic of Indonesia had conquered East Timor, taking advantage of the 1974 military coup in Portugal, prompting disagreements between East Timor's independence leaders and Washington's support for Jakarta's invasion.

It would take ten years until the next comparative study, by Zakaria bin Haji Ahmad and Harold A. Crouch, *Military-civilian Relations in South-East Asia*, was published in 1985, up to now the most comprehensive study on the subject. It was the first book in which a Southeast Asian, Dr Zakaria bin Haji Ahmad, a political scientist who was trained at the University of Singapore, McMaster University in Canada, and the Massachusetts Institute of Technology, was to have an editing role. This signaled a shift in the interpretation and production of knowledge with the arrival of more "indigenous" yet Western-trained academics who could and were willing to publish in English on matters relating to national security. It seemed that the balance had tilted towards autonomous regimes. In the meantime, the region seemed at an impasse despite socialist and communist regimes underperforming economically, and Vietnamese forces occupying most of Cambodia after their invasion in January 1979 thus ousting the Khmer Rouge from power and installing a client regime in Phnom Penh.

It was arguably the 1986 People Power Revolution in Manila, the Philippines, ending Ferdinand Marcos's tight grip on power, that reignited interest in the role and impact of militaries on regime change, although it would take a few more years until publication. In the meantime, the 8888 uprising in Burma, which began on August 8, 1988 in Rangoon, ended General Ne Win's socialist regime but maintained the Tatmadaw in power. With the end of the Cold War, those Southeast Asian states with socialist economies were confronted with a lack of financial and other inflows from their former foreign supporters. They had to explore new economic ideas. Some of them reluctantly considered new political ideas, and also created stronger regional alliances, with Vietnam, Laos, Burma, and Cambodia joining ASEAN in the 1990s.

The next series of books on armies and societies in Southeast Asia took on more explicit titles that reflected changes on the ground which, in turn, reflected the vast political changes in international politics, notably the end of the Cold War and its impact on politics, new relationships with old or new partners from the outside, and new economic policies. Hence, Viberto Selochan's 1991 book emphasized the different configurations that the military, the state, and development could take, including five Southeast Asian case studies, including the "big three," Indonesia, Burma, and Thailand, from the earliest such studies, and also Malaysia and the Philippines. Several years later, in 1998, R. J. May and Viberto Selochan shifted the emphasis to the link between the military and democracy, again featuring the big three and also the Philippines alongside five other countries from Asia and the Pacific.

Studies with a political science perspective have focused on particular themes and on political entities modeled on the sovereign state, including UN membership, as well as in the more immediate past, such as civil-military relations in post-independence Southeast Asia and Asia.[21] They usually take the nation-state and regular armed forces and a distinction between the military and civilians as their starting point, even though state- and nation-building in many parts of Southeast Asia is still an ongoing process. In contrast, this volume provides a multi-disciplinary approach, with the multinational team of authors bringing in their "disciplinary" backgrounds—history, sociology, anthropology, ethnography, and political science. This introduction brings together the papers and plays a key role in illuminating historical continuities and changes, but also identifies points of comparison between countries.

Part I, "Southeast Asian Armed Forces in the Precolonial and Colonial Periods," features six chapters, the majority of which bridge several time periods and thus provide scope for longitudinal comparisons. The first two chapters—on the mainland and the nascent Philippines—tackle indigenous traditions of warfare. In Chapter 1, Volker Grabowsky traces military traditions in Lan Na, the northernmost part of present-day Thailand, from the late thirteenth to the mid-nineteenth century. Because of low population density, control over manpower, including forced resettlement as slaves into urban centers rather than territory per se, increasingly became a key feature of warfare. Using dictionaries compiled by Franciscan friars, Felice Noelle Rodriguez, in Chapter 2, provides an indigenous account on how Juan de

Salcedo, the "Hernan Cortes of the Philippines," joined the native form of warfare and thus counters the Spanish-centric chronicles of the conquest of Luzon and the Philippines during the second half of the sixteenth century.

In Chapter 3, Kees van Dijk examines imperial anxieties as they manifest themselves in colonial armies. He brings to the fore the fears of the Netherlands, a small country in charge of a sprawling archipelago, as discussed in parliament and weighed in by newspapers in the Netherlands East Indies during the early twentieth century until the end of the Great War. These fears extended to not being able to defend itself against a much more powerful foreign enemy, but also fears, particularly during the last year of war and against the background of socialist agitation, that both indigenous and European, including Dutch, troops, especially sailors, might mutiny. However, promises of concessions towards indigenous nationalists were soon forgotten after the war and nationalists were repressed, which left the Netherlands East Indies inadequately prepared for the Japanese onslaught it had so much feared during the first two decades of the century.

In Chapter 4, Marie-Eve Blanc demonstrates that the dual identity of the Vietnamese in France, both as colonial subjects and a fighting and support force for the metropolitan motherland (*mère-patrie*), also led to ambiguous social identities by a republican French imperial nation-state that asked them to defend the independence of the French republic but denied them access to republican rights, let alone the right to self-determination. Frederik Rettig in Chapter 5 covers the French in control of Indochina and in charge of the Tirailleurs Tonkinois at a time of heightened anti-colonialism, characterized by little fear of foreign enemies but little trust, though perhaps not without anxiety about its own indigenous troops. While the French were, on the one hand, derisive of the military qualities of their Vietnamese colonial subjects and, on the other hand, unwilling to turn the army into a vehicle of Vietnamese desires for independence, the Vietnamese Nationalist Party thought it could exploit discontent among Vietnamese warrant officers about the lack of promotion chances. This would lead to a failed mutiny that fed French concerns about creating a substantial Vietnamese officer class, which eventually opened the doors for the Japanese. This chapter also articulates the other side: how and why Vietnamese civilian and military anti-colonialists rationalized their nationalist action even though many of them knew they would pay with their lives.

Joyce Lebra's contribution in Chapter 6 deals with the reverse side of Dutch and French imperial anxieties, namely how quickly the Japanese first garrisoned Japanese troops in French Indochina, an uneasy ally following French Indochina's alignment with the Vichy government in the aftermath of France's rapid defeat against Germany in 1940—before using Saigon as a launchpad for conquering the Netherlands East Indies, British Malaya, the "impregnable fortress" Singapore, and British Burma. Lebra shows how little time it took the Japanese to create independence armies, such as the Indian National Army (the first version of it relying entirely on Indian prisoners of war; the second version also integrating ethnic Indian civilians, including girls and women), the Burma Independence Army, and the Pembela Tanah Air (Defenders of the Homeland), but also many smaller self-defense units, such as the *giyuugun*, *giyuutai*, and *romusha*, which they also expected to make the return of the British and the Dutch far more difficult. The Japanese would succeed to quite an extent in Burma and in the future Indonesia, less so on the Malay peninsula, but they did not really have the time to create similar units in French Indochina because they took over power only on March 9, 1945, they were largely resented in the Philippines.

The volume's second part, also comprising six chapters, focuses on "Southeast Asian Armed Forces after Independence." The first two chapters deal with Indonesia, the first (Honna) with the victorious Indonesian armed forces, and the second (Smeets) with one of their regional-nationalist enemies (in the form of the United States of Indonesia) whose defeated soldiers (and families) were shipped to the Netherlands in the early 1950s. In Chapter 7, Jun Honna deals with the Indonesian armed forces, who trace their origins back to the Japanese-created PETA (Pembela Tanah Air). They came of age defending the new nation against the Dutch and indigenous (usually regional) enemies, to the extent of capturing all the previously Dutch territories against regionally more limited competitors, thus giving the former Netherlands East Indies a new "Indonesian" form, even though Western Papua (or Irian

Jaya) was taken over only in 1960. Honna focuses on a critical juncture: long-time President Suharto's forced abdication and the ensuing recalibration of the roles of the armed forces within the Republic of Indonesia, notably giving up its parliamentary seats (an option that was taken up about a decade later by Myanmar's military), its role in provinces aiming for autonomy or independence, such as Aceh and East Timor, and funding issues. Chapter 8 by Henk Smeets portrays an army born out of conflict in a time of historical rupture, with the main emphasis on the overseas experiences of Moluccan soldiers and their families. This chapter offers a perspective which is quite different from the experiences of Vietnamese soldiers and workers in France described in Chapter 4.

In Chapter 9, Carlyle Thayer describes how the Vietnamese were called upon from 1915, and later again in 1939, to serve the French war effort in the metropole and beyond, very rarely as combat troops due to the perception that they were inferior to other colonial troops, but in ammunition factories and in other roles far away from the battlefields. In comparison, the Moluccan experience, as outlined by Henk Smeets in Chapter 8, was an anti-climax. Traditionally regarded as "black Dutchmen" (*Belanda hitam*), but then identified as the "dogs of the Dutch" (*andjing Belanda*) for their steadfast loyalty to the Dutch during the Indonesian Revolution (1945–49), most of the Moluccans were stranded in Java when attempts to found an independent Republic of the South Moluccas turned violent in 1950. The Dutch shipped the Moluccan soldiers and their families to the Netherlands in the expectation that the situation on the ground would be settled relatively quickly. The Hague's failure to demilitarize some of their most loyal soldiers, many of whom were Christian, gave them and their offspring an ambiguous social identity, which most notoriously erupted in two highly publicized and deadly train jackings in 1975 and 1977, and other actions, that brought to attention the perceived plight of the second generation of Moluccans.

The following two chapters discuss how erstwhile revolutionary guerrilla forces transformed themselves into regular armed forces, still under the leadership of the party, but then had to rapidly adapt to the harsh realities of the post-Cold War era when a lack of resources required them to reinvent themselves as entrepreneurs and forced them to transform military-run enterprises into efficient and profit-making businesses. In Chapter 9, Carlyle Thayer provides an overview of the expanding roles of the Vietnam People's Army (VPA) in Vietnamese society since reunification in 1975. The VPA's role was enlarged to include participation in economic production, a role temporarily curtailed following the conflict with Cambodia and China in the late 1970s. As a result of reform policies (*doi moi*) since the mid-1980s, military-run enterprises and companies were put on the same legal footing as state-owned enterprises and were granted the authority to sign joint venture agreements with overseas partners. A global picture of the army and society in the Lao People's Democratic Republic (LPDR) is provided by Geoffrey Gunn in Chapter 10. In accordance with the overall structure of this book, we are also concerned to establish continuities and discontinuities with the past. While the collapse of the Soviet Union and the LPDR's embrace of market capitalism has ostensibly changed state-society relations, the real and symbolic influence of the military within the state apparatus remains entrenched. Despite the historically close ties between the Socialist Republic of Vietnam and its junior brother, the Lao People's Democratic Republic, the elder brother has been more diligent about sustaining these ties, while in more recent years Vientiane has sought closer collaborative relationships with the People's Republic of China, including dispensing lengthy land leases to Chinese companies and building casinos.

The two final chapters in Part II move away from the bird's-eye perspective taken in the previous two chapters by eschewing the framework of the nation-state (and national narratives) and instead covering regional and cross-boundary military developments in Negros Occidental in the central Philippines and in the Thai-Burmese borderlands respectively. In Chapter 11, Rosanne Rutten considers the flow of people in and out of the Philippine communist guerrilla movement in Negros Occidental, roughly 500 kilometers southeast of Manila, as an ongoing process. Thousands of women and men from towns, villages, and haciendas have successively joined the Communist Party of the Philippines (CPP) and its New People's Army (NPA) for longer or shorter periods, and then left to continue their lives "above ground" in various ways, their activist past leaving its mark on power relations, politics, and personal lives. Since the revolutionary movement began its decline in the late 1980s, this outflow has not been matched by an inflow of new activists. As former cadres left the Communist armed forces and rejoined civilian life, they repositioned themselves *vis-à-vis* the movement, the state, and political élites in ways that affected the movement and, more broadly, poor people's politics.

In Chapter 12, Amporn Jirattikorn sketches the lives of individuals who formed Jerng Laew (Freedom Way), a Shan army music band, and the roles they played in serving Shan ethno-nationalist sentiment with their songs. The chapter covers the period from the mid-1980s when Freedom Way was formed to about 2006 when the Shan armed organization the band members joined was relocated to the Thailand-Burma border. Throughout several decades of fighting, these individuals have joined multiple armed forces and have produced many musical albums. Not only do their rich personal experiences offer a rare insight into the nature of Shan armed revolt and the social dynamics along the Thailand-Burma border areas where the conflict was playing out, but their songs also reflect the evolution of the Shan-Burmese relationship and socio-political changes within the period.

Both Rutten and Amporn examine the personal revolutionary and "ethnic army" trajectories of people leaving the movement by observing and listening very closely to their protagonists, namely former cadres of the CPP-NPA in Negros Occidental, the sugar bowl of the Philippines, and former members of the Shan army's Freedom Way band, whose audiences extend beyond the Shan on both sides of the Burmese-Thai border. Amporn explains how Shan insurgents use songs to maintain a cross-border Shan identity by waging a digital and virtual war.

This volume opens new avenues to the study of the relationship between the military and society in Southeast Asia. Its longitudinal and comparative approach invites Southeast Asianists and military historians to think about the social and political history of the region's armed forces differently from earlier attempts. Historically grounded studies thus far have focused on particular eras, notably on ancient and early modern Southeast Asia, or on particular types of armies, such as Western and Asian colonial armies. Studies with a political science perspective have dealt with particular themes and the more immediate past, such as civil-military relations in post-independence Southeast Asia and Asia. In contrast, this volume provides a multi-disciplinary approach, with a multi-national team of authors bringing in their 'disciplinary' backgrounds (history; sociology; anthropology; ethnography; political science). The introduction brings together the papers and plays a key role in illuminating historical continuities and changes, but also identifies points of comparison between countries.

Notes

1. Hannah Beech, Richard C. Paddock, and Muktita Suhartono, '"Still Can't Believe It Worked': The Story of the Thailand Cave Rescue." *New York Times*, July 12, 2018, see https://www.nytimes.com/2018/07/12/world/asia/thailand-cave-rescue-seals.html (last accessed August 20, 2018).

2. SEAL is an acronym for Sea-Air-Land.

3. Apart from the principality of Chiang Mai, there were the principalities of Lampang, Lamphun, Phrae, and Nan. All were integrated into the Siamese kingdom in the decades following the second Chiang Mai treaty of 1883 between Siam and Britain. The historical region of Lan Na, however, was far larger than the present-day upper north of Thailand and also comprised border areas that today belong to Myanmar, Laos, and Yunnan (China). For details, see Sarassawadee 2005.

4. For the exact dating of the founding of Chiang Rai, see Penth 1989, 11.

5. Hannah Beech, "Stateless and Poor, Some Boys in Thai Cave Had Already Beaten Long Odds." *New York Times*, July 10, 2018 (online link, last accessed August 20, 2018).

6. On monasteries as sites for evading military service, see Charney 2004 (chapter 9).

7. The online version of Merriam-Webster defines "armed forces" as "the combined military, naval, and air forces of a nation." In Indonesia, for instance, the police forces were integrated into the armed forces in 1967 (see Honna's

chapter), only to be separated again in the late 1990s in the wake of the demise of the Suharto regime.

8. Since then (1999) rebranded as the Tentara Nasional Indonesia, with the National Police Forces separated again.

9. The 1933 Montevideo Convention on the Rights and Duties of States codified what it found to be customary international law, namely, that a sovereign state needs to fulfil four criteria, namely to have a permanent population, a defined territory, one government, and the capacity to enter into relations with other sovereign states.

10. For the concept of mandala ("circles of power") in a Southeast Asian context, see Wolters 1999.

11. At the height of its political power and cultural influence in the second half of the fifteenth century, the kingdom of Lan Na comprised roughly the upper north of present-day Thailand and adjacent areas in the eastern Shan States (the areas east of the Salween) and even Sipsong Panna in southern Yunnan. See Grabowsky 2005.

12. This could include different methods: the *ahmudan* system in the predecessor entities of Burma/Myanmar but also Siam/Thailand; plus a system where a particular territory or a particular "lord"/"vassal" had to provide a particular number of men.

13. This could include highly mobile seaborne tribes, such as the Iranun and Balangingi in the "Sulu Zone," who were organizing annual raiding expeditions. See Warren 2002 and 2007.

14. Lieberman 2003 refers to them as charter states in the sense of foundational states.

15. The acronym UNTAC stands for United Nations Transitional Authority in Cambodia; UNAMET for United Nations Mission in East Timor.

16. The final chapter of Charney's book is an excellent account of how some of the remaining major polities in the region, in particular Burma and Vietnam, responded to a new wave of European imperialism driven by the industrial revolution, technological and organizational changes, and arguably also population growth.

17. Bayly and Harper's successor volume (2007) puts the emphasis on wars for freedom and revolution rather than on armies.

18. Similar to the Guardia Civil in Spain, the Carabinieri in Italy, or the Gendarmerie in France, with their members usually barracked, for deployment in the countryside rather than in cities, and more heavily armed than regular, urban police forces. Useful for organizing mobile columns during "pacification" campaigns.

19. For an excellent overview essay relating to Asia, see Croissant 2016. For an overview of the literature on "civil-military relations," see Owens 2010.

20. The civil war in Cambodia and the final military collapse of Lon Nol's Khmer Republic is described in detail by Sak Sutsakhan (1978). As former chief of the general staff of the Khmer Armed Forces and last chief of state of the Khmer Republic, he provides a fascinating insider view.

21. See, for example, Alagappa 2001; Croissant 2015 and 2018; Croissant and Kuehn 2017; Guyot and Willner 1970; Hoadley 1975; Johnson 1962; May & Selochan 1998; Mietzner 2011; Olsen & Jurika 1986; Selochan 1991; Zakaria and Crouch 1985.

References

Ahmed, Abu Talib. 2006. "The Impact of the Japanese Occupation on Colonial and Anti-Colonial Armies." In *Colonial Armies in Southeast Asia*, eds. Karl Hack and Tobias Rettig, 213–38. London/New York: Routledge.

Alagappa, Muthiah, ed. 2001. *Coercion and Governance: The Declining Political Role of the Military in Asia*. Stanford, CA: Stanford University Press.

Bayly, Christopher, and Tim Harper. 2005. *Forgotten Armies: The Fall of British Asia, 1941–1945*. London: Allen Lane.

———. 2007. *Forgotten Wars: Freedom and Revolution in Southeast Asia*. Cambridge, MA: Harvard University Press.

Blackburn, Kevin. 2006. "Colonial Forces and Postcolonial Memories: the Malay Regiment in Malaya and Singapore." In *Colonial Armies in Southeast Asia*, eds. Karl Hack and Tobias Rettig, 302–26. London/New York: Routledge.

Charney, Michael W. 2004. *Southeast Asian Warfare, 1300–1900*. Leiden: Brill.

Croissant, Aurel. 2016. "Civil-Military Relations in Asia." In *Oxford Bibliographies*, last modified March 31, 2016. https://dx.doi.org/10.1093/obo/9780199756223-0150.

———. 2018. *Civil-Military Relations in Southeast Asia: Elements in Politics and Society in Southeast Asia*. Cambridge: Cambridge University Press.

Croissant, Aurel, and David Kuehn, eds. 2017. *Reforming Civil-Military Relations in New Democracies: Democratic Control and Military Effectiveness in Comparative Perspectives*. Berlin: Springer.

Eckert, Henri. 2006. "Double-edged Swords of Conquest in Indochina: Tirailleurs Tonkinois, Chasseaurs Annamites, and Militias, 1883–1895." In *Colonial Armies in Southeast Asia*, eds. Karl Hack and Tobias Rettig, 126–53. London/New York: Routledge.

Finer, Samuel E. [1962] 2002. *The Man on Horseback: The Role of the Military in Politics*. New Brunswick and London: Transaction Publishers (originally published New York: Frederick A. Praeger).

Grabowsky, Volker. 2005. "Population and State in Lan Na Prior to the Sixteenth Century." *Journal of the Siam Society* 93: 1–68.

Guyot, James F., and Ann Ruth Willner, eds. 1970. *The Military as Political Elites in Asia*. Beverly Hills, CA: Sage Publications.

Hack, Karl. 2006. "Imperialism and Decolonisation in Southeast Asia: Colonial forces and British World Power." In *Colonial Armies in Southeast Asia*, eds. Karl Hack and Tobias Rettig, 239–66. London/New York: Routledge.

Hack, Karl, and Tobias Rettig, eds. 2006. *Colonial Armies in Southeast Asia*. London: Routledge.

Hoadley, J. Stephen. [1975] 2017. *Soldiers and Politics in Southeast Asia: Civil-Military Relations in Asia in Comparative Perspective, 1933–1975*. New York, NY: Routledge (originally published Rochester, VT: Schenkman Publishing Company).

Huntington, Samuel. 1957. *The Soldier and the State*. Cambridge, MA: Harvard University Press.

Janowitz, Morris. 1960. *The Professional Soldier: A Social and Political Portrait*. New York, NY: Free Press.

Johnson, John J., ed. 1962. *The Role of the Military in Underdeveloped Countries.* Princeton, NJ: Princeton University Press.

Lebra, Joyce C. [1977] 2012. *Japanese-trained Armies in Southeast Asia: Independence and Volunteer Forces in World War II.* Singapore: Institute of Southeast Asian Studies (originally published Hong Kong: Heinemann).

Lieberman, Victor. 2003. *Strange Parallels: Southeast Asia in Global Context, c. 800–1830. Volume 1: Integration on the Mainland.* Cambridge: Cambridge University Press.

May, R. J., and Viberto Selochan, eds. 1998. *The Military and Democracy in Asia and the Pacific.* London: Christopher Hurst.

McCoy, Alfred W. 1999. *Closer Than Brothers: Manhood at the Philippine Military Academy.* New Haven, CT: Yale University Press.

———. 2000. "Philippine Commonwealth and Cult of Masculinity." *Philippine Studies* 48(3): 315–46.

Meixsel, Richard. 2006. "American Exceptionalism in Colonial Forces? The Philippine Scout Mutiny of 1924." In *Colonial Armies in Southeast Asia*, eds. Karl Hack and Tobias Rettig, 171–94. London/New York: Routledge.

Mietzner, Marcus, ed. 2011. *The Political Resurgence of the Military in Southeast Asia: Conflict and Leadership.* London: Routledge.

Olsen, Edward A., and Stephen Jurika, eds. 1986. *The Armed Forces in Contemporary Asian Societies.* Boulder, CO: Westview Press.

Owens, Mackubin Thomas. 2010. "Civil–Military Relations." In *Oxford Research Encyclopedia of International Studies*, http://oxfordre.com/internationalstudies/abstract/10.1093/acrefore/9780190846626.001.0001/acrefore-9780190846626-e-123.

Penth, Hans. 1989. "On the History of Chiang Rai." *Journal of the Siam Society* 77 (1): 11–32.

Quaritch-Wales, Horace G. 1952. *Ancient South-East Asian Warfare.* London: Bernard Quaritch.

Reid, Anthony. 1993. *Southeast Asia in the Age of Commerce, 1450–1680, Vol. 2, Expansion and Crisis.* New Haven, CT: Yale University Press.

Robinson, Geoffrey. 2006. "Colonial Militias in East Timor from the Portuguese Period to Independence." In *Colonial Armies in Southeast Asia*, eds. Karl Hack and Tobias Rettig, 269–301. London/New York: Routledge.

Sak Sutsakhan. 1978. *The Khmer Republic at War and the Final Collapse.* McLean, Virginia: General Research Corporation.

Sarassawadee Ongsakul. 2005. *History of Lan Na.* Chiang Mai: Silkworm Books.

Selochan, Viberto, ed. 1991. *The Military, the State, and Development in Asia and the Pacific.* Boulder, CO: Westview Press.

Taylor, Robert H. 2006. "Colonial Forces in British Burma: A National Army Postponed." In *Colonial Armies in Southeast Asia*, eds. Karl Hack and Tobias Rettig, 195–209. London/New York: Routledge.

Teitler, Gerke. 2006. "The Mixed Company: Fighting Power and Ethnic Relations in the Dutch Colonial Army, 1890–1920." In *Colonial Armies in Southeast Asia*, eds. Karl Hack and Tobias Rettig, 154–68. London/New York: Routledge.

Warren, James Francis. 2002. *Iranun and Balangingi: Globalization, Maritime Raiding, and the Birth of Ethnicity.* Singapore University Press.

———. 2007. *The Sulu Zone, 1768–1898: The Dynamics of External Trade, Slavery and Ethnicity in the Transformation of a Southeast Asian Maritime State*, 2nd edition. Singapore University Press (originally published Singapore University Press, 1981).

Wolters, O. W. [1982] 1999. *History, Culture, and Region in Southeast Asian Perspectives*, revised edition. Ithaca, NY: Cornell University Press (originally published Singapore: Institute of Southeast Asian Studies).

Womack, Sarah. 2006. "Ethnicity and Martial Races: The Garde indigène of Cambodia in the 1880s and 1990s." In *Colonial Armies in Southeast Asia*, eds. Karl Hack and Tobias Rettig, 107–25. London/New York: Routledge.

Zakaria bin Haji Ahmad, and Harold A. Crouch, eds. 1985. *Military-civilian Relations in South-East Asia.* Singapore: Oxford University Press.

Southeast Asian Armed Forces in the Precolonial and Colonial Periods

CHAPTER 1

Military Traditions and Society in Lan Na*

Volker Grabowsky

The control of manpower, not the conquest of territory, determined military strategies in precolonial Indianized Southeast Asia. The rulers of Southeast Asia, instead of fighting for incorporating weaker neighbors into their realms and administrative systems, appeared to be more interested in capturing people whom they could resettle in the heartland of their kingdoms. The main problem confronting the traditional polities in Southeast Asia, in particular those on the mainland, was not a shortage of land but of manpower. At the beginning of the nineteenth century the whole of Southeast Asia had a population of only 30–40 million inhabitants, only a twentieth of the region's present-day population. Southeast Asia as a whole was then a sparsely settled region especially when compared to the much larger population figures of China (*c.* 300 million) and the Indian subcontinent (*c.* 150 million).[1] To solve the problem of chronic manpower shortage, people had to be captured and deported in order to strengthen the workforce at the disposal of a ruler and his government.

The ancient Siamese military textbook, *Tamra Phichai Songkhram* [Textbook on the Victory in War],[2] praises the deportations of combatants as well as civilians as an appropriate military strategy: "If one has taken war captives (*chaloei*), one soldier shall take one prisoner and take him away, in the case he is a male [combatant]; and the rope has to be tightened around the [prisoner's] neck. If women are captured, one soldier can lead off three of them" (quoted in Chanchai 1984, 92).

* This article is a slightly revised and updated version of an article published in *Tai Culture*, Vol. 24, March 2015–March 2016, pp. 140–57.

In the commentary to "Letters of Luang Udomsombat," first published in 1906, on the Siamese punitive expedition against Kedah in 1841 when numerous Malay captives were resettled in Bangkok and in the central plain, Prince Damrong Rachanuphap, King Chulalongkorn's younger brother and the doyen of modern Thai historiography, made some shrewd remarks on what he perceived as an ancient Southeast Asian military tradition (Damrong 1987, 255–56). Prince Damrong defined two primarily *military* objectives of forced resettlement:

1. Weakening—temporarily or permanently—the enemy by deporting large numbers of his workforce and by creating depopulated border zones which would diminish the enemy's potential to military uprisings.
2. Rewarding generals for their loyalty and bravery by giving them war captives as personal servants.

Likewise, Prince Damrong indirectly acknowledged the *political* and *economic* objectives, among the most crucial of these being:

1. The augmentation and concentration of manpower for intensive wet-rice cultivation, which constituted the basis for agrarian surplus and economic wealth in general.
2. An additional reserve of manpower in order to recruit powerful armies in times of war and to accomplish mainly religiously motivated large-scale projects, such as temples, Buddha images, etc., in peaceful times.
3. The demonstration of the glory and charisma of the ruler who was able to increase his political power base vis-à-vis provincial elites by resettling conquered populations in the core area of his realm.[3]

During the late eighteenth and early nineteenth centuries, the northern part of present-day Thailand, also known by its historical name Lan Na (literally "[land of] a million ricefields"), was one of the region's most seriously affected by forced resettlement. *Kep phak sai sa kep kha sai müang*, which is widely regarded as an old northern Thai (Tai Yuan) saying, characterizes the forced resettlement of war captives from regions in the present-day Burmese Shan States and Sipsòng Panna to present-day northern Thailand during the late eighteenth and early nineteenth centuries. The saying, which is documented in a Lao document from Luang Prabang dated 1853, was popularized by the late Kraisri Nimmanhaeminda, who rendered it into English as "Put Vegetables Into Baskets, and People Into Towns" (1965).[4] As the present writer has demonstrated elsewhere,[5] Lan Na society during the early Bangkok period (*c.* 1782–1855)[6] was shaped by the military strategy of forcibly relocating large populations to zones under firm royal authority. By the mid-nineteenth century, up to two-fifths of the population in the five northern Thai principalities of Lan Na—Chiang Mai, Lamphun, Lampang, Phrae, and Nan—were of captive origin.

In this chapter I will first trace the military strategy outlined above, dating back to the early history of Lan Na when the region was a united independent Tai confederation under the suzerainty of Chiang Mai ruled by the kings of the Mangrai dynasty (1296–1558). During the subsequent period (1558–1775), when Lan Na came under Burmese rule or dominance, forced resettlement became an even more prevalent feature of Lan Na society. However, it was not until the reign of King Kawila of Chiang Mai (1782–1816) that this military strategy evolved and was fully adopted as an official state policy. The chapter also covers the implementation of a military strategy that depends predominantly on the willingness of the deportees to accept their destiny. A further focus will be on the recruiting of the armies involved in relocation schemes and the human experience during the process of forced resettlement.

Forced Resettlement in Early Lan Na History, pre-1558

The first record of a forced movement of population to Lan Na dates from the late thirteenth century. *The Chiang Mai Chronicle*, which dates from the early nineteenth century, reports that after a successful military campaign against Hongsawadi (Pegu) in 1288, the ruler of this Mon kingdom gave his beloved daughter to the victor, King Mangrai of Lan Na, and ordered "a group of 500 men and women and their families" to accompany the princess (Wyatt and Aroonrut 1995, 36.) A deportation in the opposite direction, from Lan Na to Siam, is mentioned in the *Royal Chronicles of Ayutthaya*. In

1385, King Bòrommatrailokanat sent troops to attack Chiang Mai, and after his victorious retreat the king "ordered that those Lao [here, northern Thai] who had been driven down from Chiang Mai be sent on to be kept in the cities of Phatthalung, Songkhla, Nakhòn Si Thammarat, and Canthabun" (Cushman 2000, 13).

Along with the fierce struggle in the second half of the fifteenth century between Lan Na and Ayutthaya for supremacy over the Sukhothai-Phitsanulok region, strategic concerns gained momentum both in Chiang Mai and in Ayutthaya to weaken the adversary by depopulating the respective border zones. In 1461, King Tilok of Chiang Mai (r. 1441–87) suppressed a rebellion in Chaliang (Si Satchanalai), at that time a southern outpost of Lan Na. As a measure of retaliation, the city's famous potters were deported to Wiang Kalòng in Chiang Rai province and San Kamphaeng in Chiang Mai province, where they established the northern Thai school of the Sangkhalok-Sukhothai pottery.[7]

Under the reign of King Müang Kaeo (1495–1526), notably after 1507, Chiang Mai extended its raids deep into territories that once belonged to Sukhothai. The rationale behind these military operations was not the conquest of the border regions and their incorporation into the Lan Na kingdom but the deportation of the local population to areas closer to Chiang Mai. A depopulated or sparsely populated buffer zone could provide a check on unrestrained northern expansion of the Siamese kingdom of Ayutthaya. The augmentation of Chiang Mai's weakening manpower base may have been another motive for the raids, which came to an end by the 1540s when Ayutthaya had gained a definite upper hand and was able to deport substantial populations from Lampang and Phrae to the southeast of Chiang Mai.

A serious shortage of manpower had prompted King Müang Kaeo to encourage migrations of Shan and Tai Khün in the Salween region to the kingdom's heartland near Chiang Mai. In 1517 alone, more than 23,000 people migrated from the Shan vassal *müang*[8] of Chiang Thòng, Müang Nai, and Müang Kai, and resettled along the northern fringes of the Ping River basin. The migrants were encouraged to resettle voluntarily in rice-growing areas, such as Fang, Chiang Dao, and Phrao, situated 80–150 kilometers to the north of the capital (Wyatt and Aroonrut 1995, 106).

One is tempted to speculate that these resettlements were motivated by the need of additional manpower to accomplish construction projects, such as the fortifications and extension of the city walls of Chiang Mai and Lampang around 1517. One might question whether the Shan had really come on their own free will or had been enticed by a combination of promises and military pressure. No matter how they were motivated, three years later, in 1520, many of the Shan, including the ruler of Müang Nai, decided to abandon their new homesteads and flee back "across the Salween [River] to the Shan domains" (Wyatt and Aroonrut 1995, 106).

Half a century earlier, in 1462–63, King Tilok launched a military campaign against the Shan State of Müang Nai, a campaign requested by rival Shan rulers. This campaign resulted in the subjugation of Müang Nai and eleven other Shan *müang* situated mainly on the west bank of the Salween River. As many of those *müang* were far beyond the sphere of intervention of the Chiang Mai ruler, he was content to be recognized as overlord and deported more than 12,000 war captives (*khòi*) to Phrao and a district situated roughly 30 kilometers west of Chiang Mai (Wyatt and Aroonrut 1995, 97).

The conquered Shan *müang* were not adversaries on a par with Chiang Mai. The forced resettlement of thousands of Shan turned out to be a twofold advantage for the victor. It disciplined the subjugated polities and, at the same time, strengthened the population potential in the core area of Lan Na. However, such a strategy could be counterproductive if the adversary possessed strong socio-political structures and was far superior in terms of demographic and economic resources. Then it was considered appropriate to act with restraint even after gaining military successes in order to avoid devastating counterattacks. Such awareness may have motivated Tilok to criticize the governor of Nan for his rash action taken after his victory against the "Kaeo" (Vietnamese) who had attacked the neighboring kingdom of Lan Sang (Laos) and were also threatening the eastern parts of Lan Na. *The Nan Chronicle*, composed around 1894, reports:

> In the *poek set* year,[9] CS 842 [AD 1480/1],[10] a Kaeo army invaded Nan. Phaña [King] Tilok ordered Tao Kha Kan to meet them with a force of forty thousand. He defeated the Kaeo and killed a large number of the enemy. Then he [gave orders to] behead them and delivered [their heads] to Phaña Tilok. He also captured large numbers of elephants, horses and families, which he presented to Phaña Tilok. Then Phaña Tilok said [to Tao Kha Kan]: "The Kaeo have suffered a defeat and fled, this should have sufficed. On the contrary, you have followed the Kaeo in pursuit and captured numerous Kaeo families. The wrath of the enemies is awful. The Kaeo [families] should not be allowed to settle in Nantaburi [Müang Nan]." Tilok then transferred Tao Kha Kan to Chiang Rai.[11]

During the second quarter of the sixteenth century, the Lan Na kingdom was in a state of decline, both politically and economically. Constant wars with Ayutthaya, its more powerful neighbor to the south, had depleted economic resources as well as manpower. Ambitious religious projects, such as the founding and renovation of monasteries, put additional strain on Lan Na society and the economy. Internal strife was rampant, exacerbating the general political crisis. When Burmese troops attacked Chiang Mai in 1558, the city surrendered without offering any serious resistance.[12]

Mangthra's War Against Chiang Mai, 1558–1788

King Bayinnaung (r. 1551–81) of Burma regarded Lan Na as a rear base where manpower and provisions of food and ammunition could be stockpiled for the imminent attack on Ayutthaya. Although the Burmese eventually had to retreat from Ayutthaya and the Siamese heartland, which they had dominated for some fifteen years (1569–84), they were determined to incorporate Lan Na into the outer belt of vassal states. According to Aye Gyaw, the Burmese kings thought Chiang Mai was strategically more essential to their survival than Ayutthaya because it gave them access to all the Tai-inhabited areas north and east of the Ping valley, including the northern part of present-day Laos.[13]

From 1578, Chiang Mai and other important *müang* were ruled by Burmese noblemen. The Yuan elite was strictly controlled by Burmese or Mon civilian and military officials. Inter-elite rivalries along regional lines resulted eventually in the political fragmentation of Lan Na. Occasional political uprisings in the first half of the seventeenth century, notably during the reign of King Thalun (1628–48), could therefore be easily suppressed because the rebels were inferior in arms and their actions were uncoordinated. Burmese retaliatory measures had always been decisive and harsh. The military strategy to quell the resistance included large-scale deportations of war captives to Pegu or Ava. The Burmese suppressed the uprisings in Chiang Mai twice in this way, in 1614–15 and 1632. These campaigns are remembered in northern Thai popular traditions as "Mangthara's War against Chiang Mai." "Mangthra" is a generic term for the Burmese king and does not refer to a specific ruler.

"Mangthra's War against Chiang Mai" is also the title of an epic poem, the *Khlong rüang mangthra rop chiang mai* (*KMCM*). This poem, comprising more than three hundred stanzas, is one of the oldest travel poems (*nirat*) of the Thai and among the most important items of Lan Na literature. The late northern Thai scholar Singkha Wannasai transliterated the poem into modern Thai script and also published a translation into the central Thai (Siamese) language (1979).[14] *KMCM* describes the deportation of the Yuan war captives from Chiang Mai to Hongsawadi (Pegu). Able-bodied men, women, old people and children had to set out on a long, difficult journey as is evocatively described in stanzas 84 and 105 (Singkha 1979, 33, 40):

> (84) The present hardships are the results of deeds in previous existences. Calamities haunt us as I am led away [and we are separated from each other]. Everything is void: the city, the palace and the rice-fields. Only the landscape, the mountains and rivers, are still there. Everything looks solitary and deserted.
>
> (105) Numerous people, elephants and horses are moving forward. En route they [reach] Nòng Khòp, a never-ending column. [They are] Tai, Mon, Burmese and Lao.[15] Relentlessly they are being forced to

> march forward. Crowded like termites on their nuptial flight they are heading for Hongsawadi (Pegu).

Burmese sources confirm the resettlement of Tai-speaking populations, including Yuan from Chiang Mai, to inner Burma. The large-scale deportations of Yuan to Pegu were obviously a response to heavy population losses in Lower Burma caused by war and political turmoil during the late sixteenth century. According to Victor Lieberman, "Anauk-hpet-lun may have settled Tai prisoners around Pegu between 1616 and 1624, but these deportations could hardly compensate for the losses of the late sixteenth century" (1984, 59; see also Lieberman 1980). Lieberman argues that Burmese sources document that resettlement of war captives to the new core area around Ava in upper Burma, to where the capital had been transferred, between 1635 and 1648, was more numerous than in all the remaining 142 years of the Toungoo dynasty combined (Lieberman 1984, 98; compare Koenig 1990, 7–8). Several royal edicts of King Thalun reflect the transfer of non-Burman ethnic groups, including Shan and Yuan, to previously deserted or sparsely populated areas in the dry zone of upper Burma.[16] The Burmese historian Daw Mya Sein summarizes the results of Thalun's policy of forced resettlement as follows (1973, 12):

> Thalun organized the revenue administration and directed the revenue inquest of A.D. 1637. He settled prisoners of war in the Kyaukse area where the families supplied the labour while they served as soldiers; other parts of Burma too were peopled in a similar way. Men from Toungoo, Zimmé (Chiang Mai), Kyaingyon, Kyainti, Tavoy, Hanthawaddy (Pegu) consisting of Shans, Gwe (Karen), Yun (Tai Yuan), Talaing (Mon), Arakanese and 250 hostages from Tenasserim were present in the Ledwin area when the inquest was made.

As Burmese sources often classify the Tai Yuan along with other Tai groups as "Shan," it is not always possible to distinguish the former from the

Tai Lü and the Tai Yai (Shan proper). At the beginning of the nineteenth century, up to one-fifth of the population in upper Burma were descendants of war captives. Thus, with an estimated population of 1.7 million in the Burmese core area, there were approximately 350,000 people whose ancestors had once been deported from various neighboring countries, including Lan Na. The Burmese distributed the deportees within a wide geographical region, in settlements interspersed among ethnic Burmese villages. As large coherent areas with a majority of migrants did not exist, the court at Ava was able to integrate these potentially rebellious populations more easily.[17] The new settlers cleared forests, reclaimed fallow land, and built irrigation channels. Thus, the population density in the dry zone of upper Burma increased gradually (Lieberman 1991, 5).

In the early eighteenth century, the Burmese transferred their administrative center in Lan Na from the old capital Chiang Mai to Chiang Saen, located further northeast on the right bank of the Mekong River. According to Hans Penth, the subsequent division of the country into "North Lan Na" (Chiang Saen) and "South Lan Na" (Chiang Mai) was conceived as part of a Burmese divide-and-rule strategy (1994, 28). Moreover, the rise of Chiang Saen reflected the growing economic importance of the upper Mekong valley, once a shift from maritime to overland trade had occurred in Burma and the surrounding regions (for details, see Grabowsky 1999, 50). A relatively peaceful period came to an end when the Kon-baung rulers initiated a new phase of political and military expansion in the 1760s. As a strategic rear base in the Burmese struggle against Siam, Lan Na suffered severe material and population losses. When a combined attack of Tai Yuan and Siamese forces expelled an increasingly repressive Burmese army from Chiang Mai in February 1775, large parts of the country were in a shambles. One version of *The Chiang Mai Chronicle* describes the complete desolation of Lan Na's former cultural and political center as follows (*Tamnan sipha ratchawong* 1989, 20): "At that time Chiang Mai was depopulated and had become a jungle overgrown by climbing plants, it turned into a place where rhinoceroses, elephants, tigers and bears were living. There were few people living in groups. Everything was overgrown leaving out the eaves of the houses and the roads to facilitate communication with each other, as there were no opportunities for clearing [the jungle]."

A similar situation prevailed in Nan, close to the border to Luang Prabang. According to Chonthira Sattayawatthana, "from 1558 until 1788, a period of 230 years, the people of Nan hardly experienced anything different from war and . . . were deported to Burma, Chiang Rai and Thoeng" (1987, 157). This may be an exaggeration. But when Nan's ruler Atthawònpanyo returned to his principality as a Siamese vassal in 1788, *The Nan Chronicle* laments that large parts of the population were hiding in the forests and mountains: "In [CS] 1145 [AD 1783/4], a *kap mao* year,[18] Nan was completely deserted. It had no ruler to care of [its citizens], and most of the people had evacuated the town fleeing into the jungle and mountains" (Wyatt 1994, 89).

Forced Resettlement in the Age of Kawila, 1775–1816

Tributary relations between the Tai Yuan princes and the Siamese king had been established between 1782 and 1788 in recognition of the crucial military support of Bangkok against the Burmese who at that time still controlled parts of Lan Na, especially the regions of Chiang Saen and Chiang Rai. The liberation of Lan Na from Burmese rule was a long struggle that had dragged on for almost thirty years and faced several setbacks as the Burmese offensive capacities remained intact until 1797. The struggle for liberation started with an uprising in the south, culminating in the recapture of Chiang Mai in 1775 by Tai Yuan and Siamese troops and ended after several setbacks in 1804 with the conquest of Chiang Saen on the upper Mekong, which the Burmese had reinforced as their main fortress in the region. This final assault was a combined attack by Tai Yuan, Lao, and Siamese troops. Burmese forces had to abandon not only the fertile valley between the towns of Chiang Rai and Chiang Saen, which became depopulated during the following decades by both voluntary migration and forced resettlement to the south, but also, temporarily, their Tai Khün and Tai Lü tributary states north of Chiang Saen, notably Chiang Tung and Müang Yòng.[19] The Tai Yuan armies were small, numbering a few thousand soldiers, but they were able to mount formidable defense positions when they were attacked by large, superior Burmese armies. As the rainy season (May–September) made military operations difficult for an invader, the beleaguered Tai Yuan troops had to hold out for a couple of months until powerful Siamese reinforcements had arrived. This was the case in 1776–77, 1784, 1787, and again in 1797, as shown in table 1.

Table 1. Large-scale Military Campaigns in Lan Na, 1774–1804

Year	Kind of War	Size of Lan Na Troops and Allies	Size of Burmese Troops and Allies
1774–75	Lan Na attack on and conquest of Chiang Mai	15,000 (Siamese from Bangkok); 20,000 (Siamese from northern provinces)	9,000 (Burmese under Po Suphla in Lampang); 4,000 (Burmese in Chiang Mai); 7,000 (Burmese in Lampang); 10,000–12,000 (Tai Yuan in Chiang Mai)
1776–77	Burmese attack on Lampang	700 (Tai Yuan defenders)	7,000
1778	Attack against Chiang Saen (near the confluence of the Kok River)	?	?
1784	Burmese attack on Lampang	1,000 (Tai Yuan defending Lampang)	30,000 (Burmese under Cao Müang Toungoo)
1787	Burmese attack on a) Pasang b) Lampang	1,000 (Yuan defending Pasang); 150 (Tai Yuan defending the passes of M. Yuan)	16,000 (Burmese attacking from M. Yuan) 30,000 (Burmese, Shan, and Yuan attacking Lampang from Chiang Rai)
1789	Battle near Chiang Saen	?	3,000 (Burmese)
1793	Lan Na attack on Chiang Saen	10,000–12,000 (Tai Yuan from Chiang Mai)	?
1797	Burmese siege of Chiang Mai	20,000 (Siamese from Phitsanulok); 20,000 (Lao from Vientiane)	80,000–99,000 (Burmese)
1802–3	Lan Na attack on Chiang Saen	3,000 (Tai Yuan from Chiang Mai)	?
1804	Lan Na attack on and conquest of Chiang Saen	20,000 (Siamese, Lao); 4,500 (Tai Yuan)	?

Source: Bòdin 2002.

In 1802, Kawila, ruler of Chiang Mai, traveled to Bangkok where King Rama I bestowed upon him the title *cao prathetsarat*, accepting him as a high-ranking vassal. The king acknowledged the supremacy of Chiang Mai over the previously separate principalities of Lampang and Lamphun. Like Chiang Mai, the latter two vassal states were ruled by members of the Kawila clan. Chiang Mai was the political center in the western half of Lan Na. In the eastern half, close to the Laotian border, the principality of Nan played a similar role *vis-à-vis* the small vassal state of Phrae.

At the beginning of Kawila's reign, the weak population base was the biggest obstacle to the final expulsion of the Burmese from Lan Na and the reconstruction of Chiang Mai as the country's political and cultural center. However, little by little people came out from their jungle hideouts and returned to their former villages in the deserted basins of the Ping, Kuang, and Wang rivers. Kawila also persuaded a group of former Chiang Mai inhabitants who had fled to Müang Yuam (Mae Sariang) in the early 1760s to return. The ruler of Nan, at that time hardly less powerful and influential than his counterpart in Chiang Mai, initiated a similar policy of voluntary remigration to the centers of state power.[20]

Voluntary migration was, however, not sufficient to create a strong demographic base necessary for social and economic recovery. Thus, the old military tradition of forced resettlement of war captives had to be resuscitated. Between 1782, the foundation of Pa Sang, and 1816, Kawila's death, the ruler of Chiang Mai led a number of small and large raids and resettled war captives in his realm. There were at least three important waves of resettlement campaigns. The first wave began shortly after the building of Pa Sang and was designed to increase the manpower at Kawila's disposal for the re-establishment of Chiang Mai. The second, in which more people were captured than in the first wave, began in 1798 and culminated in the conquest of Chiang Saen in 1804. The last wave, around 1808–10, finally attained Kawila's goals.

After 1810, there is no evidence of any further resettlement campaigns initiated by Phaya Kawila. By the time of his death in January 1816, the policy of *Kep phak sai sa kep kha sai müang* had come to an end. This does not mean that Kawila's immediate successors completely abstained from raiding neighboring territories in search of manpower. Small-scale raids against

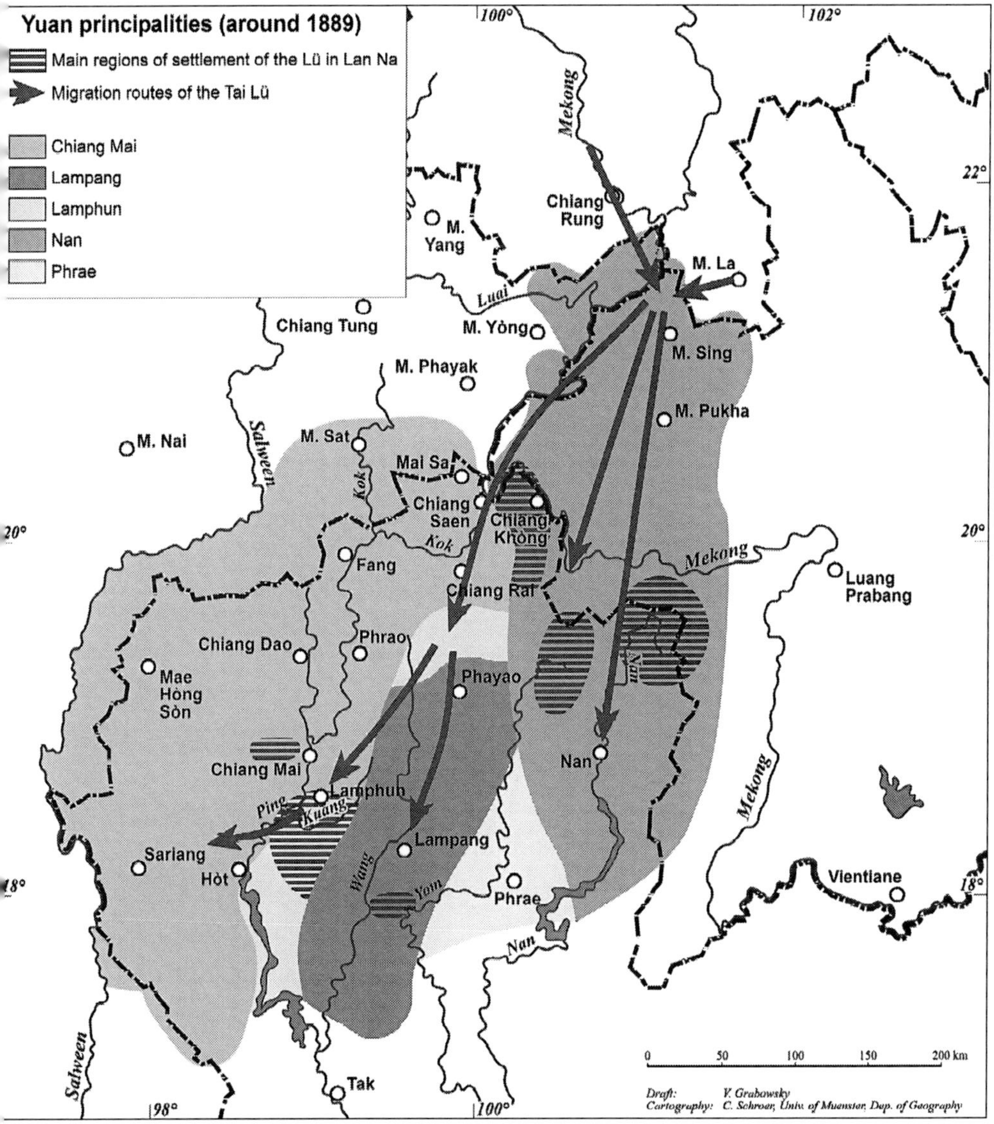

Map 1. Yuan principalities around 1889

Karen territories west of Mae Hong Son occurred occasionally during the 1820s and 1830s. For example, in 1823 a raid was launched even into Mon areas north of Martaban (for details, see Grabowsky 1999, 57).

The principality of Nan employed a similar strategy. For example, in 1812 thousands of people from from Müang La, Müang Phong and Müang Luang Phu Kha were deported to Nan in a large military campaign. Altogether 6,000 people were resettled in Nan at that time (Wyatt 1994, 105). A connection of these forced resettlements with the construction of additional irrigation canals, only two years later, seems the most plausible explanation. The building of a new capital two kilometers to the north of the old one, in 1817–18, might also have benefited from the influx of war captives. Apart from the participation of Nan in the Siamese war against Vientiane (1827–28), which yielded more than six hundred prisoners of war as "royal awards" to Nan, no hints of other resettlement campaigns are given in *The Nan Chronicle* (Wyatt 1994, 113–14).

The Expedition against Müang Sat, 1839: A Case Study

One of the most important campaigns with regard to captured manpower was an assault on Müang Tuan, Müang Pu, and Müang Sat in 1839. This military campaign, albeit conceived by the northern Thai rulers, was launched in close cooperation with Bangkok. The campaign is important for throwing light on some of the strategies employed in forced resettlement. Almost 2,000 people from the three *müang* were deported to Chiang Mai. A report from Chiang Mai and Lamphun to Bangkok dated 1839 describes the success of the campaign during the reign of Cao Phutthawong of Chiang Mai:

> On the eighth waning of the fifth month of the year *kun ekkasok*[21] (7 April 1839) Phraya Uparat (the viceroy), Nai Phimmasan and Phraya Ratchawong left Chiang Mai with 3,300 soldiers; from Lamphun Phraya Uparat [of that place] departed with nine hundred soldiers, [making up] a total of 4,300. [They marched] to attack Müang Pu, Müang Sat and Müang Tuan. The troops returned on

> the eighth waxing of the seventh month (21 May 1839). Originally they had seized 1,868 persons. The military leaders and officers got one thousand persons, the rest were presented to the ruler.[22]

It is interesting to note that the majority of war captives were not placed as commoners (*phrai müang*) under Cao Phutthawong, the then ruler of Chiang Mai, but became the personal war booty of the main military commanders, such as the viceroys of Chiang Mai and Lamphun and their bravest officers. Their status was that of "war slaves" (*that chaloei*), a reason why this inferior social group was not included in the census below which, typical for premodern census taking, also included draught animals and the weapons seized.

Table 2. War Captives and Other War Booty from Müang Tuan, Müang Sat, and Müang Pu

War Booty	Müang Tuan	Müang Sat	Müang Pu	Total
Rulers (**thao**)	2	1	1	4*
Noblemen (**khunnang**)	15	12	3	30*
Nobility (total)	**17**	**13***	**4**	**34**
Commoners (**phrai**)	69	39	28	136
Able-Bodied men (total)	**86***	**52***	**32***	**170**
Family members	422	132	144	698
Population (total)	**508**	**184**	**176**	**868**
Rifles (**pün lak**)	2	2	2	4
Wheellocks (**khap sila**)	3	15	3	21
Matchlocks (**khap chut**)	5	1	5	11
Weapons (total)	**10**	**18**	**10**	**36**
Horses (male)	?	?	?	9
Horses (female)	?	?	?	6
Horses (total)	**6**	**3**	**6**	**15**
Oxen (male)	?	?	?	184
Cows (female)	?	?	?	62
Oxen and cows (total)	**?**	**?**	**?**	**246**

Note: Population figures exclude slaves.

* Figures not mentioned in the document below but calculated by the author.

? No figures given.

Source: Hò samut haeng chat, Cotmaihet R.3, C.S. 1201, No. 6.

The majority of the deportees came from Müang Tuan as it was the first township the invading troops reached when they advanced from Chiang Dao and Müang Ngai. From Müang Tuan the Tai Yuan troops marched to Müang Sat and Müang Pu where they captured only a part of the population. Numerous inhabitants, including the local ruler (*cao fa*) of Müang Pu, had managed to escape. Müang Sat had been victim of forced resettlement campaigns twice before, in 1798 and 1801–02. It was not before 1836–37 when the ruler of Müang Pu, a vassal of the Burmese king, ordered his son to repopulate Müang Sat as well as Müang Tuan. This measure was clearly perceived by Bangkok and Chiang Mai as a security threat since Müang Sat and Müang Tuan belonged to Chiang Mai's sphere of influence.

When the British diplomat-explorer William Couperus McLeod made his pioneering journey to Chiang Mai, Chiang Tung, and Chiang Rung, he reported on his way back to Moulmein, on April 24, 1837, that the viceroy of Chiang Mai had "pledged himself to the king to reduce numerous places belonging to the Burmans, and bring them under his authority" (Grabowsky and Turton 2003, 417). Although the Siamese *Royal Chronicle of the Third Reign* does not mention the attack on Müang Sat, there is little doubt that Bangkok fully approved the military campaign as a pre-emptive strike. David Richardson, another British pioneering diplomat-explorer, who had been in Chiang Mai in August 1839, a few months after the deportees had arrived there, wrote about his encounter with the viceroy and some other *cao*: "[They had] the most lively recollection of the Birman rule. They supposed or affected to suppose (for the true reason of the attack was the fear of losing the northern people already mentioned as forming so large a portion of the population, added to the hope of obtaining slaves and plunder) that the measure was preparatory to an invasion of their country as soon as a point of assembly and depot of provisions could be formed at the new towns."[23]

Richardson informed E. A. Blundell, the British governor of the Tenasserim provinces, that he was told about the details of the military campaign by an officer who was responsible for the registration of the deportees and their belongings. This man, a native of Müang Sat who had lived in Chiang Mai since 1802, reported: "There were 1,815 miserable captives of all ages, from a few days up to seventy or eighty years old, and about five hundred cattle. He also stated that some thirty years ago, about the time his father was made prisoner, the Zimmay [Chiang Mai] people had destroyed these towns in the same way they had done now."[24]

William Melchers convincingly argues that the successful raid against Müang Sat not only bolstered the courage and self-confidence of the Chiang Mai leaders but also made them and their superiors in Bangkok believe "that a more formal invasion into the heartland of Kengtung [Chiang Tung] state would result in many more captives" (1986, 197). In fact, during the first of three wars against the Burmese tributary state of Chiang Tung, in 1850, the invaders from Chiang Mai, Lampang, and Lamphun were preoccupied with capturing inhabitants from the area as their predecessors had done so many times before. Although it was in the interests of the Tai Yuan rulers to weaken Chiang Tung, militarily and politically, its total destruction was not intended as trade with Chiang Tung had become more and more important since the 1830s. Thus, instead of joining the siege of Chiang Tung, the main Chiang Mai army of 1,500 men stayed in the areas south of the town, where they were engaged in gathering war captives in Müang Phayak, Müang Len, Müang Yòng, and, once again, Müang Sat, to resettle the captured population in the Ping-Kuang basin. As many as 5,000 captives were forced to march to Chiang Mai. As all of these *müang* combined had, in 1853, a total population of probably fewer than 15,000 inhabitants (or 2,100 households), according to contemporary Siamese sources, the deportations caused a serious drain on manpower for the affected region.[25]

The last deportation to Chiang Mai that the present writer is able to trace occurred in 1869 under Kawilorot (r. 1856–70). Mòk Mai was attacked after its ruler, Fa Kolan, refused to resettle his *müang* voluntarily in Phrao in Chiang Mai territory. These post-Kawila raids were motivated by considerations of security along the country's western border, not by a search for manpower.

Human Aspects of Implementing a Military Strategy

Military campaigns in Lan Na were in most cases not commanded by the ruler himself but by the *cao hò na*, literally "the lord of the front palace," as the viceroy was usually called in Lan Na, who was in charge of military affairs. This was the case during the reign of Kawila (1782–1816) when the king's younger brother, viceroy Thammalangka, assumed military responsibility for leading the army either together with the king or, especially after 1804, alone. The campaigns against Müang Sat in 1839 and Chiang Tung in 1850 are further examples demonstrating the crucial military role of the viceroy. As Lan Na, like Siam, had no standing army, the troops had to be levied from among the social class of *phrai müang*, commoners who had to work several months a year for the ruler and other royalty. Rare Western visitors, such as McLeod in early 1837, testify to the readiness for war which even characterized Chiang Mai society during the relatively peaceful reign of King Phutthawong (1825–46). McLeod also points to the crucial role of elephants as a means of transportation:

> The owner of each house is supposed to have a musket, and certainly no Shan [here, Tai Yuan] is met beyond the town travelling without one. Each chief may be called upon to supply, at the utmost, two-thirds of his followers during any war, these are obliged to supply themselves with provisions and carriage. Their own chiefs furnish at the rate of one elephant to five men; if the campaign is a distant one, Government occasionally gives an elephant. Two men can be exempted from going by supplying an elephant for the public service. Each man is furnished with one viss[26] of powder and fifty balls from the stores, and should he not possess a musket one is lent him. Some are also armed with spears and swords. Elephants alone are used for the transport of an army, and of these there are a great number in all the Siamese Shan towns. One branch of the army consists of elephants trained to carry two jingals[27] and four men each, but these

> are never fired over the animal's head; he is made to turn his tail to the enemy before they are discharged.[28]

We may assume that the frequent military campaigns of the late eighteenth and nineteenth centuries had certainly created a large pool of seasoned and brave soldiers among this group. The British captain, not without bias, seemed to be less enthusiastic about the Tai Yuan soldiers:

> From the materials with which their army is constructed, it can only be expected to be an undisciplined mob. The Shans [here, Tai Yuan] are considered adepts at lying in ambuscades and for night attacks. They certainly are quick of sight and hearing, and creep through the forests in a surprising and quiet way; their constant life in the woods in search of game gives them this advantage. All their attacks on their neighbours' villages have been made at night. They never wait to make a regular attack or fight by day; if they fail in their attempt, they retreat and watch a more favourable opportunity. They are not, I should say, a brave race, but boast exceedingly of their victories over the Burmans, and consider one of themselves as equal to ten Burmans.[29] They are hardy and capable of undergoing fatigue.[30]

We know very little about how the raiding troops organized the transport of the captured populations. In some instances, distances of hundreds of kilometers had to be overcome until the war captives finally reached their destination. Such a journey could take weeks or even months. Relatively large troops were necessary to guard even a handful of captured civilians. This dilemma is reflected in the *Tamra Phichai Songkhram* quoted above. The Siamese textbook on military strategy admonishes the victorious army to be most cautious during the transport of war captives (Chanchai 1984, 93):

> When taking war captives home you should hurry up during the first four hundred *sen* [*c*. 16 kilometers] in order to ward off various kinds of calamities (*het rai*). After one thousand *sen* [*c*. 40 kilometers] you

> can continue the transport of the war captives more slowly. However, if enemy troops (*kha sük*) follow in pursuit, the war captives have to march in front. In the rear a company (*kòng*) of one thousand soldiers, elephant and horse units as well as lancers have to guard the captives well.

Yet, even the best organized campaigns of forced relocation could hardly depopulate the raided territories completely. By fleeing into the jungles and mountainous areas or retreating to safe enclaves, large parts of the population could escape. Our sources do not allow us to conclude the proportion of war captives who were able to flee their guards as circumstances could vary considerably. The experiences of the Siamese campaign against Vientiane in 1827–29, however, show that it was very difficult to guard large groups of war captives over long distances. Therefore, military power alone did not suffice. The armies sent out to raid a *müang* had to apply a politico-military strategy that concentrated on capturing its ruling families. If the ruler and his relatives consented to resettlement, sooner or later their subjects would follow them. Many inhabitants of Chiang Saen who escaped captivity in 1804 returned thereafter to their ruined *müang*. But they failed to rehabilitate their agriculture. Several consecutive bad harvests convinced them that, because of the deportation of its ruler, Chiang Saen had become an ill-fated place to inhabit. Thus, the returnees decided to abandon Chiang Saen and follow their ruler to Chiang Mai (Nithi 1991, 270).

The resettlement of many thousands of people over long distances demanded that victorious armies be highly organized. The deportees not only had to take their moveable belongings with them but also any equipment they would need in their new settlements. Decent shelter and large quantities of food also had to be provided during the marches. The success of such ambitious operations depended on the cooperation of the deportees. They were often enticed by promises, such as fertile land and permanent protection against war, which made the forced resettlement appear a more attractive alternative. Escape from guards on route was not always easy and was also very dangerous. If captives did manage to escape, they would face the dangers of the jungle, hunger, and disease.

Moreover, the reconstruction of old home towns and villages was a tedious task, particularly since the victors had often resorted to a scorched earth policy before marching off. Nevertheless, time and again groups of war captives decided to escape and return to their deserted homes even if this meant even more hardship. When, in 1836, the governor of the Phuan principality of Siang Khwang in the Plain of Jars (eastern Laos), Cao San, surrendered to Siamese troops from Nòng Khai and their Lao allies of Luang Prabang, he agreed to the resettlement of the Phuan on the west bank of the Mekong river. However, this decision met resistance as revealed in the *Phuan Chronicle* (Khamman 1952, 14):

> After two or three days Thai [i.e. Siamese] and Lao troops arrived at Siang Khwang. The Siamese commander spoke to Cao San: "This is the situation. If the Vietnamese come back once again, what would you, Cao San, do? It is impossible to station Thai troops in Müang Phuan. If the Thai troops can't stay, the Vietnamese will certainly return to Müang Phuan." Thus the Thai commander forced Cao San to deport families in order to establish themselves in Phan Lam. Six thousand Phuan were enticed to come to Nòng Khai from where they would be taken to Bangkok. Having come to realise that, Cao San and Cao Sali, sons of Cao Men Nòi, could flee back with three thousand people. Thereafter, many of them died of hunger.

In most cases, a combination of military coercion and material incentives proved to be more successful. The evacuations of Chiang Tung in 1804 and Müang Yòng in 1805 are cases in point (Grabowsky 1999, 56, 58–59). Provided that the promises of better and larger paddy fields, improved social and political security, and economic prosperity were not delusions, forced resettlement of parts of the population of an area could be followed by voluntary migration of those who had stayed behind. This happened in Nan where, during the 1830s and 1840s, numerous Tai Lü refugees from Sipsòng

Panna sought shelter because their country had been plunged into anarchy and civil war.[31] These voluntary immigrants strengthened Tai Lü settlements in the core area of Nan, which had been founded a generation earlier by war captives. The immigrants were enticed not only by promises of fertile land to settle on but also by strict enforcement of just rule according to the old laws and customs of Lan Na. As a late nineteenth-century Western visitor noted, "the rulers seem more liberal, more desirous of the welfare of their people, than in any other Laos [Tai Yuan] province" (*Siam and Laos as Seen by Our American Missionaries* 1884, 541).

Conclusion

In large parts of precolonial mainland Southeast Asia, commoners were regarded as pawns by contending rulers. Like draught animals, they were destined to be captured, distributed, and resettled for various political or social reasons. Military campaigns fought for forced resettlement had become an important occupation, if not the main rationale of wars, for many rulers in precolonial mainland Southeast Asia. The Lan Na strategy of *Kep phak sai sa kep kha sai müang* had its parallels in Burma, Siam, Laos, and Cambodia, and most probably could also be found in the pristine polities of China and other regions.[32] Although local conditions may have differed, this strategy was also widespread in insular Southeast Asia. Prisoners of war were highly desirable in the Javanese kingdom of Majapahit during the fourteenth century, and four centuries later the kings of Mataram deported populations on a large scale from conquered provinces to royal domains near Yogyakarta (Ricklefs 1993, 44).[33] Muslim raids into the Visayas are another case in point. James Warren (1982, 433) estimates that "almost every year between 1770 and 1870, the Sulu sultanate sent raiding fleets of light sail craft . . . north into the Spanish Philippines, bringing back a total of some 200 thousand to 300 thousand Christian slaves."[34] Many other examples can be added to the fact that control of populations rather than territory was the key political and geopolitical rationale in Southeast Asian warfare, and the deportation of populations therefore an important technique to be mastered by attacking armies.

The military strategy of polities in the precolonial period to augment manpower has considerably shaped the linguistic and ethnographic map of modern mainland and, to a lesser extent, also island Southeast Asia. Tai Lü settlements in Nan and Lamphun, Khmer villages in Ratchaburi, Phuan settlements in Lopburi, and Lao enclaves in Saraburi have originated from deportations of war captives, mainly in the late eighteenth and early nineteenth centuries.[35] By the mid-nineteenth century, roughly 25 to 40 percent of the then 400,000 inhabitants in the five Tai Yuan principalities of Chiang Mai, Lamphun, Lampang, Phrae, and Nan were war captives or their descendants.[36] In view of these mass forced resettlements, it is necessary to point out that political scientists and social anthropologists conducting fieldwork in those areas ought not to neglect the existence of large non-Siamese ethnic groups, though partially assimilated today, in the Siamese heartland.

Notes

1. Anthony Reid (1988, 14) estimates the total population of Southeast Asia at the turn of the nineteenth century at around 33 million. Though we lack reliable population censuses in most parts of Southeast Asia prior to the twentieth century, we may calculate that Burma and Siam had a maximum population of respectively five and four million within their present-day national borders in 1800. For a discussion of pre-twentieth population figures in Thailand, see Grabowsky (2004, 15–20).

2. The *Tamra Phichai Songkhram* was in use until the first half of the nineteenth century. One of its first mentions is in the *Lilit Yuan Phai* [Poem About the Defeat of the Tai Yuan], a famous Siamese poem of the sixteenth century about the wars between Ayutthaya and Chiang Mai in the mid-fifteenth century. The Royal Chronicles of Ayutthaya mention that the ancient Siamese military textbook was initiated by King Ramathibòdi II in 1498. See Chanchai 1984, 15.

3. Based on the Javanese experience, Holt and Anderson (1972, 30) arrive at the conclusion: "Only the concentration of large populations made possible by intensive cultivation could provide the economic surplus and reserve of

manpower necessary for building monuments or armies. But the concentration of large populations around a ruler was also the best sign for his having the power, the magnetic attraction of which revealed the continuing possession of the *wahju*. This ideal may help to account for one well-known aspect of inter-dynastic conflict, not merely in Java but also in mainland Southeast Asia—wholesale deportations by victorious rulers. Bringing these conquered populations near to the center augmented royal Power that much more." According to Andaya (1992, 422) the control of manpower was a crucial instrument to determine the hierarchy among rival rulers as only through the direct control of a sufficiently large population was a ruler able to curb tendencies of disintegration in his own realm.

4. For the meaning and documentation of this saying, see Grabowsky 2001.

5. The demographic consequences of these forced resettlements are discussed in detail by Grabowsky 1999, notably pp. 66–67.

6. The periodization of Thai history is done by referring to the capitals of the main Siamese kingdoms: Sukhothai, Ayutthaya, and Bangkok. The "Bangkok Period," which has not yet ended as Bangkok is still the capital of the Kingdom of Thailand, is divided into an early and a later part. The "early Bangkok period" starts in 1782 with the founding of Bangkok and ends in 1851 with the death of King Rama III or 1855 with the Bowring treaty. The second date marks the beginning of the opening of Siam to the world market. In 1854, the third and last Chiang Tung war (see below) ended, one of the major turning points in nineteenth-century Lan Na history.

7. On Tilok's 1461–62 expedition to the region of Sukhothai and Phitsanulok, see Cushman 2000, 17. The *Lilit Yuan Phai* also mentions that Tai Yuan troops deported inhabitants of Chaliang. See Griswold and Prasert 1976, 149.

8. *Müang* is the traditional Tai polity, a term that defies precise translation. A *müang* is defined by its political and ritual center, where the ruler and his family as well as the nobility resided. The term *müang* refers both to the capital and the polity (capital plus surrounding countryside). *Müang* has many of the senses of the Greek *polis* and Roman *civis*. Moreover, a large and powerful *müang* can comprise a number of smaller *müang* which, in turn, may consist of even

smaller-sized *müang*. Even nowadays, the modern states of Thailand and Laos are called colloquially Müang Thai and Müang Lao.

9. Like other Southeast Asian peoples, the Tai Yuan use a sixty-year cycle to name years. The sexagenary cycle is a combination of a decimal and a duodenary subcycle referring to the years of a decade (in *cūḷasakarāja*) and the zodadiac of twelve animal years. *Poek set* means "year of the dog, tenth year of the decade." However, the year CS 842, confirmed by other sources, was a *kot cai* year while the nearest *poek set* year was CS 840 (AD 1478–79).

10. CS is the abbreviation for *cūḷasakarāja* or *cunlasakkkarat*, literally "the minor era," which originated in Burma and is 638 years ahead of the Christian era. This era came into use in Thailand by the mid-thirteenth century and remained popular until the early twentieth century. It is now replaced by the Buddhist era.

11. *Pün wongsa mahakhasat*. . ., Social Research Institute, Code 82.107.05.043–043, f° 105/2–4. The present writer's translation differs slightly from Wyatt's more liberal one published in 1994.

12. For an analysis of the deeper social and economic reasons for the downfall of Lan Na, see Grabowsky 2005, 52–57.

13. I am grateful to the late Ronald Renard, Chiang Mai, for this information obtained from Aye Gyaw, formerly of Rangoon University.

14. The author of the poem was probably a high-ranking Tai Yuan officer whose task was to personally accompany a princess of Chiang Mai (*cao ying*) to Pegu. After his return he was appointed governor of Thoen, a small township situated on the southern periphery of Lan Na.

15. Called "Cawa" (Lao: Sua), i.e. [the inhabitants of] Müang Sua or Luang Prabang. The mention of different nationalities should probably indicate the multiethnic composition of the deportees and not be regarded as a faithful enumeration of all ethnic groups affected.

16. See Royal Orders of Burma, Vol. I (24 May 1642, 2 April 1647), Than Tun 1983, 127, 147.

17. A similar argument was developed by the author with regards to forced resettlement in Lan Na during the late eighteenth and early nineteenth centuries. See Grabowsky 1999, 65–66.

18. The year of the rabbit, fifth year of the decade.

19. For accounts of anti-Burmese liberation efforts, see Grabowsky 1999, 51–57; Penth 1994, 28–30; Sarassawadee 1996, 259–73. The most detailed analysis of the wars from a military perspective is given in Bòdin 2002.

20. The repopulating of Nan apparently started in the early 1790s. In 1790, a group of 585 families from Müang Yòng escaped deportation to Burma and fled to Nan. A year later, the ruler of Chiang Khòng, situated 20 kilometers south of Chiang Saen, escaped Burmese rule and settled with 505 families in Nan. See Wyatt 1994, 94–95.

21. Year of the pig, the first year of the decade. The Siamese names of the sexagenary cycle differ from the respective Tai Yuan appellation.

22. *Hò samut haeng chat, Cotmaihet* R.3, C.S. 1201, No. 6. A northern Thai source confirms the arrival of the deportees in Chiang Mai: "Between the eighth and the ninth month (according to the Yuan lunar calendar May/June 1839) the families from Müang Pu, Müang Tuan and Müang Sat arrived in Chiang Mai." See "Cotmaihet lan na," in Sarassawadee 1993, 29 (f° 37/5–38/1). Compare *Phongsawadan Yonok* (Prachakitkòracak 1973, 487), which gives corresponding though slightly reduced figures, both concerning the number of soldiers involved in the campaign as well as the amount of war booty.

23. Richardson's letter to Blundell, dated August 31, 1839, in *The Burney Papers*. 1971, 38.

24. Quoted from "Extract from the Journal relative to the invasion of the Birman frontier towns by the Laos people," *The Burney Papers* 1971, 46 [May 27, 1839].

25. *Cotmaihet rüang thap chiang tung* n.d., 89. The estimated population includes Müang Phayak, Müang Sat, and Müang Yòng as well as seven other *müang*, but excludes Müang Len.

26. A *viss*, also written as *vis*, *bis*, or *bisse*, was a unit of measurement used in India and Burma. One *viss* was the equivalent of 1.417 kg in Madras, 1.512 kg in Bengal, and 1.656 kg in Burma.

27. A heavy musket fired from a rest; a light swivel gun.

28. McLeod's Journal, January 23, 1837, quoted from Grabowsky and Turton 2003, 312.

29. This boast reflects the demographic superiority of Burma whose population of more than four million in the early nineteenth century outmatched that of Lan Na at least tenfold.

30. McLeod's Journal, January 23, 1837, quoted from Grabowsky and Turton 2003, 312–13.

31. For example, in 1836 or 1837, a feud broke out among the ruling families of Sipsòng Panna regarding the acquisition of precious elephants from Laos. One group of people from Müang La in the southern part of Sipsòng Panna, led by a local nobleman, fled the fighting and sought refuge in Nan where they founded three villages in the present-day district of Tha Wang Pha.

32. Various aspects of forced resettlement schemes in traditional Southeast Asian warfare have been discussed, for example, by Lieberman (1984) on Burma; Bangòn (1986), Breazeale (1975), and Snit and Breazeale (1988) on Laos; and Puangthong (1995) on Cambodia.

33. When Pajang rebelled in 1617, Sultan Agung destroyed the town and deported its entire population to Mataram. See Andaya 1992, 432.

34. Endicott (1983) studied the impact of similar Malay slave raids against the Orang Asli, the autochthonous peoples in the interior of the Malay Peninsula.

35. In 1906–07, in the administrative circle (*monthon*) of Prachinburi, comprising the present-day provinces of Chachoengsao, Prachinburi, Chonburi, and Nakhòn Nayok, ethnic Lao constituted 30.2 percent of the population while the ethnic Thai (Siamese) made up only a slight absolute majority with 50.9 percent. See Grabowsky 1993, 35–36.

36. Roughly one-third of the population of the city of Chiang Mai were descendants of war captives and 60–80 percent of the population of the principality of Lamphun where most of the Tai Lü captives from Müang Yòng were resettled. For details, see Grabowsky 1999, 66–67.

References

Andaya, Barbara Watson. 1992. "Political Development Between the Sixteenth and Eighteenth Centuries." In *The Cambridge History of Southeast Asia, Vol. I*, ed. Nicholas Tarling, 402–59. Cambridge: Cambridge University Press.

Bangòn Piyaphan. 1986. "Prawattisat khòng chumchon chao lao nai huamüang chan nai samai rattanakosin tòn ton" [A History of the Lao Community in the Inner Provinces During the Early Bangkok Period]. MA thesis, Silpakorn University, Bangkok.

Bòdin Kinawong. 2002. "Cao luang kawila" [King Kawila]. In *Phracao kawila haeng nakhòn chiang mai* [King Kawila of Chiang Mai], ed. Bòdin Kinawong, 23–64. Chiang Mai: Monthon thahan bok thi 33.

Breazeale, Kennon. 1975. "The Integration of the Lao States into the Thai Kingdom." PhD thesis, University of Oxford.

The Burney Papers. 1971. vol. IV, pt 1 (Feb. 1838 to March 1849). Westmead, UK: Gregg International Publishers.

Chanchai Wannarong. 1984. "Kan süksa wikhrò songkhram thai rop phama chaphò rüang yutthasat lae yutthawithi thang kan thahan, ph.s. 2310–2397" [An Analysis of the Thai Wars Against Burma, in Particular the Military Strategies and Tactics, AD 1767–1854]. MA thesis, Chulalongkorn University, Bangkok.

Chonthira Sattayawatthana. 1987. *Lua müang nan* [The Lua of Nan]. Bangkok: Müang Boran.

Cotmaihet rüang thap müang chiang tung [Reports on the Chiang Tung Wars]. n.d. Bangkok.

Cushman, Richard D. 2000. *The Royal Chronicles of Ayutthaya*, ed. David K. Wyatt. Bangkok: The Siam Society.

Damrong Ratchanuphap, Prince, ed. 1987. *Cotmai luang udomsombat phròm duai athibai khòng somdet phracao bòrommawongthoe krom phraya damrong rachanuphap* [Letters of Luang Udomsombat with an Introduction by Prince Damrong Rachanuphap]. Bangkok: Krom sinlapakòn.

Endicott, K. 1983. "The Effects of Slave Raiding on the Aborigines of the Malay Peninsula." In *Slavery, Bondage and Dependency in South East Asia*, ed. Anthony Reid, 216–45. St. Lucia: University of Queensland Press.

Grabowsky, Volker. 1993. *An Early Thai Census: Translation and Analysis (Data Paper of the Institute of Population Studies).* Bangkok: Chulalongkorn University.

Grabowsky, Volker. 1999. "Forced Resettlement Campaigns in Northern Thailand During the Early Bangkok Period". *Journal of the Siam Society* 87: 45–86.

———. 2001. "Note on *Kep phak sai sa kep kha sai müang*." *Aséanie* 8: 67–72.

———. 2004. *Bevölkerung und Staat in Lan Na: Ein Beitrag zur Bevölkerungsgeschichte Südostasiens* (Population and State in Lan Na: A Contribution to the Population History of Southeast Asia). Wiesbaden: Harrassowitz Verlag.

———. 2005. "Population and State in Lan Na prior to the mid-sixteenth century." *Journal of the Siam Society* 93: 1–68.

Grabowsky, Volker, and Andrew Turton. 2003. *The Gold and Silver Road: The McLeod and Richardson Diplomatic Missions to Tai States in 1837*. Chiang Mai: Silkworm Books.

Griswold, Alexander B., and Prasert na Nagara. 1976. "A Fifteenth-Century Siamese Historical Poem." In *Southeast Asian History and Historiography*, ed. C. D. Cowan and O. W. Wolters, 123–63. Ithaca, NY: Cornell University Press.

Hò samut haengchat (Thai National Library). CS 1201, No. 6: "Banchi ken kòng thap müang chiang mai lamphun yok pai ti müang pu müang sat" [Account of the Actions Against Müang Pu and Müang Sat by the Armies of Chiang Mai and Lamphun].

Holt, Claire and Benedict Anderson. 1972. *Culture and Politics in Indonesia*. Ithaca, N.Y.: Cornell University Press.

Khamman Vongkotratna. 1952. *Phongsawadan müang phuan* [The Phuan Chronicle]. Vientiane.

Koenig, William J. 1990. *The Burmese Polity, 1752–1819: Politics, Administration, and Social Organization in the Early Kon-baung Period*. Center for South and Southeast Asian Studies, The University of Michigan.

Kraisri Nimmanhaeminda. 1965. "Put Vegetables Into Baskets, and People Into Towns." In *Ethnographic Notes on Northern Thailand*, eds. Lucien M. Hanks et al., 6–9. Ithaca, NY: Cornell University (Data Paper No. 58, Southeast Asia Program).

Lieberman, Victor B. 1980. "The Transfer of the Burmese Capital from Pegu to Ava." *Journal of the Royal Asiatic Society of Great Britain and Ireland* 1: 64–83.

———. 1984. *Burmese Administrative Cycles: Anarchy and Conquest, c. 1580–1760*. Princeton, NJ: Princeton University Press.

———. 1991. "Secular Trends in Burmese Economic History, *c.* 1350–1830, and Their Implications for State Formation." *Modern Asian Studies* 25(1): 1–31.

Melchers, William. 1986. "The Thai Invasion of Kengtung During the Reign of King Rama III." In *Anuson Walter Vella*, ed. Ronald D. Renard, 193–207. Honolulu: Center for Asian and Pacific Studies, University of Hawaii at Manoa.

Mya Sein, Daw. 1973. *The Administration of Burma*. Kuala Lumpur: Oxford University Press.

Nithi Aeusrivongse. 1991. "Ratthathammanun chabap watthanatham" [The Cultural Constitution]. *Sinlapa-watthanatham* [Arts and Culture] 13(1): 266–84.

Penth, Hans. 1994. *A Brief History of Lān Nā: Civilizations of North Thailand*. Chiang Mai: Silkworm Books.

Prachakitcakòracak, Phraya. [1907] 1973. *Phongsawadan yonok* [The Yonok Chronicle], Bangkok: Khlang witthaya.

Puangthong Rungswasdisab. 1995. "War and Trade: Siamese Interventions in Cambodia, 1767–1851." PhD thesis, University of Wollongong.

"Pün wongsa mahakhasat tanglai tangtae phaña samantalat pon ma lae pün wongsa caonai ton sawoei latcasombat nai müang pua lae müang nan" [The Chronicle of Rulers Since the Reign of Phaya Samantalat and the Chronicle of the Nobles Who Ruled in Müang Pua and Müang Nan], Wat Phranet, Müang district, Nan province (in Northern Thailand). Social Research Institute, Chiang Mai University. Code 82.107.05.043–043.

Ricklefs, M. C. 1993. *War, Culture and Economy in Java, 1677–1726: Asian and European Imperialism in the Early Kartasura Period*. Sydney: Allen & Unwin.

Saraswadee Ongsakul. 1996. *Prawattisat lan na* [A History of Lan Na]. Bangkok: Amarin.

Saraswadee Ongsakul. trans. and ed. 1993. *Lakthan prawattisat lan na cak ekkasan khamphi bai lan lae phapnangsa* [Documents on the History of Lan Na from Palm-leaf and *phapnangsa* Manuscripts]. Chiang Mai: Chiang Mai University.

Siam and Laos as Seen by Our American Missionaries. 1884. Philadelphia: Presbyterian Board of Publication.

Singkha Wannasai, translit. and trans. into Siamese. 1979. *Khlong rüang mangthra rop chiang mai* [Poem on Mangthra's War Against Chiang Mai]. Chiang Mai.

Snit, Smuckarn [Sanit Samakkhan], and Kennon Breazeale. 1988. *A Culture in Search of Survival: The Phuan of Thailand and Laos.* New Haven, CT: Yale University Southeast Asia Studies, Monograph Series No. 31.

Tamnan sipha ratchawong [The Chronicle of the Fifteen Dynasties]. 1989. Vol. 3, bundles 6–7. Chiang Mai: Social Research Institute, Chiang Mai University.

Tamra phichai songkhram [Textbook on the Victory in War]. 1969. Cremation volume for Nang Sanintharanat. Bangkok: Department of Fine Arts (quoted in Chanchai 1984).

Than Tun (Hrsg.). 1983–88. *The Royal Orders of Burma, A.D. 1598–1885* (9 vols.) [ROB]. Kyoto: The Center for Southeast Asian Studies, Kyoto University. [Vol. 1. 1598–1648 (1983)].

Warren, James. 1982. "Slavery and the Impact of External Trade: The Sulu Sultanate in the Nineteenth Century." In *Philippine Social History: Global Trade and Local Transformations*, eds. Alfred W. McCoy and Ed. C. de Jesus, 414–44. Quezon City: Ateneo de Manila University Press.

Wyatt, David K., trans. and ed. 1994. *The Nan Chronicle.* Ithaca, NY: Southeast Asia Program, Cornell University.

Wyatt, David K., and Aroonrut Wichienkeeo, trans. and ed. 1995. *The Chiang Mai Chronicle.* Chiang Mai: Silkworm Books.

CHAPTER 2

Juan de Salcedo Joins the Native Form of Warfare

Felice Noelle Rodriguez

The Filipino did not record his own story in a way that is easy for modern academics to access, that is, through the written word. However, his usual foe in battle, the Spaniard, had developed the usual habit of chronicling. We must therefore search for the Filipino face in Spanish chronicles, which remain the only source available. At the outset, it is necessary to understand that the Spaniards were intent on reporting their achievements, and occasionally explaining their failures. As a result, the records focus on themselves, the chroniclers. Though their accounts usually display the biases and self-aggrandizement embedded in the chronicle tradition, they do nonetheless reveal glimpses of native life. Furthermore, while the characters in the narrative are often one-dimensional, there is still action and movement. A nuanced and culturally sensitive interpretation of Spanish documents may thus open a door to greater historical understanding of indigenous attitudes.

One such chronicle, dated April 20, 1572, focuses on Juan de Salcedo and his exploits in the islands of Mindoro and Lubang. Its unnamed author called the piece, "Relation of the Conquest of the Island of Luzon" ("Relation" 1572, 141–72), and at the outset made his intention clear. He wished to correct or contradict earlier writings on the pacification, which he felt had presented an inaccurate picture: "I have ventured to write this relation because I have been informed that many things concerning events in this land have been written, and sent to Nueva España, which are the merest fable and conjecture." Instead, the author wanted to let the reader "know the truth with regard to what occurs here." To further stress his veracity, he emphasized his intention of "[describing] the wars between them (the natives) and the Spaniards, without useless amplification or omission." It is important, therefore, to remember that the narrator was himself a participant in the story we want to retell, since he was a member of the Salcedo expedition to Mamburao on the island of Mindoro, and to Lubang, a much smaller island fifteen leagues (*c.* 83 km) northwest of Mamburao.

There is, however, another narrative of the same event, written by Gaspar de San Agustin titled *Conquest of the Philippine Islands, 1565–1615* (1698, 531–35). This relates the story of the early years of colonization, chronicling the pacification of the native settlements. As Ambeth Ocampo remarks in his foreword to the bilingual edition published in 1998, "... it is basically a history of Spain in the Philippines, a chronicle of Spanish evangelical and military conquest of the archipelago and its people ..." (San Agustin 1698, 23). Though biased and historically bound to his own perspective, San Agustin mentions key details regarding the Salcedo story that are highly pertinent to our understanding of the event. The anonymous chronicler may have been a participant in the Salcedo expedition and provided vivid descriptions of the combat. Nonetheless, it is San Agustin's narrative that provides us with the more complete story of the expedition. Although San Agustin was not a participant, his distance from the incidents he describes enabled him to include more extensive details. He was able, for example, to obtain information about developments apart from the actual fighting, and even included a description of the role of native warriors. Though mentioned only in passing, references to *datus* (local leaders), and to their requests to Governor Miguel Lopez de Legazpi for military aid against their enemy points to their active participation in the battle.

Juan de Salcedo reached Cebu in 1567 when the Spanish colonization of the Philippines had just begun. His uncle, the famous Adelantado Miguel Lopez de Legazpi, had only arrived two years earlier, in 1565. In a footnote to the document on the pacification of the different areas of Luzon, Blair and Robertson described him as someone who "displayed ... such courage, gallantry, and ability that he soon won great renown—especially in the conquest of Luzon. He has been called the 'Hernan Cortés of the Philippines.'" (Blair and Robertson 1903, vol. 3: 73). Before the age of twenty, Salcedo figured prominently in the Spanish pacification of various indigenous towns and villages, traveling to settlements in the Visayas and Luzon and demanding that the natives pay tribute and acknowledge the king of Spain as sovereign. Understandably, this imposition was rarely welcomed and usually met initial resistance. The natives defended their settlements with their *lantakas* (cannons) mounted in forts, and with hand weapons like the *kampilan* (a type of sword) and *kali* (*kalis*). However, for a variety of reasons, these battles always resulted in the eventual surrender to Spaniards, as evidenced by Filipino payment of tribute.

In this chapter we shall look at one instance of this pacification process, placing the analysis within the context of indigenous notions of warfare. Basic to this analysis is a retelling of the story of Juan de Salcedo's triumphant conquest of the islands of Mindoro and Lubang. The Spanish account relates how the "valiant young man, full of courage, gallantry and ability" moves quickly from one town to the other, demanding subjugation to the king of Spain and asking for tribute ("Relation" 1570, 73). However, as we look more closely, we realize that the story can also be related from a different viewpoint, that of the native Filipinos. In narrating how Juan de Salcedo carried out the pacification task, this essay will attempt to interpret the same events from a perspective grounded in an appreciation of the ways in which warfare was practiced in the Philippines at the time of European contact. How, it asks, did the native understand Salcedo and his actions?

To approach the documents from the perspective of the indigenous warrior, we have to first review local methods of warfare. This would be an almost impossible task if our only documents were the highly colored Spanish accounts. However, it is possible to glean something of the indigenous understandings attached to the culture of battle because of the existence of other Spanish records which tried to explain the meanings of native words in a way that newly arrived Spaniards could comprehend. These are the dictionaries written by Spanish missionaries.

In contrast to the Christianization process in the Americas, a decision had been made to spread the word of God in the Philippines by using local languages. The dictionaries that missionaries produced were intended to help their fellow missionaries educate the natives in the ways of the Christian world. The compilation of the Tagalog–Spanish and Spanish–Tagalog dictionaries was, therefore, undertaken with care so that the dictionaries would accurately convey the "native mind" to the Spaniard priest who came to convert that mind. A description of Franciscan works in the seventeenth century specifically states that "nothing can be done in the ministry if the religious do not learn the language of the natives. The religious of this province have always occupied themselves in this with great care" (Schumacher 1979, 75).

Though the missionaries were only partially successful in conveying a sense of the native world view, the dictionaries nonetheless represent a sincere effort to project Filipino attitudes. As such, these lexicons offer us an important counter-perspective to the sometimes-bombastic Spanish chronicles. In contrast to the self-aggrandizement evident in the latter sources, these careful accounts of the native language can serve as a guide towards appreciating how the Filipinos understood many aspects of their life experiences. Although both kinds of sources inevitably reflect Spanish biases and contain the misrepresentations and creative misinterpretations that almost inevitably arise when two very different cultures meet, they can be juxtaposed to reveal the ground on which both are rooted. By playing off one genre against the other, biases are highlighted so that we are given a more careful rendition of what the Spaniard saw, and how the native fought his battles (Mintz 1996, 165–93; Rodriguez 2001, 277–97).

In the present exercise, words that directly or indirectly refer to war were compiled from the Spanish–Tagalog and Tagalog–Spanish dictionaries. Material was drawn from the following: Father Fray Pedro de San Buenaventura's 1613 printed vocabulary, Father Fray Miguel Ruiz's (1630) *Bocabulario Tagalog*, and the newly published *Vocabulario Tagalo* by Francisco de San Antonio, OFM (†1624). Words dealing with warfare were read in relation to accounts of indigenous battle tactics and the actual accounts of encounters contained in the Spanish chronicles.

The words and expressions about warfare in the Tagalog language are further enhanced by other descriptions of indigenous culture from early

Spanish writers. Available documents about early pre-Hispanic Filipinos consist primarily of Spanish reports to the king of Spain regarding native life and culture. However, these reports were so detailed that at times they were used as a guide to strategy and policy-making in the colonization process. Some of those consulted for the present essay are Francisco Ignacio Alcina's "Historia de las Islas e Indios de las Bisayas" (1668); the so-called Boxer Codex (1590); Pedro Chirino's "Of Marriages, Dowries, and Divorces Among the Filipinos" (1604); Miguel de Loarca's "Relation of the Philippine Islands" (1582); Antonio de Morga's *Sucesos de las Islas Filipinas* (1609), and Juan de Plasencia's "Customs of the Tagalogs: A Relation" (1589).

Historical research teaches us that all storytelling comes from a particular perspective. We must learn to understand this perspective and draw out what our sources say of the past and of the people who chronicled this past. In learning to sift through the chronicles, the dictionaries and the reports that speak from a particular perspective, we can also acquire the ability to enter into a dialogue with other perspectives and go on to develop our own interpretations. Accordingly, this essay shall be divided into three parts. The first presents a narrative of Juan de Salcedo's raid on the Mindoro towns; the second part explains indigenous concepts of warfare; and the third part seeks to analyze the actions related to indigenous warfare. While exploring the attitudes revealed by the sources, and while interrogating the actions they describe, we shall always refer back to the story of Salcedo, interpreting and reinterpreting the encounters inscribed therein. We shall carefully try to reconstruct what occurred, and just as carefully retell the story in terms of insights derived from contemporary scholarship. In so doing, we hope to gain not only a greater understanding of the past but a deeper experience of ourselves.

Juan de Salcedo in Mamburao

Gaspar de San Agustin begins his narrative with the account of an envoy. In January 1570, two *datus* (local leaders) from the village of Aklan in Panay and from the Bahay River visit Governor Miguel Lopez de Legazpi in Panay. They request help against their enemies, the people along the coast of Mindoro, and specifically ask for the assistance of Juan de Salcedo. Dispatched by the governor, Salcedo proceeds to the river in Aklan together with thirty of his soldiers. Awaiting him are both leaders as well as five hundred native warriors (San Agustin 1698, 531).

However, the version of the same episode provided by our anonymous writer does not mention any visit by the *datus*. The decision to send Salcedo was not a response to requests for assistance from local leaders. Rather, it was a means to "levy tribute upon the people of certain provinces" ("Relation" 1572, 142). In this chronicle, the native warriors who join Salcedo are termed "Pintados Indians" and no explanation is given for their participation in the Spanish raid against the Mindoro villages. But with San Agustin's mention of the *datus* we begin to understand that this raid was of importance not only to the Spaniards but that it also had meaning for the natives of Aklan and Bahay.

Accompanied by the local leaders and their warriors, Salcedo and his thirty men embarked on fourteen or fifteen native boats for the island of Mindoro. Shortly after midnight, the group reached the vicinity of Mamburao, a village on the island of Mindoro. Salcedo and a native leader secretly moved closer to spy on the enemy's "displacement and defense system." After rest and dinner in their encampment, these men and two hundred chosen natives from Aklan proceeded to Mamburao, where they arrived just before dawn. In the dead of night, they used the element of surprise to attack and plunder the rich town and many of the natives were captured. Some bought their freedom while others were allowed to go free. According to our anonymous document, "when the captain had departed, the natives who fled from the village returned and saw the havoc and destruction caused by the Spaniards, and were unwilling to return to rebuild it; accordingly, they themselves set fire to it, and totally destroyed it" ("Relation" 1572, 143). The intensity of the raid on the town was such that people did not think it worthwhile to resettle there.

After this destruction, Juan de Salcedo justified his actions by informing the leaders of the prisoners that "he had not come to harm them but to help the natives of Aklan and Bahay who had suffered so much under the enemy." He told them he wanted them as friends of the Spaniards, who would help them in all their needs.

In fact, it is evident that the raid in Mamburao was simple plunder. More than the taking of material goods of value like gongs or porcelain, or even *lantakas* (swivel guns), the raiders also captured enemies. Those able to pay for their liberty did so in gold. The captured leaders were told that they must ransom themselves for a stated quantity of gold to be "paid in hand." Indeed, from an indigenous viewpoint Salcedo acted less like a Spanish commander and more like a powerful *datu* who had vanquished his enemies. In other ways, too, he resembled the traditional leader of an indigenous raid, dividing the spoils among his men and the native leaders "without taking anything more than the glory of victory for himself."

Lubang

From Mamburao, Salcedo sailed to the nearby island of Lubang where he marshaled his men and the native warriors for another attack on local villages. He found, however, that news of the earlier raid had preceded him and that the Lubang men, women, and children had withdrawn to three forts. The first two of these forts are described as being "square in form, with ten or twelve culverins on each side, some of them moderately large and others very small. Each fort had a wall two *estados* high (the height of a person), and was surrounded by a ditch two and one half *brazas* (1 *braza* = 1.67 meters) in depth, filled with water" ("Relation" 1572, 143–44). Finding the village empty, Salcedo and his men made their way through a grove to reach the first fort. As in other chronicles relating Salcedo's encounters with native communities, we are told that he "negotiated with them, asking whether they desired to be friends of the Spaniards." But the natives "refused to listen, and began to discharge their culverins and a few arrows" (p. 144). From the Spanish viewpoint, this refusal of an offer of friendship justified the decision to attack. A skirmish ensued, but because the Spaniards found a boat that would carry them to the other side of the moat they were able to climb the ramparts. Seeing this, the natives fled to the next fort through a passageway. "A hundred or more of them were killed, while of our men five were wounded. In this way was the fort taken, together with fifty or sixty prisoners, ten or twelve culverins, and everything else in it" (p. 145).

After a day of continuous fighting, Salcedo was still determined to pursue and capture the remainder of the warriors. He sent a prisoner to the second fort with a message that they surrender peacefully, but "they sent back the reply that they did not desire to be friends with the Spaniards but were eager to fight with them" (p. 145). And so, together with four hundred pro-Spanish native warriors, the Spaniards besieged the second fort, bringing the boats as close to the walls as possible. "When [the natives] saw the determination of the Spaniards, and that they would not depart under any circumstances until they had conquered them, they therefore determined to make peace and become friends" (p. 146). The leaders then came out of the fort "and made peace and friendship with the captain. And as an act of friendship they gave him a hundred taels of gold which he divided among his soldiers" (p. 146).

The same process was repeated in the next fortress, located on a rocky islet near Mindoro, where more than three hundred warriors were now entrenched. The fortifications were bombarded with arquebuses for an entire day, and the next morning "the soldiers began to make ladders to scale the rock—whose occupants, when they saw the determination of the Spaniards, came to terms of peace and friendship, giving another hundred taels of gold . . ." (p. 146).

After the victory, Salcedo had the leaders brought before him, and offered them peace once more with the friendship of the Spaniards. They promised to be faithful vassals of His Majesty and asked him to impose the tribute they would have to pay henceforth in recognition of their vassalage. They gave a great quantity of gold for their ransom which, as in Mamburao, was divided among the soldiers and leaders of Aklan and Ibahais. After Captain Juan de Salcedo entered into blood compact with one of the leaders as a sign of a newly pacted friendship, he returned happily and victoriously to Panay.

Concepts of Warfare

As in other parts of Southeast Asia, raiding was common to the Philippines. In an area of abundant and fertile lands, acquisition of territory was not the reason behind raiding. Rather, it was a means of obtaining the labor needed to gather products for trade. Slaves were both a commodity and a necessity by which one affirmed one's social status (Scott 1982, 102).

Describing the Visayan islands of Samar and Leyte in the early seventeenth century, Francisco Alcina S. J. states that there are two types of warfare: *pagahat* if on land, and *pangayao* if carried out by sea.

Pagahat

According to Alcina (1668), an expedition by land was called *pagahat*, while *magahat* was the attacker. He describes *pagahat* as a means of obtaining slaves by trickery.

While most of the attackers remained hidden, when they were near the pueblos which they were going to rob, they sent on one or two of the nimblest or spirited so that those of the pueblo would believe that they came alone and they would go out with little precaution to seize them. As a consequence, either by retreating or pretending that they were defending themselves, they might be followed by the defenders into the ambush, and would fall into the hands of their companions. So those were seized who had gone out to make the seizure. This was their most common way of taking prisoners.

Alcina drew a parallel between this form of warfare and the highway robberies carried out in Spain. He described such methods as cowardly because the attack occurred under cover of darkness. In his view, no courage was required to face the attacker. The enemy was taken captive not by the strength and valor of his opponent but by reason of surprise and treachery. From this perspective, then, Salcedo is a *magahat* for he attacks and destroys Mamburao in the quiet of night, claiming captives who would only be released after the payment of a ransom. Though they may have offended the Jesuit missionary, Salcedo's actions would have been understandable and acceptable to early Philippine society.

Mangayao

Scott describes the *mangayao* as "the most celebrated form of Visayan warfare," occurring at the time of the year when "the wind is behind their backs" (1994, 154). Visayan raiders left during the so-called *bonanzas*, the period in between the monsoons, the northeast wind (*amihan*, in the months of December through February) and the southwest wind (*habagat*, in the months of June and July). In 1521, when Ferdinand Magellan offered his services to Rajah Kolambu of Cebu so that the latter could vanquish his enemies, the Rajah mentioned that he had enemies but that it was not the season for attacking (Pigafetta 1592, 71). As another observer, Martin de Rada, remarked in 1577, "Every year as soon as they harvest their fields, they man their ships to go to plunder . . . especially in October and November, and in February, March, and April, at which times a great number of corsairs go out . . ." (Rada 1577, 479; taken from Scott, 1994, 152). However, the people of the uplands, the Tinguianes, commenced their raids following the harvest (Loarca 1582, 94). According to Governor Lavezaris, "after harvest time, they plunder towns which do not trade with them or have no relation with them at all" (1575, 287).

The *datus* of the village of Aklan in Panay and from the Bahay River approached Legazpi in the month of January, which was apparently not the local season for raiding. Mamburao, which was unprepared for the surprise attack, was therefore left devastated by the raid. The people in Lubang were better warned. They must have heard of the raid in the neighboring *barangay* (village), and therefore had time to make preparations. They were able to send the women and children to a separate area, and their warriors had time to move to a defensive position in their forts.

Although Alcina, in speaking of Visayan society, had earlier described *mangayao* as going to war by sea, the Tagalog dictionaries explain its meaning as "to go and cut heads." Miguel Ruiz (1630), for example, defines it as "to go and cut heads, in the town or in the street" (*ir, a cortar cabezas, sea a pueblo, sea camino*). *Mangayao* is the act of looking for enemies to kill. There are other Tagalog words related to the cutting of heads, such as *poyoc*, *tong-ol*, and *pogot*. According to Ruiz, *poyoc* and *tong-ol* have the same meaning as *pogot*, which is to cut heads. *Pogot* is cutting the head off the body, while *tong-ol* is the word used for cutting the head in one stroke. Antonio de Morga describes this action, mentioning that the weapon used was a *balaraw* (a bladed weapon): "They are so skilled that when they go in pursuit of an enemy they clutch his hair with one hand, while with the other, in a single blow of the *balarao*, they strike off his head and carry it away with them. Afterwards they keep such heads up in their houses on show and great display is made of them, so that their possessors may appear as brave men who have wreaked vengeance upon their foes for wrongs done them" (1609, 252).

In the San Buenaventura dictionary, *sumbali* also refers to cutting of the head without totally severing it from the body (*cortar el garguero o tragadero solamente*), "to cut only the windpipe or the throat," or according to the San Antonio vocabulary, *degollamiento por delante, sin quitar la cabeza*, "to cut the throat from the front, without severing the head."

A description of the first Spanish journeys north to Luzon notes that troops passed by Balayan, Batangas in the southern part of the island and saw heads on stakes.

"According to the men of Balayan, the enmity between these towns was because a Balayan vessel, on its return from Manila, laden with merchandise, was driven by stormy weather onto the coast of Tulay, and . . . instead of helping and receiving them kindly, as neighbors should, they stole the goods of the Balayans and killed two of them, setting their heads on stakes. Similar sights were noticed by the Spaniards in these towns ("Relation" 1570, 90).

The practice of setting heads on stakes was called *bayobay*. In one of his sermons on the story of Judith in Tagalog, the priest P. Juan de Oliver described how Holofernes' head is hung from the town wall: . . . *ypinabayobay ni Judith ang olo ni Holofernes sa bacor nang bayan*. [Judith had Holofernes' head hung from the town wall] (Oliver 1599, 150).

Gobat

The dictionary compiled by Miguel Ruiz in 1630 translates *gobat* (*gubat*) as *conquistar pueblo*. However, *gobat* and *conquistar* are not one and the same. *Conquistar* implies not only going to war against a people but also the subjugation and occupation of the place conquered. *Gobat,* however refers primarily to raiding. The Manila Codex describes *gobat* as *robamiento o asolamiento de pueblo,* "the stealing or devastation of the town." *Gobat* does not convey the idea of an occupying conqueror, but of a raider. The people are unable to defend themselves and take flight, burning their houses before escaping to some safer location in the interior. However, when the raiders have gone, they return to their communities and try to rebuild their homes.

In his capture of Manila in 1570, the Spanish leader Martin de Goiti is a *conquistador,* since he burns the fort and Rajah Soliman's community within. It was a conquest made with the intention of returning to lay claim to the land. The case is different with Juan de Salcedo. After the destruction of Mamburao and the paying of ransom by the captives in Lubang, Salcedo returned briefly to collect tribute from the Mamburao captives as a sign of their vassalage to the king of Spain, but he did not intend to stay. As noted earlier, his actions may be considered in the same light as those of a *manggugubat,* a raider. After the raid, he asks for ransom, divides the spoils among the other leaders and his men, and moves on to Manila. These are actions not of a *conquistador* but of a *manggugubat.*

Conquest (*conquistar*) in the work by Miguel Ruiz is defined thus: *Naolog ang bayan*, "the town fell" (*destruicion del Pueblo por la cualquier causa de peste o guerra*, "destruction of the town for whatever cause, be it pestilence or war") and *hinilabos pinatay ang sangbayan*, "the townsfolk were ruined, killed." If there were native words to describe the destruction of Mamburao they would seem to parallel those used in the Spanish dictionaries to explain the word *conquistar.* The town was so devastated that the inhabitants did not even wish to rebuild it, preferring to burn it themselves.

The San Buenaventura work provides another example of the possible use of *conquistar*: *Conquistaron los Castillanos antiguamente este nuestro pueblo*, "before our town was conquered by the Castilians." The return to one's place of origin, possibly after its destruction in warfare, is termed *paglicas* (*volver multitud, como la gente que viene de Guerra*, "the return of a multitude, as in people returning from war"). After the fall of Manila to Martin de Goiti, the Tagalogs return, only to flee again when they see the same ships come back. The Spanish intent is not to raid but to remain and make Manila the center of their power. In the case of Mamburao, people who fled the village returned but refused to rebuild the town when they witnessed the havoc and destruction that had occurred. In Lubang, however, the natives offered taels of gold, with a promise of more upon Salcedo's return.

Mooc

Mooc is a term referring to the act of fighting. P. Juan de Oliver, in explaining the importance of preparing oneself against the evils around by making the sign of the cross, describes a warrior getting ready for battle:

> Ang tauong magpapamooc nagsasandata mona nang dalauang bagay na sandata, sinasandata mona ang ytinataquip sa canyang cataoan, ang calay baga, ang baloti, at ang calasag, yaong lahat, yngat din sa cataoan niya, nang di masugatan, nang di matimoan nang supnit nang palaso caya nang caniyang caauay, cum matacpan na niya ang kaniyang cataoan, bagho homauac nang bosog, nang Gayang, sampon nang iua, siyang ipananalo sa caniyang caauay. (Oliver 1599, 1)
>
> The person who goes to battle arms himself with two types of weapons, a weapon which covers his body, the breastplate, the armor of leather or thick cords sewn together and the shield. All these protect the body, that it may not be wounded, that it may not be hit by a wounding instrument, the arrow of his enemy, if he covers his body, before holding the bow, the lance, or the bladed weapon, will make him win against his enemy. (Translation by F. N. Rodriguez)

There are other words referring to battle: *digma* and *baca*. *Digma* is a generic term for war, for fighting (*Dinigma sa ona nang manga Castila itong aming bayan*, "in the beginning, the Spaniards went to war against our land"). *Baca* refers to the act of throwing of lances or stones and mud at the enemy (*Por tierra o mar con armas ofensivas y defensivas*, "by land or sea with offensive and defensive arms"). In the battle of Mactan, Pigafetta (1592) relates how the natives, including women and children, were continuously throwing lances, stones, and mud at the Spanish forces. The action is also evident among the people of Lubang who "discharged their culverins and a few arrows" from their forts. This action, in the native language, is *pagbabaca*.

Bangga

The act of fighting at sea, the collision of the *balangay* (boats used in warfare) was called *bangga*. In Martin de Goiti's attack in Rajah Soliman's Manila, the natives were ready for the *banggaan*: "The large ship was firing upon a Moro boat with long-bladed oars, which was far up the river. This vessel was said to have three or four hundred fighting men and rowers on board, with many culverins and large pieces of artillery. The cannon ball struck the water, for the vessel was some distance away, surrounded by more than five hundred Moro *prahus* and other large ships full of armed men, bowmen and lancers. All these were scattered by the artillery of the large junk" ("Relation" 1570, 100).

The people of Navotas wanted to engage the Spanish in a *banggaan*. Together with people from Tondo, they taunted the enemy and challenged them to a great sea battle. Martin de Goiti took up the challenge, together with seventy arquebusiers on nine *prahus*, and a few hundred Visayan warriors.

The Navotas group had between twenty and thirty *caracoas* (outrigger canoes) each equipped with a small cannon. With loud cries they discharged their cannons and arrows. However, because of the continuous shower of bullets from the Spanish arquebuses, their efforts were ineffective. As they rowed away, the Visayan warriors in *prahus* to the rear of the Spanish arquebusiers took chase and finished off those from Navotas who had taken flight. Significantly, the documents inform us that the Visayans were enemies of the Tagalogs.

In this battle, three hundred people from Navotas were killed together with their leaders. Between ten and twelve *caracoas* were captured, and around two hundred warriors were taken (*bihag*), as well as two or three hundred warriors on land. The Spanish also overcame a fort with five or six cannons. All the captives were taken to the Spanish camp in Manila, with four hundred being distributed among the soldiers as slaves, and the remainder divided among the captains and officers.

The Act of Raiding

The Preparation

On the basis of these documents, it is possible to reconstruct Juan de Salcedo's campaign from the point of view of the native participants. When the right moment has come, they make preparations to ensure the *mangayao* (raid) will be successful. Ships, weapons, and people are readied. The sea vessels—the *balangay*, *caracoa*, and *prahu*—must be strong and firm. Daggers, spears, and arrows are sharpened, armor strengthened, and shields shined. Relatives and friends in allied settlements are induced to take part in the *pangangayao* (raid). The attacking strategies are carefully planned. The *datus* of Aklan and Bahay River ally themselves with Legazpi, who in turn sends Juan de Salcedo and his men to raid the enemies of the *datus*.

The *datus* of the two towns mentioned have thus joined together against a common enemy, the towns in Mindoro. They extend their political connection to include the Spaniards, who now have settled in the same island. The chronicle stresses that the *datus* request help to fight their enemies from Miguel Lopez de Legazpi, the Spanish leader in Panay. The chronicle sees this as a simple request from native *datus* rather than a political move by which they would ally with a new power. In line with indigenous forms of warfare, the leaders were, in fact, building political connections as a necessary precondition for a raid. However, the Spanish regarded this as a sign of subjugation. The native leaders of Aklan and Bahay River were "friends," natives who had apparently accepted their presence and dominance in the area.

An important part of the preparation for winning the battle is the summoning of the *anitos* (good and bad spirits). The preparation of offensive weapons (*sandata*) and defensive weapons (*sapyao*), the marshaling of warriors, and strategic planning will all be meaningless if the *anitos* are not on one's side. The leader who sponsors the *mag-anito* ritual will receive half of what was plundered from the enemy, and the other half will be divided among the other leaders (Loarca 1582, 94).

In the Visayas, the summoning of *anitos* is called *pagdaga*, the meaning of which is given as *upang malupig naming* ("that we may conquer"). One of the *anitos* summoned during the *pagdaga* ritual is Humalgar, the serpent twin of the most eminent warriors. This serpent joins the *pangangayao*, and from him the warriors draw their courage. But there are also other *anito*s, both good and bad, who are believed to accompany warriors wherever they go (Alcina 1668, 74). Warriors also offer prayers to Varangao, the rainbow, and to other *anito*s like Ynaguinid and Macanduc (Loarca 1582, 94). They believe that the warrior who dies as a result of being shot by an arrow, sliced by a sword, or eaten by a crocodile, will go to the sun by way of the rainbow and himself become a god (p. 85).

In the *pagdaga* ritual, the natives ask for the help of the *anito*, and seek auguries that will foretell the outcome of the raid. They hurl a tooth of the crocodile or wild boar and determine the strategies they should adopt according to its position when it falls. If they see omens of victory, they pursue the plans in hand. However, if the perceived outcome is not positive, they will delay their actions until the auguries tell them the time is auspicious (Boxer Codex 1590, 224). All those involved must be alert to the smallest sign, for the number of knots tied in a rope can foretell the destiny of their *pangangayao* (Loarca 1582, 93). If the person who prepares for war or a voyage should sneeze (*pagkabahin*), he will abandon any plans in train, since it is thought that this bodily phenomenon portends a bad fate (p. 99). A good omen is a heron flying from the right part of the horizon or one perching on a riverbank or any paths where the warriors may tread. If such good signs eventuate, the raid will continue, with participants certain of their victory (Boxer Codex 1590, 190).

There are numerous other omens that can be of great importance. While sea vessels are being constructed, the natives are said to shoot their arrows upwards and fire their *astinggals* (native arquebuses) towards the sky so the vessel may be light (Boxer Codex 1590: 213). They also have a ritual to ascertain whether a knife or any sharp object is lucky (Plasencia 1589, 118).

An individual's name is similarly highly significant, and natives believe that a different name must be used in traveling so that they not be defeated or captured. Indeed, it may be possible that the right name can even render them invisible (Boxer Codex 1590, 190). The modern commentator can perhaps speculate here about the value of enunciating names; if a name is pronounced by the enemy, would his spirit be captured as well?

According to Alcina (1668), the slippage of the ship over the body of a slave is believed to bestow luck on the planned *pangangayao*. The ship that has been stained with the blood of a slave becomes the vessel of a warrior who is courageous and ready to take life. The slave offered usually comes from the town about to be attacked.

The Act of War

The *bodong* (bamboo with large hole) and the *tambor* (the *tambuli*, large shell that is blown like a flute) are sounded by the warrior while attacking a town. People leave their homes, spouses, and even their children because of the terrifying chorus made by these instruments (Alcina 1668, 163). In the *caracoa* the *caratong* is played. This is an elongated drum made from the trunk of the *pugahan* (wild palm), with the tympanum made from a cloth or animal hide (p. 169). Accompanying the sound of the *caratong* is that of the *tambuli* or *caracoles*. All these sounds stir fear in people, who flee (*tomagactagac*) in panic, and are thus more easily captured. In defending themselves against the Spaniards, the people of Nagcarlan played the *canlang* and the *gimbal*, both drum-like instruments (Quirino and Garcia 1958, 324–423).

Warriors holding their weapons ride on the *buralones* (the second level of the battle vessels), with their *kalis* or *kampilan* at their side for hand-to-hand fighting, and different types of spears, arrows, and *supnit* available for hurling. From the descriptions of the *caracoa* or *balangay* in the battle of Manila against Martin de Goiti, it seems that the *lantakas* were placed at the front. At times, only a few *caracoa* or *balangay* were involved in a *pangungubat*. On the other hand, in another narrative by Alcina regarding a *pangungubat* in Bingi, the leader Dumaraug had a fleet of one hundred vessels (Alcina 1668, 163).

Stories of the *pangungubat* of the people of Ibabao, Samar, and even the pueblos of Bantaian on the island of Cebu, can be heard in ancient songs, represented as vendetta against the capture of a *principala*, a native woman of high rank. Sometimes these raiding parties traveled considerable distances. Bohol once engaged in a *pangungubat* as far away as Maluco. And in one folk song, a *datu* went to war in Jolo, Mindanao, and Brunei and reached even the beaches of China (Alcina 1668, 173). However, for the people of Ibabao, the usual target was Albay, the area from Manila to Casiguran, and Catanduanes. Here they were able to procure numerous captives at different times, including *principalas* whom the warriors took as wives. Indeed, Alcina said he knew of grandchildren of captured *principalas* from the town of Bobon (then Viri) up to Borogan. In Borogan, Alcina recognized several who had been taken from the beaches of Manila (p. 174).

Laws in War

When Miguel de Loarca wrote his report in 1582, he had behind him ten years' experience as an *encomendero* on Panay, the island from whence the *datus* who joined Salcedo came (Scott 1982, 97). In his account, de Loarca gives a detailed list of laws followed by the people of Panay in conducting warfare.

In particular, a captured leader or *datu* was treated well. When he was ransomed by a friend, the *datu* should each contribute according to the closeness of their relationship. If the ransom was not paid, the *datu* remained a slave (p. 94). Another law was applied to the capture of enemies. The preference was to take captives alive, and those who had killed a captive who had previously surrendered were required to make the equivalent recompense. If they were unable to pay, they became a slave.

In this context, we need to reconsider the Spanish interpretation of local actions, particularly those of the chiefs who first resisted Salcedo but surrendered and paid tribute in the face of impending defeat. Given the law requiring the payment of ransom for the freedom of the chiefs, was it then possible that instead of paying tribute they were effectively buying back their lives? When the document comments that the leaders came out of the fort "and made peace and friendship with the captain and as an act of friendship they gave him a hundred taels of gold," this may not have been a gesture of friendship. Rather, they were doing what they always did when a stronger force captured them—they were ransoming themselves.

Another instance concerns the relationship of *datu* and follower. The ruling *datu* offered a prize to his men as he wished, but he also had rights over those who attacked. The *datus* owned whatever was plundered from the *pangungubat*, but other portions were given to the *timawa*s or bondsmen who served as oarsmen. Should a naval force be formed, the datu who was able to fulfill the offerings for the *anitos* of war received half of the *dangin*, the human captives, and the *taban,* the material plunder. Spanish accounts called Salcedo a magnanimous leader who distributed the taels of gold taken from the "tribute" of captive leaders from Mindoro and Lubang among his own men and the native leaders who participated in the raid. But from the indigenous perspective, his actions would have been seen as normal: it was an accepted practice for the booty to be divided among the leaders of the raid and others who must have offered rituals to the *anitos* in an effort to ensure victory.

Receiving News of Victory

Everyone celebrated the return of the victor. Feathers of gold were put in the crowns worn by those who beheaded enemies. Percussion instruments were played, and the people danced to the music. Everyone drank, including the women. This celebration was held over a span of two or three days (Boxer Codex 1590, 190, 214). Those who died in war were celebrated in chants and burial rituals, and numerous offerings were made to the *anitos*. A great feast was held.

Other ceremonies were required for those who had died. The Tagalogs believed that a living slave must accompany a dead warrior in his tomb and there meet his own death (Plasencia 1589, 122). The deceased warrior was also accompanied by his weapons so that he could maintain his status as a great warrior in the next life. If the warrior were a part of the *pangungubat*, the shape of his coffin would be that of a *balangay*, a boat (San Antonio

1977, 152). Alongside the coffin could be two goats, two pigs, two deer, and, if willed by the community, two oarsmen, a male and a female. One of the slave leaders would be chosen to lead the journey to the next world. There are stories about a Boholano chief who was buried in a *balangay* surrounded by seventy slaves, weapons, and food. He was indeed prepared to engage in *pangungubat* in the afterlife (Colin 1660, 174). When the motivation for the *pangungubat* was vengeance or the withdrawal from mourning because of the death of a mother, father, or other relative, the return was followed by several days of feasting, culminating in the mourning ritual. In other victorious returns, the indigenous priests and priestesses, or *babaylan* were summoned to chant the *pagdaaig*, a paean of praise to the raiding heroes. The *tagumpay*, a song of triumph, was also sung (Alcina 1668, 172, 173).

The Destruction of the Town

What might be the probable effects of *digma*? The definition of the word *lupig* explains that *digma* refers to the capture of a *hacienda* and the possible destruction of the surrounding area: *nabagbag doon sa bayan naming, iguinigiba ang lahat na bahay at pinagsira lahat naari* ("every house was brought down and all properties destroyed"). What would happen when a town was attacked (*ginubat*)? The people would run everywhere, *tumagac-tagac*, looking for a place of refuge. If the town was plundered, *sinamsam,* they would become captives, or could be injured and killed, *hinilabus pinatayang sangbayan* ("the whole town was harmed and killed"). The town would be abandoned (*baying quinapocsaan*). Finally, the town would fall (*naolog ang bayan*). This is the reason for people to abandon their homes (*lilicas*).

Casi-casi or Sanduguan

Casi-casi or *sanduguan* is a ritual of agreement or friendship of two people. Each takes a few drops of blood from any part of his body. These are then mixed in some form of liquid, with both parties drinking from the goblet. This symbolizes the creation of a bond of friendship and alliance between the two sides, and agreements which cannot be violated (Boxer Codex 1590, 233; Loarca 1582, 98). The vocabulary lists, which include the word *magkasandugo* (derived from *sanduguan*), indicate that the game of war allowed towns to become "blood relatives." These connections were made possible because rituals like the *sanduguan* formed fictive family ties. Another term for friendship was *casi*, as used in the following sentence: *Nagcacasi silang dalawa* ("they are becoming friends").

The Retelling of the Story

Let me present here an alternative reading of Salcedo's conquest based on our understanding of the rules of native warfare. Although some of this is speculative, the basis is still provided by historical evidence that provides a glimpse of the native *imaginaire*, a reconstruction of a point of view that was of no interest to the Spanish chroniclers.

As early as January 1570, the *datus* of Aklan and Bahay River had been plotting their raid against Mindoro. They had been harassed continuously by their enemies and would have been preoccupied with the goal of retaliation. In pursuit of this goal, they approached the newly arrived peoples who had settled on their island, Panay. The Spanish leader, Miguel Lopez de Legazpi, then sent Captain Juan de Salcedo and his soldiers to join the *datus* in their fight against the people of Mindoro.

Around five hundred warriors, together with their leaders, readied themselves for the *pangungubat* and were joined by Salcedo and his men. They reached the enemy's settlement, Mamburao, and under cover of darkness they spied out the artillery placements. This completed, they launched a surprise attack as dawn broke. The entire town was devastated, and it was only after a ransom was paid that the group moved on to the next settlement. Here, however, the inhabitants had heard of the attack and readied themselves against the raid. They retreated inside their forts and defended themselves with *lantakas*, arrows, and cannons. However, the fort was more vulnerable than they had thought, for the attackers were able to cross the moat and climb the ramparts. The warriors defending the fort died and the remainder were captured. The same strategy was followed in encounters in the next two forts, whence the people of Lubang had retreated. In the end, the people of

Mindoro paid a ransom in gold taels that was divided amongst Salcedo's soldiers and the *datus*.

This retelling of the basic story considers the contrasting perceptions of power relationships in the Spanish-Filipino alliance when viewed from the standpoint of the Spanish chronicler (the Spanish reading of native action), and that of the *datus*, the local leaders. In indigenous forms of warfare, the making of an alliance was part of the political negotiations in trading and raiding. Alcina mentions alliances made not only through marriage but also through the *sanduguan*, the blood compact, so that neighboring towns could be sworn enemies or close allies. The *datus* of Aklan and Bahay River on the island of Panay may not have been as dominant as the people in Mindoro, who were described as having forts and cannons, but they were nonetheless preparing for a surprise raid on Mindoro. Presumably, they saw the Spaniards, Legazpi and his men, as potential and promising allies. However, the Spanish chronicle assumes that the Spaniards were uppermost in the power equation and that the request for help came about because of their military superiority. Those asking assistance were seen simply as "friendly natives," people who had accommodated to the Spanish presence. In the Spanish chronicle, Salcedo is the leader of the raid and his dominance is unquestioned. The chronicler has forgotten that this conflict is not the Spaniard's war. Rather, it is a conflict waged by the people of Aklan and Bahay River against their Mindoro enemies.

Against this background, it is possible to see that Salcedo may have been viewed merely as a participant in a native conflict, and not necessarily as the leader. After the fighting, when the outcome was already clear, Salcedo demanded "tribute," which in the Spanish world view was indeed a meaningful form of subjugation, symbolizing subservience to a higher social order. "After the victory, [Salcedo] had the leaders brought before him, and offered them peace once more with the friendship of the Spaniards. They promised to be faithful vassals of His Majesty, and asked him to impose the tribute they would have to pay henceforth in recognition of their vassalage" (San Agustin 1698, 533). The chronicler even emphasizes the willingness of the captured leaders to pay the tribute and that the tribute was indeed a form of vassalage. But was this really the case? In the indigenous culture of warfare, such payments could also signify "ransom," since it was common for captured leaders to pay ransom, or for someone else to pay the ransom and later receive a hundred percent interest in capital. It could be argued, then, that Filipinos would have interpreted the presentation of taels of gold less as an act of vassalage than as a form of ransom.

One of the "laws" of indigenous warfare dictated that all the *pangungubat* plunder was the possession of the *datus* or the leaders. It was they who decided what should be distributed among their warriors. As we have seen, the document praises Salcedo for sharing the spoils amongst his soldiers and the *datus*: "He distributed it among the soldiers and leaders, without Juan de Salcedo taking anything more than the glory of victory for himself." (San Agustin 1698, 531). Similarly, "They gave a great quantity of gold for their ransom which, as in Mamburao, was divided among the soldiers and leaders of Aklan and Ibahais." From the Spanish perspective, it was a generous act to divide the spoils among the other leaders and the participants in the raid. However, in a *pangungubat* or a *pangayao*, the spoils went to leaders who spent their resources in supporting the expedition—those who had sponsored the *pag-anito*, those who gathered men together. In this context, Salcedo was simply one of several leaders of the raid. Although he is said to have taken nothing for himself, the mere act of dividing the spoils among the other leaders and his own men means he had in effect accepted that he was sharing in a joint enterprise.

The Spanish chronicle ends with a triumphant note: ". . . after Captain Juan de Salcedo entered into a blood compact with one of the leaders as a sign of a newly pacted friendship, he returned happily and victoriously to Panay" (San Agustin 1698, 533). The actor at center stage is the victorious Salcedo. Neither the local leaders of Aklan and Bahay River nor their five hundred warriors figure in the story. They remain merely cardboard characters mentioned in passing as supporters of the heroic Salcedo. And yet, in retelling the same story against the Spanish grain, other forms of evidence can provide the ethnohistorian with valuable alternative perspectives. Through this means it is possible to suggest that the *datu* essentially incorporated Salcedo into their own world view. Though unrecorded in the Spanish sources, we can perhaps envisage their triumphant return to their own villages where they were greeted with joy and where their success was celebrated as the *babaylan* chanted the song of victory (*tagumpay*).

References

Alcina, Francisco Ignacio. 1668. "Historia de las Islas e Indios de las Bisayas." In *The Munoz Text of Alcins's History of the Bisayan Islands*, ed. and trans. Paul S. Lietz. 3 vols. Chicago: Philippine Studies Program, University of Chicago, 1960.

Blair, Emma, and J. A. Robertson, eds. and trans. 1903–9. *The Philippine Islands 1493–1898.* 55 vols. Cleveland: Arthur H. Clark.

Boxer Codex. 1590. "The Manner, Customs and Beliefs of the Philippine Inhabitants of Long Ago, Being Chapters of 'A Late 16th Century Manila Manuscript.'" In *The Philippines at the Spanish Contact*, ed. F. Landa Jocano, 188–235. Manila: MCS Enterprises, 1975.

Chirino, Pedro. 1604. "Of Marriages, Dowries and Divorces Among the Filipinos." In *The Philippines at the Spanish Contact*, ed. F. Landa Jocano, 125–46. Manila: MCS Enterprises, 1975.

Colin, Francisco. 1660. "Native Races and Their Customs: Of the Origin of the Nations and Peoples Who Inhabit These Islands." In *The Philippines at the Spanish Contact*, ed. F. Landa Jocano, 147–87. Manila: MCS Enterprises, 1975.

Goyti, Martin de, and Hernando Riquel. 1570. "Act of Taking Possession of Luzon." In *The Philippine Islands 1493–1898, Vol. 3*, trans. Emma Blair and James Robertson, 105–7. Cleveland: Arthur H. Clark, 1903–9.

Jocano, F. Landa, ed. 1975. *The Philippines at the Spanish Contact.* Manila: MCS Enterprises.

Lavezaris, Guido de. 1575. "Slavery Among the Natives." In *The Philippine Islands 1493–1898, Vol. 3*, trans. Emma Blair and James Robertson, 286–87. Cleveland: Arthur H. Clark, 1903–9.

Loarca, Miguel de. 1582. "Relación de las Islas Filipinas." In *The Philippines at the Spanish Contact*, ed. F. Landa Jocano, 81–107. Manila: MCS Enterprises, 1975.

Mintz, Malcolm W. 1996. "Prehispanic Terms for War and Conflict." *Pilipinas* 26: 165–93.

Morga, Antonio de. 1609. *Sucesos de las Islas Filipinas*, ed. and trans. J. S. Cummins. Cambridge University Press and Hakluyt Society, 1971.

Oliver, Juan de. 1599. *Declaration de Doctrina Christiana en Idioma Tagalog*, ed. Jose M. Cruz. Quezon City: Pulong Sources for Philippine Materials, 1995.

Pigafetta, Antonio. 1592. *Magellan's Voyage: A Narrative Account of the First Circumnavigation*, ed. and trans. R. A. Skelton. New York: Dover Publications, 1994.

Plasencia, Juan de. 1589. "Customs of the Tagalogs: A Relation." In *The Philippines at the Spanish Contact*, ed. F. Landa Jocano, 108–24. Manila: MCS Enterprises, 1975.

Quirino, Carlos, and Mauro Garcia. 1958. "Narrative of Mr. Juan Masolong, First Christian of Lilio, Laguna, and the Founding of the Town in 1572: An 18th Century Manuscript." *Philippine Journal of Science* 87(4): 325–453.

"Relation of the Voyage to Luzon." 1570. In *The Philippine Islands 1493–1898, Vol. 3*, trans. Emma Blair and James Robertson, 73–104. Cleveland: Arthur H. Clark, 1903–9.

———. 1572. "Relation of the Conquest of the Island of Luzon." In *The Philippine Islands 1493–1898, Vol. 3*, trans. Emma Blair and James Robertson, 141–72. Cleveland: Arthur H. Clark, 1903–9.

Rodriguez, Felice Noelle. 2001. "Words of War: Philippine Warfare in the 17th Century." In *Imperios y Naciones en el Pacifico, Vol. 2*, eds. Ma. Dolores Elizalde, Josep M. Fradera, and Luis Alonso, 277–98. Madrid: Consejo Superior de Investigaciones Cientificas.

Ruiz, Miguel. 1630. *Bocabulario Tagalog*, ed. Jose Mario Francisco. Quezon City: Pulong Sources for Philippine Materials, 1997.

San Agustin, Gaspar de. 1698. *Conquistas de las Islas Filipinas: Conquest of the Philippine Islands, 1565–1615*, ed. Pedro G. Galende, 531–35. Manila: San Agustin Museum, 1998.

San Antonio, Francisco de. (†1624).2000. *Vocabulario Tagalo*, ed. Antoon Postma. Quezon City: Pulong Sources for Philippine Materials.

San Antonio, Juan Francisco de. 1977. *Cronicas de la Provincia de San Gregorio Magno*, trans. D. Pedro Picornell. Manila: Casalinda and the Historical Conservation Society.

San Buenaventura, Pedro de. 1613. *Vocabulario de la Lengua Tagala*. Pila, Laguna.

Santiago, Luciano P. R. 1990. "The Filipino Indios Encomendores (ca. 1620–1711)." *Philippine Quarterly of Culture and Society* 18(3): 162–84.

Schumacher, John. 1979. *Readings in Philippine Church History*. Quezon City: Loyola School of Theology.

Scott, William Henry. 1982. *Cracks in the Parchment Curtain*. Quezon City: New Day Publishers.

———. 1994. *Barangay: Sixteenth-Century Philippine Culture and Society*. Quezon City: Ateneo de Manila University Press.

CHAPTER 3

The Fears of a Small Country with a Big Colony: The Netherlands Indies in the First Decades of the Twentieth Century

Kees van Dijk

In the nineteenth and early twentieth centuries, the Dutch had to come to terms with the fact that they were inhabiting a small and militarily weak country in Europe that ruled over a large colony in Asia. Aware that the Netherlands would almost surely be defeated in any armed international dispute, their apprehension over the fate of the motherland and her incommensurably bigger eastern colonial possession increased whenever interstate tensions in Europe mounted. Any upset in the international society of states, be it in terms of the balance of power or of the rules governing international relations, might threaten the territorial integrity of the Netherlands Indies as well as that of the Netherlands. People entertained fears that an occupation of the motherland would invite other mightier powers to seize the chance to grab the Dutch colonial possessions. Equally worrisome was the threat of an enemy snatching away the colony without actually trying to conquer the metropolitan Low Countries.

Pessimism about the possibility of a successful defense of the colony prevailed. In civilian and military circles of the Netherlands Indies, this sentiment was the rule rather than the exception, as the army and navy in the Netherlands Indies were considered too weak to repel an enemy determined to conquer Java or any other Dutch possessions in the archipelago. Initially it was European powers, who since the 1880s had been busy carving up Africa and Asia amongst themselves, that figured prominently in the doomsday scenarios of the Dutch, but around 1900 Japanese "Jingoism" and expansionist ambitions began to encroach on the minds of the Dutch. Japan had defeated China in the Sino-Japanese War of 1894–95, its troops had made an excellent impression during the march on Beijing after the Boxer Rebellion, and soon Japan was to take on and defeat Russia in the Russo-Japanese War of 1904–5.

Taiwan, ceded by China in 1895, might prove to be the first step for Japan on its march south. The Philippines, poorly defended by Spain, would then be next. In view of this, the speedy build-up of the Japanese fleet after the Sino-Japanese War was observed with awe and dread. Japan's formidable navy with its "fighting machines", the "floating citadels", which had a far greater battle capacity than any of the warships in the Dutch navy, inspired admiration as well as anxiety (*De Locomotief*, January 6, 1900; March 8, 1900).[1] The awe only increased when Japan began to build impressive dreadnought battleships in its attempt to follow the example of the other naval powers and as part of the international arms race. Since Japan had made immense advancements in the intellectual and material sphere, the correspondent of the *Schlesische Zeitung* in The Hague wrote, "It is an indisputable article of faith in the Dutch Archipelago that the bold, assertive state, having succumbed to the urge of expansion by force, would have designs on the annexation of parts of the Dutch colonial possession" (February 2, 1904).

In a sense, the threat envisaged from Japan transformed discussions about the defense of the Netherlands Indies. In the past, the most likely form of foreign aggression had seemed to involve small-scale occupation of a limited piece of territory, either to function as a commercial settlement or as a coaling station. Far more than in the past, the Japanese specter presented people—politicians, army and navy officers and planners, and the lay public alike—with the heightened prospect of a full-fledged invasion.

The Colonial Army

If a foreign enemy was to land its troops in the Netherlands Indies, it was the duty of the colonial army to repel them. Unfortunately, this army was not a paragon of power and might. Having difficulties in conquering the sultanate of Aceh in the north of Sumatra, there were serious doubts about its ability to defend the country against foreign invaders. The chronic shortage of officers and men, as well as uncertainties regarding the capability of the army to perform as a reliable instrument of defense, were inseparably linked with a low regard for its soldiers. Some of these soldiers were Europeans, some Indonesians. The European soldiers, who numbered some 14,000 in 1900, and some 8,500 in 1914, were despised by the white European community. Many of the European soldiers who had been recruited in Europe had been enticed by the bounty they received on enlisting. They saw enlistment as a chance to escape poverty, with some of them also motivated by the opportunity to run away from the law, and so the prospect of being transported thousands of kilometers away was to them heaven-sent. The European soldiers were considered riffraff and were treated as such, as they hovered on the fringes of European colonial society. Even in the eyes of the Indonesian population, they were deemed inferior to other Europeans. As a newspaper noted around the turn of the century, every Dutchman was a "sir" (*tuan*) to the natives. The exception was the soldiers, who were simply called *soldadoe* (soldiers) (*De Locomotief*, August 2, 1904).

An additional reason to doubt the trustworthiness of the colonial army, in particular after the eighteenth century, was that, almost from the days the Dutch had established themselves in the archipelago, the number of foreigners in the European military force had been disproportionately large. During the nineteenth century, the influx of foreigners still remained high. After a separate colonial army, the Oost-Indische Leger or the East Indies Army, had been established in 1830, men from all over Europe continued to enlist. It was not a comforting thought for the Dutch community in the Netherlands Indies that their safety in part depended on foreign soldiers, a feeling that was exacerbated whenever tension in Europe was on the rise. With some apprehension, *De Locomotief* (December 28, 1870) observed at the time of the Franco-Prussian War that alien soldiers had offered invaluable service to the colony but that it would be safest if the defense of the Dutch flag were to be laid in Dutch hands. At that moment, 2,700 of the 13,000 European soldiers were of non-Dutch nationality. The commander of the army appeared slightly more confident about the loyalty of these troops. He maintained that there was nothing to worry about, at least "as long as no

European enemy appears in these possessions and even then, without doubt there will be found among them a very large proportion of good soldiers who will not desert their flag or turn their weapons against us." Nevertheless, he did recommend that for political reasons, the foreign element should gradually be eased out of the colonial army (Nationaal Archief, The Hague. NA, Kol., Mailrapport 1871/111).

Not much had changed by the end of the nineteenth century due to the Aceh War and other military operations in the archipelago. Therefore, the influx of foreign soldiers remained indispensable. In 1900, still almost one-fifth of all Europeans serving in the army of the Netherlands Indies, some 3,000 soldiers, were foreigners. In 1904, at the time of the Russo-Japanese War, the number of foreign soldiers had dropped to 2,400, but proportionally their ratio remained the same. At that time, fearing the consequences of the war for the Netherlands Indies, it was even deemed necessary to take measures to facilitate the recruitment of foreigners for the colonial army. Only in the years thereafter did the colonial army become less dependent on non-Dutch soldiers. In 1916, their numbers had dropped to fewer than 800, or about 10 percent of the European soldiers, the majority of them (625) being of German origin (Koloniaal Verslag 1901 and 1905, Bijlage A Table 3; Zwitzer and Heshusius 1977, 12–13).

If European soldiers were regarded lowly by civil society, perceptions of the Indonesian soldiers proved to be even worse. A note from the Colonial Office in 1906 observed that such soldiers came from the bottom-most layers of society (NA, Kol. Openbaar, Vb. 13-7-1906 Q15). Of the Indonesian soldiers, the majority were Javanese, that is, men from central and east Java. In 1900 (and in 1914), there were over 16,000 Javanese soldiers serving. The next largest group was that of the so-called Amboinese, soldiers from the Moluccas and from Menado in the north of Celebes, a term which also came to denote all Christian native soldiers. In 1900, there were some 4,000, and in 1914 some 9,000 of them. Except at times when their services were needed, all the prejudices the white European community nurtured about the Indonesian population and its various ethnic groups surfaced in full force when their performance in battle was discussed. There were widely held doubts about the fighting spirit and military qualities of the Javanese. The fact that Javanese soldiers went barefooted, as did the majority of the population, made them appear even less soldierly in the eyes of many white men. Shoes, it would seem, made a good soldier. When the matter of Dutch troops joining the expeditionary force in China had come up, it was argued that there was nothing wrong with sending Indonesian troops as long as they were Amboinese soldiers, who wore shoes, and not others who still went about barefooted (*De Locomotief*, July 20, 1900).

Those from the Moluccas and the Minahasa were considered to be the product of more warlike ethnic groups, and were consequently also better paid and treated than the Javanese. One of the moments when serious consideration had to be given to the performance of Indonesian soldiers was after the Boxer Rebellion, when the possibility of the Netherlands sending a military contingent to China was raised. In Java, the newspaper *Java Bode* (cited in *De Locomotief*, July 23, 1900) pondered the question of which indigenous troops should accompany the European soldiers. The answer was ready enough, in that no native troops at all should be sent to China. The Javanese were simply perceived to lack the aptitude to fight the Chinese. The Amboinese, on the other hand, were good soldiers but had the disadvantage that "they never want to take up arms without women," a reference to the fact that their wives accompanied them on all their missions. Both groups, moreover, regardless of their professional abilities, were "children of the hot sun" and would not be able to endure the severe northern Chinese climate.

The perception that there were differences among the colony's various ethnic groups in their capacity to become good soldiers, either due to nature or nurture, was an issue that acquired urgency in the years leading up to World War I. The official view at that time was that an army with a large proportion of native soldiers was essentially weak. For fighting a foreign enemy or for action in regions in the archipelago with a belligerent population, military experts had decided that no more than half of the troops should consist of native soldiers (*Rapport* 1913, 92). It was also argued in the Dutch Senate that the colonial army could not be expanded by simply recruiting more soldiers from among the Indonesian population, as that would be detrimental to its fighting capability (*Handelingen* 1913–1914, I 65). These views were still widely shared, also in the East Indies. In Java, even the progressive *De Locomotief* (October 20, 1913; November 1, 1913), wrote that the Amboinese and Menadonese soldiers could become good soldiers under the guidance of capable Dutch officers. This was a completely different matter with regard to the Javanese, as most of them lacked the required physical and intellectual endowments. Yet, there was a glimmer of hope. The newspaper went on to observe that until recently the Javanese had been deprived of physical and mental training in their youth, but times were changing. The emergence of a nationalist movement also manifested itself in an increased care of their bodies by the Javanese.

The Dutch Navy

European sailors were perhaps even more despised by the civil European society than the soldiers (Tichelman 1985, 15). The navy did not inspire much confidence, with its image tarnished by desertion and by the many sailors who suffered from venereal diseases. And, most disturbing of all, its fighting strength was small. When it was observed that countries all over the world were ordering and building dreadnoughts in the years leading up to World War I, the realization hit home that the Dutch fleet guarding the Netherlands Indies counted for nothing. It was no match for the fleets of the great powers, nor would it become so in the foreseeable future. This fact had already been established in the years prior to the Russo-Japanese War, but since then warships had only grown bigger and were armed with increasingly heavy guns. The Dutch fleet had none of these new large battleships and its warships were dwarfed by the modern dreadnoughts. The defense of the archipelago in the 1910s was entrusted to a number of torpedo boats and a few ironclads and armored deck vessels, of which maybe one, in the most pessimistic evaluation, was still to some extent battleworthy (*Handelingen* 1913–14, II 1355). Another gloomy assessment was the common observation that the combined firing power of all the Dutch battleships put together was less than that of one single modern battleship, of which countries like

Great Britain, Germany, and Japan had many (Anon. 1914, 6). On December 30, 1913, *De Locomotief* thus stressed that the colonial fleet was "in such a sorry state that, independent of any international fleet frenzy, the necessary measures for the naval defense of our colony should have already been taken long, long ago." Naval command agreed, calling the Dutch fleet a *quantité négligeable* (*Handelingen* 1913–14, II 1339). Even the minister of the navy, J. J. Rambonnet, himself a former naval officer, had to admit that the Dutch fleet did not amount to much, and in expressing this view was treading the well-trodden path of his predecessors, who almost without exception had stressed this point in an attempt to have the navy budget increased (*Handelingen* 1913–14, I 418).

Armaments, or the lack thereof, were not the only problems upsetting such people. The establishment considered leftist agitation among the ratings to be at least as alarming. The "undermining class struggle," as it was sometimes castigated, had produced what in the minds of some amounted to a "red fleet." The Bond van Minder Marine-Personeel (Union of Lower Naval Personnel) had gained considerable support among sailors and had earned itself a name by organizing actions to protest against arbitrary decisions and excessive demands for the maintenance of discipline from the side of the officers. Its periodical, *Het Anker* (The Anchor), was widely read. This had been so since the beginning of the twentieth century despite the efforts of some of the naval officers to check their crews' mail in order to confiscate the magazine. If people in the Netherlands were concerned regarding the activities of the Union of Lower Naval Personnel, the colonial authorities had even greater cause for concern. The Union of Lower Naval Personnel had a branch in the Netherlands Indies. Its office was in Surabaya, the main base of the Dutch fleet in the colonies. The branch was generally considered, as was indeed the case, to be more radical than its head office in the Netherlands, and during World War I was led and inspired—or incited, some would say—by J. A. Brandsteder, H. J. F. M. Sneevliet, A. Baars, and other hardline social democrats, all members of the Indische Sociaal-Democratische Vereeniging (ISDV, Indies Social Democratic Association), who were later to give the initial impetus for the founding of the Communist Party of Indonesia.

Such was the apprehension of the naval authorities about the influence of socialist propaganda even before World War I that in March 1914, when sailors at the naval base in Surabaya were invited to attend a full-dress rehearsal of a play, their commander forbade them to march from the union building to the theater as a group. Such a procession was seen as a violation of the ban on sailors participating in demonstrations.

When the sailors, 175 in all, disregarded the ban and marched to the theater as a group, they were kept under close observation by an armed patrol (*De Expres*, March 11, 1914). From time to time, senior officers, among them the commander of the navy in the Netherlands Indies, Vice-Admiral J. A. M. Bron, called for stern action against the union and its activists. In doing so, they could count on the support of Rambonnet, a convinced enemy of *Het Anker* and all the magazine stood for, who had been qualified by *De Expres* (June 17, 1914), a newspaper produced by Indo-Europeans striving for emancipation, as "the god of war of the Dutch fleet, the fierce opponent of the red ghost on board of ships."

The navy was not only red, it also suffered from a shortage of sailors. The implication of this was that expanding the fleet and building dreadnoughts would mean that part of the crew would have to consist of conscripts. The idea of recruiting Indonesians for the auxiliary fleet, that is, the war fleet with a duty to protect the colony from an external foe—there was also a so-called Indies Military Navy made up of even smaller warships employed to impress native coastal states—in order to make up for at least some of the shortages in navy personnel, was not readily welcomed by all. It was a new field of employment for Indonesians, and the Dutch argued, as they would invariably do whenever Indonesians entered or wanted to enter a field of employment previously closed to them, that Indonesians lacked the requisite mental or physical qualifications for the job. Reliability, honesty, discipline, said to be prerequisites for certain jobs, and in this instance also sexual abstinence, were traits reserved for their own race.

Confronted with a shortage of crew in March 1913, the navy began to recruit Indonesians as "war sailors" in the auxiliary fleet, even though they had to date only served in very minor positions as servants to naval officers and the like. Even when properly trained, these first Indonesian sailors were considered inferior to their Dutch colleagues and, consequently, the minister of the colonies, Th. B. Pleyte, was to stress that they were to receive less pay but this was only temporary. The experiment offered the extra advantage that, if it were a success, Indonesians could take the place of some of the European sailors who considered their long stay in the colony an "irrevocable disaster" (*Handelingen* 1913–14, II 2254). Opinions about the prospects of recruiting Indonesian sailors were mixed. Some Dutch people had difficulty in admitting that Indonesians could qualify. Officers argued that the Indonesians were too indolent and lacked the necessary energy. A Dutch sailor could do three times as much work (*Handelingen* 1913–14, II 2554–5). Such critics saw no contradiction with the fact, stressed by Pleyte in parliament, that Indonesians made excellent gunners as they often outperformed Dutch sailors in target practice (*Handelingen* 1913–14, II 2561).

Agitation and moral conduct also played a role in the evaluation of the experiment to train Indonesian sailors. Some feared that mixing with the Dutch crew could contaminate Indonesian sailors with the "wrong spirit" of socialism, with dire consequences for the authority of Dutch rule in the colony (*Handelingen* 1913–14, II 2455). Sex was also a problem. A discussion of the sexual habits of Indonesians was triggered by an interview in a Dutch newspaper with a naval officer stationed in the Netherlands Indies, who had suggested that serving as a sailor would be a healthy occupation for people from north Celebes. Referring to a statement made by the local Dutch Resident, he postulated that early and frequent sexual intercourse coupled with bad food (sago was their staple) had resulted in heart disease and had made 80 percent of the young men in that region unfit for service in the army, a remarkable observation indeed, because many Indonesian soldiers in the colonial army came from this region. The isolated life on board a warship and the healthy food in the navy would redress this undesirable situation (*Handelingen* 1913–14, II 2566).

Later, he disclaimed his words, but others took up the issue of the sexual habits of Indonesians. Of the ethnic groups from which the government intended to recruit Indonesian sailors, one member of parliament remarked that it was common knowledge that they had sexual intercourse at a very young age. While welcoming the efforts to recruit Indonesians into the navy as a chance to reform their sexual habits, he warned that isolation on board ship should not last too long as this might otherwise lead to "other sexual practices, which are perhaps worse" (*Handelingen* 1913–14, II 2556). For natives, he continued, could not endure sexual continence, citing as proof the newspaper *Java-Bode* in which this argument was advanced as one of the reasons why Indonesians probably could never be recruited for the navy in great numbers. In the army, sex was less of a problem, as women accompanied their husbands to their posts. This armed forces practice, however, would be impossible in the navy and might dissuade many Indonesians from enlisting. Without ample shore leave and without an effort on the part of the government to promote marriage, the cases of venereal diseases therefore looked set to multiply if Indonesian sailors were to be enlisted in the navy.

Our Fleet

The realization that both the Dutch army and the Dutch navy in the Netherlands Indies were weak invariably prompted discussions about the improvements to be made to the defense of the Netherlands Indies in order to safeguard the colony against an invasion. On hindsight, it was an amusing discussion spiced with varied opinions. On the one side of the spectrum were those who suggested that the navy should be scrapped altogether as it would never be a match for a foreign fleet. Defensive efforts should entirely be concentrated on land and all the money available thus be spent on the building up of the colonial army. Others expressed exactly the opposite opinion: the colonial army should gradually be disbanded to make money available for the building up of the navy. Against a seaborne invading force, the army would never be able to defend a territory as large as the Netherlands Indies. It followed that the defense of the colony depends on the fleet rather than the army; the former should consequently be expanded by providing it with powerful modern battleships. In 1913, it seemed that the latter opinion was adopted when a report was presented by the state commission set up to investigate the steps to be taken to strengthen the defense of the Netherlands Indies. The task of the commission, which had been instituted in June the previous year, was, in the words of *De Locomotief* (October 10, 1913), to study how the defense of the colony could be ensured, even though both the required manpower and money were lacking. The newspaper concluded that this was an absurd task.

The state commission nevertheless produced an ambitious plan: an artillery fleet of which nine large battleships would form the core. The nine vessels would preferably be of at least the same speed and armed with the same heavy caliber guns as the dreadnoughts constructed by the British, Germans, and Japanese. Four such vessels should be ready at all times to engage the enemy in colonial waters. The first was planned to come into service in 1917, the last in 1921. It was also essential that a fifth extra reserve vessel, to be launched in 1923, be stationed in the Netherlands Indies. Its additional presence would allow for longer and shorter repairs to be carried out efficiently and without endangering the perceived minimum strength of battle-ready dreadnoughts.

The conclusions of the state commission were wholeheartedly supported by the association Onze Vloot (Our Fleet), which had been founded in May 1906. The call for a large fleet appealed to them, as did the glorification of Dutch power and the idea that the Netherlands was still held in high esteem all over the world because of its large and rich colony. These were clearly the sentiments that permeated the pages of the report. Like its counterpart and example in Germany, the Flottenverein founded at the instigation of Krupp, and a similar league in France, Our Fleet aimed to mobilize public opinion in favor of a naval build-up. By organizing lectures all over the Netherlands, its members spread the message that a powerful fleet was a vital prerequisite to the defense of the Netherlands Indies. Pamphlets supporting the campaign warned the Dutch public that the loss of its rich overseas possessions would bring ruin to the Netherlands. The first of these, sketching the disastrous economic consequences of the loss of the Netherlands Indies for the home country, was published in October 1913. An alarming title and subtitle were chosen: *'s Lands welvaart in gevaar!* [Our Country's Prosperity in Danger: A Serious Message to the Dutch People . . .] Its author was W. A. van Aken, a former naval officer and first secretary and treasurer of Our Fleet. A second pamphlet in 1914, written by Jonkheer C. G. S. Sandberg who had given his lectures the same motto, was even more alarmist: *Indië verloren, rampspoed geboren* [The Indies Lost, a Catastrophe Born]. The title captured the public imagination. It became a well-known slogan, used alike by friend and foe of the fleet movement, and reemerged between 1945 and 1950 when Dutch forces were fighting Indonesian nationalists in the war of independence.

Army circles were shocked when the conclusions of the State Commission were published in its *Rapport* of August 1913. They were appalled by the fact that the State Commission had little faith in the ability of the colonial army to act as an effective deterrent. In view of the cost to be incurred in building the fleet, the commission seemed determined to do away with almost the entire army and to put its trust completely in the navy of the Netherlands Indies. The members of the committee had argued that should the Netherlands be attacked in the event of a European conflict, land-borne warfare would decide the fate of the motherland. In the colony, by contrast, the confrontation at sea would be decisive. The report of the State Commission stressed the likelihood that the decisive battle for the Netherlands Indies would be that waged for control of the seas. Once the enemy commanded these waters, not even a large and well-equipped army would be able to do much. At most, it could temporarily keep some of the islands of the archipelago in Dutch hands. Java, for instance, once cut off from the outside world, would eventually certainly fall into enemy hands because the island lacked the necessary natural resources to keep its economy running and to sustain a prolonged resistance. Having the army to defend Java was a utopian misconception, moreover, as half of its forces were made up of "elements (*Natives*) of presumably less battle-worthy quality than those in the ranks of the enemy" (*Rapport* 1913, 19, 24). Predicting an invasion by a force of 100,000 men, the State Commission concluded that it would be impossible for the Netherlands to raise an army of equal strength. It was "self-deceit" to think that the army stood any chance of success in the repulsion of such an assault (*Rapport* 1913, 86). Once the navy had been defeated, no second line of defense could be brought into play.

For army officers, the idea that an army could not defend Java was not such an open and shut conclusion. In their view, a strong fleet was fine but a strong army was equally important and an even more important asset for the defense of the colony. They maintained that it was a folly to assume that a Dutch fleet could command the seas and straits of the archipelago. The navy should concentrate on guarding neutrality and on inflicting heavy losses on an enemy fleet, which in fact was what the State Commission had argued.

Opponents of the fleet plans also pointed out that it would be madness to try to join the race contested by the naval powers for ever larger and better armed warships, which Rambonnet, who himself had been one of the advisors to the State Commission, assured was not at all the intention of the Dutch government (*Handelingen* 1913–14, 289). They were convinced that the best guarantee against foreign aggression remained competition between the great powers as none of them would ever allow a rival to occupy Holland or the Netherlands Indies.

Opposition was also launched by the left. One of the people who voiced his disagreement was H. H. van Kol. On behalf of the socialist party, Sociaal-Democratische Arbeiderspartij (SDAP), he recollected that since the close of the nineteenth century it had always been the same old song: the government, referring to the weakness of the navy, asked for extra money to build new ships, which, once commissioned, were soon declared to be obsolete. Between 1904 and 1913, he calculated, 70 million guilders had been spent on a fleet that was now considered to be virtually obsolete (*Handelingen* 1913–14, 418). Van Kol even argued that a weak fleet was much better than a strong one to guard Dutch neutrality. Nobody would have raised a protest during the Russo-Japanese War should the Russian Baltic Fleet on its way to do battle with the Japanese fleet have violated Dutch neutrality. Were the Dutch cockleshells to be replaced by impressive battleships, the situation would change. A strong fleet would mean that the Dutch navy had to do battle in such a situation and this still without any chance of victory (*Handelingen* 1913–14, 419).

Advocates and opponents of the fleet plans in the Netherlands and in the Netherlands Indies were still strenuously debating the issue when World War I broke out, upon which the plan had to be shelved. The defense of the colony had to rest upon the navy as it was, and on the army. An immediate problem, and due to the imminent threat of war a very pressing one, was that the colonial army was chronically undermanned. There was a shortage of 3,000 European men, a quarter of its original strength, and over 1,700 native soldiers. To promote fresh recruitment of European and Indonesian soldiers, the financial incentives to prompt people to enlist were improved, a step, it was claimed a few years later, which had resulted only in an influx of "undesirable elements" among the European and Indonesian soldiers (*Soerabaiasch Handelsblad* cited in *De Indische Gids* 1917, 1248).

With respect to the recruitment of the latter, and in conformity with prevailing views about which ethnic groups made good soldiers and which not, special attention was paid to Amboinese and Menadonese recruits. In the case of the Indonesian soldiers, the campaign was successful, at least with regard to numbers. The training time of these new soldiers was, however, shortened to about half of what it would have been under normal circumstances. Standards of recruitment also seem to have been lowered. When a group of over 200 recruits from Yogyakarta arrived at the training depot in the colonial capital Batavia (present-day Jakarta), they were initially assumed to be migrant laborers on their way to the plantations in Deli/east Sumatra because of the way they were dressed. Among Europeans, the campaign was less successful. Because sea traffic between Europe and Asia would become disrupted during the war, the shortage of soldiers and officers was only to increase in the years to come.

The Internal Foe

There was yet another reason why people had argued in 1913 that the army should not be reduced in strength. Should the plans of the State Commission become a reality, the downsized army would cease to be strong enough to suppress a large-scale rising in Java. Five years earlier, it had taken three and a half battalions to suppress a rebellion in west Sumatra, in a region with a population of little over one million inhabitants. What would happen in Java with its population of thirty million people? Just how sure the Dutch felt about their hold over the population of Java and of the other islands is impossible to reconstruct. What is certain is that the nervousness in this respect increased after 1910. One of the reasons for this was that modern nationalism had begun to make its mark in the Netherlands Indies. The year 1911 saw the birth of Sarekat Islam (SI), the Islamic Union, which soon would attract a mass following, especially in Java but also in other parts of the colony. It was a new and, for many, a fearful development about which ordinary Dutch people were in a quandary. Within years of the founding of Sarekat Islam, rumors started to circulate on Java that a day of judgment was at hand and that all Europeans would be massacred. Such rumors were especially rife in the summer of 1913 when it became a hotly debated topic of conversation at the clubs. Dutch people speculated about the impending murder of Europeans in August of that year, during the Islamic fasting month of Ramadhan. Dutch newspapers in the Netherlands Indies also wrote about the prospects of a St. Bartholomew's Night. In Batavia, people spoke in retrospect about the "fearful" days (*De Locomotief*, November 29, 1913).

The mass following that Sarekat Islam had acquired and the occasional riot that erupted allowed the commander of the colonial army, Major-General J. P. Michielsen, to reconsider his previous position on the matter of the importance of the colonial army. As a member of the State Commission, he had assented to the suggestion of doing away with the armed forces under his own command but only now did he fully realize the implications of his unusual position. In May 1914, he wrote to Governor-General A. W. F. Idenburg that, had he been able to foresee developments like those manifested in Sarekat Islam at the time when the Commission discussed the cuts to the army budget, he would never have been in favor of the Commission's recommendations (NA, Kol. Openbaar, Vb. 23-7-1914 S13). Others warned that should the Netherlands Indies be made to pay for the expansion of the Dutch fleet, Sarekat Islam would exploit this in its propaganda among the Indonesian population who had so many pressing needs, and who were not at all perplexed by talk of a foreign invasion (*De Locomotief*, November 28, 1913).

World War I would add an additional specific element of worry. Were the Netherlands to engage in a war with Germany, the Germans might try to take over the Netherlands Indies. Speculations about such an eventuality not only led to doubts about the loyalty of the German soldiers in the colonial army but rumors also abounded that German residents were plotting to bring down the colonial government. The implications went much further. The loyalty of the Indonesian soldiers, and in fact of a large part of the Indonesian population, was at stake. These Indonesians were Muslims and it was clear to everyone that their sympathy in the war lay with Germany, which had the Ottoman Empire as its ally, and not with Great Britain or France. Defeatist Dutch people were sure that the Germans in the Netherlands Indies had made good use of the ties of friendship between Germany and Turkey which had developed before the turn of the century and that they had done all they could to turn the colonial army into a bulwark of pro-German sympathizers.

During a lecture in The Hague in 1918, one Dutch captain even ventured to express the opinion that since the beginning of the century, portraits of the Kaiser (and of the Turkish sultan) had adorned barrack walls all over the archipelago (*De Locomotief*, May 15, 1918). An illustration of what the dangers of relying on Islamic soldiers could mean had been provided by the mutiny of Indian Muslim soldiers of the Fifth Light Infantry Battalion in Singapore in February 1915, who were almost the only soldiers in the city at that time. The mutiny had made a great impression in the Netherlands Indies. A new foe had made its appearance: mutinous native soldiers. The composition of the colonial army, with its many Indonesian soldiers, became an acute cause of concern for some. Others realized that the larger cities no longer had fortresses in which the whole European population could take shelter should the native troops rise up and mutiny (*De Locomotief*, March 15, 1915).

The Indies Resilient

At the outbreak of World War I, the colonial authorities and the Dutch people living in the Netherlands Indies anxiously awaited the Indonesian reaction to the conflict. The Netherlands might become involved in the war and Indonesian nationalists and those who abominated Dutch rule (which was not the same) might exploit the situation. It was also considered not unlikely that Turkish agitators would stir up the population or that dissatisfied Indonesians, as they had done before, might turn to the Ottoman Empire for help in getting rid of the Dutch. Nothing of the sort happened, however, as all those fears proved to be nothing more than phantasmagoria. There was a plethora of declarations by Indonesian administrators, by branches of Sarekat Islam, and by others in support of Dutch rule. Muslims also prayed that the Netherlands would be spared from war and would survive as an independent nation.

In view of this sudden and also unexpected wave of pro-Dutch sentiment among the Indonesian population, a novel instrument for the defense of the Netherlands Indies was contemplated: a native militia (the contemporary term for an army of conscripts). In the years immediately before the war, the possibility of native conscription had been raised a number of times but had not been received with much enthusiasm by the colonial authorities. The idea was rejected not only because of security reasons but also because compulsory military service could well be used by nationalist agitators to set the colonial population against Dutch rule. Again, it was doubts about the martial qualities of Indonesians, and especially of the Javanese, which colored the situation. The State Commission, for instance, had been against the conscription of Indonesians for fear that it would become a lengthy process. Based on experience, the report noted, it took as much as six years to turn a native into an "employable battle soldier" (*Rapport* 1913, 94).

Shortly before the outbreak of World War I, mounting international tension imbued the matter with a new urgency. In February 1914, the minister of the colonies in The Hague, Th. B. Pleyte, asked Governor-General Idenburg to mount a new investigation into the feasibility of a native militia, without, the subsequent instructions to army command read, incurring extra costs (van der Weijden 1916, 10). One of the consequences was that, after the outbreak of the war, conscription became a hotly debated issue in the Indonesian as well as the European community. The idea was for a militia for Europeans and natives, not for the Chinese, who, as the immediate prewar years had shown, on the whole formed too restless a group, nor for the Arabs, who were distrusted for religious reasons and for the alleged adverse influence they were supposed to have on the Muslim population. The colonial administration and the Dutch government in The Hague were both now clearly in favor of a native militia, albeit under certain conditions. A native militia should be instituted only in Java and the Minahasa, a largely Christian area (significantly, not in the Moluccas with its mixed Christian and Islamic population), and in Java the militia should be confined to youths with a certain level of formal education. Making no restrictions on the recruitment of Europeans and of people from north Celebes, but doing so for Javanese, was, in the eyes of some Europeans, an insult to the Javanese (van der Weijden 1916, 10).

The formal reason for demanding a certain level of education in the Javanese conscripts-to-be was that they should have a fair knowledge of Dutch. This, in turn, was inspired by the notion that it would take a long time to transform a simple farmer into a soldier, in particular urgent at a time when the period of military service should remain as short as possible. Initially proposed was eight and a half months, later one year. Rural Javanese, moreover, had the additional handicap of not understanding the language of instruction used in the army for the Indonesian troops, which was Malay. The proposed condition left eligible for recruitment a category of Javanese, who, like the Europeans some countered, was too small a group to provide a significant number of conscripts. Moreover, the small group of Dutch-educated Javanese included many civil servants whose administrative services would be difficult to replace and hence strongly missed (*Bataviaasch Handelsblad* cited in *De Indische Gids* 1916, 962). A more important reason remained unspoken, at least in official correspondence, and this was the danger posed to European and Dutch rule by a large group of Javanese with access to arms.

Realizing that intellectuals would form too small a group to establish a viable militia, senior officers of the colonial army contemplated a general conscription, not confined to the intelligentsia. This was also the way in which the lay public imagined the conscription to be. The editor of *De Locomotief* (September 15, 1914; November 26, 1914) speculated about a defense by millions of Indonesians and conjured up an image of savages, suggesting that "the people not inhibited by Western civilization [would] present the intruder with a defense, which would appear to be an invincible obstacle for many of their operations." Without arming the natives, it was later also stated in Holland in the *Algemeen Handelsblad* (cited in *De Indische Gids* 1916, 611), that the colony would be lost, but "if a fleet of submarines were to lie on guard in our Indies waters, backed up by an army of 3 million Javanese, and several hundreds of thousands more Malays, Menadonese, Amboinese, Timorese, then the evil designs of whomsoever it might be, would certainly be somewhat tempered..."

The idea of a native militia, all the more so because the plans concerned only the island of Java, meant that a *volte face* had to be made in the perceptions of the martial qualities of the indigenous population, in particular those of the Javanese. Apace with nascent dreams among Dutch people in the Netherlands Indies and in Holland about a "people's army" of Javanese resisting a foreign invasion, the image of the Javanese as temperamentally unsuitable soldiers faded into the background, at least momentarily. A Javanese can make a good soldier, major J. van der Weijden, a member of the general staff of the colonial army, commented in 1916, recalling the fierce resistance put up against Dutch troops by Diponogoro's followers during the Java War almost a century earlier. When they realized that their very existence was at stake, they would fight as bravely as the Japanese. "The Javanese is not inferior, he is being made inferior by us" (van der Weijden 1916, 31). Nevertheless, proponents of conscription had not completely discarded the idea that the Javanese were not ideally suited to military service, an opinion which had been voiced so frequently before by the Europeans. Adherents of this view argued that the ordinary population should be excluded from conscription as the military would not be pleased if it had to cope with "a great many stupid fellows" (*De Locomotief*, November 26, 1914).

Public discussion focused on political and security implications. At least a portion of the Dutch general public still harbored ambiguous feelings towards the idea of a native militia. Some were even appalled by the idea of the Javanese population being kitted out with guns. Everybody agreed that the defense of the colony had to be strengthened, yet they were cautious of the dangers involved in arming the natives to accomplish this. In a letter to the editor of a newspaper in Holland, a reader who had lived in the Netherlands Indies wrote that the Indonesians were unsuited to the task of defending the colony and that this situation was unlikely to change in the near future. But this, he said, was not the weakest link in the conscription plan: "The brown brother . . . with weapons in his hand is simply not to be trusted" (*De Maasbode* cited in *De Indische Gids* 1917, 789). One of the Dutch language newspapers in the colony summarized the dilemma facing the Dutch as follows: "Without the energetic support of a Native militia, we will lose our colony to a *foreign* enemy and with that Native militia to an *internal* enemy" (cited in *De Indische Gids* 1917, 664). People voicing such an opinion were not very impressed by the manifestations of loyalty in the weeks following the outbreak of World War I, and at times even made fun of them. They were convinced that in a real crisis, it remained to be seen whether the Indonesian population would rally to the assistance of the Dutch. Some regarded the vows of loyalty as having been merely a gesture by a few intellectuals, because, they said, the mass of the people had no opinion at all. Others, furthermore, did not trust these intellectuals who were the proponents of nascent nationalism.

Among leading members of Javanese society and prominent figures in the nationalist movement, conscription became a symbol of loyalty to Dutch rule, partly inspired by the apprehension that the power most likely to replace the Dutch was Japan, which, in China, had not earned itself a reputation of being a benign nor an emancipatory occupying power. With such ideas at the back of their minds, they joined the colonial administration in promoting the idea of a native militia. In the eyes of the nationalist leaders, the militia campaign was first and foremost a political instrument. Political reforms were what they wanted and their support for a militia was only a means to accomplish this. The left was less enthusiastic, while on the whole the ordinary Javanese abhorred the idea that they themselves or their sons could be drafted. Indicative of the mood is the word "conscript," which was sometimes translated as *soldadoe paksaan*, or coerced soldier.

The drive for a native militia culminated in the so-called Indië Weerbaar (Indies Resilient) campaign that propagated the idea of a native militia as part of a larger plan of action to improve the defense of the Netherlands Indies. The campaign reached its peak when an Indonesian deputation visited the Netherlands where it expressed support for native conscription but also demanded political reforms and full emancipation. In Holland, the members of the deputation addressed a wide range of meetings, were received in audience by the Dutch Queen, and were also celebrated in commercial and army circles.

The campaign had some unexpected consequences. In their patriotic zeal to demonstrate reasons for a strong defense, for instance, Dutch campaigners in the Netherlands Indies lashed out at Japan. This was precisely one of the things which the Dutch government was highly apprehensive about as Japan should by no means be rattled. Dutch diplomacy in those days was skilled at lodging protests with the governments of world powers, whether it was Great Britain or Japan, in the kindest and friendliest way possible in order to avoid eliciting the anger of a mightier nation, which at times of international crises could take offense and use the insult as an excuse to act against the Netherlands. The latter was exactly what the fierce speeches demanding a better defense might well accomplish.

Much more important was the fact that a native militia became the topic of meetings of nationalist organizations and this resulted in a radicalization of the nationalist movement, adding to the already existing doubts of the Dutch people regarding the establishment of a native militia. Even the more moderate leaders spoke out fiercely as they demanded an elected parliament in the Netherlands Indies and equal rights for Indonesians in all fields of life, and complained bitterly about the discrimination and oppression they had to endure. Nationalist proponents of a militia were tireless in arguing that if Indonesians were asked to share in the defense of the colony, they should be treated as equal citizens. They should feel that they were defending something that was their own, instead of a colonial possession that belonged to the Dutch.[2] Not all Dutch people, however, found this link between ownership and eagerness to defend quite so evident. Many were convinced that Dutch rule was beneficial to the population, and that, as the Indonesians had also indicated themselves, colonized and colonizers alike would suffer if Dutch rule were to be replaced by that of another state. In their eyes, such prospects rendered the demand for political concessions irrelevant. Further displeasure was generated by the fact that the Indonesians had not hesitated to present their point in plain, uncompromising language.

Disgruntlement

By 1916, the reassuring expressions of solidarity made by the leaders of the nationalist movement in the closing months of 1914 had been drowned out by vocal attacks on Dutch rule, while in some regions—Jambi and Palembang on Sumatra, south and east Kalimantan, and south Sulawesi—the colonial army had to be employed to quell rebellions. Among the Indonesians, the anti-Dutch undercurrent, which the authorities and Dutch public alike feared might be exploited by agitators, was also once again as strong as ever. If they had not yet been aware of this, the campaign for a native militia had also reinforced to the Indonesians the realization that the Dutch in the Netherlands Indies were incapable of withstanding a Japanese invasion. At an anti-Indië Weerbaar manifestation in Semarang on August 31, 1916, a member of Sarekat Islam argued that Japan would inevitably emerge as the victor in a war with the Netherlands in the East, and that being the case, the proponents of a militia were throwing in their lot with the fall of the colony. It was useless, the Sarekat Islam newspaper *Oetoesan Hindia* wrote a few months later, to defend the Netherlands Indies against Japan. It would be more beneficial to promote the spiritual and material wellbeing of the country instead and pray to God to be spared an invasion (*Sinar Djawa and Oetoesan Hindia* cited in *Koloniaal Tijdschrift* 1917 I, 100).

People even began to wonder if the colonial army could still be counted upon not just to defend the colony against a foreign enemy but even against a domestic foe. Even worse, they doubted whether the soldiers and sailors could still be relied on. Discontent in the army ran high among both officers and other ranks. Officers were displeased—according to some, very displeased—because plans to improve their financial position had been shelved for years, and this was at a time when war had driven up the cost of living to unprecedented heights. Officers, it was reported, had begun to study in their spare time in order to prepare themselves for a civilian career (*Nieuwe Soerabaia Courant* cited in *De Indische Gids* 1919, 251; van Heekeren 1919, 146).

Non-commissioned officers also had their fair share of complaints. A newspaper report from Surakarta in July 1916 spoke of discontent on all sides among the 3,000 non-commissioned officers. One of the reasons was that, in an effort to combat concubinage, married NCOs had been given privileges (*De Locomotief*, July 13, 1916). Such privileges included better housing and an extra crossing premium (when the European wife indeed traveled along), whereas concubinage (with Asian women) was forbidden in the barracks.

Discontent among the soldiers—and civilians were well aware of this—ran even deeper. Desertion among European soldiers had taken on, to use the words of a military journal in 1917, "really serious dimensions" (Note department 8, NA, Kol. Openbaar, Vb. 19-4-1918 1; *Algemeen Militair Weekblad* cited in *De Locomotief*, November 24, 1917). One reason presented for this was the presence of recruitment agents of the belligerents in the archipelago. But, even if such persons really existed, there was no actual proof of this. Their presence was not the major cause of desertion. Desertion thus seems to have been caused by other factors, many of them not difficult to pinpoint. For instance, food left much to be desired, the living quarters in the barracks were a cause for complaint, the medical service was inadequate, and the pay had not kept pace with inflation.

Even more important was the inexorable fact that discipline was strict and brutally enforced. Punishments included caning with the rattan stick. This was such an institutionalized practice that a special rank of *korporaal stokkenknecht* (corporal stick servant) had been created. Further punishments included the penalty to carry a heavy metal ball of twenty-six kilograms, and the binding with barbed wire. The most notorious punishment was the *kromsluiten*, the tight shackling of a person in such a way that he was forced to remain in a bent position for hours at a stretch. Only when World War I drew to its close were the more extreme forms of punishment forbidden, partly because of agitation by members of the Indies Social Democratic Association (ISDV) and partly because of what was described as the urge to take action, which possessed the Governor-General, J. P. Count van Limburg Stirum, who ignored protests lodged by the army command.

Feelings of unrest in the colonial army and navy had reached such a level in the closing years of World War I that the Dutch public and government alike had started to doubt the reliability of the armed forces in the colony. Due to developments in Russia, people at this stage were very well aware of the possible consequences of a rebellious mood in the army and navy. As was pointed out in the *Sumatra-Post* (cited in *De Indische Gids* 1918, 895), Russia had shown people who were determined to start a revolution that the best thing to do was to try getting the army on their side. Although the newspaper considered the chance that soldiers in the Netherlands Indies would refuse to obey orders as slight, this was of little comfort. An army in which some of the soldiers were "constantly sulking and bearing grudges and employing passive resistance" was not a reliable force, and this was a reality at a time when the army and navy might have to act "at any moment."

In the closing months of 1917, Dutch-language newspapers published numerous pleas to improve the lot of ordinary European soldiers. Various solutions were contemplated to buoy up the mood in the army. The most impressive initiative was the establishment of a Society for the Improvement of the Social Status of the Soldier, at the end of 1917. The patron was Governor-General van Limburg Stirum. The society observed that soldiers were mere outcasts and that their lives had been pared down to the "greatest possible austerity." The result had been "bitter resentment" which manifested itself in "acts of violation of order and discipline," and in a flight into liquor and into the "dark hideaways of society." On the basis of this conclusion, a plan of action was developed. Concubinage and alcohol abuse should be combated and housing improved. In their spare time, soldiers should be presented with opportunities for "sound work and decent repose" (*De Indische Gids* 1918, 848–52).

The Dutch-language press commented that the founding of the society was a forlorn hope which had come far too late. Agitation by the ISDV and by the Union of Lower Naval Personnel had struck a much more favorable chord among the men. Soldiers and sailors attended meetings at which Sneevliet and his leftist associates spoke, and individual communists received soldiers and sailors in their houses to discuss the political situation (Morrien 1984, 76). This had left its mark and had made the soldiers more defiant. It was not difficult to come to this conclusion as soldiers had started to vent their anger against rich white Europeans, who, in the past, had not hidden their distaste for the lower ranks. In Bandung, a fusilier threw his food into the car of a European. It was remarked in Parliament in The Hague by a sympathizer of the ISDV that this, of course, was a pity for the dress of the lady in the car who received the whole consignment in her lap. In Semarang, a soldier shouted at a lady in a car that she and those of her kind would soon be thrown out, and that he and his friends would then be the ones driving around in motor cars. Indeed, the mood among the soldiers in the local garrison of Semarang had become so relentless that the commander decided to hold secret patrols in the city on a regular basis in May 1918. (*Handelingen* 1918–19, II, 2068; *De Locomotief*, November 4, 1918; *Neratja*, May 15, 1918). In the spring of 1918, when Java experienced "a season of strikes," Dutch-language newspapers—the *Locomotief*, *Preangerbode*, and *Bataviaasch Handelsblad*—also called for extraordinary government measures to prevent strikes by soldiers and laborers.

Although the discontent of the European soldiers attracted the most attention, the native soldiers were not immune to the spirit of the day. Semaoen, a communist Sarekat Islam leader, claimed that his organization had a large following among indigenous soldiers, even though this may have been just wishful thinking (*Sinar Hindia* cited in *De Indische Gids* 1919, 643). Like European soldiers, Indonesian soldiers were often not happy with their fate. Differences in payment, pensions, and treatment fueled their resentment. This was especially true for the Javanese soldiers who were ranked lowest on the ladder and who received less pay than the soldiers from the Minahasa and the Moluccas. Minahasans and Moluccans also had their complaints. First, they were paid less than their European equivalents and conditions in the barracks were poor. Secondly, as moral uplift was part of the nationalist call, protests could also be heard about the demeaning fact that a group of soldiers, each with his wife and children, had to live in one *chambrée* (one common room) in the barracks, without virtually any privacy.

Desertion was also frequent among Indonesian soldiers. The premium for enlistment was one thing but staying put in the army was another. One reason for running away was financial as soldiers deserted to become estate laborers. To prevent Indonesians from deserting immediately after they had cashed in their recruitment premiums, it was suggested that the fingerprints of new recruits should be taken. Accompanied by a photograph of the person in question in his "native dress," these fingerprints should then be sent to the recruitment offices of the estates in the pursuit of these culprits (*Soerabaiasch Handelsblad* cited in *De Indische Gids* 1917, 1248). Some recruits and soldiers resorted to drastic methods in order to be discharged from the army. At the end of 1917, a warning went out against the practice of dripping gonorrhea fluid into the eyes in an attempt to have oneself declared medically unfit for military service (*Nieuwe Soerabaia Courant* cited in *De Locomotief*, December 14, 1917). The fluid inflamed the eyes, with often disastrous consequences. This can be deducted from a warning that was issued after it had come to the attention of army headquarters that many Indonesian soldiers in Malang had been discharged because they had gone blind.

In the navy, a similar atmosphere of unrest prevailed. Discontent, at times finding its expression in acts of sabotage on board Dutch warships, was even greater than in the army. European sailors were also better organized.

They had their Union of Lower Naval Personnel, with Brandsteder as its administrator, leader, and inspirator.

Indonesian sailors also nurtured grudges. Differences in racial and ethnic background created animosities. Some Dutch officers had a low opinion of the seamanship of the Javanese, and crew members from the Minahasa equally looked down on the Javanese. They hence protested when shortly after the outbreak of World War I, in October 1914, the differences in treatment (and food) between Minahasan and Javanese sailors were abolished. There was no justice in the navy, one Javanese sailor wrote in May 1916, as he complained about the treatment he and his fellow Javanese sailors had received (*Oetoesan-Hindia*, February 1, 1916; February 18, 1916; March 20, 1916; May 5, 1916). Indonesian sailors also had their own organization, Sinar Laoetan (Ray of the Sea), which was closely linked to Sarekat Islam. It had been set up by a Javanese able seaman of the second class, M. Argawidjaja, and was greatly distrusted by the colonial authorities. As in the case of European sailors, naval command did its utmost to prevent Indonesian sailors from reading what it considered inflammatory literature on board warships, and this included the confiscation of leftist books. An Indonesian sailor wrote to *Oetoesan Hindia* (May 29, 1916) that he had been punished for having seditious literature, including *De Anker*, the journal of the Union, and the rules of Sarekat Islam, in his possession. He also wrote that he could endure this because he knew that "those who are right dare, and those who wrong fear" (a slogan popular with the nationalist movement at the time).

Discontent in the navy boiled over in the middle of 1916. On May 7, 400 sailors—according to some rumors about half of them armed—staged a march in Surabaya, the city where the naval base was located. They sang socialist songs and carried banners protesting "about the dirt, about the poor food, about the bedbugs." Another banner depicted money bags with the text "war profits" written under them. The police reacted resolutely. Pistol shots were fired and policemen charged with their unsheathed *klewang*. Subsequently, the sailors roamed around the city in small groups. The following day, warships could not sail because 300 sailors had refused to reboard (Morrien 1984, 69). Among the sailors who did embark were seven, one of whom had been hurt the previous day, who had discharged themselves from the military hospital "because they were tormented there by hunger and wanted a square meal for once." The seven sailors, still in their hospital clothes and barefooted, were cheered on by the other sailors (*De Locomotief*, May 10, 1916).

The incident alarmed the commander of the navy in the Netherlands Indies. Vice-Admiral Bron, the commander of the navy in Batavia, concluded that there was a spirit prevalent in the navy which was "absolutely incompatible with the objective of a military naval force." The spirit had resulted in "gross unmilitary conduct, yes in some instances even in the foulest acts of sabotage" (*De Locomotief*, September 21, 1916). There could only be one response: rigid disciplinary measures, which meant that all shore leave was cancelled. Within days, fifty-nine sailors were told that they were no longer needed in the navy in the Netherlands Indies. They were shipped back to Holland where some deserted on arrival and others were dishonorably discharged from the navy.

More Agitation

Towards the end of 1917 and the beginning of 1918, the Union of Lower Naval Personnel began attempts to win over soldiers to its cause. At the end of January 1918, when sailors marched through Surabaya after they had attended a meeting addressed by Sneevliet, one of the slogans they carried read "Soldiers join us!" (*Neratja*, February 2, 1918). For the authorities, this was an alarming development. They had grown deeply distrustful of the Union of Lower Naval Personnel, which was by now even more radical than before. The distrust was shared by sections of the Dutch European community in the Netherlands Indies. According to the minister of the colonies, the union displayed "very anarchical" tendencies (*Handelingen* 1918–19 II, 2153). This view was shared by Bron (*Neratja*, December 4, 1918).

In Java, as in many other places in the world, soldiers' councils and unions were formed. At the instigation of the Union of Lower Naval Personnel, a soldiers' union was founded in the garrison city of Malang in March. In almost every barrack, soldiers flocked to join, and within three months the union claimed a membership of 3,000 (Perthus 1953, 58). Vocal local soldiers' unions began to spread their wings in many garrisons. Parallel to these Dutch unions with their European members, Indonesian soldiers began to organize themselves as well. In Batavia, a union of native soldiers, Djawa-Setia (Faithful to Java), was formed in April 1918. Some 600 of its members staged a protest meeting demanding higher pay, equal status with their European counterparts (they were not even allowed hammocks), and better education for their children (*Oetoesan-Hindia*, April 24, 1918; *De Locomotief*, May 11, 1918).

In the midst of these protests, the authorities tried to create the impression that all remained well. The commander of the colonial army, Lieutenant-General C. H. van Rietschoten, publicly and vehemently denied, as concluded by civilians, that the "general unrest" in the army had any real basis. He admitted that living conditions in the barracks were deplorable and that the food soldiers had to eat left much to be desired, but this was as far as he would go. As grousing was normal among soldiers, he attributed the increase in manifestations of discontent to troublemakers who tried to impress upon the soldiers that they were being treated unfairly. Van Rietschoten claimed that the propaganda of the rabble-rousers had not influenced the "experienced soldier." Only the "many inexperienced ones and the weaklings, and not the least the bad elements" were contaminated (*Handelingen Volksraad* 1918–19, 463, 481–82).[3] The Governor-General also did not give the impression that he was particularly upset. He wired to the minister of the colonies at the end of May that the social democratic movement among soldiers should not be taken too seriously. It was "symptomatic of present world circumstances" (van Limburg Stirum to Pleyte 29-5-1918, NA, Kol. Openbaar Vb. 17-6-1918 62).

Nevertheless, the military authorities implemented measures to quell the unrest. Soldiers were forbidden to attend public meetings addressed by radical leftist orators. Initially, no names were mentioned and it was left to the discretion of the local army commanders to identify the firebrands. In March 1918, the army commander of Surabaya forbade soldiers to attend meetings of the Union of Lower Naval Personnel or any other meeting where Brandsteder, Sneevliet, and others who called themselves "friends and defenders" of the ordinary soldiers, were among the speakers (*Neratja*, March 11, 1918). In early April, a general order went out banning European and Indonesian soldiers from attending ISDV meetings. Sarekat Islam meetings and even celebrations were also occasionally declared off limits to soldiers. When contested events took place, patrols were sent out into the streets to ensure that no soldiers or sailors were present. Meetings with Sneevliet and other ISDV members among the speakers were raided by the police if they were attended by soldiers. Such was the case at a meeting in the City Theatre of Batavia on November 5, 1918, at which Sneevliet was one of the speakers. The premise was cordoned off by loyal soldiers. To elude the military authorities, sailors and soldiers met in restaurants, in the houses of ISDV members, and elsewhere to discuss plans to organize the soldiers and to coordinate action.

It was also made clear that those unions "which set their course in propaganda in a purely anarchistic direction" were unacceptable (*Handelingen Volksraad* 1918, 581). The colonial authorities also left no doubt that they were determined to combat "the making of propaganda setting out revolutionary principles in the barracks" (*Handelingen Volksraad* 1918, 545). In Surabaya, the building housing the Union of Lower Naval Personnel, which in the past had also been frequented by soldiers in search of recreation, was declared strictly out of bounds. In the eyes of the authorities, the building had become a center of agitation and a place where soldiers hatched subversive plans. Soldiers who tried to enter the building by disguising themselves as sailors were sentenced to detention upon being discovered. In Surabaya, three members of the board of a corporals and soldiers union were given almost two weeks of close arrest for eluding the ban at the end of April. A two-week sentence seems to have been the ordinary punishment for such offences, often repeated in the months to come. Action was also taken to prevent the reading of leftist literature. The authorities tried to ban *Het Vrije Woord*, the magazine of the ISDV, *Soldaten-en Matrozenkrant*, the Soldiers and Sailors Paper, of which Brandsteder was the editor, and other socialist periodicals and pamphlets from places frequented by soldiers and sailors.

Even the Protestant Church came to the assistance of the authorities. During a service for soldiers from the Moluccas and the Minahasa held in Surabaya in June 1918, the minister appealed to his audience not to join the soldiers' unions.

Acknowledging that there were grounds for discontent, army command made efforts to eradicate the causes. Recreation rooms were set up in barracks, although initially profiting only the European soldiers. By the end of 1918, no such facility had yet been offered to Indonesian soldiers. European soldiers were even moved *en bloc* to garrisons outside Java. It was hoped that a change of environment would make the troops more sanguine. At the same time, vague promises were made to abolish the differences in treatment between the European soldiers and their Menadonese and Amboinese brothers-in-arms. This had to be done gradually as it would otherwise prove too costly (*Handelingen Volksraad* 1918, 585). Javanese soldiers, by contrast, who earned twelve cents a day less than the Amboinese, were still not considered to deserve the same rise in status as they were still perceived to be poor military material.

A Red Navy and a Red Army

Meanwhile, a confrontation was brewing in the navy. The crew of the warship *Koningin-Regentes* refused to go on duty on June 5, 1918. This strike had begun when their captain had disregarded protests about having to eat brown rice at breakfast. The sailors had wanted white rice in the morning and in the afternoon. The captain tried to convince them that this was impossible in view of the limited stock of white rice on board, and proposed that the crew eat white rice at breakfast only every second day. Convinced that there was enough rice on board, the sailors rejected the compromise. They then got out of hand and officers had to draw their revolvers in order to force the sailors into line. Eighty-five crew members were sentenced to between three and twelve months imprisonment, but because such a large number of prisoners could not be accommodated elsewhere, they had to be interned on the island of Onrust. A scandal erupted when one of the internees, J. Bezema, had to be taken to hospital in Surabaya where he died of dysentery a fortnight after his release. Onrust had a reputation for being an extremely unhealthy place and was considered a graveyard for those who worked there. After Bezema's death, stories about the deplorable conditions on Onrust abounded.

To counter such stories, the civil and military authorities stressed the fact that much had changed on the island over the years. They praised the fresh sea breeze, said that the island was influenza and malaria free, and claimed that a transfer to Onrust had cured other prisoners of pneumonia. Or, as Vice-Admiral Bron stated in a telegram to the minister of the colonies, "Island very healthy, no malaria, no mosquitoes, good water, cool climate, is used as recuperation place for prisoners" (*Handelingen Volksraad* 1918–19, Aanhangsel 145, 175). All this made people wonder why the Europeans living in nearby Batavia had not migrated to the island *en masse* if what they claimed was true.

Bezema's funeral was indicative of the mood of the day. Brandsteder and Baars announced their intention to attend. This reinforced the naval command's fear that "revolutionary elements" would seize upon the occasion to demonstrate. Only seventy sailors were permitted to go to the funeral and they were marched to and from the ceremony. All other sailors in Surabaya were refused leave. No wreaths bearing a red ribbon were allowed to be carried in the funeral procession. Speeches were also prohibited. In defiance of the ban, one of Bezema's comrades, D. Kraan, stepped forward and spoke a few words. Kraan mentioned the word "graveyard" in relation to Onrust and said that Bezema was a victim of the conditions on the island. He added, "This is the way in which the government treats you men!" (*Handelingen Volksraad* 1918–19, II 2152). Kraan was immediately silenced by the officer on parade despite the protests by the other sailors. On the evening of Bezema's funeral, 400 of them attended a meeting in Surabaya. They deplored the fact that Kraan had not been allowed to continue with his speech and declared the internment of sailors on Onrust after they had served their sentence (awaiting a ship on which they were to be sent off to Holland) to be "in violation of the most fundamental feelings of humanity" (*Handelingen Volksraad* 1918–19, 495–96).

Disgruntlement in the army also seemed to come to a head in the middle of 1918. The occasion which prompted this was a new Indië Weerbaar drive. All over the Netherlands Indies, local committees organized activities within the framework of an Indië Weerbaar week held in September. Antagonists also did their best to make the week a memorable one. In Batavia, where the week lasted eleven days, posters formulating the demands of the soldiers—better food, a better legal position, no corporal punishment, and leave in Europe—were pasted up everywhere in the city. Pamphlets were distributed and demonstrations planned. Much went wrong in Batavia during the Indië Weerbaar week. Cavalrymen, machine gunners, and other soldiers had trained for two days for a military tattoo to be held on September 2. *De Locomotief* (cited in *De Indische Gids* 1918, 93) rapturously described the parade that passed the palace of the governor-general as "marvelous." Nevertheless, it was not "the buglers, the drummers, the staff music, the battalion music, the flute players" who made an impression on and excited colonial society. Demonstrating soldiers singing the "Internationale" who preceded the tattoo stole the march. The cavalry had to disperse them, and fearing further protests, the military authorities stepped in to take control of the situation. Instead of enjoying leave or a Sunday roster during the festivities, soldiers and NCOs were confined to barracks. Dutch officers kept watch to prevent mischief and armed patrols were out on the streets.

In an atmosphere of unrest and agitation, news about the socialist revolutions in Europe sent shockwaves throughout the Dutch community in the Netherlands Indies. Rumors about the proclamation of a socialist republic Holland, and even about a revolution in the Netherlands Indies, did the rounds. Socialists were to march to the palace of the governor-general to demand a transfer of power (McVey 1965, 31).

Counter Forces Prevail

The exciting political situation in the Netherlands Indies during World War I, partly colored by the revolutionary threat in western Europe and Asia, was exciting in more ways than one. After the war, however, it gradually gave way to the restoration of the old colonial relationships. No revolution took place in Holland or the Netherlands Indies. This provided the colonial authorities with the courage to set things right and act against those who had incited soldiers and sailors, and those who were also held responsible for the turn to the left taken by the nationalist movement. Sneevliet and Brandsteder were banned from the colony, while Baars left of his own free will. Socialist teachers were transferred to outposts. The old order really set in when sea and telegraph links between the motherland and colony were restored, allowing the motherland to take firm control of the colony once again and to nullify any independence of action the Netherlands Indies had gained in the political and economic sphere as a result of the war. Most, if not all, promises made to nationalist leaders during World War I were forgotten. A native militia was never instituted. The reason was not that war had ended or that a foreign invasion was no longer thought likely. The deciding argument was that it was too dangerous to give the Indonesian population access to arms. Discarding the idea that cooperation with broad sections of the Indonesian population was needed to foil an invasion meant that one of the main reasons to at least consider demands for political reforms and full emancipation had thereby also disappeared.

Indonesian nationalists remained active in the decades to come but their room to maneuver was limited. The policy of repression, which set in, produced a false sense of security in Dutch colonial society. Many Dutch people in the colony were thus not aware of the intensity of the population's desire for independence and also how explosive the domestic situation was. They seemed untouched by the fears that had gripped Dutch society in the Netherlands Indies in the 1910s. It was a rude awakening for them when Indonesian Independence was proclaimed on August 17, 1945 and was given massive support all over the colony. This was closely related to the events of 1942 when the Dutch fear of Japanese aggression and even conquest had become a reality. Japanese success was arguably facilitated by the failure to build up a better, more numerous, and more motivated indigenous armed force. True enough, whilst the Netherlands indeed was a country too small and too weak militarily to repel an invasion of its colony, fears of the internal, in particular Javanese, enemy had considerably facilitated the conqueror's and then the nationalists' endeavors.

Notes

1. *De Locomotief* was a progressive daily with some sympathy for the calls for the social, political, and economic emancipation of the Indonesian population. It was printed in Semarang.

2. Initially turning the argument around, the progressive colonial newspaper *De Locomotief* (September 15, 1914) had argued that conscription should be restricted to the intellectuals and the well-to-do in the cities. Implicit in their aspiration to full civil rights was that they therefore assented to fully shoulder the resulting civic duties.

3. The Volksraad was the colonial parliament in Batavia.

References

Aken, W. A. van. 1913. *'s-Lands welvaart in gevaar! Een ernstig woord tot het Nederlandsche Volk door De Nederlandsche Vereeniging "Onze Vloot"* [Our Country's Prosperity in Danger: A Serious Message to the Dutch People by the Dutch Association "Our Fleet"]. n.p.: Onze Vloot.

Anon. 1914. *Neerland's ondergang kan en moet voorkomen worden* [The Ruin of the Netherlands Can and Must be Prevented]. n.p.: Onze Vloot.

Handelingen. Verslag der handelingen van de Staten Generaal [Proceedings of the States General]. Gedurende de zitting van [. . .]. 's-Gravenhage: Algemeene Landsdrukkerij.

Handelingen van den Volksraad Vol. 1 – [. . .]. [Proceedings of the People's Council]. 1918–19 – [. . .]. Batavia: Volksraad van Nederlandsch-Indië.

Heekeren, E. A. A. van. 1919. "Nederlandsch Oost-Indië in 1918" [The Netherlands East Indies in 1918]. *De Indische Gids* 41(1): 137–47.

Koloniaal Verslag. Bijlage by Handelingen der Staten Generaal 1850– [. . .]. [Annual Colonial Report]. 's-Gravenhage: Landsdrukkerij.

McVey, Ruth T. 1965. *The Rise of Indonesian Communism*. Ithaca, NY: Cornell University Press.

Morrien, J. 1984. *"Aroen": Jan Stam, rebel in Indonesië en Nederland* ["Aroen": Jan Stam, Rebel in Indonesia and the Netherlands]. Amsterdam: Pegasus.

Perthus, M., ed. 1953. *Voor vrijheid en socialisme: gedenkboek van het Sneevliet Herdenkingscomité* [For Freedom and Socialism: Commemorative Book of the Sneevliet Memorial Committee]. Rotterdam: Gramo.

Rapport van de staatscommissie voor de verdediging van Nederlandsch-Indië [Report of the State Commission for the Defence of the Netherlands Indies]. 1913. 's-Gravenhage: Nijhoff. [Hereafter *Rapport*]

Sandberg, C. G. S. 1914. *Indië verloren, rampspoed geboren* [The Indies Lost, a Catastrophe Born]. 's-Gravenhage: D. A. Daamen.

Tichelman, F. 1985. *Socialisme in Indonesië: de Indische Sociaal-Democratische Vereeniging* [Socialism in Indonesia: The Indies Social Democratic Association]. Vol. 1, 1897–1917. Dordrecht, Cinnaminson: Foris Publications.

Weijden, J. van der. 1916. *Weerplicht voor inlanders en samenstelling van de weermacht in Nederlandsch-Indië* [Compulsory Military Service for Natives and the Composition of the Armed Forces in the Netherlands Indies]. Amsterdam: Van Holkema & Warendorf.

Zwitzer, H. L., and C. A. Heshusius. 1977. *Het Koninklijk Nederlandsch-Indisch Leger, 1830–1950.* [The Royal Netherlands-Indies Army, 1830–1950]. 's-Gravenhage: Staatsuitgeverij.

Newspapers and Periodicals Consulted

De Expres

De Indische Gids

De Locomotief

Koloniaal Tijdschrift

Neratja

Oetoesan-Hindia

Schlesische Zeitung

CHAPTER 4

Vietnamese Soldier-Workers during the Two World Wars under French Social Controls

Marie-Eve Blanc

Focusing on the social and political processes common to colonial states and colonized people, my chapter will demonstrate how imperial relationships and encounters can facilitate mutual learning opportunities, including the adaptation of democracy and the learning of new forms of association, but also how not only imperial power structures but also class differences among the colonized can constitute serious hurdles in the learning of democracy. Specifically, we will try to see how the experiences of the Vietnamese soldier-workers, who were hired or conscripted to boost the French war economy and made to work largely along military lines, impacted the political education of two generations of Vietnamese. Even if Indochina was considered a reservoir of manpower, the great majority of Indochinese battalions comprised service troops (Gunn 2014). Even though historians have worked a lot on the soldiers' role as instrument of war, less is known about their role as workers and their relationship with their "employer," the state (Coates and Morrison 1993). During World War I, or the Great War, roughly 48,000 of these soldier-workers came to their French *mère-patrie* (motherland) and approximately 20,000 at the beginning of World War II.

The main part of this chapter is divided into four sections, the first of which will compare the modern French legal construct of an association with the traditional Vietnamese one. The next section will describe the situation and the French interest in this "Indochinese labor force" (*main d'œuvre indochinoise*, MOI) during and immediately after World Wars I and II. I will then expose how the French authorities established institutions that systematically aimed to control the Vietnamese associative movement, largely to ensure a compliant labor force but also to prevent anti-colonial subversion. Finally, we will show how social control and migration were important factors in the emergence of a movement that, in particular during the German occupation of southern France during World War II, combined anti-colonialism with an incomplete learning of democracy.

Comparing the 1901 French Law Regulating Associations with Traditional Vietnamese Associations

When I began my historical-sociological research on Vietnamese associations in France in the early 1990s, my main question was comparative. Why did Vietnamese expatriates not use and adapt their traditional social organization the same way that Chinese people in the diaspora did, notably by reconstructing their social space abroad, keeping their ethnicity and power intact? Although many "Chinatowns" exist in France, "Little Saigons" are unheard of. While it is true that there are some ethnic Vietnamese enclaves in France's large cities, they pale in comparison with the Vietnamese communities in certain states and counties in the United States, such as in Orange County near Los Angeles, California. We are thus justified in wondering about the colonial contact organized by the French and its impact on Vietnamese culture not only in French Indochina but also in France, including how it impacted Vietnamese encounters with French models of democracy and association.

Moreover, it also seemed to me that the Vietnamese associative practices I encountered during my research on France's Vietnamese associations were very close to the French associative tradition related to France's 1901 law that limited associative practices to those that do not endanger the sovereignty and secularism of the French state. In their traditional social organization, Vietnamese villagers would create associations and organizations to accomplish a variety of collective endeavors, such as village festivals, community self-help following natural disasters, or the rebuilding of a village temple. During the colonial period, they tried to continue this practice but faced many obstacles due to a new foreign law being enforced on their land, which was neither that of a democratic France nor a true adaptation of the customary principles of Vietnamese villages. Hence, while the 1901 law was not enacted in Indochina until 1933, it was very far from the spirit of freedom of association, as it was intended to prevent any possibility of anti-colonial activism or the development of secret societies trying to topple the foreign power.

Modern French associations are very different from the Vietnamese *hội*, a social institution that literally means a "celebration with a banquet." It is part of the lifestyle of the villagers, who, when celebrating the village and reproducing its ancient rituals, are at the same time practicing the community and family ritual of *ăn nói*. The latter, which literally means "eating and chatting," is related to the expression *ăn tết* (literally "eating the celebration"), which means "celebrating the new year." Thus, it is easy to understand how a gathering of Vietnamese people is incomplete without the added pleasure of food, tea, or the traditional betel quid.[1] The very numerous village associations were thus part of the process of managing village life and public and communal affairs and quite distinct from the nature and history of modern French associations.

While religious, ritual, and festive aspects, as well as a strong connection with the village (the native land) characterize Vietnamese associations, modern-day French associations are defined by their secularism. In contrast, under the *ancien régime* in pre-revolutionary France, their legitimacy derived from their religious, parochial, and local context. This already changed at the end of the *ancien régime* with freemasonry and the development of a social life among both the bourgeois and the working classes (Agulhon 1968).

In France, particularly in the late nineteenth and early twentieth centuries, associations had become tools for developing secularism, social work, and education for the middle or working classes. The 1901 law restricted the goals associations could have and aimed to prevent any type of political or even religious activism that could have endangered the sovereignty of the state or the republic. Associations thus were tools for developing the republican and democratic concepts of the state. The common interest developed in France was more that of the state, even though the interest of the people came first.

Of course, before becoming tools for secularism, associations, fraternities, and mutual societies in France had been places for sociability and local and regional identity, which they still are. But in Vietnam, the associative tool did not undergo the same change. Associations were independent tools for managing village matters, very far from those of the centralized Confucian state. And it seems that during the colonial era, the Government General of French Indochina,[2] which had replaced the Confucian state, continued to consider associations of the Vietnamese, both village and indigenous associations, as "foreign" and dangerous for the colonial authority, without really wanting to make them tools for democracy.

How did this play out in metropolitan France where Vietnamese often encountered a more liberal jurisdiction than back home? The first significant wave of migrants from Vietnam to France started during World War I when the Ministry of War decided to bring Indochinese people to France to have them work in munitions factories and to make up for France's war-depleted labor force more generally.[3] The example of the Vietnamese soldier-workers in France shows us how associating was first perceived as a force of opposition even though an association of fellow countrymen first and foremost means nothing more than thinking about one's homeland, family duties, traditional rituals, and ancestor worship.

French Wartime Interest in Indochinese Soldier-Workers

The recruitment of Vietnamese soldier-workers started in April 1915, with many of the men staying in France until 1920, long after the armistice of November 11, 1918. This aimed at making up for a substantial decrease in the French male workforce, which was caused by wartime mobilization and significant French losses on the battlefields. The recruitment was made on a voluntary basis and brought together men of different social origins, primarily peasants, but also members of the families of high-ranking court officials and civil servants in the colonial and imperial bureaucracies (Eckert 2000; Hill 2006). The volunteers received wages and pensions if they became disabled or died (Hill 2006, 2015; Vu-Hill 2011), with an additional incentive, at least for the soldiers, a legislative proposal in 1915 that promised to offer French citizenship (Fogarty 2008). A little more than twenty years after the end of the Great War, a second recruitment wave, patterned after the first but involving far fewer men, was implemented in late 1939 and early 1940 but ground to a halt following France's defeat against Germany. The great majority of the workers remained stranded in France until well after the war, often in very poor and regimented living conditions and frequently without access to regular work (Cavenne n.d.; Daum 2009; Liêm-Khê Luguern 2010; Rettig 2012; Rives and Deroo 1999).

First, it is essential to look more closely at the statistics concerning the Indochinese migrants during the Great War, the vast majority of whom came from the three Vietnamese jurisdictions of French Indochina: the colony of Cochinchina in the south and the protectorates of Annam in the center and Tonkin in the north.[4] Between 88,000 and 93,000 men left Indochina to be recruited as "soldier-workers" and as soldiers in France from 1915 to 1920 (Blanc 2003, 54, 392).[5] Rives and Deroo (1999) estimate there to have been 43,430 soldiers[6] and 49,890 non-specialized workers who set sail to serve in France. In 1918, 30 percent of France's wartime colonial labor force was Indochinese. The city of Marseille, as a large port city and bridgehead for trade with the rest of the colonial empire, emerged as one of the main transit and management centers for the Indochinese soldier-workers and troops.

It is nearly impossible to say how many soldier-workers were killed during this period. However, in many cemeteries in Marseille and the south of France a few hundred graves and monuments honoring the memory of the Vietnamese soldiers exist. Although Bernard Le Calloc'h (1983) estimates that 8,000 Vietnamese died in France during the Great War, including 2,700 workers, Xu Guoqi (2017) indicates that 1,548 workers had died by the end of the war in France. At the end of 1919, when most of the soldiers had already been repatriated, the colonial labor force was gradually decreasing but a large and sustained number of Vietnamese workers remained, representing 50 percent of this entire workforce. How did such a situation come about?

Fig.1. The Indochinese Labor Force in 1919

Sources: Archives Nationales (AN); Blanc 2003, 56; Centre des Archives d'Outre-Mer (CAOM), Affaires politiques 1462.

A report written in 1919 by Pierre Guesde of the General Control of Indochinese Workers and Infantrymen allows us to understand the interest in this type of labor force on the part of the French, who defended it for its productivity, provided of course that the men were "intelligently and paternalistically" managed. It was clear that the Indochinese workers represented an advantage for the war and immediate postwar industry and a true economic benefit. They were particularly appreciated for their docility, obedience, agility, and precision work, as confirmed by Guesde:

> I recently had the occasion to observe, at the munitions storage station in Miramas [about 60 kilometres northwest of Marseille], our Annamese unloading wagons and lugging on their backs, in the European fashion, crates of cartridges weighing between 115 and 120 kilos, which they would carry 40 meters and stack in piles 5 to 6 meters high. The mere fact that they managed to do such a task steadily for several hours without seeming to struggle more than the Europeans, chatting and joking among themselves, proves the wonderful potential of this labour force when it is intelligently and

> paternalistically managed, as is the case with the group at Miramas. (Guesde 1919)

Not surprisingly, the War Ministry continued to act "paternalistically" at the end of the war to prevent revolts and riots within the workers' camps. The repatriation of the Vietnamese soldier-workers to Indochina took time and lasted until August 1920. The Vietnamese would have wanted to return to their native land earlier, but after the war the French government lacked sufficient logistical resources to ensure the return of these soldier-workers to Indochina. For this reason, in January 1919, the War Ministry decided to organize a Lunar New Year celebration in the workers' camps in keeping with their tradition, with better meals and time for relaxing. We should reiterate that working and living conditions were harsh and sometimes dangerous.

Most of the Indochinese soldier-workers were based mainly in the south of France (Haute Garonne, Bouches-du-Rhône, Gironde, Tarn, Vaucluse, etc.). Many produced weapons, gunpowder, explosives, and chemicals in state-run factories, such as the Saint-Chamas and Salins de Giraud gunpowder works. Others worked in the ports and in the transportation sector, in agriculture as farm laborers, as well as for the railroads and health services.

Finally, in 1920, the situation was becoming increasingly explosive due to the concentration and inactivity of the Vietnamese soldier-workers stationed in the Marseille colonial depot before returning to their homeland. In this postwar environment, as we will see later, the Indochinese began to establish small groups and associations to organize the entire labor force and make certain demands on the authorities on whom they depended.

When war in Europe arrived, the French drew on their experience during World War II. In late 1939 and early 1940, Vietnamese soldier-workers arrived in Marseille and the French authorities placed them together in temporary camps where conditions were very rudimentary and sometimes unhealthy. The labor allocation system was basically the same as during the World War I. Maurice Rives (1994) describes in detail that roughly one-third of the 19,276 workers who came to France during the 1939–40 juncture had volunteered while the rest had been coerced. In contrast, *Le Monde Colonial*

Illustré (1939) claimed that a very large number of Indochinese had answered the call to French patriotism made by the Ministry of Colonies. According to Pham Cong Anh (1974), in 1940, 18,634 specialized workers were assigned to the Indochinese labor force (Ministry of the Interior).

After the armistice and the creation of the Germany-aligned Vichy regime, and the effective division of France into a northern zone occupied by the Germans and a southern "free" zone initially remaining free of German troops, the great majority of the soldier-workers remained in France because Britain controlled the sealanes to French Indochina. In July 1941, 15,000 Indochinese workers were stranded in France, divided into sixty divisions or camps (Cavenne n.d.; Le Huu Khoa 1990; Simon 1986). Each division consisted of people native to a single province, which made it much easier for the men to faithfully reproduce the social organization of their native village.

At first, the Vietnamese were directed to rural areas in the "zone libre" (free zone) that remained free of German occupying troops. Then, in late 1942 and early 1943, after German and Italian forces had occupied the zone libre, some of the Vietnamese began to work in factories. At the end of 1943, nearly 10 percent of the Vietnamese workers, equivalent to almost 1,300 men, were forced to work for the German authorities for the Todt Organization, causing the geographic dispersion of the men in January 1944. Ten Vietnamese worker camps had to move to the Mediterranean Coast (to Sète, Port-de-Bouc, Marseille, La Ciotat, Toulon, Fréjus, Théoule-sur-Mer, and Antibes) and also to the Atlantic Coast, along the "Atlantic Wall."

During this historic juncture, some of the Vietnamese workers refused to submit to the orders of the occupying forces and some even decided to establish contact with the French resistance network, which could either be close to the communist, socialist, anarchist, royalist, or catholic groups. In contrast, a few Vietnamese even agreed to work in Nazi Germany, believing that "the enemies of my enemies are my friends," while some France-based Vietnamese students accepted German scholarships to further their studies in Germany. At the same time, under German occupation, the time was ripe to act and think about the birth of an independent Vietnamese homeland by putting an end to colonial domination by a defeated French *mère-patrie*.

Even more so than after World War I, when repatriation of the workers was not complete until 1920, neither the liberation of France in August 1944 nor the reopening of shipping lanes to French vessels put an end to the stay of soldier-workers in MOI camps in France. Instead, because the French authorities prioritized the transportation of French, Foreign Legion, and African colonial troops to reassert French imperial control over French Indochina (Témime and Deguigné, 2001), the return was a long drawn-out process that often ground to a halt.

The Great War and the Institutionalization of Socio-Political Control over Indochinese Soldier-Workers

How did the French administration assert a metropolitan-imperial order over the Indochinese troops and the soldier-workers? During World War I, the French authorities had already seen a need to organize social and moral control over the Indochinese troops. The management of the Indochinese in France became thoroughly institutionalized, affecting all aspects of these displaced people's metropolitan stay, from education to health to their social lives. In line with the French *mission civilisatrice*, which in the colonies did not extend to more than a very small proportion of the population, the French administration and patronage associations in wartime France established an educational system. This included the Alliance Française, which distributed books to teach French, mathematics, and hygiene in all camps, but the foundations of this educational system were laid in Paris in March 1916 through the Committee to Assist Indochinese Workers (Comité d'Assistance aux Travailleurs Indochinois, or CATI). The CATI, created by administrative representatives from the banking, agriculture, and business sectors and from the Government General of Indochina, henceforth organized "free" or convalescence time for Vietnamese soldier-workers by offering classes and "healthy" distractions.

Controlling the health and productivity of the soldier-workers was the key focus and objective of this management undertaking. The War Ministry, the Government General of Indochina, the CATI, and the Association of

French Ladies (Association des Dames Françaises) founded hospitals for the Indochinese in Marseille and other cities in the south of France, such as Fréjus and Bordeaux. Starting in 1916, these hospitals, for Vietnamese patients only, were staffed by Vietnamese doctors trained at the Ecole de Médecine Indigène (indigenous medical school) in Hanoi. Nguyễn Văn Hiên, the *bố chánh*[7] or official representative of the royal court of Annam, visited France from 1916 to 1918 and reported that four Vietnamese doctors were working at the Saint-Louis Hospital in Marseille. A pagoda, headed by a monk from Tonkin, was built nearby.

Medical care aside, another type of control was the inspection of mail being sent to Indochina, an initiative begun in Marseille in November 1916 by the Ministry of Colonies. The main idea was to gauge the state of mind and mood of the Indochinese soldier-workers living in France and to prevent negative news and anti-colonial ideas from reaching French Indochina. In March 1918, 40,000 letters out of a total of 300,000 were inspected, representing approximately 13 percent of outgoing mail. After that, the French administration moved from simply taking the pulse of the Indochinese to recording and archiving the words and actions of any individual considered suspicious. Thus, the institutional foundations for the systematic police control of the Vietnamese migrants on French soil were being laid, which would further expand in the 1920s and 1930s and remain until the period of decolonization.

This institutionalization of moral and social control was made possible due to the cooperation of the War Ministry and the Ministry of Colonies. Together, they created the Department for the Organization and Surveillance of Colonial Workers in France in December 1915, in order to avoid any disruptions to France's manpower-depleted war economy. In addition, the French administration was aware of the potential for the outbreak of turmoil due to the displacement of large numbers of colonials. They trained specialized staff, members of the colonial administration, in order to control and keep an eye on the Indochinese soldier-workers. Two types of workers and managers were trained: inspectors and interpreters.

The inspectors were charged with enforcing a five-part regulation: implementing the regulation in all the labor camps, overseeing living conditions and discipline, improving moral and material circumstances, ensuring the protection of the troops, and providing information to the War Ministry when requested. According to an excerpt from instructions for the Department for the Control of Colonial Workers in France, dated March 20, 1916:

Inspectors are responsible for:

1. Ensuring that the regulations and instructions concerning colonial workers issued by the Central Department are observed and implemented;
2. Overseeing the conditions of the facilities, housing, food, clothing, and discipline experienced by the indigenous soldier-workers, both in detachments and in military or private establishments;
3. Seeking, with the agreement of the local military authorities, employers and private organizations, measures likely to improve the material and moral circumstances of the indigenous soldier-workers;
4. Carrying out their duties as moral guardians, which devolve to the protecting country, by guiding and advising the indigenous soldier-workers in their behavior and relationships;
5. Undertaking any investigation or mission prescribed by the War Ministry in the interest of the service.

The French inspectors were in charge of setting up [social] clubs for the Indochinese workers with an eye to enhancing their stay and overseeing them so that they would not fall "under the influence of crooks, hoodlums or other union activists." These clubs would be places where the workers could get together to have a cup of coffee, play cards, or write letters home. Among the first to open was the Indochinese Workers' Circle in Marseille's downtown area near la Canebière, the old quarter's high street stretching to the Old Port. The motivation for this paternalistic initiative was to protect the Indochinese workers by keeping them from "all the temptations of city life." Upon visiting the Bordeaux and Toulouse regions, Inspector du Vaure decided to build and establish these clubs near the workers' places of work and far from the cities in order to shield the Indochinese from negative city influences, notably prostitution and venereal disease. Thus, in 1916 clubs were built in Toulouse, Tarbes, Bergerac, and Sorgues near, or even inside, the gunpowder factories to which the workers had been assigned. The Indochinese soldier-workers were thought of as children, fragile and naïve, incapable of leading their own lives. The paternalism of the French with respect to the Indochinese became particularly difficult to tolerate. This relationship between the French and Vietnamese was so fraught that it triggered complaints, revolts, and even suicides in the camps.

Besides a very small number of French inspectors at the very top of this system of control, Vietnamese interpreters played an important role by interpreting and acting as intermediaries between the French administration and the workers. They transmitted the complaints of the workers and explained the decisions of the administration to their fellow countrymen. A few schools were opened for the more educated of the new recruits, usually sons of the intelligentsia or mandarins. After the armistice, the more educated among them wanted to remain in France to continue their studies. The interpreters also contributed significantly to the associative movement that was emerging at the end of World War I. The associations created during the war or soon after already constituted an embryonic network for a newly established Vietnamese community. The main goal of these first associations was to organize mutual assistance among the migrants and their families. Only a few had political goals.

As for the Department for the Organization and Surveillance of Colonial Workers in France, even though it was a system of control that was set up for all the colonial troops (from Africa, Madagascar, and Indochina), it was mainly centered on the Vietnamese soldier-workers because they were more numerous, but also because a relatively homogeneous ethno-nationalism had already emerged. Not surprisingly, the department's general inspector, Jules Bosc, was an Indochina hand who had recently worked in the colonial administration in Indochina. In the beginning, the socio-political control was intended for the soldier-workers but it was extended to the other migrants from Indochina, such as students, servants, and others. The following diagram provides a detailed view of the institutional system of social control that the Vietnamese lived under (Blanc 2003, 69).

Fig. 2. System of Socio-Political Control over the Vietnamese in France, 1915–1930

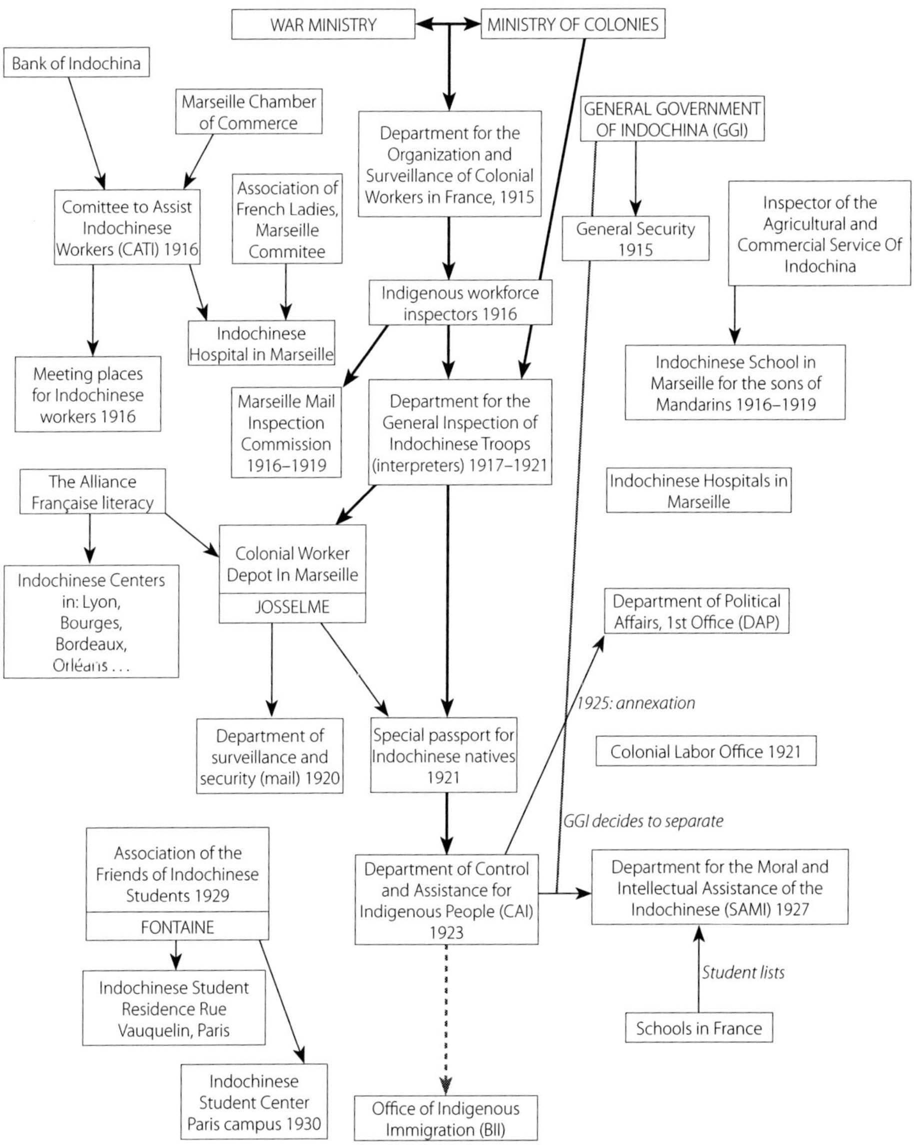

The Anti-colonial Movement, the Learning of Democracy and Its Limits

This system of socio-political control over the Vietnamese evolved over time, in particular from the late 1920s, as one can see in the diagram below on Vietnamese associations and political relationships, and according to the needs of the French authorities who strove to stay on top of developments among the Vietnamese community in France and in French Indochina.

Fig. 3. The Vietnamese Associative Movement and Its Political Relationships, 1930–1945

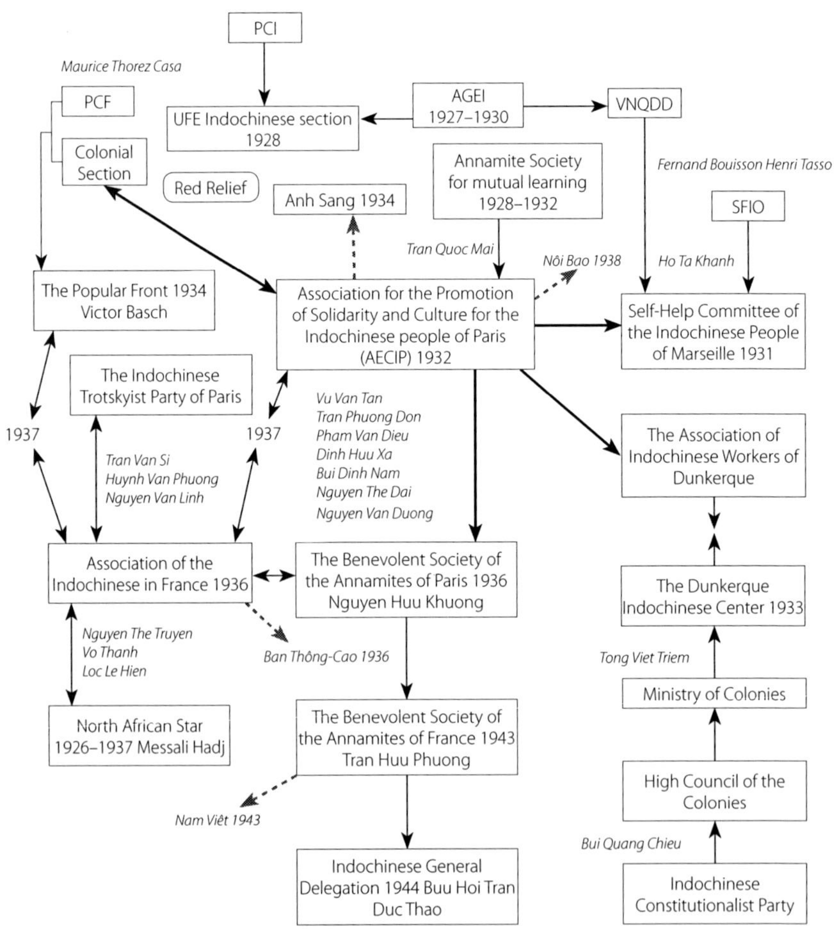

This had definite consequences on the organization of the Vietnamese associative movement. The harsher the system of control, the less visible was the Vietnamese anti-colonial movement. Security was so efficient in Indochina that the only nationalist movements able to survive were those established outside Indochina (Goscha 1995). But the Vietnamese groups also knew how to adapt to the circumstances. This flexibility and creativity was one of the hallmarks of a political movement against a state or an empire and was familiar to the North Vietnamese who had become accustomed to using it in the past in the form of secret societies and triads, such as those used by the Chinese (Chesneaux, Davis, and Nguyen 1970). Sometimes the French authorities appeared to be very provocative and suspicious when confronted with the invisibility of the meetings and other political activities of the Vietnamese. Acting out of paranoia, they would literally push some young Vietnamese men into revolutionary action by wrongly charging them with crimes of anti-colonial activism and subversion, which they had not yet committed. The youngest men were unable to protect themselves and often chose to join the anti-colonial movement of their older fellow countrymen.

A more modern Vietnamese anti-colonial movement, one that adopted modern political ideas and forms of organization, developed throughout the 1920s and 1930s, with the trends in France and in French Indochina largely mirroring each other. In the beginning, the associations focused on mutual assistance activities but political objectives were gradually added. In a nutshell, at the end of the 1930s there were roughly two main factions: one, founded in 1930, was close to the Indochinese Communist Party, while the other had a nationalist orientation. The communist group claimed to fight for democracy and against any form of "fascism." In France, from 1943 to 1944, Vietnamese close to the communists participated in the Maquis guerrilla movement after the German occupation of the "zone libre." The nationalist group was more broadly anti-colonial and felt closer to France's "enemies." Most of the students in the nationalist camp accepted scholarships from Goebbels. Alongside these factions had appeared a third small group in 1937, the Trotskyists, who gradually won over a portion of the soldier-workers who saw that the communists had set aside the anti-colonial objective in favor of the fight against fascism (Hémery 1975, 401). Also worth mentioning is the largely Cochinchina-based constitutionalist party, which attracted Francophiles—frequently Cochinchinese who had the French nationality—and wanted to develop the idea of greater participation by the Indochinese in colonial institutions and find an institutional and constitutional solution.

After 1920, the Vietnamese community in France consisted mainly of students and the social composition of this community gave specific goals to its associations. This is arguably the main reason why the communists and nationalists in the metropole did not always have the problems of the soldier-workers in mind after the 1940 armistice. Because of the predominance of intellectuals within the community, the objectives of political activism focused more on political aspects rather than practical ones. They sometimes forgot to fight to improve the conditions faced by the Indochinese labor force. The context of the war and the defeat of the French after the armistice gave wings and confidence to the Vietnamese intellectuals to make headway on the political front.

This social divide also ran through the soldier-workers. Many of the interpreters of the MOI had come to France with the idea that they could continue their studies or that they would have better job and life prospects. They had something to look forward to. In contrast, the other soldier-workers, at least during World War II, had been recruited in a more or less coercive fashion. They lacked the skills and the confidence to organize in the same way and they wanted to return home. More passive than the intellectuals, and experiencing more precarious living conditions and more restrictive regulations in the camps, they suffered as migrants even though they would have made just as good militants as the intellectuals and had additional reasons to fight.

However, within the MOI, information and propaganda circulated rather easily because of changes in the very structure of the soldier-workers group as well as in the management of the MOI. The soldier-workers organized associations and published their own newspapers to broadcast information and other news about their native land and about revolutionary Vietnamese organizations. Among such publications was the magazine *Cong Binh Tap*

Chi, distributed in 1941 (Rives 1994) and the newspaper *Viêt Nam Công Nông Doàn*, which played an important role in the political activism of the Vietnamese workers. This newspaper was printed by Louis Jean in Gap (in the Hautes Alpes region), but it was written in the Mazargues MOI camp in Marseille (1946). There was also a Trotskyist newspaper, the *Vo San*, which was still in existence in 1948.

The MOI, which at the time was under the jurisdiction of the Ministry of Labor, was an independent department but in wartime France its administrators were not always able to give the Vietnamese workers enough work or income to live on. Life in the MOI camps also lent itself to considerable abuse, including torture and incarceration, and cases of desertion or even suicide were not unheard of. After the liberation of France in August 1944, the inspectors of the Ministry of Colonies wrote harsh reports, which resulted in a major reform among the management and staff of the MOI.

A big change occurred in terms of salaries, the right to unionize in accordance with the Brazzaville Conference (February 1944), the right to elect delegates to have a share in the administration of the camps with the French, training, and the authorization to work for the private sector, thus avoiding unemployment. Most of the Vietnamese workers chose to become members of the leftist General Confederation of Workers (Confédération générale du travail, CGT).

A few months after the liberation of France, the General Convention of the Indochinese Peoples of France was held from 15 to 17 December 1944 in the city of Avignon, in relative proximity to the more "agitated" camps of the Vaucluse region's MOI. It established a General Delegation, which called for the independence of Indochina, which would come in conflict with de Gaulle's plans to keep Indochina in the French Union. After the events of August Revolution and the Independence declaration on September 2, 1945, the General Delegation was dissolved by the French government on October 18, 1945, as an illegal organization, subject to the 1936 law against militias and political associations. The suppression of the anti-colonial movement saw an increase in the number and rate of repatriation of Vietnamese militants and workers. Although the Ho-Sainteny agreement of March 6, 1946 made

Vietnam a free state within the French Union, deep divisions remained between the different factions, all led by intellectuals, of the Vietnamese community (communist, nationalist, Trotskyist, Catholic, royalist, etc.) in France.

The French authorities did not know how to respond to this new period of unrest. With the help of General Le Bris they tried to reach a consensus in November 1946, but to no avail. General Le Bris demanded that the French Communist Party stop supporting the Vietnamese propaganda. He also, demanded that the CGT (Labour Union) calm down the soldier-workers (Rives 1994). Consequently, many workers were accused by their fellow countrymen of "collaborating with the French colonialists." The year 1947 was marked by violent confrontations between communists, Trotskyists, and members of the administration in the Grand Arénas Camp in the southern outskirts of Marseille, about control of the camp. The violence ended with the resumption of the repatriation of soldier-workers to Indochina (Témime and Deguigné 2001). This was the end of the last utopian Franco-Vietnamese relationship. Communism and the Việt Minh were the only groups able to attract consensus within the Vietnamese community in France. The nationalist group disappeared because of a lack of organization and clear credo. However, it was not until July 1950 that the last ship returning the remaining Vietnamese soldier-workers departed for Indochina, more than ten years after they had arrived in France.

Conclusion

What did the Vietnamese soldier-workers learn as a result of their wartime experiences in France during World War I and World War II, including the postwar months or even years when many of them remained stranded in France? For those who were in touch with the French working class, such as in ammunition factories during World War I, there was an opportunity to become familiar with a new type of associative organization, the union, which was not allowed in the colonies. During World War II, following the German occupation of southern France, some of them also learned how to form a French-Vietnamese common front, for instance, with their fellow communist resistant fighters in the Maquis.

Although these experiences were far from representative, did the Indochinese soldier-workers residing in the motherland of the French Revolution learn anything about democracy? The control and censorship system that the French authorities created and institutionalized during World War I suggest that the French Republic, let alone the Vichy regime during World War II, had its imperial interests at heart rather than any desire to extend a favorable version of democracy to the Indochinese it had brought in to defend the "motherland." Likewise, in the area of training the soldier-workers in modernity and transferable job skills, the vocational training system was not adapted to develop the workforce within the MOI camps.

These restrictive issues aside, Vietnamese associations did emerge, but were they genuinely democratic, and whose interests did they reflect? The solidarity between fellow countrymen was shortlived from 1944 to 1946, not least because of a considerable social divide between those who were educated and those who were not. For many, democracy was more a means to achieve the goal of independence rather than an end in itself. The Vietnamese used democratic slogans and structures with an eye to freedom. In terms of traditional values and class interests, the main obstacle was getting the workers' messages to correspond with those of the intellectuals because the expatriate community reflected traditional Vietnamese social hierarchies and inequalities. It is true that the experience of both the French army and the very particular organization of the MOI accentuated the alienation felt by the soldier-workers, who came from more disadvantaged backgrounds. Within the General Delegation, only the students were able to negotiate with the French authorities due to their ability to speak and their knowledge of the language, even though they were far fewer in number than the workers. This reproduced the old Confucian model of intellectualism being associated with power and the literati expected to lead.

The French social control over the Vietnamese soldier-workers, coupled with the lack of education among the majority of the latter, reinforced socio-economic inequalities among the Vietnamese. Moreover, class-based confrontations occurred among them, as was typical in Indochinese society at that time. In this sense, the associations were not democratic but rather the vehicles of the educated elite. This is why it cannot be claimed that the associations were democratic. On the other hand, this associative movement did move them one step closer to political "modernity." Yet, active participation in this associative modernity was generally reserved only for intellectuals, further proof that Confucian formalism would continue to influence the history of the Vietnamese state for several more years.

Fig. 4. Battalion of Annamese sharpshooters with their commanders and deputy officers during the 1914–17 war

Fig. 5. Distribution of letters at Indochinese Camp of Angoulême, 1918

Fig. 6. A traditional Indochinese theater performance (called *tuồng* or *hát bội* to entertain the troops at the Toulouse Section of the Assistance Committee for Indochinese Workers)

Fig. 7. The Office of the Indochinese Group of Colonial Workers at the Military Aviation School of Istres (Bouches-du-Rhône)

Fig. 8. Indochinese sharpshooters in their study room during the 1914–17 war

Notes

1. Traditionally, betel quid is made up of a piece of areca nut (the seed of the areca palm), a fresh betel leaf, and a bit of slaked lime. In some areas, other ingredients are added, such as tobacco or maybe a piece of red root from a banyan tree. Betel quid is offered to all guests visiting a house in the village. It is also offered during a wedding banquet and is among the traditional engagement gifts. Betel quid can also be found in neighboring Southeast Asian countries and the Indian subcontinent.

2. French Indochina comprised three Vietnamese entities—the colony of Cochinchina in the south, the protectorate of Annam in the center, and the protectorate of Tonkin in the north—and the protectorates of Cambodia and Laos, and the territory of Kouang-Tchéou-Wan.

3. It also brought over Vietnamese as soldiers—see, for example, Farve 1986; Eckert 2000; Hill 2006; Forgarty 2008; Vu-Hill 2011; and Hill 2015—but I will focus here on the soldier-workers because they were subject to different experiences and to specific controls from the colonial administration. Not only did they amount to a significant number of people but they were located mainly in urban areas like Marseilles and had more contact with civilians.

4. Cambodia and Laos constituted the other parts of French Indochina.

5. According to work by Pham (1974), Farve (1986), and my compilation of data from the archives of the War Ministry's Colonial Labor Organization Service (Service de l'Organisation des Travailleurs Coloniaux en France).

6. The cohort of Indochinese soldiers consisted not only of Vietnamese natives (Annamites, Cochinchinese, and Tonkinese at the time) but also included some Cambodians. For this reason, we are unable to be very precise as to the number of worker-soldiers who were of Vietnamese origin.

7. Second provincial mandarin, responsible for financial affairs.

References

Agulhon, Maurice. 1968. *Pénitents et Francs-Maçons de l'ancienne Provence: Essai sur la sociabilité méridionale* [Penitents and Freemasons of Ancient Provence: Essay on southern sociability]. Paris: Fayard.

Blanc, Marie-Eve. [1994] 2003. *La pratique associative vietnamienne: tradition et modernité du "Tương Tế Hội"* [The Vietnamese associative practice: tradition and modernity of "Tương Tế Hội "]. Villeneuve d'Ascq: Presses Universitaires du Septentrion, ANRT.

Cavenne. n.d. *Les travailleurs annamites en France: 1939–42* [Annamese workers in France: 1939–42]. Mémoire de L'Institut International de l'Administration Publique, Paris.

Chesneaux, Jean, Feiling Davis, and Nguyen Nguyet Ho. 1970. *Mouvements populaires et sociétés secrètes en Chine aux XIX° et XX° siècles* [Popular movements and secret societies in China in the nineteenth and twentieth centuries]. Paris: François Maspéro, CNRS.

Coates, Kenneth S., and William R. Morrison. 1993. "Soldier-Workers: The U.S. Army Corps of Engineers and the Northwest Defense Projects, 1942–6." *Pacific Historical Review* 62(3): 273–304.

Daum, Pierre. 2009. *Immigrés de force: Les travailleurs indochinois en France, 1939–52* [Forced immigrants: Indochinese workers in France, 1939–52]. Arles: Actes Sud (Editions Solin).

Department for the Control of Colonial Workers in France. 1916. AN, CAOM, Service de Liaison avec les Originaires des Territoires de la France d'Outre-Mer (SLOTFOM) I, 4.

Eckert, Henri. [1998] 2000. *Les militaires indochinois au service de la France, 1859–1939* [The Indochinese military in the service of France, 1859–1939]. Villeneuve d'Ascq: Presses Universitaires du Septentrion, ANRT.

Favre, Mireille. 1986. *Un milieu porteur de modernisation: travailleurs et tirailleurs vietnamiens pendant la première guerre mondiale* [A modernizing medium: Vietnamese workers and skirmishers during the First World War]. Thèse d'archiviste paléographe, Ecole Nationale des Chartes.

Fogarty, Richard S. 2008. *Race and War in France: Colonial Subjects in the French Army, 1914–1918.* Baltimore, MD: The Johns Hopkins University Press.

Goscha, Christopher. 1995. *Vietnam or Indochina (1887–1954)? Contesting Concepts of Space in Vietnamese Nationalism.* Copenhagen: Nordic Institute of Asian Studies.

Guesde, Pierre. 1919. AN, CAOM, Fonds Indochine, NF 21–225.

Gunn, Geoffrey C. 2014. "Mort pour la France: Coercion and Co-option of 'Indochinese' Worker-Soldiers in World War One." *Social Scientist* 4(7/8): 63–84.

Hémery, Daniel. 1975. *Révolutionnaires vietnamiens et pouvoir colonial en Indochine: Communistes, trotskystes, nationalistes à Saigon de 1932 à 1937* [Vietnamese Revolutionaries and Colonial Power in Indochina: Communists, Trotskyists, Nationalists in Saigon from 1932 to 1937]. Paris: François Maspéro, CNRS.

Hill, Kimloan. 2006. "Strangers in a Foreign Land: Vietnamese Soldiers and Workers in France during World War I." In *Viet Nam: Borderless Histories*, eds. Nhung Tuyet Tran and Anthony Reid, 256–89. Madison, WI: University of Wisconsin Press.

———. 2015. "Sacrifices, Sex, Race: Vietnamese Experiences in the First World War." In *Race, Empire and First World Writing*, ed. Santanu Das, 53–69. Cambridge: Cambridge University Press.

Le Calloc'h, Bernard. 1983. "La communauté Vietnamienne en France" [The Vietnamese community in France]. *Acta Geographica* 54: 1–14.

Le Huu Khoa. 1985. *Les Vietnamiens en France, insertion et identité* [Vietnamese in France, insertion and identity]. Paris: L'Harmattan.

———. 1990. "Communauté Vietnamienne 1940–6: Diversité des stratégies collectives dans l'enjeu de l'indépendance du Vietnam" [Vietnamese Community 1940–6: Diversity of the collective strategies in the stake of the independence of Vietnam]. *Approches Asie* 10.

Le Monde Colonial Illustré. 1939. "En masse les Indochinois ont répondu 'présents!'" [Together, the Indochinese answered 'present'!]. December, No. 198.

Liêm-Khê Luguern. 2010. *Những người lính thợ/Les travailleurs indochinois requis: parcours 1939–2006* [Indochinese workers recruited: itinerary 1939–2006]. Đà Nẵng: NXB Đà Nẵng.

Nguyễn Văn Hiên. 1918. AN, CAOM, General Government, 1887.

Pham Cong Anh. 1974. *Les Vietnamiens de Paris* [The Vietnamese of Paris]. Thèse de 3ème cycle, sous la direction de Georges Condominas, Paris.

Rettig, Frederik Tobias. 2012. "From Subaltern to Free Worker: Exit, Voice, and Loyalty among Indochina's Subaltern Imperial Labor Camp Diaspora in Metropolitan France, 1939–1944." *Journal of Vietnamese Studies* 7(3): 7–54, http://dx.doi.org/10.1525/vs.2012.7.3.7.

———. 2016. "The Politics and Consequences of Mobilising Overseas Service: Vietnamese Workers and Soldiers During and After WWI, 1915–2015." In *Re-visiting World War I: Interpretation and Perspectives of the Great Conflict*, eds. Jarek Suchoples and Stephanie James, 85–114. Bern: Peter Lang.

Rives, Maurice. 1994. "1939–1954, les travailleurs Indochinois en France" [1939–1954, Indochinese workers in France]. *Hommes et Migrations*, 1175: 24–29.

Rives, Maurice and Eric Deroo. 1999. *Les Lính Tập: Histoire des militaires indochinois au service de la France (1859–1960)* [Lính Tập: History of the Indochinese military in the service of France (1859–1960)]. Paris: Editions Charles-Lavauzelle.

Simon, Jean-Marc. 1986. "Des Vietnamiens en Vaucluse: le Camp de Sorgues" [Vietnamese in Vaucluse: the Camp of Sorgues]. *Etudes Vauclusiennes* 36, juillet-décembre: 19–24.

Témime, Emile, and Nathalie Deguigné. 2001. *Le camp du Grand Arénas. Marseille, 1944–1966.* [The Grand Arenas camp. Marseille, 1944–1966]. Paris: Autrement.

Vu-Hill, Kimloan. 2011. *Coolies into Rebels: Impact of World War I on French Indochina.* Paris: Les Indes Savantes.

Xu Guoqi. 2017. *Asia and the Great War: A Shared History*. Oxford: Oxford University Press.

CHAPTER 5

A Mutiny with Vietnamese Characteristics: The Yen Bay Mutiny of 1930

Frederik Rettig

The relationship between armed forces and societies can become particularly visible in a situation of crisis, such as a mutiny. In an imperial situation, in which colonial and indigenous organizations, interests, and cultures might intersect, this dialectic relationship can become particularly pronounced, especially if there also is a transnational element. In its 1923 handbook for officers and non-commissioned officers of "Indochinese" soldiers and workers serving in France, the French Ministry of War emphasized the support in men provided to the metropole by its colonies and protectorates during World War I (Ministère de la Guerre 1923, 7), including French Indochina.[1] It then provided the reader with a wide range of information on the psychological and physical characteristics of, in particular, the "Annamites" among the Indochinese soldiers, their cultural background, how to command and train them, and how to keep them in good health. Interestingly, perhaps assuming it would not matter in the metropole, the handbook did not alert its readers to the fact that the Annamites also had a reputation for mutiny that was arguably rooted in a strong sense of patriotism, if not awakening nationalism.

This chapter begins with some background information on a series of mutinies in Tonkin and Annam in the period 1908–18 in order to locate the Yen Bay mutiny of 1930 in its immediate historical and geographical context. In terms of a wider "Southeast Asian" perspective, the 1908–18 series of Vietnamese mutinies was far more deadly in intent than the demonstrations and unionization of disgruntled European and Indonesian soldiers and sailors in the Netherlands East Indies towards the end of World War I discussed by Kees van Dijk in Chapter 3 of this volume. The Vietnamese mutinies were also quite different in character from the "loyal" mutinies of African soldiers from the Gold Coast in the Netherlands East Indies during the 1838–41 period (van Kessel 2003) or the Philippine Scouts in 1924 (Meixsel 2006) because their acts of insubordination primarily protested unfair service conditions. While deadly determination was not amiss in the Singapore Mutiny of 1915 (Ban Kah Choon 2001) and the 1932 coup in Siam that ended the kingdom's absolute monarchy, the mutinies in Tonkin and Annam followed their own repertoire, and so did French repression.

What then was specific about the Yen Bay mutiny of 1930, and earlier mutiny attempts? The first section of this chapter provides some historical background of various failed Vietnamese mutinies during the 1908–18 period. The next two sections will briefly touch on the radicalization of Vietnamese society in the 1920s and then focus in particular on the goals of the Vietnamese Nationalist Party (Viet Nam Quoc Dan Dang, VNQDD),[2] which was partially modeled on the Chinese Nationalist Party, of ridding the country of French rule in order to set up an independent republic. The recruitment of Vietnamese warrant officers was of key tactical importance to the VNQDD because its leaders firmly believed that the Vietnamese republic could be achieved only by violent means. France's monopoly of violence in French Indochina was seen as the key barrier that stood in the way of an independent Vietnamese republic. As a consequence of considerable French reliance on Vietnamese soldiers for maintaining the *pax gallica*,[3] party leaders expected that they could exploit the dual identity of indigenous soldiers, as guardians but also subjects of the French "imperial nation-state,"[4] for their own ends.

In this chapter's central sections, which cover the run-up to the Yen Bay mutiny and further mutiny attempts that were part of a Tonkin-wide insurrection plan, I will show how the exalted importance of Vietnamese warrant officers exposed the party to infiltration by individuals loyal or beholden to the colonial military authorities. The final sections deal with the mutiny itself and the pursuant French repression that not only targeted the VNQDD and disloyal soldiers, but further tried to ensure that the mutineers and VNQDD leaders would not become popular heroes and thus role models for the Vietnamese.

The findings of this article are based on original archival research in the French overseas archives, the Centre des Archives d'Outre-Mer (CAOM) in Aix-en-Provence in southern France.[5] They are complemented by additional sources such as interviews with VNQDD members conducted by French journalist Louis Roubaud ([1931] 2010), the English translation of Hoang Van Dao's history of the VNQDD ([1970] 2008), and additional secondary literature. Some of these sources are problematic as they are based on incomplete and sometimes inaccurate information. Some sources are also interlinked (Hoang Van Dao, for instance, often draws on Roubaud), and at times clearly portray events from a partisan perspective in terms of omission, emphasis, or interpretation. The comparison of these sources nevertheless allows for the identification of some of these problems and to come as close as possible to understanding what really happened.

A Decade of Mutiny and Insurrection Attempts, 1908–18

Less than a decade after the late 1890s, when the French had declared the conquest and pacification phase of Tonkin and Annam as over, a series of mutinies would remind the French colonial authorities that the *pax gallica* could not be taken for granted, not even among its indigenous soldiers. In particular, the first mutiny during the 1908–18 period, the unsuccessful poisoning attempt of the European garrison in Hanoi on June 27, 1908, struck considerable fear into the French population in Tonkin. Among those pulling the threads from behind the scenes was the classically trained scholar Phan Boi Chau (1867–1940), the leading exponent and practitioner of violent Vietnamese anti-colonialism of the first quarter of the twentieth century (Fourniau 2002, 704–6). Also heavily implicated was the veteran of the anti-French Can Vuong (Aid the King Movement, 1885–96), Hoang Hoa Tham (1858–1913), who had submitted twice to the French on condition that the land under his control remain autonomous (see Duiker 2000, 64; Ngo Ngoc

Trung 1998, 152). His troops were to descend to Hanoi and take the weapons of the poisoned garrison in order to start an insurrection in Tonkin.

Four years later, less than half a year into World War I, the military wing of Phan Boi Chau's Vietnam Quang Phuc Hoi (Vietnamese Restoration Society), the Quang Phuc Quan,[6] was implicated in a poisoning and bombing attempt at Mong Cay garrison in the northeastern part of Tonkin bordering China, which was foiled in December 1914 (Morlat 1995, 193). A potentially far more serious mutiny attempt, in which boy-emperor Duy Tan (1900–45) was implicated, occurred on the night of May 3–4, 1916, in the protectorate of Annam. It was part of an ill-fated insurrection attempt that was prepared with considerable time and effort by scholars already implicated in the Tax Revolt of 1908 in Annam and who had remained in touch with Phan Boi Chau's Restoration Society (Nguyên Thê Anh 1992, 239–40). A key precipitating factor for the insurrection was the temporary presence in Hue and Tourane of recruits for overseas service in France who the plotters aimed to win over.

Slightly more than a year later, in August 1917, Luong Ngoc Quyen (1890–1917), Phan Boi Chau's first Dong Du participant and close associate, took a leading role in the Thai Nguyen Rebellion by exploiting the appalling conditions in the provincial capital's penitentiary.[7] It was started when a *garde indigène* contingent collaborated with the prisoners of Thai Nguyen penitentiary, which included Quyen, after the brutal French Resident had made the mistake of mistreating not only the inmates but also the militia guard forces who were guarding the prison.[8] After having killed their French commander and a number of French and Vietnamese *garde indigènes*, administrators, and civilians, they held the city for several days. It took the French authorities a further six months to dismantle the movement (Daufès 1933, 245–51; Officiers de l'Etat-Major 1930, 233–38; Zinoman 2000).

Finally, in November 1918, at the tail end of World War I, ethnic Chinese *tirailleurs* (riflemen) of Binh Lieu near the border of China killed their French officers, though rumors about a mutiny had been circulating since July of that year (Daufès 1933, 252–56; Officiers de l'Etat-Major 1930, 238–39). In fact, Army Headquarters had not taken these warning signals seriously, and failed to help the garrison's commander whose decorations won on Europe's battlefields could not make up for his lack of experience in Indochina. The mutiny was linked to a wider insurrectionary attempt in which German agents were said to be involved. The mutineers convinced the soldiers of Hoanh Mo garrison to join them, and then crossed the border into China. It was only in June 1919 that the French restored order in the region.

It is interesting to note that of the five mutiny attempts mentioned above, only two succeeded, which was arguably largely due to very particular shortcomings. In the case of Thai Nguyen, the brutality of Resident Darles most likely was the key factor. At Binh Lieu, the commanding officer's lack of experience and the misinterpretation of intelligence appear to have been key factors. In both cases, Lieutenant-Colonel Bonifacy's (1856–1931) advice that "a leader who knows how to handle the Tonkinese will obtain everything that one can ask for from his soldiers" was not heeded (Bonifacy 1911, 31).

Perhaps more interesting than the Thai Nguyen and Binh Lieu mutinies was that the other three mutiny attempts had been nipped in the bud. The poisoning attempt of the Hanoi garrison in 1908 was subverted because some of those in charge of mixing the potentially deadly hallucinogen datura into the food of the "white soldiers" did not do so, while four Catholic soldiers informed the French so that the authorities could take countermeasures (Fourniau 2002, 705). The causes for the foiling of the mutiny attempt at Mong Cay are not known, but the mutiny attempt of May 1916 in Annam was reported by an interpreter (Nguyên Thê Anh 1992, 239), as a result of which we do not know for sure whether the Vietnamese headed for war in Europe would have been willing mutineers. However, the examples of Thai Nguyen and Binh Lieu suggest this would have been unlikely unless the warning signals were ignored and the soldiers (or militia) guards were not handled properly. As a result, the organization of a mutiny was far more difficult than patriotic leaders such as Phan Boi Chau had hoped for.

The likely calculation of Phan Boi Chau that the ambiguous identity of Vietnamese soldiers, as agents and subjects of colonial domination, could be exploited by appealing to patriotism and anti-French sentiments was thus suspect. It did not consider that army service inculcates a strong sense of discipline, obedience, and hierarchy in its members, out of which a strong sense of loyalty and brotherhood in arms can arguably emerge. In fact, Bonifacy had emphasized that "patriotism is not the motivation of the *tirailleurs*, but their affection for their leader, the desire to distinguish themselves in front of their comrades" (1911, 31).

Moreover, the risks of participating in a mutiny are likely to have been very clear to even the most junior *tirailleur*. Unlike a civilian participant of an insurrection, a mutineer was relatively easy to identify because of his uniform and because knowledge of his personal particulars allowed for an easy tracking down. A return to his home village was thus almost impossible, also because the village authorities and even the villagers would have felt compelled to turn him in to the army in order to avoid severe penalties for the village. Moreover, the likely punishments for mutiny were severe. Immediately after the 1908 poisoning attempt, a Criminal Commission was convened that pronounced a total of sixteen death penalties.[9] Among the first to be publicly executed were three of the ringleaders whose severed heads were locked up in chicken baskets that were hung for three days in front of the entrance to Hanoi as a warning (Fourniau 2002, 706). As a result, the risks were considerable whereas service in the army had benefits such as regular food and pay, the opportunity to learn new skills, including reading and writing for the illiterate, and opportunities to rise through the ranks, although the positions of sergeant and adjutant were the highest that Vietnamese soldiers could aspire to until the late 1920s.[10]

The Emergence of a New Generation of Anti-colonialists from 1925

Following French victory in World War I, the temptation to launch mutiny and insurrection attempts was far reduced because the favorable moment to strike had passed. The French had maintained their control over French Indochina despite a significant reduction of European troops and despite German propaganda, so that a strike in peacetime would have been far more audacious. Moreover, at least some Vietnamese elites, such as the Constitutionalists in Cochinchina, hoped that the French would reward them for their loyal support during wartime. However, their strong opposition to Vietnamese World War I veterans, most of them of peasant or worker stock, becoming naturalized French citizens prevented the constitutionalists from connecting with a wider group of people and creating a mass movement (Hue-Tam Ho Tai 1992, 42).

Possibly the last major Constitutionalist attempt to draw attention to Indochina's immense contribution to the French war effort was Duong Van Giao's PhD thesis, defended in the Law Faculty of the University of Paris in early 1926. It was dedicated "To the memory of my Indochinese compatriots who gave their life to France for the Law (1914–1918)," by which he must have meant legal equality because a few pages later he would draw attention to the advantages of dominion status along British lines and emphasized a people's right to self-determination as put forward by the League of Nations (Duong Van Giao 1926, 22–23). By the time of Giao's PhD defense, however, massive changes in Vietnamese society, in particular among the anti-colonial elite, were underway.

Among the most crucial changes was that the older generation of anti-colonialists was on its way out. Thus Phan Chau Trinh (1872–1926), a strong opponent of the Vietnamese monarchy and advocate of social transformation having to occur before independence could be claimed, returned to Vietnam in 1925 only to pass away in 1926. His more violence-prone and conservative counterpart, Phan Boi Chau (1867–1940), who had been sentenced to death *in absentia* due to his hand in many of the anti-French plots of the last two decades (see above), was arrested in 1925 in Shanghai but eventually put under house arrest in Hue after a large-scale public outcry. His considerable expectation that acts of collective or individual violence would get rid of the French had evaporated as quickly as his hope that Asian powers such as Japan and later China would become involved in the liberation of Vietnam. What remained was the model of his steadfastness in the face of failure and his many writings that exalted Vietnamese heroism (de Tréglodé 2001, 54–64), but arguably also a certain blueprint for anti-colonial action that could be tapped into.

Emerging now was a new elite that was at least partially socialized through French educational institutions. It had to find newer solutions to French rule than those attempted by the older, mostly traditionally educated generation. According to Hue-Tam Ho Tai (1992), this generation was characterized by their radicalism towards French domination and their own cultural roots. Strikes of school students were not uncommon and such radicalism was often accompanied by a disinterest in compromising with the French, but at this stage it was not evident that radicalism would eventually filter into communism, although proto-communism was clearly an emerging option. A career in the French Indochinese army was almost inconceivable for this generation.

Hence, many of these radicalized youths left for southern China where Nguyen Ai Quoc (the future Ho Chi Minh), by now a Comintern agent, had created the proto-communist Thanh Nhien (Youth League) in mid-1925 in Canton, which would soon contain a small, secret communist cell. Its training was primarily political even though dozens of Thanh Nhien members went through the military academies at Whampoa and Nanjing, and a few also received some military training in Moscow. This primacy of the political over the militaristic was very different from the military training provided by the French to the Vietnamese. Career opportunities in the French Indochinese army were mostly limited to the position of warrant officer until the late 1920s, with an emphasis on loyal service under the French rather than on military leadership at the company or even battalion level.[11] In contrast, the emphasis in China and the Soviet Union was to mold a political party soldier who could lead and mobilize.

For the Thanh Nhien, the emphasis was on building up its own political and military expertise, although its "combat program" at the organization's first national congress in Hong Kong, May 1–9, 1929, marked a clear, although third-level interest in Vietnamese soldiers in French service (Eckert 2000, 662–63). This was a minor issue, however, in a party being torn apart by larger concerns that emerged at the Hong Kong congress. As a result, the Thanh Nhien was thrown into serious disarray when a radicalized faction, intent on the proletarianization and transformation of the organization, walked out of the congress. By mid-June 1929 this group had founded the Dong Duong Cong San Dang (DDCSD, Communist Party of Indochina). Their rivals in the Thanh Nhien then drew level with the creation of the Annam Cong San Dang (ACSD, Annamite Communist Party) in October 1929 (Duiker 2000, 159; Smith 1998, 784). Because a rival organization, the Tan Viet Cach Menh Dang (New Vietnamese Revolutionary Party), had changed its name to the Dong Duong Cong San Lien Doan (DDCSLD, Indochinese Communist League), there were now three communist parties where there had been none just months before (Sampson 1975, 259). None of these parties were recognized by Moscow, and it would take until early February 1930 for Nguyen Ai Quoc to convince their representatives to form a Vietnamese Communist Party (Viet Nam Cong San Dang), which would maintain a third-rate level interest in soldiers.

In contrast to the trend of the abovementioned parties competing for official recognition from Moscow, who were primarily interested in workers and peasants, the Viet Nam Quoc Dan Dang (VNQDD, Vietnamese Nationalist Party) was mainly interested in Vietnamese soldiers. With a name and key ideas inspired by the Chinese Nationalist Party, the Guomindang, the VNQDD emerged from a fusion of the Nam Dong Publishing Society (Nam Dong Thu Xa) and various provincial groups on December 25, 1927, in Hanoi (Hue-Tam Ho Tai 1992, 184). A key figure in the newly founded party was Nguyen Thai Hoc (1902–30), who had attended a French primary school and three years of Pedagogy School, which he did not finish, and eventually a business college but was frustrated by the lack of response to his two letters to Governor-General Varenne in 1925 and the French refusal in mid-1927 to give him a permit to publish a monthly magazine (Hoang Van Dao 2008, 477–81, 12–13).

However, from 1928 at the latest, when the Confucian scholar Nguyen Khac Nhu (1883–1930) joined the VNQDD, along with members of his own organization, a direct revolutionary lineage was established with the veteran revolutionary Phan Boi Chau. Hence, Nguyen Khac Nhu had gone to China in 1907 as part of the Dong Du Movement and thereafter remained close to the various movements set up by Chau. He knew their militant goals very well and above all understood the "importance of the revolutionary role of indigenous soldiers in the colonial army" (Goscha 1994, 30). In a document attributed to him, Nguyen Khac Nhu offers a violent solution to the problem of colonial oppression, stating that "it is better to die than to lead" the lives of "beasts of burden."[12] Its author argued that it "is indispensable to do away first with the [French] pirates of the nation" by "wait[ing] for the opportune moment to strike," and by "killing the enemy in order to regain our rights."

It is possible to see the continuity between the VNQDD's acceptance of violence and Vietnamese traditions of violent insurrection, such as the anti-French "Aid the King Movement" (Can Vuong, 1885–96) or the phase of violent patriotism that followed, which was largely influenced by Phan Boi Chau. Several of the VNQDD's revolutionary strategies were in line with Chau's revolutionary ideas, including his exaltation of Vietnamese anti-foreign heroism, and the party had apparently asked for, and received, advice from Chau even though he was, since 1925, living under house arrest in Hue. The party even featured the veteran revolutionary, who as early as July 1924 had discussed the setting up of a Vietnamese Nationalist Party, as one of their honorary members (see Duiker 2000, 119, 144n 154). These influences aside, from mid-1929 the party also adapted the Thanh Nien's Leninist organizational structure in which party cells played a considerable role.

In keeping with its political orientation and lineage, the VNQDD was committed from the beginning to achieving its political goals through violence with the support of subverted Indochinese soldiers, although there was disagreement about the most suitable timeframe (Goscha 1994, 29; Marr 1981, 377–78). The party's program formulated three key goals, and indicated the sequence in which they were to be achieved: "(1) Make a racial revolution; (2) Form a direct republican movement; (3) Help other oppressed peoples" (Gouvernement Général de l'Indochine 1933, 42). Although some of these goals were rather broad, three years later the head of the party's execution committee, Ky Con (1908–30), gave the metropolitan journalist Louis Roubaud the following answer in June 1930 when Roubaud asked him whether he was a communist: "I am simply a republican, like you. I desire [*souhaite*] for my country what you have achieved for yours; a democratic government, universal suffrage, freedom of press, recognition of the rights of man and the citizen, and, to start with, independence!" (Roubaud 2010, 75).

However, what clearly stood in the way of the party's goal of a racial revolution, that is independence, and the formation of a republic, was the French colonial regime. If the colonial military could not be eliminated straightaway, it could crush the Vietnamese Nationalist Party's insurrection in its initial stages and doom it to failure. It was, therefore, of crucial importance that the French military threat to the party's insurrection be eliminated.

In line with these ideas, the VNQDD recruited heavily among Vietnamese troops (Huynh Kim Khanh 1982, 94), especially warrant officers (Hy Van Luong 1992, 88). The latter were apparently given member status whereas the former appear to have been organized "into party-affiliated associations" (p. 88). The party's particular interest in warrant officers seems to have derived from the perception that they not only occupied the nodal point between French officers and Indochinese troops, but also that they had enough authority over their Indochinese subordinates to make them join the ranks of the nationalist insurgents. As we will see in the next section, this was not much of a conceptual stretch, as French training manuals for officers and warrant officers confirmed some of these ideas.

The VNQDD's Interest in Warrant Officers

The nodal position of indigenous warrant officers was clearly recognized by the French, as is evident in Lieutenant-Colonel Auguste Bonifacy's advice to French warrant officers (1911, 8–15). Bonifacy, a scholar-officer who was also a corresponding member of the Ecole Française d'Extrême-Orient, devoted a quarter of his booklet to the "conduct with regarded to [the indigenous] warrant officers": adjutants, sergeants, corporals, and 1st class *tirailleurs*. He emphasized that French NCOs should not rely on "their direct influence on the *tirailleurs* [because] it will only exist if the adjutant, if the indigenous sergeants are of one heart with you" (p. 9). He devoted particular attention to the sergeants, who occupied a "somewhat sham" position because they were only in direct command in the absence of the two French sergeants. Nevertheless, emphasized Bonifacy, the indigenous sergeant "absolutely needs to be on our side, and this depends enormously on how we treat him, have confidence in him" (p. 11).

This importance of the Indochinese sergeant derived from the fact that he "absolutely needs to thoroughly know [and] monitor all the corporals and *tirailleurs* of his section and that he provides you, and the *chef de section*, with all the information that you ask him" (pp. 10–11). This did not only apply to the barracks, but also beyond with information such as "where they are lodging [*prendre pension*], if they regularly pay for their lodgings, who their acquaintances are." However, a later publication by the Ministry of War (Ministère de la Guerre 1923, 18), which drew heavily on Bonifacy, advised that the "information provided by indigenous warrant officers regarding the *tirailleurs* has to be frequently checked and their enquiries verified because of a tendency by some warrant officers to 'exploit' their subordinates." From all of the above it resulted that, in particular, the "sergeants need to be selected carefully, with a very scrupulous conscience" (Ministère de la Guerre 1923, 17).

The party's key focus on Indochinese soldiers distinguished the VNQDD from other contemporary revolutionary patriotic groups, resulting in a virtual monopoly of recruitment among the indigenous military (Huynh Kim Khanh 1982, 94). By early February 1929, the "[p]arty was making headway in recruiting members in the population at large, and was particularly successful among colonial troops" (Hue-Tam Ho Tai 1992, 219). However, this success was threatened by one party member's apparently unauthorized initiative to kill René Bazin, the head of the Office Général de la Main-d'Œuvre Indochinoise (General Office of Indochinese Manpower) that recruited plantation laborers, on February 9, 1929, in Hanoi when he stepped out of his French-Vietnamese mistress's home (Hoang Van Dao 2008, 38–40). Subsequent investigations led to a crackdown on the VNQDD and even prompted Governor-General (GG) Pierre Pasquier to initiate the Criminal Commission of Tonkin (Commission Criminelle du Tonkin) on February 24, 1929 (Resident Superior Robin to GG Pasquier, Yen Bay Report [hereafter Robin's Yen Bay Report], 9-3-1930, CAOM, NF, Dossier 2936, 49; Morlat

1990, 114). It soon became clear that the largest socio-professional group (40 out of the 227 individuals) investigated by the Commission were soldiers, predominantly warrant officers. These numbers were mirrored, although to a lesser extent, in the overall number of soldiers identified by the intelligence services as affiliate members of the party—120 out of 1,500 (Gouvernement Général de l'Indochine 1933, 12).[13]

Of the forty soldiers brought to the attention of the Criminal Commission, twenty-seven did not undergo further prosecution because they were deemed to have "played but a secondary role" (General Aubert to Minister of Colonies, 29-6-1929, CAOM, GGI, CM 209). The report by the president of the Criminal Commission, Jules Brides, provides valuable information about the thirteen soldiers put on trial (Criminal Commission Report, 9-7-1929, CAOM, GGI, 65517). Five of the soldiers were condemned to five years of detention each, another to five years of imprisonment, and the final three to two years of imprisonment each. Then again, the two-year imprisonment of another three soldiers was suspended, and one soldier was found not guilty and released. The thirteen soldiers who were most seriously implicated in the affair were soldiers ranking from corporal to sergeant, with only two of the accused identified as *tirailleurs*. This suggests that higher-ranking soldiers were targeted by the VNQDD because they occupied a key position in the colonial army, and perhaps also because they were more receptive towards its propaganda.

The party's interest in warrant officers is confirmed by additional statistics on the 121 soldiers who were punished by the military authorities (General Aubert to Minister of Colonies, 29-6-1929; Criminal Commission Report, 9-7-1929). Aubert's statistics concern the 121 soldiers who were punished by the military authorities, and they seem to include the 40 caught by the Criminal Commission. They show that four adjutant chiefs and adjutants, 38 sergeants, 23 corporals, and 56 *tirailleurs* were punished. Although more *tirailleurs* were involved, it is the higher ranks, in particular the sergeants, which are overrepresented. According to Aubert, the "culprits all belong to relatively educated or evolved categories," which was in line with the VNQDD's targeting of indigenous warrant officers, as they were better qualified than ordinary soldiers and also commanded more authority.[14] In addition, it is likely that the VNQDD particularly targeted some services because of their strategic utility. Thus, according to Louis Marty, the VNQDD targeted the air force because it intended "to destroy the aircraft on the day of the insurrection" (Gouvernement Général de l'Indochine 1933, 12).[15]

The VNQDD's recruitment success in the armed forces suggests that soldiers were fairly easy to attract. The party's relatively simple program, with its nationalistic goal, certainly had potential appeal. It did not require long explanations or even, as in the case of the proto-communist Thanh Nhien, demand a complete change in one's world view. One could further argue that the prominent and flattering role that the soldiers played in the VNQDD's revolution could have appealed to other soldiers, whose interest might have been propelled by expectations of occupying high positions in the republic's post-independence army. It is not entirely clear, however, whether the soldiers who became affiliated with the VNQDD fully understood the extent of revolutionary commitment and sacrifice required of them. Thus, even the party's core members disagreed on the exact nature of the party program with regard to the timing and the ultimate goal of revolution. Under these circumstances, it was not clear whether all indigenous warrant officers, let alone their subordinates, realized that their alliance with the VNQDD might eventually place them under the guillotine. Moreover, were the soldiers and warrant officers not socialized and trained to serve professionally rather than get involved in anti-French politics?

Availing the party of the services of warrant officers, however, was not without its dangers given the high French expectations that they function as a source of intelligence. Hence, the Sûreté's highest-ranking informer was Pham Thanh Duong, the party's head of military affairs and eventually its provisional military affairs minister (Hy Van Luong 1992, 33, 235). According to one of the VNQDD's historians, Duong came from a privileged background, demonstrated by his graduation from high school, but he dropped out of medical school "in his second year" (Hoang Van Dao 2008, 79). He then worked in the office of the French Resident Superior (RS) in Laos, but quit because of gambling problems. This setback did not prevent him from enrolling in the air force at Bach Mai, near Hanoi, which permitted him to join the "Air Force Non-Commissioned Officer Academy" in Chua Thong, Sontay province, from where he graduated in early 1929. In 1928, Nguyen Thai Hoc had come to Sontay "to motivate and admit Duong into the VNQDD." In 1929, based at Bach Mai airport, Duong "was sworn in and officially admitted as a Party member" and was soon to replace Sergeant Mon who had been arrested by the Criminal Commission, as head of the party's "military sub-committee" in which capacity he "recruit(ed) many soldiers and proved to be a warm, worthy partisan."

From the VNQDD's perspective, Sergeant Duong was a prize target due to his high rank and key intermediary position in the military, but most notably because of his position in the air force, which was sometimes used to repress unrest.[16] However, towards the end of 1929, Sergeant Duong's warm attitude changed when his father, Pham Huy Du, a teacher, realized that his son had become an important VNQDD member (Hoang Van Dao 2008, 80). Du shared his concern with the "director of the French-Vietnamese primary schools," who in turn alerted the Sûreté [literally, Security], the feared political police, which recommended that his son leave the party. Du pleaded with Duong and even threatened to hand him over to the authorities, who would surely send him to the infamous Poulo Condore prison island off the coast of Cochinchina. Having Duong's father on their side gave a crucial advantage to the French because they could exploit the young revolutionary's filial obligations towards his father. Seeing the high potential of using Sergeant Duong against his own party, the authorities invited father and son, awarded the former with a prestigious medal and a "title of nobility," and the latter with a monthly stipend. The shadow of Duong's betrayal not only threatened the VNQDD but also hung over his own head because the party punished treason with death.

Surging Ahead with the Insurgence Plans

Less than two weeks after the Thanh Nhien's May 1929 conference, an equally turbulent VNQDD meeting accelerated the latter's insurrection plan

(Hue-Tam Ho Tai 1992, 221; Hy Van Luong 1992, 89). The recruitment of new members and the mobilization of the local population were to be intensified as the uprising was actively prepared (Hy Van Luong 1992, 89). Concerns about the further erosion of the VNQDD's strength as the result of French repression, the decline of prestige, and a loss of members to other parties seem to have been the party's main motivations. Nonetheless, differences within the party had come to the fore again, because not all members present at the meeting had initially agreed on the new strategy of speeding up the preparations for revolt. It is not clear from secondary sources whether the arguments within the VNQDD were based on an aversion to violence, a preference for more solid, long-term planning, or the realization that the chances of success were slim.

Although the majority also considered the chances of success to be dismal (Hy Van Luong 1992, 89),[17] they might have won over the minority by arguing that the morally noble action itself would be more important than its concrete results—"even if victory were not achieved, we would fully mature as human beings with our [heroic] efforts"—an argument deeply embedded in the Vietnamese cultural logic (p. 89). Party leaders also seem to have been aware that a failed attempt would create symbols of resistance for future generations of Vietnamese anti-colonialists.

In a more general sense, the mobilization process of winning over non-party members for the insurrection had begun. The conversion of soldiers, and occasionally native guards, was one aspect that included the distribution of leaflets to "French, legionnaire, and Vietnamese soldiers, as well as to the Vietnamese populace at large" (p. 89).

On December 7, 1929, the Sûreté discovered the hiding place of Nguyen Thai Hoc, Nguyen Khac Nhu, and Hoc's lieutenant Pho Duc Chinh in Vong La village (Phu Tho province) and ordered Sergeant Pham Thanh Duong to arrest them (Hoang Van Dao 2008, 76–77). One day later, having learned from another party member how best to enter the village undetected, Duong and a Vietnamese "detective [who was] disguised as a non-commissioned military officer" accessed the village via the unprotected riverbank while Sûreté agents led by Inspector Riner took up positions outside the village.

Sergeant Duong and the disguised detective managed to gain access to the party leaders' location, but Duong "acted unnaturally," which gave the leaders the chance to mentally prepare for the worst while having tea with their guests. When Duong suddenly got up to draw his weapon, Nguyen Khac Nhu kicked the table towards Duong and the detective and the VNQDD leaders ran for their lives. Although Duong and his companion succeeded in wounding the party's "shadow" interior minister, Pho Duc Chinh, all three party leaders managed to escape (Gouvernement Général de l'Indochine 1933, 16; Hoang Van Dao 2008, 76–77; Hy Van Luong 1992, 33–34, 89).

Pham Thanh Duong was now revealed as a traitor and the party's leadership finally realized how well-informed and determined the Sûreté was. The psychological impact on the party was a sense of urgency and a desire to strike before the Sûreté could strike again, although the party's organization and coordination were far from adequate (Gouvernement Général de l'Indochine 1933, 16). Moreover, the botched arrest set in motion attempts to punish the traitors, including Pham Thanh Duong, who had done further damage by "denounc[ing] the soldiers in the Party military cells" in Hanoi (Hoang Van Dao 2008, 81, 101). On January 20, 1930, the party's "Highest Revolutionary Court . . . sentenced father and son to death" and the party's Death Squad Subcommittee designated the executioners (Hoang Van Dao 2008, 81). Pham Huy Du was assassinated by a single gunshot in a street in Hanoi on January 22, 1930, by Nguyen Thai Hoc's younger brother, seventeen-year-old Nguyen Van Nho (Hoang Van Dao 2008, 81–82). Pham Thanh Duong, who had been promoted to the rank of Sûreté Inspector, was eventually seriously wounded by another party affiliate who fired a shot into his back on May 30, 1930 (Hoang Van Dao 2008, 83–84). The gunshot perforated Duong's bowels, but he managed to return fire and survived. He was awarded a medal while still hospitalized and was subsequently sent to France for additional treatment. It was not until late 1945 that Duong was killed by party members.

Although the Sûreté could no longer rely on the services of its most eminent informer, a series of discoveries indicated that preparations for an insurrection were still underway. On December 26, 1929, 100 bombs were found at Noi-Vien (Bac-Ninh province) with a further 184 discovered in Thai-Ha-Ap, an immediate suburb of Hanoi. On January 12, 1930, jars full of tracts to be distributed on the day of the insurrection were found in Luc-Nam by the Resident of Bac-Giang. On January 20, 1930, a blacksmith from Vinh Yen was surprised while making sabers (Robin's Yen Bay Report, 9-3-1930, 53) and on January 21, 1930, six VNQDD affiliates boarded the Hanoi-Sontay bus and robbed the other passengers in order to fill the party's war coffers (Gouvernement Général de l'Indochine 1933, 16).

Nguyen Thai Hoc called an emergency conference on January 26, 1930, again in Vong La village, to deal with the new situation (Hoang Van Dao 2008, 84; Hue-Tam Ho Tai 1992, 221). Hoc argued that the VNQDD could not wait for the reorganization before launching its insurrection, although he told the assembled party members that defeat was very likely. The reported content of his party address reflected the spirit of the party leaders as well as their belief that even a defeat could be a victory in the sense that it would serve as a reference point for future generations of Vietnamese anti-colonialists:

> Life is only a game of cards; in an unlucky game, a person can lose everything.
>
> If we wait, our Party's forces will continue to erode. When fear makes its way into people's minds, they lose their enthusiasm to serve the Party and their confidence in its success; the revolutionary movement of the Party would be as cool as a cinder. Material resources would vanish and arrests would eat away at our human resources. We would be leading our comrades to a lonely and worn out death in prison cells.
>
> It is time for us to act! If we die, we will provide good models for the next generations. If we fail to succeed, we will become virtuous men. "Không Thành Công Thì Thành Nhân." There is no dilemma in our decision. (Hoang Van Dao 2008, 85)

The conference unanimously followed Hoc's recommendation to wage a general insurrection throughout Bac-Ky [Tonkin], scheduled to take place on the night of February 9, 1930 (Huynh Kim Khanh 1982, 95). Because the party's initial plan for an uprising in Kien-An had been discovered, the VNQDD decided, according to General Aubert, "to attempt their first strike in another center chosen for being far away from cities as protected and under surveillance as Hanoi and Haiphong, but also close enough to the regions where the VNQDD's leaders possessed the support of numerous and loyal supporters" (General Aubert, Service note, 11-3-1930, 2). This new plan placed substantial importance on the garrisons of Yen Bay and Lao Kay, with the former situated just beyond halfway on the 296-kilometer rail track linking Hanoi with Lao Kay on the border with China, even though these two garrisons had not figured at all in the party's earlier insurrectionary plans.[18]

Among those involved in the effort to mobilize the six hundred soldiers of the 2nd Battalion of the 4th Tirailleurs Tonkinois Regiment, an ethnically Vietnamese unit which had been stationed there since 1928 and also comprised a disciplinary section (Officiers de l'Etat-Major 1930, 89), were Nguyen Thi Giang and two other "female comrades," Nguyen Thi Bac and Nguyen Thi Tam (Hoang Van Dao 2008, 73). Giang and Bac were the sisters of a Confucian scholar in Ha Giang province and had joined the VNQDD in 1928 with Nguyen Khac Nhu's "secret revolutionary organization" (Hoang Van Dao 2008, 488). As such, they would become the party's first full female members. Nguyen Thi Giang, in particular, was soon noted as an "effective and efficient comrade" who served as a messenger and provider of intelligence and also excelled at propaganda (Hoang Van Dao 2008, 73, 488). Eventually, Giang and Nguyen Thai Hoc would become companions whose fate would be indelibly related to the success or failure of the VNQDD (pp. 488–90).

Yen Bay as a Place of Mutiny

The sudden importance given to Yen Bay and Lao Kay was partially a response to the measures taken by the colonial authorities, in particular

Sergeant Pham Thanh Duong's betrayal, which had so strongly affected the party's mutiny plans in Hanoi and its surroundings. Duong's treachery clearly had resulted in the VNQDD's postponement of their initial insurrectionary plan and now led to the new emphasis on striking first in peripheral regions. However, the VNQDD's change in priorities was also related to the fact that Nguyen The Nghiep, one of the party's most important leaders, had managed to escape from prison and cross the border into Yunnan. There, according to Louis Marty:

> He attempted to organise a party section among the numerous Annamite colony in Yunnan and, at the same time, to infect our troops stationed in the frontier area. He informed Nguyên Thai Hoc that he had worked the exclusively Annamite garrison of Lao-Kay and organised a cell of eighteen members, composed almost entirely of warrant officers. He affirmed that he could, if necessary, stir up the garrison and participate in the attack in Tonkin provided that the passage in the Red River Valley was opened to him by eliminating the centre of resistance at Yên-Bay.
>
> Even though this garrison on the periphery had been touched only a little by the VNQDD's propaganda, Nguyên Thai Hoc decided to provoke its rebellion. (Gouvernement Général de l'Indochine 1933, 17)

The sudden importance given to Lao Kay, a garrison without European troops apart from some European officers, similar to Yen Bay, meant that Yen Bay was given a privileged position in the VNQDD's revolutionary plans, even though the party was not strongly represented there. Moreover, the party's planners, in particular Pho Duc Chinh who appeared to have been in charge of the overall plan, did not seriously consider contingency plans in the case that something might go wrong (Roubaud 2010, 95–96). This backfired because of the problems contacting Nguyen The Nghiep in Yunnan and the resulting lack of party discipline:

> The uprising was fixed for the morning of 10 February. The plan was as follows: Nguyên Thê Nghiêp had to take Lao-Kay. Nguyên Khac Nhu . . . and Pho Duc Chinh had to attack Yên-Bay, Hung-Hoa, Lâm-Thao and Son-Tay. Nguyên Thai Hoc had to provoke the uprising at Bac-Ninh, Dap-Câu, Sept-Pagodes and at Hai-Duong. Vu Van Giâng remained in charge of starting the rebellion in Kiên-An province . . . .
>
> A messenger was immediately despatched to Yunnan to inform Nguyên Thê Nghiêp of these plans. But he failed to meet him and Nguyên Thai Hoc told his lieutenants that the general attack was postponed to 15 February.
>
> Nguyên Khac Nhu . . ., however, who had taken all dispositions for the attack of Yên-Bay on the 10th, refused to give a counter-order. (Gouvernement Général de l'Indochine 1933, 18)

According to other accounts, however, Nhu did not receive the counter-order in time (see Hy Van Luong 1992, 93) because the messenger was arrested en route (Pham Hong Tung 2002, 245). These communication problems, and perhaps even some discord, remained unknown to both the French authorities, who were relieved but also apprehensive that Tet, the Vietnamese lunar new year, had passed without major troubles, and the party's affiliates in Yen Bay who had been preparing since mid-January. "Between 19 January and 2 February, five reunions were held . . . [at Yên Bay]. They were assisted by five or six *tirailleurs* and a civilian affiliate of the Phu Tho *thin bo*. The meeting on 2 February seems to have been the last one" before the mutiny (Massimi's Second Report, 16-2-1930, 5–6).[19] This increase in the frequency of meetings went ahead despite the fact that the cell's president, Adjutant Cam, had fallen sick and had been "evacuated to a hospital in Hanoi."[20] In the meantime, Corporal Thuyet had taken over the interim presidency.

At the same time, aside from these meetings, the garrison's party affiliates approached those soldiers with whom they had established contact earlier. Tran Uc Sinh, the central Military Intelligence Service's informer, was approached a second time by Corporal Hoang, about a fortnight before Tet

(Interrogation of Tran-Uc-Sinh, 16-2-1930, CAOM, NF, FM, Dossier 2936, 1–2). Corporal Hoang took Sinh, a 2nd class *tirailleur*, aside during their guard duty and told him: "I have always been good to you, whereas the French warrant officers punish you for the slightest mistake; if you want to come with me, we will start the revolution. Numerous are those who will join us. You have been a victim of the French, you must take revenge." Hoang might have been referring to Captain Jourdan, who commanded the Seventh Company in which Sinh served.

According to one of his French colleagues, Jourdan was a small man with an occasionally vicious temper who commandeered his indigenous troops with a rattan stick or riding whip. These methods were inadmissible, but apparently tolerated by Commander Le Tacon (Paillat 1981, 484–85).[21] Hoang did not speak about money, but confided that the party owned many grenades and a lot of traditional weapons, but few guns. Hoang seemed to immediately regret his words and asked Sinh to keep everything secret. He did not ask Sinh to swear an oath of loyalty, but instead relied entirely on his higher rank and the power of his own speech to win Sinh's participation. In a society in which respect for hierarchy and authority was deeply ingrained, it was arguably unlikely that someone in a subordinate position would openly have contradicted Corporal Hoang. But it made it far more difficult for the mutiny's leaders to gauge the extent of commitment of their followers.

Tran Uc Sinh, however, dutifully wrote a letter to Lieutenant Slouchez, his contact officer within the Military Intelligence Service, but received no reply. The Lieutenant had left for France without informing Sinh or his replacement, and Sinh's letter was sent by ordinary mail (Eckert 2000, 652). Sinh wrote a second letter, which also went unanswered. On February 5, Tirailleur Sinh finally wrote to Sergeant Giau, a relative of his whom he knew to be in contact with the Head of the Service de Renseignement ([Military] Intelligence Service], Commander Carles (Eckert 2000, 653). By this time, Sinh knew that the mutiny was scheduled for February 9. Sergeant Giau, however, did not understand what Sinh wanted from him and demanded further information in addition to hesitating to contact Carles.

While one avenue for uncovering the mutiny was foreclosed by communication and organizational problems within the Military Intelligence Service, the other possibility was obstructed by a lack of communication between the military and civil authorities in Yen Bay. Less than a week prior to the mutiny, Yen Bay's Resident, Massimi, received a confidential circular sent to all Residents (No. 80-SCB) on February 3, 1930 (Robin's Yen Bay Report, 9-3-1930, 32–33). It called on the Military Commander and the civil authorities of each location to exchange information about revolutionary propaganda among the troops and military establishments. Surveillance outside military barracks was expected to involve close collaboration between civil and military authorities. The instructions then defined the duties of both authorities. The military would communicate intelligence about suspected military personnel to the responsible civil authority, and residents were asked to contact their military commander to guarantee the strict application of surveillance measures.

Most local civil and military authorities complied, at least partially, with this new instruction, despite their traditional rivalry. In Yen Bay, however, the situation was different because of a profound animosity between the province's Resident, Massimi, and the garrison's military commander, Le Tacon. In his report to Resident Superior Robin, written after the mutiny, Massimi wrote: "I have never personally been able to obtain precise intelligence from the Commander [Le Tacon] about the frame of mind of his troops. I would even say that my demands constantly seem to indispose this high-ranking officer who does not miss any occasion to make me understand how inopportune my questions are, (which are) almost insulting for such a splendid troop, praised by the Commandant Superior [Aubert] himself" (16-2-1930, CAOM, SLOTFOM, Series III, Dossier 9).

Robin, in his report, asks why the *chefs de quartier* and the mandarins of Yen Bay did not find out about the soldiers' meetings with VNQDD civilian members. The secret meetings had taken place in a quarter that was beyond civilian control, as Commander Le Tacon "jealously reserved its surveillance" and could not bear intrusion by the residential police. A further reason was that the regiment "inspired real terror in the civilian population" and behaved like "in conquered territory," so that the subaltern indigenous authorities did not dare intervene (Resident Wintrebert to RS Robin [hereafter Wintrebert's Report], Report on civilian authorities of Yen Bay, 20-2-1930, 11–12; Robin's Yen Bay Report, 9-3-1930, 34). Even so, Robin noted, they should at least have reported these suspicious movements, which they could not have failed to notice. He also regarded it unlikely that Commander Le Tacon had not been told of these movements by his military informants (Robin's Yen Bay Report, 9-3-1930, 21–22, 25).

At dusk on February 8, the *chi bo* (party cell) of Xuang Lung was assembled by its president, Hop, at Tiep's place. Twelve members attended the meeting and listened to Hop's speech:

> According to the tong-bo's instructions transmitted to us by Ngoc-Tinh, and with the assent of Yên-Bay garrison's tirailleurs, with whom Ngoc-Tinh had come to an understanding, we have to take the province of Yên Bay tomorrow. The tirailleurs only ask us for thirty [party] soldiers. As another chi-bo has to furnish a certain proportion of soldiers, according to Ngoc-Tinh's instruction, we will complete that number according to the number of soldiers provided by the first chi-bo. (Massimi's Second Report, 16-2-1930, 7–8)

According to Massimi (p. 8):

> It was thus only then that the revolutionaries learned the place and the time chosen for their action. They had only twenty-four hours to execute it.

Final Mutiny Preparations: Sunday, February 9

On the morning of Sunday, February 9, 1930, VNQDD members and supporters from the Lam Thao district, many of them women,[22] converged by train on Yen Bay. Not wanting to arouse French suspicions, they boarded the train at different stations and at different times, and some of them got off the train at the stations directly before and after Yen Bay. Thus, the twenty-two members and affiliates of the Xuang Lung *chi bo* boarded the train at Kieu Tien station (Massimi's Second Report 16-2-1930, 8–9). According to Resident Wintrebert, 50–60 more revolutionaries from Phu Tho boarded the train at Phu Tho (Wintrebert's Report, 20-2-1930, 14–15).[23] The transport of weapons, organized by the *chi bo* of Son Duong village, took place on the evening train. Sabers were hidden in cases and bombs in baskets covered with onions or paddy, with flags, bandoleers, and badges transported in suitcases. Neither the train personnel nor the civilian authorities noticed any suspicious movements.

The lack of suspicion on behalf of the civilian authorities was not too surprising because customs only checked trains going down to Hanoi, rather than those going up to Yunnan, since the opium trade moved from China to Indochina (Robin's Yen Bay Report, 9-3-1930, 25–26). The arrival of about sixty VNQDD members at Yen Bay went equally unnoticed by the garrison city's civilian French and indigenous authorities because Yen Bay was a transit location for coolies from the Tu Le mines, and a large number of pilgrims also came to pray at the pagoda of the goddess Thanh Mau during the first month of the Vietnamese lunar year. Another reason the revolutionaries' arrival went largely unnoticed was because they were welcomed at the station by fellow *tirailleurs* and then spread out in very small groups to the town's taverns. Thosc who did not disembark at Yen Bay went to the wood at the foot of the hillock close to the barracks.

At nightfall, corporals and *tirailleurs* gathered the civilian plotters and three corporals gave the following speech:

> We have prepared everything; the keys to the weapons magazines are ours; all in all, there are only twenty-nine Frenchmen to massacre and the tirailleurs are numerous, very numerous. We only need to demonstrate that military and civilians are of the same mind. Your role is limited to assure order and to appease the population once the fort is taken.

> The civilians asked what exactly their mission was and when the projected operation would be executed. The NCOs replied that the role of everyone would be determined in the deliberative assembly. They went to a small wood near the new European cemetery, about 300 meters from the fort.
>
> There the civilian plotters, about thirty, joined the tirailleurs who were already waiting. Together they made up a force of sixty to seventy people.
>
> The deliberative assembly then gathered in a straw hut with six arches in immediate proximity to the fort.... (Massimi's Second Report 16-2-1930, 9–10)

Unheeded Last-minute Warnings from Loyal Soldiers

The VNQDD's preparations at Yen Bay were almost uncovered when two of the battalion's soldiers informed Commander Le Tacon about suspicious movements among the civilians and military planning to take the fort. Tirailleur Tran Uc Sinh, the Military Intelligence Service's informer who had still not received a reply from his contact officer, Slouchez, had decided to warn his superiors. In order to avoid exposing his identity as an informer, he asked his direct superior to present him to Commander Le Tacon. His difficulty in alerting them to the impending danger was partly related to the pidgin French common in the barracks (see Eckert 2000, 881–90; Love 2001, 52–63), and the skeptical attitude of his interlocutors, with both factors working together to prevent his warnings from being passed on more cogently:

> I have to tell you that I went to see Adjutant Cuneo at seven o'clock in the evening in order to inform him about what was happening, and told him in French: "*Mon Adjutant*, I have come to speak about a personal matter." The adjutant came out. I added: "During the night, there is a very difficult matter. I am presenting myself to ask to be led to the Commandant, because you are my Company's Adjutant." The

> Adjutant replied: "What difficult affair." [Sinh:] "I ask you to go to the Commandant to present me, because I am tirailleur, it is difficult to present to the Commandant personally, I fear that the boy knows."[24] The Adjutant told me that I could go on my own. "You go alone to Commandant, I come with you, it is the same thing." I answered: "Careful! You look out this night [for] the guns' keys, do not give the corporal on duty to take the keys this night." The Adjutant said: "All right." (Interrogation of Tran-Uc-Sinh, 16-2-1930, 3)

Cuneo and Sinh then went to Commander Le Tacon who, according to Reul, was completely disinterested in the country and people he was serving (Paillat 1981, 485):

> The Commander asked me to enter; it was about 19:30. The Commander finished his dessert; he sent away the boy, made me come nearer and I told him: "*Mon Commandant*, during this night, there is a very difficult thing; corporal 3351[25] makes communist, he make pirate."[26] The Commandant asked me in which company 3351 was serving. I replied: "Seventh company. Now I see there are three civilians who sleep at corporal 3351's." I had forgotten the exact number of civilians because I was panic-stricken. I continued after the Commandant had asked me to. "What they do, the civilians?" [Sinh:] "They make pirates also with corporal 3351." "Where ask [i.e. "is"] 3351" asked the Commandant. "Next to the non-commissioned officers' canteen, in the military village. At ten p.m., he has an assembly at his place to eat, so at midnight he has assembly at the end of the mountain, even many more pirates, civilians, and military." The Commander told me: "This is sure." I replied: "It is sure, *mon Commandant*" (Interrogation of Tran-Uc-Sinh, 16-2-1930, 3–4).

Shortly afterwards, at 7.40 p.m., further information about a mutiny was provided by an actively loyal soldier. An indigenous sergeant asked to see Captain Gainza and told him that a *tirailleur* with the matriculation number X had informed him that numerous meetings of *tirailleurs* and pirates had taken place in the afternoon in houses situated within the train station quarter.[27] A minimum of about ten *tirailleurs* per company had been there. The Europeans would probably be attacked during the night and the arms and ammunitions magazines would be pillaged. The sergeant seemed very nervous, so Gainza verified that he was not drunk and took him to Commander Le Tacon. On the way there, the sergeant advised him not to eat anything that evening as the food could be poisoned (Robin's Yen Bay Report, 9-3-1930, 28–30).

Ten minutes later, at 7.50, Gainza presented the sergeant to Le Tacon, clearly remarking that Sergeant X was a serious warrant officer of a balanced nature, and that it took severe circumstances for him to risk his life by coming to inform them. The Commander asked several questions, such as whether the sergeant had seen these meetings himself, and the sergeant had to answer "no" because he had received all of the information from *tirailleur* X, to whom the sergeant was related according to Gainza.[28] Le Tacon then sent the sergeant away, congratulating him for coming and assuring him that nobody would find out that he had reported the information.

The Commander then told Gainza that he had already been informed by a certain *tirailleur* (i.e. Sinh), and that the situation was less serious than the sergeant, who seemed completely panic-stricken, had indicated. Tirailleur X had said that a meeting of ringleaders would take place at ten o'clock in a cabin in the fort belonging to the seventh company. The Commander suggested that the *tirailleur* had wanted to gain some importance by informing Sergeant X, and had imagined the rest; advising that one need not attach too much importance to this kind of declaration. Captain Gainza remarked, once more, that the sergeant was a particularly calm individual and not easily impressed, but Le Tacon stuck to his point. The Commander dismissed Gainza shortly thereafter and gave him a note instructing Captain Jourdan to take measures to surprise the ringleaders (Robin's Yen Bay Report, 9-3-1930, 30).

Le Tacon's inspection tour began at eight o'clock in the evening (Robin's Yen Bay Report, 9-3-1930, 30). Two hours later, the tour uncovered the civilian and military plotters who, after an initial meeting at the corporals' house at nine o'clock, had gathered in the small wood near the barracks to hold their secret general assembly. According to Resident Massimi, "[t]he plotters dispersed instantly and very likely returned to the small wood where, even though they felt the operation exposed, they fixed the rebellion's details" (Massimi's Second Report, 16-2-1930, 10). Le Tacon saw two men fleeing from the wood, but did not pay any further attention to them, arguing later that he had not received any specific instructions from Resident Massimi. Yet, according to Wintrebert, Le Tacon's men fired "one or two gun shots and one revolver shot to disperse the band; but believing they were gamblers he retreated calmly" (Wintrebert's Report, 20-2-1930, 16). At about 11.15 p.m., Le Tacon ended the tour and he and his men went to bed without informing the Resident or taking any security measures (Robin's Yen Bay Report, 9-3-1930, 27, 30). They did not even inform the remainder of the French officers and warrant officers. Thus, Captain Gainza, who had not been on the inspection tour, later testified that he "ignore[d] the results of the tour. At this moment everything seemed calm and we decided to go to bed" (p. 30).

According to Wintrebert, Le Tacon's assessment of the situation at Yen Bay, as well as his security measures, were lacking in several respects (Wintrebert's Report, 20-2-1930, 21–22). An experienced *garde indigène* inspector would never have committed Le Tacon's mistakes, which were partly due to the latter's "insufficient knowledge of the Vietnamese mentality and of the country." An experienced individual would have taken his informants' intelligence seriously, because under normal circumstances indigenous soldiers would never dare to request an interview with their Commander during his dinner time and doing so would indicate that the information was of the utmost importance. In addition, as a basic rule, messengers' advice was always to be taken seriously. Even if one took unnecessary precautions in many cases, such vigilance was better than being taken by surprise. Le Tacon's conclusion that those he had surprised in the wood were gamblers was erroneous because ordinary gamblers would "never have played in such an isolated spot, but in the huts opposite the barracks, where the *tirailleurs* could play without risks." Finally, Le Tacon failed to inform his company commanders and the province's chief about the information he received.

The Mutiny

During this time, the final preparations for the mutiny at Yen Bay continued. Sinh reports on the final phase and the means used by the mutiny's leaders to ensure absolute obedience among the participants:

> At about half past twelve, the military and civilian groups declared that we had to hurry up as the night would be over soon and the affair risked failure. The [fifth or sixth company's] white-teethed corporal asked the civilians' leader to make a proclamation.[29] I do not remember the terms, but he said that because the country of Annam was under the yoke of the French, one had to address people of good will to destroy this yoke [and that] those who recoiled from it would be executed. The word "executed" (*chêm*) was repeated continually.
>
> It was then the white-teethed corporal's turn to make a speech to the tirailleurs. "We ask," he said in substance, "our *tirailleurs*' good will; the French have to be killed, otherwise they will kill us." He changed his machete from hand to hand while making his speech, speaking with a low voice like the civilian.
>
> The distribution of weapons began; the assembly was done in columns of two. I received a machete and three hand grenades. I was given a tall and strong man as comrade in arms, a civilian whom I would recognize. I gave the machete and one hand grenade to the civilian and kept two hand grenades—which I recognized as being made of cement[30]—and asked 3351 how to handle it. He told me to press the hand grenade's nail, to move it, and then throw it.
>
> At about one o'clock, the groups began to move in the direction of the lower barracks; 3351 and his group, which was mine, were given charge of the attack on the upper barracks. Each soldier was paired with a civilian; if one flinched, the other had the mission to kill the

> person abandoning the attack. I believed that the Commander had taken all steps to ward off the danger I had reported to him and I thought that my death was near. I also cried. But no precautions had been taken; the guard on duty did not see us, we were crawling to advance. There was complete silence and the sentry was untroubled. I did not know whether they were informed about what would happen. We arrived at the citadel door and took a small dike to enter the barracks at the place where the French warrant officers lived; six people, including me, passed via the small dike. I was volunteering for this mission, because a small passage led from there to the Commander whom I still hoped to warn. The six others [from the original group of twelve] were in the small passage, around the citadel, in order to be able to enter Adjutant Cuneo's lodgings. I had been charged by 3351 to destroy [sic!] the house of chief-sergeant Renaudet; on 3351's order, a soldier and a civilian were placed at each of the warrant officers' doors. Then 3351 left in an unknown direction. (Interrogation of Tran-Uc-Sinh, 16-2-1930, 6–7)

By then, the insurgents were waiting for the signal to begin the mutiny. At about 1.30[31] in the early hours of Monday, February 10, 1930, one of the plotters gave the general alarm for the weapons and ammunition magazines to be opened by warrant officers, so that the mutineers could gain access to the firearms. At the same time, French officers and warrant officers were attacked.

After an hour of confusion, a stalemate had developed that allowed the attackers and the attacked to make a first assessment of the situation, which remained chaotic until about 3 a.m.[32] The rebels had succeeded in gaining control of the lower barracks of the fifth and sixth companies. Some hand guns and machine guns had been secured. Of the twenty-nine French soldiers, five had been killed and four more wounded while four loyal indigenous soldiers had lost their lives. Among those killed was Lieutenant Robert, who lived in part of the Seventh Company's barracks. He managed to grab a weapon, but upon reaching the veranda he was struck down by an attacker's machete and died in the arms of his wife, who managed to pull him back into their room. A similar scenario unfolded in front of Captain Gainza's pavilion, where Gainza was seriously wounded but saved by his wife, who dragged him back into their room where no one dared enter and finish him off.

Adjutant Cuneo, who had been informed about the impending mutiny only hours before by the informer Tran Uc Sinh, was killed in his room, whereas Sergeant-Major Renaudet had his arm severed by a machete and only survived by feigning death. Adjutant Trotoux and Chief-Sergeant Deschamps were wounded and were not found until the morning. Sergeant Damour, who held the keys to his company's weapons room, was killed and the weapons were taken. Sergeant Chevalier, who held the keys to the Eighth Company's weapons room, was also killed. His assassins, however, left the keys on his body, which meant that the Eighth Company was armed by the French. Captain Jourdan appeared to be the only French officer killed in action while trying to assemble his men in the yard.[33] Sergeant Reynaud and his wife, who had taken refuge in Sergeant Huruguen's room and who defended themselves all night, were not freed until around 7.30 a.m.

While the losses inflicted on the French were severe, the mutiny had not unfolded according to plan. Most of the French officers and soldiers had not been killed and were either barricaded or had been able to rally to Commander Le Tacon. The fort, apart from the lower barracks, remained in the Commander's control. The number of modern weapons captured by the mutineers was relatively small. Thus, the Eighth Company's weapons remained secure because the insurgents, for reasons unknown, had not taken the keys from the slain Sergeant Chevalier. Most crucially, the indigenous soldiers' loyalty to the French had held. Thus, about half the indigenous troops and the Eighth Company, in particular, had rallied to the French. Four native soldiers had proved their loyalty with their lives. Moreover, according to Lieutenant Reul, the "sang-froid of an Annamite adjutant" seems to have played a crucial role in arming the Eighth Company.

As for the remainder, namely those who did not join the French immediately, it is not clear whether they were on the insurgents' side or caught in circumstances that did not allow them to take a clear position. Thus, Tran Uc Sinh testified that "[t]he Seventh Company's *tirailleurs* did not dare intervene, because they had heard the threat from [Corporal] 3351 that they would be killed in case of their intervention" (Interrogation of Tran-Uc-Sinh, 16-2-1930, 8–9). This threat, as well as the possibility that some found themselves without weapons to resist the mutineers, could explain their behavior. According to others, however, it is also possible that some soldiers observed the development of the mutiny before making a clear commitment. Thus, Resident Massimi, Le Tacon's bitter rival, writes that "between two and three a.m. it is without doubt that almost the entire battalion's stance was very precarious, and I have the feeling that it was only by little that the rebellion spread to the whole battalion" (Massimi's Second Report, 16-2-1930, 12).

The situation in the city was less tumultuous. Some revolutionaries had spread into Yen Bay's center, announcing the massacre of the whole French garrison and the beginning of a general uprising in Indochina. The town's inhabitants, however, stayed in their homes, perhaps because they had been terrorized—as Wintrebert and Robin would note in their reports—by the garrisons' troops since the Foreign Legion had left the city in 1928 (Paillat 1981, 482; Robin's Yen Bay Report, 9-3-1930, 34–35; Wintrebert's Report, 20-2-1930, 12–13).[34] More importantly, the *garde indigène* did not join the uprising because the VNQDD did not conduct propaganda among them, and also perhaps because their relations with the garrison's tirailleurs were not good. Instead, the militia gaurds protected the city's French inhabitants who were sheltered, together with Resident Massimi, in the *garde indigène*'s blockhouse. Finally, the VNQDD's fighters did not cut the telegraph wire or seize the train station and other strategic points within the city, and the communication infrastructure remained intact.[35]

Beginning at approximately 3 a.m., the attackers' situation deteriorated rapidly.[36] During the last hours before dawn, numerous *tirailleurs* of the 5th and 6th companies who had been based in the lower barracks rallied to the French. They handed over the revolutionary armbands that had been distributed to them and claimed that they had not used their guns or ammunition, which was verified by their French officers. At around 7.30 a.m., three colonial troop sections counterattacked and took back the lower barracks where the VNQDD's yellow and red flag had been hung. The revolutionaries fired two shots during this attack. One group of mutineers, among them five civilians, were arrested in an arms magazine. The remaining mutineers and revolutionaries managed to flee. Patrols were immediately sent into the town and many rebels who had hidden in houses were arrested. At 9.30 a.m., less than half a day after the outbreak of the mutiny, order was re-established at Yen Bay.

A few hours later, at about 5 a.m., a special train carrying two companies of the Ninth Colonial Infantry Regiment (Régiment d'Infanterie Coloniale) and a shipment of machine guns arrived in Yen Bay (Robin's Yen Bay Report, 9-3-1930, 11, 13). It had been set in motion by Resident Superior Robin, who had started organizing the repression in consultation with Governor-General Pasquier and General Commandant Superior Aubert and other key personnel immediately after receiving Resident Massimi's first telegram at 5.30 a.m. The two Colonial Infantry companies occupied the fort, the lower barracks, and all points of access to the city. They also reinforced the guard for the local prison, in which a large number of captured rebels were being held.

Brief Summary

By February 14, the final count at Yen Bay was as follows: five French and warrant officers killed and five wounded; four loyal *tirailleurs* killed; and, on the mutineers' side, at least four *tirailleurs* killed, thirty arrested, and four fugitives (Cabinet of the Director, Annex to Secret Note, 14-2-1930, CAOM, FM, DAM).[37] The mutiny was over rapidly for a number of reasons. It was badly organized and coordinated, and the VNQDD had only been at Yen Bay for a mere three months to gather supporters. Moreover, the party's subversive activities at Yen Bay had not included the town's *garde indigène* and population at large. Even within the garrison itself, the party was hindered by the fact that the conversion of party supporters among lower-ranking indigenous soldiers, beyond the relatively limited number belonging to the party cell, was risky and did not allow sufficient opportunity for thorough indoctrination. The fact that attempts to win supporters remained "secret" was more a failure of the local and central French intelligence systems than the party's sophisticated recruitment methods. The participants' lack of weapons and failure to get access to more also doomed their chance for success.

Neither the military nor the mutiny's civilian leaders had enough tactical knowledge to carry out a successful operation. More crucially, their military and civilian followers did not have the experience or stamina to execute the tasks given to them. In addition, the mutiny's leaders underestimated the amount and extent of propaganda and subversion it takes to overturn well-established military hierarchies, discipline, routines, and reflexes. As a result, the expected subversion of military discipline and loyalty, particularly of those not directly indoctrinated, did not materialize. This was perhaps due to the soldiers' ingrained discipline and devotion to their profession and superiors, but perhaps also due to the fact that most of them identified neither with the party's goals nor its rather crude recruitment methods. Alternatively, the soldiers simply may not have deemed the mutiny a worthy cause after having made a realistic assessment of the party's chances of success. The VNQDD's key assumption, that it would suffice to convert warrant officers to the nationalists' ideals and they would then mobilize their native subordinates and turn them against the French, had proven erroneous.

French Repression and the Capture of Top VNQDD Leaders

The garrison of Yen Bay was not the only place where VNQDD members and affiliates in the sector under the command of Nguyen Khac Nhu were actively engaged in an attempt to end French colonial rule. However, the attack on Hung Hoa, where the local *garde indigène* post had to be neutralized, failed despite the propaganda campaign the VNQDD had conducted among the post's militias (Hy Van Luong 1992, 24–26). According to VNQDD historian Hoang Van Dao (2008, 95), this failure was because the "unit there had been broken during the betrayal of... Sergeant Duong.

As a result, there was no force faithful to the Party at this post." Another group of VNQDD fighters briefly managed to take the district seat of Lam Thao but were heavily defeated by a twenty-strong *garde indigène* detachment under the command of the Deputy Resident that had arrived from Phu Tho (Robin's Yen Bay Report, 9-3-1930, 8). A gunshot to Nguyen Khac Nhu's chest severely wounded the VNQDD leader responsible for the events of Yen Bay, Hung Hoa, and Lam Thao.

Nguyen Khac Nhu's last moments are significant in that there are several accounts of his death, each of which offers a different meaning. According to the French, Nguyen Khac Nhu was taken prisoner and died the following day after "throwing up his hatred of France with ignoble swearwords" with his dying breath (Gouvernement Général de l'Indochine 1933, 18). According to Hoang Van Dao (2008, 97), Nguyen Khac Nhu preferred to kill himself rather than fall into the hands of the French, but his first suicide attempt by means of a grenade failed. His second attempt involved escaping from being bound in a hammock and jumping into a river while being transported to Hung Hoa, but he was pulled out of the river and had to face the ignominy of interrogation by the Deputy Resident of Phu Tho province, Chauvet, who asked him why he had revolted: "I am a Vietnamese citizen. I have a duty to protect my country. It is reasonable for me to achieve that noble civil responsibility. Why do you say, 'revolt'?"

After Chauvet's departure, Nguyen Khac Nhu "repeatedly hit his head on the wall of stone, finally achieving his death." These two versions are not necessarily contradictory.[38] The Sûreté's version deprives Nguyen Khac Nhu of dignity by depicting him as someone full of hatred, whereas the other version portrays the VNQDD leader as bound by a moral code of virtue that he preserves in the face of the utmost adversity (Smith 1968, 5)—a code of honor where suicide is a way of preserving face in failure and in front of the enemy (Nguyên Van Ky 1995, 338). In fact, the hatred displayed by Nguyen Khac Nhu was one of the five generic characteristics identified by Phan Boi Chau for someone to be a hero (de Tréglodé 2001, 61–62). Moreover, death in action for Chau was the ultimate gift of oneself but also eternal proof of an ideal, hence the importance he paid to the "last hours of the hero" (p. 63) in his prolific writings. It is arguably for these reasons, as we will see again later, that the party and the French colonial administration devoted considerable attention to "managing" the death of revolutionaries.

With order re-established in Nguyen Khac Nhu's revolutionary sector, it was therefore not too difficult for Robin to deduce that the party's next strike would occur in the third sector, for which Nguyen Thai Hoc was responsible. This sector comprised Haiduong, Bacninh, Thaibinh, and Kien An. Robin's precautionary measures effectively pre-empted any VNQDD strikes in the urban centers, of Kien An, Thaibinh, Haiduong, and Bac Ninh all of which had substantial military garrison. Thus, at Kien An, a VNQDD attack, in which the garrison's *tirailleurs* were to have played an important role, had been planned for February 15, but no such action materialized (General Aubert, Service note, 11-3-1930, 6). The same held true for Sept-Pagodes where a similar plot was unearthed, considerably limiting the strategic options of those militant party members still at large:

> Nguyên Thái Hoc organized an attack on Sept-Pagodes, scheduled to take place on 18 February. He counted on the support of the *tirailleurs* won over to his cause, and hoped, if the attack was successful, to procure for his troops the indispensable armaments for his revolutionary activities.
>
> But the measures taken at Sept-Pagodes by the military authorities (arrest of suspects, reinforcement of the garrison by detachments of the Foreign Legion) showed Nguyên Thái Hoc [by 15 February 1930] the impossibility of pursuing his attack plans and the revolutionaries withdrew to the *huyen* [subdistrict] of Vinh-Bao [Haiduong province]. (General Aubert, Service note, 11-3-1930, 5)

With their final chance for mutiny at Sept-Pagodes frustrated and the outcome of the insurrection decided, the two final VNQDD attacks on the administrative posts of Phu Duc and Vinh Bao focused on revenge, aiming to punish Vietnamese officials rather than drive away the French. On the evening of Friday, February 15, a group of roughly fifty insurgents "managed to capture the administrative seat of Phu Duc by surprise, wounded the mandarin's daughter, and disarmed the *linh co* [guards under the local mandarins] who were deceived by the khaki uniforms worn by the rebels" (Gouvernement Général de l'Indochine 1933, 19; Robin's Yen Bay Report, 9-3-1930, 10). The attack on Vinh Bao was also successful and had severe consequences for the local mandarin in charge of the subdistrict, Hoang Gia Mo (GG Pasquier to Minister of Colonies, Telegram, 13-3-1930, CAOM, GGI, 65517, 5). The VNQDD leaders sentenced him to death "[a]fter a simulacrum of justice" on grounds not only of corruption but also for being the grandson of Hoang Khao Khai, the last *kinh luoc* (viceroy) of Tonkin, who had played a key role for the French in the pacification of Tonkin (Gouvernement Général de l'Indochine 1933, 19; Hoang Van Dao 2008, 109–10; Paillat 1981, 494).

The VNQDD's success at Phu Duc and Vinh Bao was shortlived as *garde indigène* units took control of both places in the morning of February 16. On the same day, in response to these last-ditch nationalist efforts, Resident Superior Robin ordered a police column of 200 *garde indigène* to sweep the region and further instructed the air force to bombard Co Am village, the party's last stronghold (Robin's Yen Bay Report, 9-3-1930, 16–20). One day later, on Sunday, February 17, Robin reported that order had been restored everywhere in Tonkin, even though the police operation was still ongoing. By this time, Nguyen Thai Hoc's lieutenants, Pho Duc Chinh and Nguyen Thanh Loi, had been arrested in Sontay. Hoc's brother, Nguyen Van Nho, who had executed Pham Huy Du, had also been arrested together with other VNQDD members still at large. Finally, on February 21, Nguyen Thai Hoc himself was wounded and arrested by lookouts from Co Vit village, located between Dong Trieu and Mao Khe in Haiduong province. The following day, February 22, 1930, a mere twelve days after its start, Governor-General Pasquier officially proclaimed the insurrection to be over (Robin's Yen Bay Report, 9-3-1930, 22).

The Criminal Commission and the Guillotine

Two days after the mutiny, on February 12, Governor-General Pasquier had already set up the Criminal Commission (Commission Criminelle) of Tonkin to investigate VNQDD actions (Morlat 1990, 123). The Commission gathered twice at Yen Bay, and in three more places in Tonkin during 1930. It prosecuted 547 soldiers and civilians, delivering 80 death penalties (not all of which were carried out), 102 life terms of forced labor, 243 deportations, and many lesser terms of forced labor and detention. There were 18 acquittals, and 58 individuals could not be prosecuted due to a lack of evidence (p. 122). Moreover, in January 1931, the Criminal Commission at Kien An found 189 individuals guilty of the attacks in Haiphong in 1930. In addition to the main Criminal Commission, provincial tribunals were also involved in the repression (p. 123), and military authorities took a whole range of additional measures to punish soldiers and prevent future mutiny attempts (Rettig 2002).

The largest number of death penalties was pronounced by the first Criminal Commission, which gathered at Yen Bay to judge those involved in the mutiny and nearby insurrectionary attempts.[39] In two separate trials, the Criminal Commission pronounced 52 death penalties against 101 defendants. At the first Yen Bay trial, on February 27 and 28 1930, 13 of the 15 defendants were sentenced to death (Telegrams by GG Pasquier to Minister of Colonies, 28-2-1930 and 3-5-1930, CAOM, GGI, 65517). A second trial, on March 22–28, condemned 87, of whom 46 were servicemen (Eckert 2000, 659; 44 according to Ngo Van 1995, 144).

At the first trial, according to Hoang Van Dao (2008, 139–40), Corporal Ngo Hai Hoang revealed his motivation when interrogated by the Commission's presiding judge, Poulet Osier. For Hoang, the choice was easy. If he had betrayed the VNQDD, he would have been sentenced to death, and death would have been the worst outcome of participating in the mutiny. When asked why he shot Captain Jourdan, who "has always been nice to you," he distinguished between private sentiment and public responsibility, completely neglecting to consider his duty as a professional soldier:

"I was glad that the captain was always kind to me, but it was our private sentiment. Killing him was my duty towards my Party. The Vietnamese have long believed that public responsibility should take priority over private sentiment."

At the second trial, only three corporals did not deny active participation in the mutiny. Most forceful amongst those who readily "confessed" was one Corporal Nguyen Van Tinh, who declared that "I admit that I am simply a revolutionary who wants to save my country" (*L'Avenir du Tonkin*, 28-3-1930, CAOM, GGI, 65517). Some of those who could not deny involvement argued instead that they had been "surprised and forced to take part" (Paillat 1981, 499–500, in particular note 11). Thus, Commander Le Tacon's orderly, Ha Cap, declared that "I am not of the Viet-Nam [Quoc-Dan Dang], but if I had refused to participate, I would have been killed" (*L'Avenir du Tonkin*, 28-3-1930).[40] Many of those whom the judges considered to have participated in the mutiny and then fled after its failure argued that they had become frightened and abandoned their military duties. Tirailleur Trinh Van Tung declared that "I got afraid and, because of the gunfire and because I was caught in between two fires, I ran away."

Others claimed that they had been unjustly arrested while on their way to join or rejoin the troops. Two defendants argued that they had been unjustly denounced by fellow soldiers. The Criminal Commission was seldom impressed with such excuses. It sentenced 39 of the 87 convicted at the March trial to death, 5 to deportation, 33 to life terms of forced labor, and 10 to lesser penalties (Morlat 1990, 123). Among those sentenced to death, 24 were civilians and 15 were servicemen (Eckert 2000, 659).

Because of the high number of death penalties, the Minister of Colonies, François Piétri, intervened with Governor-General Pasquier to establish that executions could only be carried out after the case had been examined by a pardoning commission (Morlat 1990, 123). The first presidential pardon regarding the sentences handed down on February 28 was decreed on May 1, 1930 (GG Pasquier to Minister of Colonies, Telegram, 3-5-1930). It commuted nine of the death sentences into lesser penalties, but maintained four more. These were implemented on May 8, 1930, at dawn, when Medical

Corporal Nguyen Thanh Thuyet, Corporal Ngo Hai Hoang, the former Tirailleur Dang Van Tiep, and another civilian were executed (GG Pasquier to Minister of Colonies, Telegram, 8-5-1930, CAOM, GGI, 65517).

A second presidential pardon on June 10, 1930, reduced the number of death penalties handed down at the second Yen Bay trial from 39 to 13, by commuting the remainder into life terms of forced labor (GG Pasquier to RS Robin, Telegram, 16-6-1930, Saigon, CAOM, GGI, 65517). Pardons were refused to those who had killed a French officer, warrant officer, or an indigenous soldier, however, so the civilians profited proportionately more (Eckert 2000, 660–1; RS Robin to GG Pasquier [in Saigon], Telegram, Hanoi, 17-6-1930, CAOM, GGI, 65517). The presidential decision appears to have been kept secret to make sure the executions were carried out with a minimum of public disruption (Hoang Van Dao 2008, 143).

In the evening of June 16, the thirteen death row candidates were taken out of their cells at Hoa Lo prison in Hanoi and put into heavily guarded motorcars. On the way to the Hang Co train station, according to Hoang Van Dao (2008, 144), people in the street heard them cheer "'Vietnam forever' and 'VNQDĐ forever'." On the train, one of the thirteen claimed he was innocent as two others fearfully squatted in silence, but the rest encouraged each other that they would be welcomed at Yen Bay by their comrades "Hoang, Tiep, Thuyet, and Long" who had been executed there five weeks earlier (Roubaud 2010, 100–1). Someone else claimed that they were "not criminals but vanquished," while Ngoc Tinh regretted that he had not been able to finish off Sergeant Bouhier despite thirty machete blows. Meanwhile, Nguyen Thai Hoc rejected the chaplain of Hoa Lo prison, Father Dronet's attempts to get him to repent his crime by citing from a well-known poem by the author of the *Marseillaise*: "Mourir pour sa patrie, c'est le sort le plus beau . . ." [To die for one's fatherland, is the most beautiful fate . . .].

At Yen Bay, the authorities had made sure that the public would not know about the executions to prevent any unwanted "incidents." The train arrived just before midnight, and the executions began before sunrise. The guillotine, which was lit by electrical lights and established on the ground rather than on a pedestal as in revolutionary France, was quietly set up during the night

(Roubaud 2010, 98, 100). Four hundred soldiers were present to ensure that the executions went smoothly (Hoang Van Dao 2008, 145; Roubaud 2010, 98), upsetting Nguyen Thi Giang's desperate rescue plans (Hoang Van Dao 2008, 491). Separated in individual cells, the death candidates had the right to a glass of rice wine, and most wrote a last letter that Fathers Mechet and Dronet promised to deliver to their families (Roubaud 2010, 99). The two missionaries even convinced nine of the thirteen to be "baptized *in extremis*" by sprinkling "water on their foreheads" and "putting salt on their tongues" (p. 101).

Between 4.55 and 5.35 a.m., one by one the eight mutineers and five insurgents were taken from their cells and escorted to the guillotine. Once there, they were handled by the Vietnamese executioner, Cai Cong, from Hoa Lao prison, who encouraged them in their last steps by putting a hand on their shoulder and assuring them that they would feel no pain (pp. 98–99). Cai Cong would then operate the deadly mechanism while his assistant, Cai Long, also a supervisor at the same prison, would lift the severed head and pronounce the execution to be successful (Hoang Van Dao 2008, 148). According to Hoang Van Dao, all but one shouted "Viet Nam" or "Viet," depending on how fast a legionnaire could cover their mouths, then the blade came down (pp. 146–7). The second to last person to be brought to the guillotine was Pho Duc Chinh who, as stated by Hoang Van Dao, requested to be executed looking up at the blade, although it is not clear whether his last wish was granted (p. 147). Finally, it was Nguyen Thai Hoc's turn. He walked confidently to the guillotine, smiled freely, nodded to the crowd, and "shouted with a strong and sonorous voice: 'Viet Nam! . . .' before the legionnaire's hand stifled his shout" (Roubaud 2010, 102).

The thirteen heads were photographed and then placed in the thirteen coffins with the bodies (see in Hoang Van Dao 2008, 147, and Roubaud 2010, 94). They were buried in a common grave at the bottom of a hill near the Tran Quan temple, about one kilometer from the train station, and instructions were given that the military watch their last resting place "day and night until the end of 1930" (Hoang Van Dao 2008, 147). A similar fate awaited Nguyen Thi Giang, Nguyen Thai Hoc's companion. After having witnessed the executions and after she had paid Nguyen Thai Hoc's family her respects, she shot herself on June 18, 1930 (pp. 491–94). Her body was also photographed (see photo in Ngo Van 1995, 170), and despite pleas by Nguyen Thai Hoc's family she was buried "in a grave three meters deep and covered ... with a mound to prevent the exhumation of her corpse," which was furthermore guaranteed by the nearby erection of a watch-house.

The family members were thus denied the right to bury their loved ones close to home according to Vietnamese customs, although it is unlikely that a Vietnamese emperor would have acted more humanely. The main French rationale, nevertheless, was that the authorities wanted to prevent the graves from becoming a pilgrimage site akin to the one erected for the revolutionary Pham Hong Tai (1893–1924) in the outskirts of Canton (southern China). It commemorated his failed assassination attempt on Governor-General Martial Merlin on June 19, 1924, in the Victoria Hotel, during which he had killed five Frenchmen. His memory was also kept alive in all kinds of patriotic publications that were avidly read by schoolchildren and workers (see e.g. Roubaud 2010, 33–36). In fact, Phan Boi Chau had written about Pham Hong Tai's heroic feat in 1924 or 1925 (de Tréglodé 2001, 55, 59).

The civilian prosecution of *tirailleurs* alleged to have been involved in the VNQDD insurrection plan continued throughout the year, though the two Yen Bay Criminal Commissions of February and March 1930 remained the main trials. On July 15, another Criminal Commission decided that it could not sentence the seventeen soldiers referred to it by the military authorities on the grounds that the soldiers' acts were not serious enough.[41] Fifteen of them were then sentenced by the General Commandant Superior, receiving punishments ranging from demotion to forced unpaid leave. On July 18, the Military Tribunal at Hanoi dismissed, for the same reason stated by the Criminal Commission, the cases against thirteen soldiers allegedly involved in the mutiny plot at Langson. The ordinary military authorities then inflicted disciplinary sanctions on them, including demotion and dismissal, dispatch to disciplinary sections, and forced unpaid leave.

The last soldier implicated in the Yen Bay mutiny was sentenced to a life term of forced labor by the Criminal Commission in Hanoi on August 9, while sixteen other soldier-defendants received less severe sentences.[42] Finally, the Criminal Commission of November 15 sentenced six soldiers and NCOs to lifelong deportation from Indochina. By the end of the year, the Criminal Commission still had to examine the cases of twenty-four soldiers alleged to have been part of the VNQDD plot at the Kien An garrison.

Although the scale of the civilian and military investigations suggested that the identification and elimination of undesired soldiers and the monitoring of the rest was the key priority following Yen Bay, General Aubert nevertheless acknowledged the active participation of Indochinese soldiers in suppressing the mutiny. On April 5, 1930, he recommended several of them for metropolitan military honors. Though the highest honors were generally reserved for European officers, three among the four NCOs proposed for the prestigious "médaille militaire" were Vietnamese.[43] Seven more Indochinese, including a first-class militia guard, were awarded citations. Hence, Sergeant Tran Van Man was proposed for citation at the division level on the grounds that he was "A warrant officer who had always been appreciated by his chiefs throughout his fourteen years of service; during the Yen Bay rebellion, he imposed himself over his men by his energetic attitude and his active collaboration in the defense of the fort."[44] Intriguingly, the scale of Indochinese participation in putting down the revolt seems to have attracted relatively little attention, both at the time and in later literature, in addition to having made little impression on the overriding feeling that Indochinese troops had shown themselves to be unreliable.

Conclusion

The mutiny of parts of the second Battalion of the fourth Tirailleurs Tonkinois Regiment at Yen Bay and the pre-empted attempts in other garrisons and militia posts in Tonkin had shown that it was possible for nationalist organizations such as the VNQDD to exploit the ambiguous identity of the *tirailleurs*. As guardians of the French imperial nation-state, they were agents but also subjects of French imperial domination. However, the botched Yen Bay mutiny and the averted attempts elsewhere demonstrated that playing the nationalist card was no guarantee for winning over the French imperial nation-state's Vietnamese guardians. Deeply ingrained mechanisms that ensured military discipline, obedience, and even loyalty were extremely difficult to overcome. In fact, if not for a unique combination of security and intelligence shortcomings, it is likely that the mutiny at Yen Bay would have been averted at the last minute as in the other garrisons and militia posts.

The VNQDD's failure and the subsequent repression demonstrated the extent of the French monopoly of power, which included the active participation of Vietnamese soldiers. Nevertheless, it was a shock to the French psychologically. The mutiny demonstrated the continued anti-colonial resolve of Vietnamese nationalists and, even more worryingly, of some soldiers. If power consists not just of coercion but also consent, then clearly the VNQDD and its members and affiliates within the military deemed French colonial rule as illegitimate. This was a sentiment widely shared by many Vietnamese, in particular with regard to what many perceived as the excesses of French repression, even though not all agreed with the VNQDD's violent means and tactics. While the party had clearly failed to achieve its goal of overthrowing French rule and the setting up of a Vietnamese republic, from its own moral point of view Nguyen Thai Hoc, Nguyen Khac Nhu, or Corporal Ngo Hai Hoang had prevailed even in death. Had Nguyen Thai Hoc not argued in favor of insurrection on January 26, 1930, even though he knew that defeat was likely, on the grounds that "It is better to die now and leave behind the example of sacrifice and striving for later generations" (Hue-Tam Ho Tai 1992, 221–22), immediately adding that "If we fail to succeed, we will become virtuous men" (Hoang Van Dao 2008, 85)?

They did not succeed at Yen Bay, but the sacrifice of Nguyen Thai Hoc and fellow mutineers was so powerful that the Vietnamese communists, the sworn enemies of the VNQDD, considered it prudent to integrate him into the officially accepted pantheon of heroes, arguably to better control his legacy while profiting from his nationalist appeal. Hence, major cities of the Socialist Republic of Vietnam, such as the symbolically significant historical center of Hanoi, feature a Nguyen Thai Hoc Street. At Yen Bay, an impressive memorial commemorates the seventeen men who were executed on May 8 and June 17, 1930. The memorial plaque fails to mention any party affiliation and simply reads "Here rest the bodies of the fallen heroes who participated in the Yen Bay insurrection of February 1930 who were executed by the French colonialists."

While arguably being virtuous models of anti-colonialism whose ultimate sacrifice put them in a long line of heroes, the VNQDD's failed mutiny and insurrection attempt also served as a model lesson of what any revolutionary organization should avoid. Instead of entering the pantheon of patriotic heroes and becoming a role model, was it not better to survive and achieve success? The VNQDD had shown the considerable power of new means of organization that had allowed it to subvert a far greater number of garrisons than the more traditional secret society style mutinies and insurrection attempts of the 1908–18 period, but it also widely exposed the party to infiltration and counter-intelligence. In fact, the betrayal of the party's provisional military affairs minister, Sergeant Pham Thanh Duong, had led the fledgling party to accelerate rather than postpone or even abandon its insurrection plans.

Witnessing the demise of the VNQDD is likely to have confirmed to the Vietnamese communists that their strategy of reaching out to the masses by means of agitation and propaganda among workers and peasants was superior, although this did not prevent the Cochinchinese branch of the Indochinese Communist Party launching an uprising in late 1940 in the vain hope that the Vietnamese soldiers of the Saigon garrison would pull along. It was not until the Japanese *coup de force* of March 1945 against the French-Indochinese military that conditions were ripe for the communist-led Viet Minh. When Japan surrendered five months later, the Viet Minh skillfully exploited the brief window of opportunity created by a temporary vacuum of power to launch the countrywide August Revolution and declare independence on September 2, 1945, with Ho Chi Minh's proclamation of the Democratic Republic of Vietnam.

Notes

1. For an overview of "Indochinese" metropolitan service, see Marie-Eve Blanc's contribution in chapter 4 of this volume and Blanc (2003); Duong Van Giao (1926); Hill (2006); Vu-Hill (2011); and Le Van Ho (1996; 2014). The Union of French Indochina was composed of five constituent territories. Besides the protectorates of Cambodia and Laos (Luang Prabang), the three "Vietnamese" territories were the protectorates of Tonkin (North Vietnam) and Annam (Central Vietnam), and the colony of Cochinchina (South Vietnam). The French used the term "Indochinese" for any indigenous inhabitant of French Indochina, even though the French Indochinese army mainly drew on the "Annamites," the ethnic Vietnamese majority. To complicate matters further, the "Annamites" were sometimes also divided into the "Tonkinese" from Tonkin, the "Annamites" from Annam, and the "Cochinchinese" from Cochinchina. A final complication was that the Tirailleurs Annamites units came from Cochinchina rather than from Annam, while the Tirailleurs Tonkinois units in the north could also contain ethnic minority units.

2. Written Vietnamese in its romanized form, *quoc ngu*, has undergone tremendous changes over the last century or so. I will therefore write the names of people, places, and organizations without the diacritics of this tonal language, and by starting each syllable with a capital letter, with the exception of places like Hanoi or Saigon that are conventionally written together, or when directly citing from French primary sources.

3. As a general rule, indigenous troops outnumbered their European counterparts by three to two. In practice, the racial ratio and overall troop numbers varied due to changes in the global and regional arenas. In 1916, there were sixteen indigenous and six European battalions but by 1930 their number had increased to nineteen and ten, respectively. Most of these units were based in Tonkin and in Cochinchina. See Eckert 2000, 323–24, 328.

4. I borrow this useful term from Wilder (2005) because service in France during World War I, in the interwar period, and then in World War II clearly makes the Indochinese soldiers more than mere guardians of "empire."

5. There I consulted the Nouveau Fonds (NF), which contains the Fonds Ministériel (FM), which in turn contains the Direction des Affaires Militaires

(DAM). I further consulted materials from the Service de Liaison des Originaires des Territoires Français d'Outre-Mer (SLOTFOM) and from the Gouvernement Général de l'Indochine (GGI), which also has documents from the Cabinet Militaire (CM).

6. Set up in 1912 in China, after Chau's expulsion from Japan in 1908, it aimed at establishing an independent Vietnamese republic. The Restoration Society closely mirrored the Guomindang of Sun Yat Sen, whose support he sought to elicit. Duiker 2000, 273–75.

7. Chau's Dong Du (Eastern Travel Movement), begun in 1905, exhorted young Vietnamese to travel eastwards, in particular to Japan, to acquire Western military and scientific training. Luong Ngoc Quyen had graduated from the Shimbu [Gakko] Military Academy in Tokyo in 1908 and "pursued further military studies in Kwangsi and Peking" in 1909 (Zinoman 2000, 63).

8. Although the *garde indigène* is a militia guard directly under the civil authorities rather than a military force, I include it here because of similar dynamics and overlaps with the military. Hence, former soldiers would join this rural policing force, while discipline and weapons were similar to the French gendarmerie and thus differentiated it from a conventional urban police force.

9. Morlat (1990, 123) defines it as an extraordinary judicial institution of last resort. Galembert (1931, 380) calls it a "special repressive jurisdiction" unique to Tonkin. We will encounter it again later in this chapter.

10. A small number of Indochinese officers, usually from families supportive of French colonial rule, were the exception after the conclusion of the conquest and pacification phases. Trained in the metropole, they were mostly prevented from serving—and in particular from commanding—in Indochina, so as not to upset the "racialized" hierarchies in the colonial military. There were only four in 1912. See Eckert 2000, 818–89.

11. It was not until 1928 that three Indochinese medical doctors were given the rank of medical second lieutenant in order to serve in French Indochina (see Deroo and Rives 1999, 78). In mid-1929, two Tonkinese NCOs were promoted to the rank of second lieutenant (Eckert 2000, 847). By 1938, the number of Indochinese officers had risen to no more than twenty-eight (Eckert 2000, 78; Hesse d'Alzon 1985, 27).

12. Truong Buu Lam 2000, 248–50. His source is the French translation of a document entitled "Proclamation to the People," contained in a "file sent by the governor-general of Indochina to the French minister of colonies in Paris on 3 August 1927" in CAOM, SLOTFOM, Series III, Dossier 8. Evidence that the original was written by Nguyen Khac Nhu is based on a handwritten statement on the document which states that it bears Nhu's handwriting. As the VNQDD was not officially launched until late December 1927, this raises questions about the accurate date and provenance of the document.

13. This number is probably the 121 soldiers identified by the military authorities and the Criminal Commission in the summer of 1929, following the post-Bazin murder investigation and crackdown on the VNQDD.

14. Eckert (2000, 648–49) draws the same conclusions.

15. As head of the security police, the Sûreté, Marty was the unnamed author of the source cited here.

16. Military aviation was first used in April 1924 to bombard an ethnic minority village upon request of Annam's Resident Superior. In March 1929, again in Annam, several villages were aerially bombarded to repress the troubles of Kontum. See Officiers de l'Etat-Major 1930, 276, 289.

17. While these doubts about the chances of success may have been dominant among leading VNQDD members attending the meeting, lower-ranking party members such as Nguyen Dac Bang—Hy Van Luong's chief inspiration—genuinely seem to have believed in the chances of this enterprise.

18. With a population of less than five thousand inhabitants, the market town of Yen Bay was a major settlement and administrative center in the sparsely populated "middle region" of Tonkin. Located on the left bank of the Red River, Yen Bay differed from the highly populated Tonkin Delta in that most of the middle region's population was composed of ethnic minorities. See Madrolle [Travel] Guide 1930, 189–91; Naval Intelligence Divisions 1943, 220–21, 239, 437.

19. February 2, 1930 was also the date on which the more active of the two civilian *chi bos* in Xuang Lung village was informed about the projected uprising, but did not receive any indication as to which province would be its focus. Massimi's Second Report, 16-2-1930, 7.

20. According to Hoang Van Dao (2008, 91), he suffered from "serious heart disease" and "would die after receiving news that the uprising had been unsuccessful."

21. Paillat relies on an interview with Albert Reul, then a junior officer based at Yen Bay.

22. Hoang Van Dao (2008, 90) mentions there were fifteen women from the VNQDD's women's cell that Nguyen Thi Bac had created.

23. The number of 200 Phu Tho party members and sympathizers noted by Nguyen Hai Ham (cited in Hy Van Luong 1992, 235 n4) is probably exaggerated. Hoang Van Dao (2008, 90) even mentions three hundred men.

24. Sinh very likely referred to Ha Cap, 1st class *tirailleur* from the Sixth Company, who was Le Tacon's orderly and an active VNQDD member; orderlies were also referred to as "boys."

25. For reasons of superstition, *tirailleurs* were usually designated with their matriculation number rather than their full name (Bonifacy 1911, 16).

26. "Pirate" was a term used by the French, particularly during the conquest and pacification phases, to designate those who opposed colonial rule. It was a way of denying the legitimacy of Vietnamese patriotic efforts to resist foreign domination, but the use of the term was not a French invention. In fact, Bruce Lockhart (1993, 9) reminds us that "[t]he Vietnamese have a sardonic proverb to the effect that those who emerge victorious from a conflict become rulers, while the underdogs end up being labelled 'bandits' or 'pirates'."

27. Roubaud (2010, 13–14) also narrates this episode, although slightly differently, and identifies the sergeant as Sergeant Vinh.

28. Roubaud (p. 14) suggests that Sergeant Vinh's relation was his cousin, one ethnic Tai *tirailleur*.

29. At this time, many Vietnamese apparently still had their teeth lacquered black in order to protect against tooth decay. See Bonifacy 1911, 17.

30. The Sûreté's book on the VNQDD describes the various grenade models constructed by party members. See Gouvernement Général de l'Indochine 1933, 15, 22, 25. The model described in Tran Uc Sinh's account has a cement exterior. It is a very primitive and unreliable device, as many of them would not explode, and some would even injure or kill the person handling them. At least

one newspaper speculated that the bombs had been constructed by Vietnamese soldiers who had served in France during World War I, or the Vietnamese who had worked in metropolitan ammunition factories (Gouvernement Général de l'Indochine 1933, 76), but Hoang Van Dao (2008, 76) denies this connection.

31. The exact time varies in different accounts. Robin's Yen Bay Report (9-3-1930, 4) mentions 1.30 a.m.; Roubaud (2010, 15) suggests it was 1 a.m.

32. This paragraph and the two following are based on a synthesis of various sources: Eckert 2000, 652–58; Massimi's Second Report, 16-2-1930, 10–12; Paillat 1981, 489–92; and Robin's Yen Bay Report, 9-3-1930, 4–7.

33. Corporal [Cai] [Ngo Hai] Hoang had vowed to kill him and apparently shot him. See Hoang Van Dao 2008, 91, 94.

34. In contrast, Hoang Van Dao (2008, 95) claims that "People flocked to the city streets when they heard the revolutionary soldiers' cheers and they shouted their support eagerly."

35. Hy Van Luong (1992, 29–30), citing from CAOM-NF, 323-2626. Hoang Van Dao (2008, 94), instead suggests that all lines of communication were cut with the exception of the one to Lao Kay.

36. This paragraph synthesizes various sources: Eckert 2000, 652–58; Massimi's Second Report, 16-2-1930, 10–12; Paillat 1981, 489–92; and Robin's Yen Bay Report, 9-3-1930, 4–7.

37. Sergeant Trotoux, who died shortly thereafter, would be the sixth French victim.

38. A third version would be more difficult to reconcile with the above two accounts. Based on two Vietnamese sources, including Nhu's son, Nguyen Khac Dam, it claims that the French executed his father on the spot. See Goscha 1994, 41.

39. Among them was Nguyen Dac Bang. His eyewitness account of four torture sessions, of punches and kicks from his two French interlocutors, has him knocked unconscious at least once. See Hy Van Luong 1992, 98–100.

40. According to Hoang Van Dao (2008, 90–91), Ha Cap had been instructed to kill Le Tacon, but the latter had "ordered a close watch on him" with the result that the VNQDD's "communication with him has been lost for two days."

41. General Billotte's 2nd Semester Military Intelligence Service Report, 31-12-1930, CAOM, SLOTFOM, Series III, Box 22, 1–2.

42. Ibid. Of the sixteen, two corporals got ten years of forced labor and a ten-year order banning them from frequenting certain places, and two corporals and ten *tirailleurs* were to be deported. Most of these sixteen had been involved in the military party cells of Bach Mai, Tong, and Bac Ninh.

43. Photocopy of *Le Journal des Coloniaux et l'Armée Coloniale Réunis*, 8 (n.d.) [May or June 1930] kindly made available to me by Colonel (retd.) Maurice Rives.

44. Ibid. The other soldiers at Yen Bay who were not implicated in the mutiny apparently received a certificate attesting their innocence. This was made known to the aforementioned colonel when a Yen Bay veteran brandished this certificate at him in a chance encounter during the French Indochina War (1946–54) in northern Vietnam.

References

Ban Kah Choon. 2001. *Absent History: The Untold Story of Special Branch Operations in Singapore, 1915–1942*. Singapore: Raffles.

Blanc, Marie-Eve. [1994] 2003. "La pratique associative vietnamienne: tradition et modernité." PhD thesis, University of Aix-en-Provence, 1994.

Bonifacy, Auguste. 1911. *Conseils aux sous-officiers des troupes indigènes d'Indo-Chine*. Paris: Henri Charles-Lavauzelle.

Cabinet of the Director, Annex to Secret Note, 14-2-1930, CAOM, FM, DAM.

Criminal Commission Report, 9-7-1929, CAOM, GGI, 65517.

Daufès, E. 1933. *La garde indigène de l'Indochine de sa création à nos jours*. Tome Premier. Tonkin. Avignon: Imprimerie D. Seguin.

Deroo, Eric, and Maurice Rives. 1999. *Les Lính Tập: Histoire des militaires indochinois au service de la France, 1859–1960*. Paris: Lavauzelle.

Duiker, William. [1998] 2000. *Historical Dictionary of Vietnam*. 2nd edition. New York: Hyperion (originally published London: Scarecrow Press).

Duong Van Giao. 1926. *L'Indochine pendant la Guerre de 1914–1918: Contribution à l'étude de la colonization indochinoise*. Paris: Jean Budry et Cie.

Eckert, Henri. [1998] 2000. "Les militaires indochinois au service de la France, 1859–1939." PhD thesis, University of Paris IV, 1998. Reprint, Villeneuve d'Ascq: Presses universitaires du Septentrion.

Fourniau, Charles. 2002. *Vietnam: Domination coloniale et résistance nationale, 1858–1914*. Paris: Les Indes Savantes.

Frémeaux, Jacques. 2006. *Les Colonies dans la Grande Guerre: combats et épreuves des peuples d'outre-mer*. Paris: Editions 14–18.

Galembert, J. de. 1931. *Les administrations et les services publics indochinois*, 2nd edition, revised E. Erard. Hanoi: Imprimerie Mac-Dinh-Tu.

General Aubert to Minister of Colonies, 29-6-1929, CAOM, GGI, CM 209.

General Aubert, Service note, 11-3-1930. See Officiers de l'Etat-Major du Général de Division Aubert.

General Billotte's 2nd Semester Military Intelligence Service Report, 31-12-1930, CAOM, SLOTFOM, Series III, Box 22.

GG Pasquier to Minister of Colonies, Telegrams, 28-2-1930, 13-3-1930, 3-5-1930, CAOM, GGI, 65517.

GG Pasquier to RS Robin, Telegram, 16-6-1930, Saigon, CAOM, GGI, 65517.

Goscha, Christopher. 1994. "Tradition militante et rénovation culturelle au Vietnam: Réflexions sur le VNQDD, le Tu Luc Van Doan et la rupture d'un courant non-communiste, 1927–1946." DEA, University of Paris 7.

Gouvernement Général de l'Indochine, Direction des Affaires Politiques et de la Sûreté Générale. 1933. *Contribution à l'histoire des mouvements politiques de l'Indochine française*. Documents. Volume II. *Le "Viêt Nam Quôc Dân Dang" ou "Parti National Annamite" au Tonkin, 1927–1932*. Hanoi: Imprimerie d'Extrême-Orient.

Hesse d'Alzon, Claude. 1985. *La présence militaire française en Indochine, 1940–1945*. Vincennes France: Service historique de l'Armée de terre, 1985.

Hill, Kimloan. 2006. "Strangers in a Foreign Land: Vietnamese Soldiers and Workers in France during World War I." In *Việt Nam: Borderless Histories*, eds. Nhung Tuyet Tran and Anthony Reid, 256–89. Madison, WI: University of Wisconsin Press.

———. See also Vu-Hill, Kimloan.

Hoang Van Dao. [1970] 2008. *Viet Nam Quoc Dan Dang: A Contemporary History of a National Struggle, 1927–1954*, transl. Huynh Khue. Pittsburgh, PA: RoseDog Books (originally published Saigon: Hoang Van Dao).

Huynh Kim Khanh. 1982. *Vietnamese Communism, 1925–1945*. Ithaca, NY: Cornell University Press.

Hy Van Luong (with the collaboration of Nguyen Dac Bang). 1992. *Revolution in the Village: Tradition and Transformation in North Vietnam, 1925–1988*. Honolulu: University of Hawaii Press.

Interrogation of Tran-Uc-Sinh, 16-2-1930, CAOM, NF, FM, Dossier 2936.

Kessel, Ineke van. 2003. "African Mutinies in the Netherlands East Indies: A Nineteenth-Century Colonial Paradox." In *Rethinking Resistance: Revolt and Violence in African History*, eds. Jon Abbink, Mirjam de Bruijn, and Klaas van Walraven, 141–69. Leiden: Brill.

L'Avenir du Tonkin, 28-3-1930, CAOM, GGI, 65517.

Le Journal des Coloniaux et l'Armée Coloniale Réunis, 8 (n.d.) [May or June 1930].

Le Van Ho, Mireille. 1996. "L'Indochine. Un milieu porteur de modernisation: les travailleurs vietnamiens en France pendant la Première Guerre mondiale." In *Mémoires d'outre-mer: Les colonies et la Première Guerre mondiale*, eds. Marc Michel and Thomas Compère-Morel, 80–89. Péronne: Historial de Péronne.

———. 2014. *Des Vietnamiens dans la Grande Guerre: 50,000 recrues dans les usines françaises*. Paris: Vendémiaire.

Lockhart, Bruce McFarland. 1993. *The End of the Vietnamese Monarchy*. Lac Viet Series no. 15. New Haven, CT: Yale Center for International and Area Studies.

Love, Susan. 2001. "Le tây bôy: Un pidgin français du Vietnam." DEA thesis, University of Provence–Aix-Marseille I.

Madrolle [Travel] Guide. 1930. *Indochina. The Traveller's Handbook to French Indochina and Siam: Cochinchina, Annam, Yünnan, Cambodia, Tonkin, Laos*. Paris: Libraire Hachette.

Marr, David G. 1981. *Vietnamese Tradition on Trial, 1920–1945*. Berkeley, CA: University of California Press.

Massimi's Second Report, 16-2-1930.

Meixsel, Richard. 2006. "American Exceptionalism in Colonial Forces? The Philippine Scout Mutiny of 1924." In *Colonial Armies in Southeast Asia*, eds. Karl Hack and Tobias Rettig, 171–94. London: Routledge.

Ministère de la Guerre, Etat-Major de l'Armée. 1923. *Manuel élémentaire à l'usage des officiers et sous-officiers appelés à commander des indigènes coloniaux (Indochinois-Sénégalais-Malgaches) dans la Métropole*. Fascicule No. 1: Indochinois. Paris: Imprimerie Nationale.

Morlat, Patrice. 1990. *La répression coloniale au Vietnam, 1908–1940*. Paris: L'Harmattan.

———. 1995. *Les affaires politiques de l'Indochine, 1895–1923*. Les grands commis: du savoir au pouvoir. Paris: L'Harmattan.

Naval Intelligence Divisions, Geographical Handbook Series. 1943. Indo-China. Cambridge: University Press.

Ngo Ngoc Trung. 1998. "De Tham." In *Encyclopedia of the Vietnam War: A Political, Social, and Military History*, Vol. 1, ed. Spencer C. Tucker. Santa Barbara, CA: ABC-CLIO.

Ngo Van. 1995. *Viêt-nam 1920–1945: Révolution et contre-révolution sous la domination coloniale*. Paris: L'Insomniaque.

Nguyên Van Ky. 1995. *La société vietnamienne face à la modernité: Le Tonkin de la fin du XIXe siècle à la seconde guerre mondiale*. Paris: L'Harmattan.

Nguyên Thê Anh. 1992. *Monarchie et fait colonial au Việt-Nam, 1875–1925: Le crépuscule d'un ordre traditionnel*. Paris: L'Harmattan.

Officiers de l'Etat-Major du Général de Division Aubert. 1930. *Histoire militaire de l'Indochine française. Des débuts à nos jours*. 2nd edition. Hanoi-Haiphong: Imprimerie d'Extrême-Orient.

Paillat, Claude. 1981. *Dossiers secrets de la France contemporaine*. Tome 3. *La guerre à l'horizon*. Paris: Robert Laffont.

Pham Hong Tung. 2002. *Die Politisierung der Massen in Vietnam, 1925–1939*. Berlin: Logos.

Resident Wintrebert to RS Robin, Report on civilian authorities of Yen Bay, 20-2-1930.

Resident Superior Robin to GG Pasquier, Yen Bay Report, 9-3-1930, CAOM, NF, Dossier 2936.

Rettig, Tobias. 2002. "French Military Policies in the Aftermath of the Yên Bay Mutiny, 1930: Old Security Dilemmas Return to the Surface." *South East Asia Research* 10(3): 309–31.

Robin's Yen Bay Report. See Resident Superior Robin to GG Pasquier.

Roubaud, Louis. [1931] 2010. *Viêt Nam, la tragédie indochinoise, suivi d'autres écrits sur le colonialisme*. Paris: L'Harmattan (originally published Paris: Librairie Valois).

RS Robin to GG Pasquier [in Saigon], Telegram, Hanoi, 17-6-1930, CAOM, GGI, 65517.

Sampson, Cedric Allen. 1975. "Nationalism and Communism in Viet Nam, 1925–1931." PhD thesis, University of California, Los Angeles.

Smith, Ralph B. 1968. *Viet-Nam and the West*. London: Heinemann.

———. 1998. "The Foundation of the Indochinese Communist Party, 1929–30." *Modern Asian Studies* 32(4): 769–805.

Tai, Hue-Tam Ho. 1992. *Radicalism and the Origins of the Vietnamese Revolution*. Cambridge, MA: Harvard University Press.

Tréglodé, Benoît de. 2001. *Héros et révolution au Viêt-Nam*. Paris: L'Harmattan.

Truong Buu Lam. 2000. *Colonialism Experienced: Vietnamese Writings on Colonialism, 1900–1931*. Ann Arbor, MI: University of Michigan Press.

Vu-Hill, Kimloan. 2011. *Coolies into Rebels: Impact of World War I on French Indochina*. Paris: Les Indes savantes.

Wilder, Gary. 2005. *The French Imperial Nation-State: Negritude and Colonial Humanism between the Two World Wars*. Chicago: University of Chicago Press.

Wintrebert's Report. See Resident Wintrebert to RS Robin.

Zinoman, Peter. 2000. "Colonial Prisons and Anti-Colonial Resistance in French Indochina: The Thai Nguyen Rebellion, 1917.". *Modern Asian Studies* 34(1): 57–98.

CHAPTER 6

Japanese Military Policies in Southeast Asia during World War II

Joyce Lebra

A significant factor in effecting the end of Western colonial rule in Southeast Asia during World War II was Japanese military occupation and the creation and training of a far-flung series of independence and volunteer units. The impact of these Japanese-trained units could still be felt in the postwar military bureaucracies of Indonesia and Burma until the 1980s. A whole generation of nationalists were trained in a wide range of military units, from independence armies such as the Indian National Army and Burma Independence Army, through a homeland defense force on Java and Bali, to volunteer "armies" and units with policing or defense functions in Malaya, Sumatra, North Borneo, and the Philippines, and less highly structured guerrilla units and auxiliary forces that verged in some cases on forced labor. In some cases, existing policing institutions were maintained, such as the Philippine Constabulary, whereas the militia and armed forces in French Indochina were left intact only until March 1945.

Three distinct stages can be identified in Japanese motives in creating and training these armies and armed organizations. In the early phase of political warfare (1940–41), the creation of the Indian National Army (INA) and the Burma Independence Army (BIA) was achieved by sending intelligence officers to Southeast Asia to foster disaffection from Britain. An intermediary phase in Japanese motivation is represented in the formation of the Volunteer Army of Defenders of the Homeland (PETA, Sukarela Tentera Pembela Tanah Air), at least in name a homeland defense army on Java and Bali in Indonesia in 1943, but unlike the INA and the BIA without unified command structure. Japan's increasingly weak defense capability in Java and the protection of its economic resources, as well as pressure from Indonesian nationalists on Java, were crucial factors in its inception. Economic factors were predominant there, and access to essential oil sources was a factor that inhibited Japanese officers from using the rhetoric of independence. In a later and third stage, 1943–45, Japan sought to shore up its deficient regional coastal defenses in British Malaya, North Borneo, and Sumatra by the creation of volunteer *giyuugun* and *giyuutai* forces that were geared to resist the reoccupation of these parts of Southeast Asia by England and Holland. In these regions, there was no Japanese intent to foster or encourage nationalism or independence among the inhabitants or the need to create such units as part of political warfare. The territories of French Indochina and the American Philippines were not affected to the same extent by Japanese attempts to locally raise armed organizations.

Having said this about Japanese motivation, a major caveat is in order. It was more the lack of coherent policy goals towards Southeast Asia than clear policy directives that led to the creating and training of independence forces in 1941. This absence of cogent policy goals enabled a few young intelligence officers staffing *tokumu kikan* (special or intelligence agencies) to exercise a free hand in creating military units without prior reference to Tokyo.

The outbreak of war in Asia and the Pacific in December 1941 caught Japan ill-prepared in policies and strategies for dealing with Southeast Asia. There were some cogent reasons for this lack of preparedness. For one thing, the Imperial Japanese Army, which was several times more powerful politically than the Imperial Japanese Navy, was oriented towards North China and Manchukuo out of a long-held army conviction that Russia was Japan's hypothetical enemy number one. Southeast Asia in the years immediately preceding the war was a navy concern.

Once war erupted, nevertheless, some early Pan-Asianism came into play and enabled Japan to construct the ideological framework that generated a wartime propaganda appeal to Southeast Asians. The initial geographic target during the 1930s was the "core area," Japan, China, and Manchukuo, in the terminology of the East Asia Federation and East Asia Cooperative Body. By July 1940, however, Japan had proclaimed the Greater East Asia

Co-Prosperity Sphere. The Sphere was to embrace Asia through geographic ties, ethnic affinity, and cultural bonds, including Buddhism. This ideological construct took shape politically in the creation, in 1942, of the Greater East Asia Ministry, which in 1943 called Southeast Asian leaders to Tokyo for the Greater East Asia Conference. Japan's call of "Asia for the Asians" evoked some resonance among Southeast Asian nationalists, many of whom recalled Japan's startling victory in 1905 over the Western giant, Russia.

The question in Tokyo was how much of Southeast Asia should Japan occupy militarily? How far should the boundaries of the Greater East Asia Co-Prosperity Sphere extend? How should the often feeble Japanese military presence be boosted by resort to locally available human resources? There were contradictions in policy pronouncements on these issues even as Japan advanced into Southeast Asia. These contradictions and ambiguities enabled three young Japanese intelligence officers to have a free hand in their projects in propaganda warfare as they headed different *tokumu kikan*. Major Fujiwara Iwaichi, Colonel Suzuki Keiji, and Lieutenant Yanagawa Munerari were able to act apart from upper-echelon policymaking in Tokyo, at least long enough to create what became independence armies capable of fighting Western forces and the later attempted return of British and Dutch rule in Burma and Indonesia. These men were mavericks in the Japanese military bureaucracy, each committed to the goal of Southeast Asian independence and imbued with a self-image that led them to compare themselves to Lawrence of Arabia.

The roles of Fujiwara in the INA, Suzuki in the BIA, and Yanagawa in PETA were exceptional. That they were given a free hand speaks to the function of field-grade officers in the Imperial Japanese Army and Navy. When Fujiwara's and Suzuki's fostering of independence armies came to the attention of higher ranking officers in Tokyo, however, they were replaced by officers under closer surveillance from Tokyo. Yet, Tokyo could not reverse the nationalist sentiment or the military imprinting created by Japanese training in Burma or Indonesia. Moreover, these Japanese-fostered armies could be justified as part of the propaganda goal of encouraging anti-Western sentiment. Apart from Fujiwara and Suzuki, the young intelligence officers on their staffs shared the same committed zeal to encourage Southeast Asian aspirations. Many of these individuals retained nostalgic ties with their Southeast Asian trainees and revisited them after the war.

Major Fujiwara and the Indian National Army (INA)

Major Fujiwara, then a 33-year old officer, was sent to Bangkok in October 1941 with instructions to contact nationalists and independence movements. As with Colonel Suzuki a year earlier, his contact in Bangkok was a Colonel Tamura, a military attaché there, who introduced him to Indian and Burmese nationalists respectively. While Tokyo did not contemplate incorporating India into the Sphere, a November 1941 policy goal called for the "separation of Australia and India from Britain and stimulation of the Indian independence movement." This policy pronouncement and Fujiwara's instruction to contact leaders of the independence movement were the imprimatur for the steps Fujiwara devised. His lack of information about India and Southeast Asia as he embarked on his mission reflected the low level of intelligence on India in Tokyo. In Thailand, Fujiwara met overseas Indians under the leadership of Pritam Singh and the Indian Independence League and learned of their disaffection from the British Raj.

Once Japan advanced into Malaya in December 1941, Fujiwara contacted captured Indians in the British Indian Army. The key Indian officer captured in December 1941 was a Sikh, Mohan Singh, who was then either a lieutenant or a captain. Fujiwara and Mohan Singh took an instant liking to each other. Mohan Singh was convinced by the sincerity of Fujiwara's appeal to fight for independence rather than remain a prisoner of war. Together they ushered into being the INA, a revolutionary force that was British by conditioning and experience, partly Japanese in inspiration, and more Indian in character than the British Indian Army. This force numbered approximately 2,500 before the capture of Singapore.

With the surrender of Singapore in mid-February 1942 and capture of an estimated 45,000 Indian troops being used to defend the British bastion, Fujiwara and Mohan Singh addressed the men, exhorting them to fight for independence rather than be prisoners of war. About half the number rallied to this call, some of them abandoning long traditions of loyalty to the British Raj.

One problem Fujiwara faced was a schism in Tokyo due to the presence there of a radical Bengali nationalist, Rash Behari Bose who, because of his Japanese wife and a son in the Japanese army, did not have the right nationalist credentials to be accepted by Southeast Asian Indians. This split was not resolved until the arrival in Singapore of another Bengali nationalist, Subhas Chandra Bose. Bose had escaped British house arrest in Calcutta and made his way via Afghanistan to Nazi Germany. Both Fujiwara and Mohan Singh urged Tokyo to bring Bose from Germany to Southeast Asia and this was achieved in the summer of 1943.

When Bose arrived, both Fujiwara and Mohan Singh were no longer in charge of the INA. Fujiwara had been replaced by the politically powerful and higher ranking Colonel Iwakuro Hideo. Iwakuro and his enlarged staff of some 250 members operated from a Tokyo attitude of limited and grudging support of the INA and Indian independence. Mohan Singh pushed Iwakuro with specific demands and was finally placed under house arrest for the duration of the war, putting the INA into limbo without leadership until the arrival of Subhas Chandra Bose in mid-1943. Iwakuro, in turn, was replaced in 1944 by the still higher ranking Lieutenant General Isoda.

When Bose arrived in Southeast Asia, he created the Free Indian Provisional Government and became its head. Although he had never been a military man, he assumed command of the INA and created a women's regiment whose members initially were Singaporean, later Malayan, Indians. The Rani of Jhansi Regiment was named after the legendary heroine of the Sepoy Rebellion. This and the unprecedented participation of women in the INA helped create a national character and revolutionary image for the INA. Bose's arrival gave impetus for a campaign into India. Bose insisted that the INA fight in units of regimental size commanded by Indians. The reason Japan agreed to fight jointly with the INA was Japanese respect for British military discipline and a long tradition in the Japanese army and navy of British inspiration. Bose's leadership and charisma was another factor that overcame Japanese army reluctance to fight joint campaigns with Asian forces. However, the campaign was badly timed for Japan and the INA: without supplies or air cover, it turned into a fiasco.

The Imphal campaign, which was to last for five months until July 1944, was the only major campaign fought jointly by Japan and a Japanese-fostered army. This contrasted with Japanese dealings with the BIA, the predominantly Javanese PETA, and volunteer forces elsewhere in Southeast Asia.

Colonel Suzuki and the Burma Independence Army (BIA)

The BIA originated in a somewhat different set of circumstances from the INA. Burma attracted the attention of Japanese individuals and the navy because of natural resources, in particular rubber and teak. A former navy man, Captain (retd.) Kokubu Shouzou had spent nineteen years in Burma and was involved with the independence movement there. He plied his former navy classmates with information about Burma and, in 1944, published a two-volume study of Burma during the war. A Burma lobby of sorts consisted of research groups that focused on this British colony, a lobby that had no counterpart for India or Indonesia. In September 1940, the National Policy Research Institute recommended that Burma be included in the Greater East Asia Co-Prosperity Sphere and also that Burma be liberated. A War Ministry review of 1941 also viewed Burma as within the Sphere and essential to Japan because the "Burma Road" was the wartime supply route to the Chungking government of Nationalist China.

Despite these goals and policy recommendations, however, Japan had no coherent Burma policy. A number of disjunctions and disagreements over Burma policy laterally divided the Southern Theatre Headquarters and the 15th Army Staff Headquarters, but divisions also ran vertically between levels in the command structures. Two contradictory goals were advanced, often simultaneously: promoting Burmese independence but almost simultaneously avoiding stimulating Burmese independence.

Initiative in creating the BIA came from two men, Colonel Suzuki Keiji (b. 1897) from the Army General Staff Headquarters, and Kokubu Shouzou with his navy connections. Suzuki had been given orders in February 1940 to contact the Burmese nationalist movement and to disrupt the route supplying Chiang K'ai-shek in Chungking. The swashbuckling Suzuki took the name Bo Mogyo (Thunderclap) to identify himself with a folk belief that lightning would one day shatter the umbrella rod, that is, British rule, and liberate Burma. A rumor also spread that Suzuki was descended from a prince who had fled to Thailand. Even if it meant taking up arms against the Japanese, Suzuki's advice to nationalist U Nu was "Independence is not the kind of thing you can get by begging for it from other people. You should proclaim it yourselves."[1]

Suzuki got his orders from the Tokyo Imperial General Headquarters in February 1940 and did research on Burma in Japan and in China for three months. He also secured a front as a Yomiuri correspondent. In late May 1940, he flew to Bangkok, and from there to Rangoon, where he would stay until January 1941. In both places, he met other Japanese long resident in Burma as well as Burmese nationalists, as he realized that the best means to accomplishing his mission was to win over the latter to disrupt Chinese nationalist supply routes. In particular, he contacted young students in the anti-British Thakin (Masters) Party and arranged the passage of Aung San and Hla Myaing, who had escaped to Amoy and Tokyo, respectively. Suzuki avoided the party faction supported by Kokubu, partly for security reasons but largely because the two men did not get along. The latter, for instance, was convinced that Aung San was a communist.

In 1940, some young Burmese were in jail, others had gone underground. Suzuki's arrival precipitated a debate about whether to accept Japanese aid or whether to look for Chinese or Russian help. One argument in winning them over was to give them military training.

The Minami Kikan (Southern Agency), an intelligence agency that would operate in Burma, was created in February 1941 as a joint army-navy venture. Aung San and Hla Myaing were smuggled back into Burma where they collected Thakin Party members who were to be given training and arms abroad before being smuggled back into Burma. The "thirty comrades" were sent first to Tokyo, then to the Naval Training Center on Hainan Island, with the main aim still to train them to cut the Burma route supplying Chungking and, as an ancillary aim, to aid Burmese independence. Actual training began in May 1941 under the direction of Captain Kawashima Takenobu, a graduate of the Military Academy and intelligence school, the Nakano Gakkou. This was the first exposure of the thirty to military discipline, rigors they endured out of their strong political convictions. The trainees were divided into three groups, given training respectively in command of soldiers, guerrilla tactics, and espionage, and as leaders of the independence movement.

Within the Minami Kikan, friction between Suzuki and the former navy man Kokubu led the navy to withdraw in August 1941, leaving the army officers in control. Suzuki envisioned not only training the thirty as the nucleus of the BIA but also establishing a political authority at Tenasserim and driving the British from Burma. In July 1941, by which date the thirty were to be infiltrated into Burma, they were still on Hainan. In October, the thirty were given marching orders to a camp in Taiwan rather than Burma. In December 1941, the BIA formally came into being. It numbered about two hundred men, most of whom had been recruited among Burmese nationalist émigrés in Bangkok. On December 31, 1941, these troops, commanded by Suzuki and led by the trained thirty, crossed over into Burma. The following April, after Japan had secured control of Rangoon on April 7, 1942, Suzuki created the Baho Government in Rangoon under Thakin leadership.

Disagreements between Suzuki, on the one hand, and the 15th Army and Southern Theater Army, on the other, arose as the BIA reached a strength of 200 thousand. As occurred later in Indonesia, recruits did not belong to those ethnic groups that had been disproportionately present in the British colonial armed forces because the Japanese were unsure about the loyalty of such ethnic minority groups. Most recruits belonged to the Burmese ethnic majority population, and the rapid growth of the BIA was in no small part due to this, as well as their nationalist sentiment and the local tradition of dacoity (banditry). However, the rapidly developing troop numbers were more than the Japanese and the BIA command could handle organizationally.

Fujiwara, the initiator of the INA and by this time staff officer of the Southern Army Headquarters, suggested that Suzuki reduce and restrain the BIA, but this only angered the latter. The 15th Army conceived the BIA's role to be harassing the enemy to the rear as part of an intelligence operation. This did not sit well with Suzuki, who was also dissatisfied that independence was not granted. Thus, the Baho Government was dissolved in May 1942 and the Japanese army turned to Ba Maw, who had been jailed by the British for political activities. His leadership as the chairman of the Preparatory Committee on Administrative Control, as well as his nominal leadership as the supreme commander of the BNA at this point relied more on Japanese sanction than on popularity among Thakin nationalists, who felt underrepresented in the Ba Maw Administrative Council.

Finally, on July 10, 1942, the Southern Theater and 15th Armies dissolved the Minami Kikan and sent Suzuki back to Japan. By this time, the Japanese occupation of Burma and the imposition of military government had in any case rendered the Minami Kikan obsolete as a liaison agency. On July 27, the BIA was dissolved to build a more tightly organized army, the Burma Defence Army (BDA), which came into being on July 27, with Aung San as commander. A nucleus of 2,800 men for this more disciplined force was selected by examination from between seven thousand to eight thousand candidates. Three battalions were formed under Ne Win, Yan Naing, and Zc Ya, all from thc original thirty. Four more battalions were added later. In addition to this, a staff training school was established in September 1942 at Mingaladon in the suburbs of Rangoon. Instruction at the Mingaladon academy was carried out in Japanese. The first class graduated in March 1943. Thirty of these were sent to Japan for further study, followed by a second group and another ten to the Air Force Staff School in Japan. All liaison with the BDA was carried on through the Southern Theater Army. By April 1943 there were 55,000 new recruits in the BDA. A military prep school was created at the same time to foster a martial spirit and give preliminary training to boys aged fourteen to sixteen from whom BDA candidates could be recruited later. A class of airforce pilots were also trained in wartime Burma.

In September 1943, following the Burmese "independence" ceremony on September 15 (independence had been granted on August 1), Commander-in-Chief Ne Win announced a change in name from Burma Defence Army to Burma National Army (BNA, Bama Tatmadaw). General Kawabe of the new Burma Area Army staff had no plan to use the BNA in combat until 1945, by which time it was too late. The BNA was used only in garrison duty, a factor that led to frustration and ultimately to revolt.

Ba Maw wrote General Kawabe, "I am convinced that the Japanese policy of creating an armed force in, for them, a totally new country and keeping it idle and exposed to all kinds of political contacts and frustrations was one of the worst blunders the Japanese committed in Burma."[2] Japanese procrastination in dealing with the BNA as a genuine combat unit, plus some training practices that offended Burmese soldiers, such as slapping, also contributed to the revolt by BNA men against their Japanese officers in February 1945.

Lieutenant Yanagawa and the Volunteer Army of Defenders of the Homeland (PETA)

Although the Japanese had wrested power from the Dutch in the East Indies in early March 1942, a Japanese-sponsored military unit was created in Indonesia later than the INA and BIA, a reflection of the difference in Japanese motives. Japan was primarily concerned about the inadequacy of its ten thousand strong troop presence in Java, which, in 1943, was a logistical and supply base for all of Southeast Asia. The division of the Dutch East Indies into territories administered by the navy and various Japanese armies, divergences between and within the navy and the army, but also in Tokyo ministries, made a unified Japanese stance with regards to local independence aspirations extremely difficult to arrive at. A January 1943 announcement of "independence" for Burma and the Philippines gave further fuel to local aspirations.

It was rather at the local level, in Java, that Japan provided the greatest positive stimulus to the nationalist goal of independence. This incentive was provided through the organization and training of a volunteer army, the Sukarela Tentera Pembela Tanah Air, or Volunteer Army of Defenders of the Homeland, abbreviated as PETA, on October 3, 1943. The creation of this army was the work of an intelligence agency, the Samboubu Tokubetsu-han, or Beppan for short. Like the *tokumu kikan*, it was staffed with graduates of the Nakano Gakkou, but a different name was chosen in Java.

One of the Beppan officers, Lieutenant (later Captain) Yanagawa, collected six young Indonesians in Bandung in early 1942 and taught them judo, sumo, kendo, and some Japanese language. This was an early predecessor to PETA prior to the call for volunteers from Java and Bali that went out in the press in 1943. Yanagawa met with Indonesian National Party (PNI) leader Gatot Mangkupradja and asked him to put a proposal in writing. Gatot pricked his finger and wrote in blood. Yanagawa was aware that Beppan could not use the rhetoric of independence, and further wished to create the impression that the initiative for PETA was Indonesian, not Japanese. He decided to promote Islam as the spiritual basis for a volunteer army.

Volunteers with a strong national consciousness were selected through interviews by Japanese recruiting officers. It was Japanese policy to avoid candidates who had been trained by the Dutch in the Royal Netherlands East-Indies Army (KNIL, Koninklijk Nederlands-Indisch Leger) or who had had Dutch-style education. Traditional recruiting grounds for the KNIL were also avoided, measures designed to assure anti-Dutch sentiment.

Yanagawa taught sumo, military science, intelligence, espionage, and Japanese language in the training center at Tanggerang. When that center closed, some star pupils were transferred to Bogor for officer training in late 1943. Seventy were trained as battalion commanders, 200 as company commanders, and 620 as platoon commanders. One battalion commander, Kasman Singodimedjo, a law professor and later attorney general, had been jailed by the Dutch. All those trained recalled the emphasis on discipline and spirit in the Japanese training.

Despite Japanese policy not to recruit former Dutch trainees, a few such men were recruited. One of these, General Djatikusumo, was well placed to compare Dutch and Japanese training. "The Dutch were better in theory, but the Japanese were more practical. We didn't learn from the Dutch how to make an army. What we learned from the Japanese was more important: how to create an army from scratch and lead it. We learned how to fight at company level, how to recruit soldiers, and how to devote yourself to your country," he said in an interview.[3]

Unlike in the "independence armies," the INA or BIA, there was no direct communication between battalions, and there is some disagreement about whether the Japanese actually intended to train a general staff or were afraid to do so. Three battalions were trained on Bali by a group that included Zulkifli Lubis and Kemal Idris. After the war, Lubis served as deputy chief of staff and was a leader of the Outer Islands Revolt in 1956, for which Sukarno imprisoned him; Lubis was later to serve as Suharto's head of military intelligence.

By August 1944, PETA on Java was 33 thousand men strong, with another 1,500 on Bali. In late 1944 and early 1945, the 16th Army took emergency measures to train more military and paramilitary units as a precaution against the anticipated invasion by Allied forces. A plan was drafted for guerrilla units to defend Java. Specialized guerrilla techniques, such as infiltration, liaison, communications, and disguise, were included, and no uniforms were worn by trainees. Boys and young men between the ages of sixteen and twenty-five were selected through recommendations of Muslim schools and teachers. Wooden and bamboo spears and guns were used in training. Instruction was given in making Molotov cocktails, explosives, and bombs. These units were called Hizbullah (Muslim Youth Corps) and grew to a strength of 50 thousand by the end of the war. Guerrilla training was not a feature of Dutch training and was acknowledged by trainees as a significant Japanese legacy.

Giyuugun and Giyuutai Volunteer Forces

Throughout Southeast Asia, Japanese motives in training *giyuugun* volunteer forces were strictly military, without reference to local nationalist aspirations, whereas *giyuutai* were for preservation of peace and order. *Giyuugun* units were recruited in Malaya, Sumatra, Indochina, Borneo, and the Philippines as Japan's military situation deteriorated, in order to supplement Japan's deficient troop strength for coastal defense.

In Malaya, though some journalists expressed nationalist sentiment, the communal divisions among the multiethnic population made a united nationalist movement against the British impossible. Japan planned no recognition of Malayan independence until the near end of the war, in July 1945. Only one Malay graduated from the Shihan Gakkou, the Military Academy in Japan, by contrast with seventeen Indonesians, sixty Burmese, thirty-five Indians, and fifty-three Filipinos.

In Malaya and Sumatra, which together were administered by the 25th Army, plans for creating *giyuugun* were conceived by September 1943, pursuant to a year-old order from Tokyo Imperial General Headquarters. Both types of volunteer corps, *giyuugun* and *giyuutai*, were organized in Malaya. *Giyuutai* were for defense of the coastline and preservation of public peace and order. Units were organized at the city, town, and village level, with no central training camp. Training was sporadic, often only once a week, with small arms captured from British forces. Japanese officers traveled from village to town to city to conduct training. In effect, the *giyuutai* functioned as super-police units. No Indians or Chinese were recruited in these units. One recruit described making long marches followed by running, followed by jumping into a cold pool, something also described by PETA trainees. These recruits were given lectures on *seishin* (spirit) and taught to sing the Japanese national anthem. A few recruits were sent to Singapore for military intelligence and espionage training. By March 1944, the *giyuutai* numbered about five thousand members.

The Malay *giyuugun*, by contrast, was created in early 1944 following a January 1944 call in the local press. They were to assist in the defense of all Malaya and were trained as a single unit of two thousand at Johore Bahru, and provided with food and uniforms. *Giyuugun* forces, which were more disciplined than the decentralized *giyuutai*, did see combat with the Japanese army in the last defense of Singapore. Compared with the number of troops and auxiliary forces raised in Burma and Java, however, numbers raised in Malaya were small. This was partly due to the fact that neither the Chinese half of the population, nor the Indian sector could be drawn on. Furthermore, the recruitment of about 100 thousand young men for the Thai-Burma Railway had depleted the pool of men such defense forces could have relied on.

The number of Japanese-led defense forces on Indonesian Sumatra, combined with Malaya, under the jurisdiction of the 25th Army, was also comparatively small. The rationale for this territorial arrangement was that the Japanese army avoided treating Indonesia as a single political unit. The threat of invasion from the West through the Malacca Straits also provided a serious geopolitical rationale for this strategy.

Several *tokumu kikan* (special agencies) operated throughout Sumatra. Aceh state was treated separately, having fought its own war of independence from Holland from 1875 to 1908. Part of Major Fujiwara's 1941 mission there was to encourage pro-Japanese, anti-Dutch sentiment. A few Acehnese cooperated with Fujiwara and the "F" Kikan in beaming broadcasts from Malaya to other parts of Sumatra. A plan was concocted to infiltrate Sumatra to protect oilfields and refineries from Dutch sabotage. The Palembang Kikan, for instance, trained a hundred Sumatrans to protect that region's rich oilfield. A few Acehnese wearing the "F" insignia of Fujiwara's Kikan did infiltrate from Selangor and carried out espionage against the Dutch.

Giyuugun raised in Sumatra included some ex-KNIL officers and men, educated in Dutch and English, and therefore useful as interpreters. Several officer training centers were established and a force of between five thousand and six thousand was trained. Candidates selected were sons of Muslim teachers and leaders. The curriculum included military drill, judo, kendo, Japanese language, and *seishin* lectures. After three months, officers became platoon commanders. *Giyuugun* units were attached directly to units of the Japanese 25th Army. In Aceh state, trained officers were dispersed with Japanese officers to sixteen locales to train recruits. Training continued until the end of the war.

Late in 1944, a small guerrilla unit of Japanese disguised as Sumatrans was created. These men helped fishermen and farmers while they collected intelligence. A few actual Sumatrans were trained in intelligence and reconnaissance. A few Japanese individuals were dispatched from the Nakano Gakkou in Japan on specific intelligence missions. Some of these men organized small groups on the spot and trained small numbers of Sumatrans.

Giyuugun were not called on to fight until the Indonesian war of independence. At the end of the war, violence erupted in Sumatra against the Japanese, the returning Dutch, and between groups of Sumatrans, for example in Aceh against an aristocratic class through whom the Dutch had ruled Aceh. Although there were numerous clashes between Sumatrans and Japanese, there were also Japanese soldiers who fought in the war of independence on the Sumatran side. Some of these men remained in Sumatra after the war.

In north Borneo in 1944, a small *giyuugun* of 1,300 men was recruited from the Dayak ethnic group. One battalion of about five hundred men was stationed at Kuching. Four other areas—Miri, Jesselton, Sandakan, and Sebau—each had one company of from 150 to 200 men. Placed under the Japanese Garrison Army, the duty of this *giyuugun* included the preservation of public peace and some defense and guard duty.

The pattern for Japanese-raised armed organizations in French Indochina and in the American Philippines differed considerably from the rest of Southeast Asia. In Indochina, Japanese and French-Indochinese forces coexisted uneasily as a result of the 1940 defense treaty of Japan with the Vichy French regime. This did not allow for the raising of volunteer forces such as the *giyuugun* or *giyuutai*, let alone an independence army, as this would have violated the agreed terms of the treaty. It was feared that Governor General Decoux's regime and Free French forces would eventually side with the advancing Allied troops. The Normandy landing of June 1944 had put an end to the French metropolitan Vichy government, and the Southern Army Headquarters moved from Manila to Saigon in November 1944. An intelligence unit was created in January 1945.

The Yasu Butai (Annam Unit), headquartered in Saigon with branches in Hanoi, Hue, Haiphong, and Phnom Penh, was to collect intelligence on French forces there and to contact underground groups dedicated to

Vietnamese independence. Young Vietnamese nationalists were used to gather intelligence but did not receive any military training. Intelligence also involved participation in the Japanese military coup planned for March 9, 1945. Japanese forces on that date moved to take over all government offices and garrison camps, interning the French and confirming Emperor Bao Dai. In the imperial city of Hue in central Vietnam, Yasu Butai men dressed as Vietnamese were to ensure the emperor's safety and to confirm his sovereign rights. The Japanese coup de force was so successful that on March 10 the Japanese ambassador in Saigon declared Vietnam independent.

The Yasu Butai, headquartered now on the Annam-Laos border, carried on guerrilla warfare against the French but also against Britain's Force 136. It was not until after the coup that Japan could envisage creating a small *giyuutai* for public peace and self-defense. The plan called for organizing five units of one thousand men each in Tonkin, Annam, Cochinchina, Laos, and Cambodia. A call for volunteers went out in May 1945. Training began in Tonkin, Annam, and Cochinchina in July, but was not completed when hostilities ended in August. Training had not even begun in Cambodia and Laos. The implications of this were that there were no Vietnamese-controlled combat forces in French Indochina other than those under Ho Chi Minh.

The Philippines had been promised independence from American rule before the war, scheduled for 1946. Military occupation presented the Japanese with a critical problem in popular resistance, in part through underground guerrilla activities. At the end of 1942, all political parties were abolished and a supraparty, the Kalibapi (Kapisanan Sa Paglilingkod Sa Bagong Pilipinas, Association for Service in the Philippines), created in their place. In May 1943, furthermore, the Japanese organized Saipilnip, a constabulary based on former residence in Japan. Unlike the Japanese-occupied former British and Dutch colonies in Southeast Asia, where the Japanese were reluctant to rely on former colonial forces and native personnel, the Philippine constabulary forces were maintained and even remained under the same leadership. This was an attempt to maintain control over a popular resistance against the Japanese that was carried out through underground activities.

In November 1943, one month after independence had been granted, the Japanese pressed José Laurel II, secretary-general of Saipilnip, to increase the size of the constabulary to 40 thousand and to establish regional training schools. Former officers of the Philippine army were given automatic commissions. A basic problem was Japanese reluctance to arm the constabulary out of fear that the arms would end up in guerrilla hands. The constabulary in prewar days was a unit organized in 1901 for police purposes. They had been underpaid and had to supplement their salaries through graft. Wartime allegiances shifted mercurially through the constabulary and the guerrillas. One problem for the Japanese was that the US had already promised the Philippines independence for 1946.

Japan did not intend to create an army and navy after granting the Philippines independence in October 1943, but rather strengthen the police power to maintain public peace. After US Army Chief of Staff General Douglas MacArthur landed on Leyte on November 19, 1944 and because the Japanese distrusted the constabulary, on December 8, 1944 they accordingly created the Makapili (Kalipunang Makabayan ng mag Pilipino, Patriotic League of Filipinos). It was an armed political organization under General Artemio Ricarte, father of José Laurel II and president of Saipilnip, though neither of them was enthusiastic about this organization. Commander-in-Chief General Yamashita of the 14th Army overcame the opposition of other Japanese to the formation of this league. The Japanese deemed this organization pro-Japanese and armed it when arms could be spared. The hope was to recruit twenty thousand men, but in the end only between three thousand and five thousand were collected, primarily in two Luzon and southern Tagalog provinces. By this time, Japan could not spare officers and weapons to train the Makapili, and members functioned therefore as jungle guides and trench diggers, in other words more as *heiho* (auxiliary forces) and in some cases almost as forced labor (*romusha*), rather than as a genuine *giyuugun*.

In addition to the Makapili, after October 1944 Ricarte organized a more genuine *giyuugun*, the Houan Giyuugun (security force). It was more independent of Japanese control and more loyal to Ricarte, but its membership did not exceed more than two hundred to three hundred soldiers.

Most Filipinos regarded the Makapili—the term had been used during Spanish rule to designate the guards of the governor-general who were of Mexican Indian extraction—as traitors. Makapili members were tried for treason after the war, whereas the wartime constabulary and even the Houan Giyuugun were not tried. Generally, it was men who fought and led anti-Japanese guerrilla units rather than Makapili men who rose to postwar leadership, men such as Ferdinand Marcos and Ramon Magsaysay.

Revolt of the Independence Armies and Defense Forces

By 1944, following over three years of military occupation, many Southeast Asian nationalists harbored doubts about Japan's role as liberator. Japan as an occupying power began to take on some of the repressive features of Western colonial powers. Throughout Southeast Asia, incidents of violence against Japanese forces erupted. As the war situation deteriorated for Japan, Japanese forces became increasingly dependent on local supplies and this exacerbated shortages of rice and other necessities.

Another grievance against the occupying power was the mobilization of forced labor, the *romusha*. These so-called volunteers, who included women, were used in Java, Thailand, Burma, and Malaya, some to work on the dreaded Thai-Burma ("death") railway. Between 140 thousand to 300 thousand *romusha* are estimated to have been sent abroad. Forced labor had a disastrous impact on village life, depriving the economy of the most vigorous age group.

The first significant revolt erupted in the PETA battalion in Blitar, east Java, whose members were appalled that the *romusha* and populace generally were suffering from malnutrition and disease. Another grievance was that PETA battalion commanders had to salute the lowest Japanese non-commissioned officers. Slapping of officers and men, a normal form of discipline in the Japanese army, was furthermore offensive to Muslims. Blitar, in addition, was home to nationalist leaders, including Sukarno, and east Java was moreover the stronghold of the Indonesian Communist Party (PKI).

In Blitar, some PETA officers worked with *romusha* in the second half of 1944. Junior ranking PETA officers began secret meetings in September 1944 to prepare to revolt. In early February 1945, one of their leaders, a PETA officer named Suprijadi, urged immediate action because the Kempeitai military police were aware of the plan, but his ideas initially met with objection. Revolt ignited on February 14 with the firing of mortars at the hotel where Japanese officers were billeted. Kempeitai headquarters were hit with machine gunfire but the buildings had already been evacuated, indicating Japanese foreknowledge. A total of 360 officers and men participated in the revolt, which killed some twenty-five Japanese officers.

Because there was no communication between PETA battalions, the Japanese were able to restrict and suppress the revolt by a combination of conciliation and force. Despite Japanese promises that responsibility for the revolt would not be questioned, seventy-eight officers and men were sent to Jakarta to be court-martialled, but Suprijadi managed to escape and disappeared. Although he never reappeared, this "phantom general" was first named public peace minister and supreme commander of the National Army of the Republic after the war. By special presidential order, participants in this revolt came to be regarded as "fathers of independence." Despite the lack of inter-battalion communication, the revolutionary energy of Blitar was transferred to the battalion at Rengasdengklok, where soldiers, in combination with youth groups (*pemuda*) and the support of leading nationalists, kidnapped the nationalist leaders Sukarno and Hatta and demanded that they proclaim independence on the night of August 16, 1945. They also arrested all Japanese officers in the area.

In spite of these local incidents, PETA was successfully disbanded though there were some skirmishes by the Japanese. Most of its weapons, in fact, were in Japanese hands at the cessation of hostilities because Indonesian PETA officers did not believe the news of Japanese surrender. PETA would, nevertheless, feed into the Badan Keamanan Rakjat (BKR, or People's

Security Agency), and then into the Tentara Keamanan Rakjat (TKR, or People's Security Army), which was the regular army until June 1947.

In Burma, revolt was far more widespread owing certainly to unified command structures and the earlier organization of the Burma National Army (BNA), infecting the whole of the BNA. Deterioration of material conditions, requisitioning of labor and materials, epidemics and air raids all contributed to the malaise of the populace generally. As in Indonesia, furthermore, the Japanese disciplinary form of slapping as well as the often arrogant, insulting behavior of Japanese soldiers had created an unhealthy psychological climate. Among the Thakins and BNA, dissatisfaction with Ba Maw's leadership and his cooperation with the Japanese were contributing factors. The discrepancy between Japan's announcement of independence and the reality was obvious to nationalists. "Our independence exists only on paper," said Aung San.[4]

Some officers saw the reorganization of the then Burma Independence Army (BIA) as the Burma Defence Army (BDA) in mid-1942 as a Japanese attempt to exert more direct control over Burmese officers. But since the BDA was under unified command, this gave Burmese officers an advantage those in PETA did not enjoy. As early as October 1942, nineteen of the younger officers held secret meetings and distributed anti-Japanese leaflets. Kempeitai intelligence reports mentioned preparations for revolt at least by 1943, but the Burma Area Army command did not deem them serious enough. The anti-Japanese mood heightened as a result of the disastrous Imphal campaign in early 1944, partly because the Japanese army virtually ignored the BNA throughout. Ne Win and Aung San seldom agreed on anything and they disagreed over the timing of revolt and whether to revolt against Japan and Britain simultaneously. Aung San objected to some army officers' plans for revolt scheduled for June 22 and then July 22, 1944. With the formation, in September 1944, of the Anti-Fascist Peoples' Freedom League (AFPFL), which also included ethnic minority groups, plans for revolt became more widespread and open but still had to be postponed. By early 1945, the British-sponsored Force 136 was contacting AFPFL guerrillas and distributing weapons to them and to Karen units, but giving four times as many to Karen units as British military intelligence was suspicious regarding the reliability of the BNA.

Japanese countermeasures in 1945, including a proposed expansion in the size of the BNA, came too late to alleviate tension or avert revolt. British forces were pushing beyond Singapore across the Irrawaddy into Burma. Japanese commanders tried to sabotage Burmese cooperation by declaring that the revolt was directed at the unpopular Ba Maw rather than the Japanese. General Sakurai also made a last-ditch proposal to restore the Burmese monarchy.

Between late March and May 1945, BNA members killed several Japanese officers. The earliest sign of disaffection was when the BNA commander at Mandalay, Bo Ba Htut, declared war against the Japanese and joined the invading Allied forces. Although quarrels and incidents between Japanese and Burmans were now erupting everywhere, the Japanese regarded them as isolated incidents. In May, Aung San met with General Slim, commander of the 14th Army in Burma in World War II, who recognized the BNA as the Patriotic Burmese Forces (PBF). Aung San objected to the return of Governor General Dorman-Smith to Burma and wrote Mountbatten, admiral of the British fleet, that he could not agree to the resumption of British rule. Mountbatten then disbanded the BNA and announced the creation of a Burma army. Aung San refused to take a leading role in it and instead founded the People's Volunteer Organisation, describing it to the British as a home guard rather than an army, with officers and men from the BNA.

The BNA and PETA revolts against the Japanese officers who had trained them demonstrated the metamorphosis of these armies into genuine independence armies able and eager to fight for freedom from colonial rule by any nation. Japanese training and organization of these armies hence did not translate into Japanese control over their armed creations. From a Japanese perspective, though, the decentralized nature of PETA proved to be less dangerous than the centralized command structures in the BNA, both in terms of the coordination of anti-Japanese action as well as negotiation with the advancing Allied forces. After the Japanese capitulation, however, this would lead to the war of independence in Indonesia, and in particular Java, whereas in Burma negotiations with the British led to independence. The INA, whose officers had been professional soldiers in the British Indian Army, was a case apart. Even though less tightly controlled by the Japanese than the BNA or PETA, it was predicated on the absolute leadership of Bose, who never officially turned his back on the Japanese or contemplated negotiation with the British. Moreover, unlike the other independence armies, the INA found itself outside India and hence could not draw on populations within India.

Significance of the Japanese Military Model for Southeast Asia

Japanese military training affected a whole generation of leadership in Southeast Asia, and in Burma and Indonesia led to the creation of military bureaucracies that remained highly influential until at least the early 1970s. How this Japanese wartime training affected Asians varies from one nation to another. Variants include the wartime role of indigenous armies, the impact of Japan's collapse on independence armies, and the postwar career profiles of Japanese trainees as they integrated into postwar political elites. In the following, one needs to differentiate between Burma and Java/Indonesia, the special position of the INA, and the rest of Japanese-occupied Southeast Asia.

The total impact of Japanese training of Southeast Asians went far beyond Japan's motives in recruiting and training them. Japan's wartime initiatives were predicated on the political goal of weakening the colonial powers through propaganda warfare, on requirements for vital natural resources to support Japan's war effort, and on the military's need to shore up deficient coastal defenses.

Revolutionary potential was generated by the Japanese policy of selecting for training young men who had been excluded from Western colonial regimes, including those who had been imprisoned or had engaged in nationalist activities. In Burma, young members of the Thakin Party were favored and members of ethnic groups that had served in colonial forces were avoided. Similarly, in Indonesia, the Japanese recruited those imprisoned by the Dutch or men with strong Islamic faith and shunned sectors of the populace who had served in the KNIL and the Dutch bureaucracy. The result of this policy was that in both Burma and Indonesia disenfranchised nationalists rose to the top militarily and in the postwar era also politically.

The BIA and the PETA, the various *giyuugun* and *giyuutai*, and the Hizbullah, were all recruited and trained from scratch, without military antecedents. The Philippine constabulary was exceptional in that it was a colonial militia force that was not disbanded, whereas the INA was formed from members of the British Indian Army. The INA, moreover, was the only one of these armies with a highly trained staff with whom Japanese officers felt confident in conducting joint strategic planning. Even with the INA in joint combat with the Japanese, some Japanese harbored reservations. The Philippine constabulary, based at home rather than stranded in Malaya, was held in much lower esteem, not only because it was a militia force but because the loyalty of its members to the Japanese was far more ambiguous.

In postwar Burma and Indonesia, however, these volunteer and independence forces assumed a significance far greater than most Japanese imagined or foresaw. These armies fed directly into the armies of the postwar years and inhibited the return of British and Dutch colonial control. In Indonesia and Burma, staff officers could function in the new armies of independent nations. According to an Indonesian general, "The Japanese taught us something far more important [than the Dutch]: how to create an army from scratch."[5] Such skills had not been fostered by the colonial powers that were far more concerned with the maintenance of colonial rule and internal security than defense against a modern army of a major military power. Staff officer training was conducted in wartime Japan at the Military Academy for sixty Burmese, thirty-five Indians, several Thais, seventeen Indonesians, one Malay and fifty-three Filipinos.

Another innovation of the Japanese military model was guerrilla training, a universal feature of Japanese training programs in Southeast Asia and a contrast with training by previous colonial powers. Some Indonesian generals attributed the brevity of Dutch resistance to Japanese invasion of Java and Sumatra to this factor.

Still another Japanese legacy to postwar Southeast Asia was a group of Japanese soldiers who "stayed on" after defeat to join the independence struggle and remained even after independence. Although French Indochina had seen very little Japanese effort to create locally recruited militia or even armed forces, a certain number of Japanese remained, some of them joining the Viet Minh. In Indonesia, the Japanese who stayed on numbered between 350 and 400, most of them infantrymen rather than officers. Among the latter was Yanagawa, who had been involved in all stages of training of PETA and remained there until his death. He said, "My six children in Bandung became fifty people, then a hundred, a thousand, ten thousand, a hundred thousand. Those who fought in the war of independence scattered as flowers, fought to the last, and won Indonesian merdeka [freedom]."[6] Other Japanese officers involved in training these armies held nostalgic memories of their wartime activities and returned for postwar visits to Southeast Asian trainees. This is particularly true of members of the Fujiwara Kikan and their INA students, and Minami Kikan and 15th Army veterans with regard to Burma. Some of these Japanese became businessmen in Southeast Asia or advisers to postwar governments.

Two basic assumptions underpinned Japanese training programs in Southeast Asia, as in Japan itself. One was that spirit (*seishin*) is more important than any technological advantage in military weaponry. The other is that self-discipline must be absolute, precluding other values. The Japanese sought thus to foster bravery in battle when all technical advantage might lie with the enemy. The Japanese were convinced that the *élan* of the warrior was able to overcome any obstacle, no doubt in part a legacy of the samurai tradition. Many Southeast Asians commented that they still felt the effects of this spiritual training decades after the war. In Indonesia, emphasis on these traits produced what became known as the "PETA officer type."

Burmese and Indonesian trainees did not regard themselves as professionals in the sense of British- or Dutch-trained officers as, under different circumstances, they would never have considered entering a military career. Instead, they were nationalists first and professional soldiers second.

"We didn't become soldiers for money," in the words of General Bambang Sugeng, who became postwar chief of staff of the Indonesian army.[7]

The postwar profiles of INA veterans differ from the career trajectories of the Japanese-trained individuals. Since INA officers were for the most part already trained in the British Indian Army, the Japanese experience had for these Indians a basically political rather than military impact. After the war, most of them were interrogated and dismissed, barring INA veterans from continuing their military careers. Instead, they became politicized, absorbed into government positions, the diplomatic corps, or the lower echelons of the bureaucracy. Some of them distinguished themselves as labor leaders. Most of those from India returned to India.

In Burma and Indonesia, Japanese training was a two-edged sword, enhancing nationalism and providing the military potential that could be used both against Japanese tutors and against British and Dutch attempts to return. In Burma, the Revolutionary Party was staffed after 1962 by Ne Win and the "second generation" officers of the BDA rather than the original "thirty comrades," though some of the former had studied at Mingaladon or in Japan during the war. By 1962, some of the original thirty had been killed, assassinated, or died, while others had retired from politics or joined the resistance against Ne Win. Some BDA veterans were given ambassadorial appointments, sometimes as military attachés.

In Indonesia, by contrast to Burma, three-quarters of the top ranks of the Indonesian army in 1971 were still staffed by PETA veterans, most of them former company commanders. Although some *giyuugun* members who had risen to prominence in postwar Sumatra had lost out in the Outer Islands Rebellion, as did their fellow Sumatran in Java, Zulkifli Lubis, some of them re-entered the military bureaucracy under Suharto. In addition, some Dutch-trained officers still survived, while the new generation was partly trained under American influence. Others received ambassadorial appointments or became businessmen.

Veterans of volunteer units in Malaya, Indochina, and the Philippines, on the other hand, have not played as prominent a role as the independence army veterans. Those who became prominent in Malaya/Malaysia, for example, have not wished to publicize wartime Japanese connections if they had them. The same is true in the Philippines. And in French Indochina, wartime coexistence of the French with the Japanese until March 1945 meant that their numbers were too insignificant. The relative anonymity of this group of Southeast Asians reflects also the limited goals of these units and the relative obscurity of the Japanese who trained them. The latter generally were not Nakano Gakkou graduates and sometimes not even commissioned officers.

The total Japanese military impact on Southeast Asia, from the formation of paramilitary youth groups to the recruitment and training of volunteer and independence armies, and finally, to sending select officers from these armies to Japan for further training, was of crucial significance for the independent nations of postwar Southeast Asia. In the case of Indonesia and Burma, a whole generation of men whose nationalism was already incubating were given rigorous military discipline and training which equipped them to wage wars of independence and to staff and train the military bureaucracies that persist today. A double revolution took a generation of young Burmese and Indonesian nationalists through a metamorphosis as military officers who were at the same time politicized. Japanese occupation provided a positive example in its modernizing aspects and a negative example in its repressive features. In both cases, the catalytic result was to stimulate nationalist aspirations for independence. The self-confidence, military training, and political expertise that were acquired during the Japanese interregnum could now be mobilized against attempts at reassertion of Western colonial rule. The myth of colonial omnipotence was exposed both by the defeat of Western colonial powers by Japan and then by Japan's own defeat. In the case of Indonesia and Burma, but also in regard to French Indochina, British Malaya, and the Philippines, Southeast Asians gained the confidence that they would never again have to submit to foreign rule and the means to ensure that it did not happen again. This was a Japanese legacy beyond measure.

Notes

Besides the sources noted below, full bibliographical references can be found in the author's book on which this chapter is based: Joyce C. Lebra. 1977. *Japanese-trained Armies in Southeast Asia: Independence and Volunteer Forces in World War II*. New York: Columbia University Press.

1. U Nu, *Burma under the Japanese* (New York: St. Martin's Press, 1954), 24–25.

2. Ba Maw, *Breakthrough in Burma: Memoirs of a Revolution, 1939–1946* (New Haven, CT: Yale University Press, 1968), 370.

3. Interview with General Djatikusumo, Jakarta, January 19, 1971.

4. Quoted from the newspaper *New Light of Burma*, August 6, 1944, by Maung Maung in *Burma in the Family of Nations* (Amsterdam: Djambatan), 1956, 98–101; John F. Cady, *A History of Modern Burma* (Ithaca, NY: Cornell University Press, 1958, 480.

5. Interview with General Djatikusumo.

6. Yanagawa Munenari, "Jawa no Beppan" [The Beppan of Java], *Shekan Yomiuri, Nihon no himitsu sen* [Weekly Yomiuri, Japan's secret war], Special issue, 1956, 155.

7. Interview with General Bambang Sugeng, Jakarta, January 19, 1971.

Southeast Asian Armed Forces after Independence

CHAPTER 7

Dominance, Twilights, and Legacies of Power: The Politics of the Indonesian Army during and after Suharto

Jun Honna

Politik militer adalah politik negara (Politics of the military is politics of the nation). This is a favorite manifestation of Indonesia's military in explaining its political role. It was originated by Indonesia's first army commander, Sudirman, who led the revolutionary war against Dutch colonial forces in 1945–49. Identifying the army as a hero of independence, Sudirman and his soldiers constructed the army's self-image as "guardian of the nation," whose responsibility was not limited to the narrow field of defense but extended to the total wellbeing of the nation. Like other Southeast Asian countries, such as Myanmar and Vietnam, which had experienced wars of independence, Indonesia's patriotic military has traditionally claimed that its role should embrace political engagement as its historical right.[1] How has such self-image been projected after independence? During the parliamentary democracy period (1949–58), the military participated in politics as a political force competing with various political parties. Under Sukarno's "Guided Democracy" (1958–65), the military emerged as one of three dominant powers, together with President Sukarno and the Indonesian Communist Party (PKI). During Suharto's authoritarian "New Order" government (1966–98), the military became a single powerful political force dominating the polity.[2] After Suharto's fall, the country's democratic experiment forced the military to be one among equals. In this way, the military's historical claim as "national guardian" has ensured the constant role of the military in politics after independence, although its mode of involvement has varied over time.[3] This chapter focuses mainly on the Suharto era but also discusses what followed. It examines how the military consolidated its political rule during the first twenty years of the Suharto regime, how its dominance was challenged during its last ten years, and how the military lost its political hegemony but preserved significant legacies of power in the democratization of Indonesia after the fall of Suharto. Before examining these developments, however, it is useful to briefly look at the origins of the Indonesian army in order to understand the historical reasons for its political activism.

The Military and the State before the New Order Regime (1949–1965)

The Indonesian army was born during the struggle for independence against the Dutch colonial power. After Indonesia's national leaders Sukarno and Hatta proclaimed independence on August 17, 1945, the nation went into a revolutionary war (Kahin, 1952). Prior to 1945, fighters were recruited nationwide and were led by trained soldiers during the period of Dutch colonialism and the subsequent Japanese occupation (1942–45). Lacking the ability to conduct conventional warfare, Indonesia's independent fighters engaged in guerrilla struggles against the Dutch who continued to rule Indonesia after the defeat of Japan in the Pacific War. The four-year armed struggle, which ended in 1949 with the recognition of Indonesia's self-sovereignty, greatly contributed to the formation of military thinking and the role of the military in the newly independent nation. In fact, the nature of guerrilla warfare barely differentiated the boundary between military and non-military affairs as soldiers tended to lead in various fields of national life all over the archipelago, such as economic, administrative, political, and social activities. From the beginning, therefore, the Indonesian army was not merely a defense force but a multifunctional one, and this experience encouraged the army to play non-military roles even after independence rather than create a professional army. Moreover, the war of independence effectively constructed the self-perception of the Indonesian army as the guardian of the nation, and it led the post-revolutionary army to claim its "historical legitimacy" to engage in the political decision-making of the new nation-state. It was against this background that the army was treated both as a military and political force in post-independent Indonesia.

The achievement of independence, however, did not guarantee a stable management of the new nation-state. The system of parliamentary democracy that was adopted did not function well as a political mechanism for accommodating different societal interests. Reflecting the country's ethnic, religious, and regional diversity which had, to some extent, been camouflaged by the wartime nationalism, post-independent national politics revealed the difficulties in handling the social diversity that was now brought into the formal political process via various political parties established along ethnic, regional, religious, and ideological lines. The country's first general election in 1955 brought into focus the social conflict represented by the political parties rather than providing stability in politics. The rise and fall of weak coalition governments also revealed the vulnerability of parliamentary democracy in Indonesia.

The army as an institution had a limited role in politics during this period. It participated in parliament via its political party, created by A. H. Nasution, the army chief at the time. The army had been intensively engaged in the suppression of uprisings and secessionist attempts, but when it came to assuring that the country needed stronger political leadership to counter these attempts, it moved to lobby President Sukarno, asking him to dissolve parliament and create a strong authoritarian government based on the presidential system. The army's concern about territorial disunity, caused by the lingering Islamic (Darul Islam) separatist movements in west Java, Aceh, and South Sulawesi since 1949, was caused by the breakout of regional rebellions (so-called PRRI/Permesta) in Sumatra and Sulawesi in 1956–58, which were covertly supported by the United States government in an attempt to block the increasing penetration of communist influence in the archipelago (Kahin and Kahin 1995). Following the imposition of martial law in March 1957 and the subsequent army crackdown of rebels in 1958, President Sukarno declared Indonesia's return to the 1945 Constitution, which granted strong presidential power, and then established an authoritarian government under the slogan of "Guided Democracy" in 1959. Indonesia's experiment with parliamentary democracy had failed.[4]

Under Sukarno's Guided Democracy (1959–65), the political role of the military was enhanced. However, it was not to dominate the government. As Nasution explained in his famous 1958 speech about the desired role of the army as a "middle way" (*jalan tengah*), the military took the position somewhere in between "dominating government" and "subordinating civilian political authority." Nasution insisted that Indonesia's army would not follow either Latin American militaries that often established military governments, or Western professional militaries that endorsed the civilian supremacy principle.[5] The "middle way" concept reflected Indonesia's political reality in not allowing the army to control the government. The army gained political influence after martial law, but Sukarno—the father of independence—sought constant mass mobilization in consolidating Indonesian nationalism and territorial integrity. He believed that the Communist Party of Indonesia (Partai Komunis Indonesia, PKI) could be the driving force to this end (Mortimer 1974).

On the other hand, Sukarno saw the army as significant in furthering his bold foreign policies that reflected anti-Western nationalism, evidenced by the military campaigns to "liberate" West Irian in 1961–62 and to crush the formation of Malaysia in 1963.[6] In this way, the army and the PKI emerged as two political pillars during the Guided Democracy period, competing with each other to gain influence in the Sukarno government. The competition reached a peak in the alleged communist-led abortive coup in September 1965. This event provided an opportunity for the army to defeat the PKI, finally emerging as the most powerful institution in the polity. After this 1965 incident, Sukarno's leadership was fated to end in the face of the growing assertiveness of the army.

Military Dominance: Motivations, Programs and Power Consolidation (1965/66–1985)

Military rule in Indonesia was constructed after the collapse of the Guided Democracy period (Crouch, 1988). The abortive coup in September 1965 resulted in the concentration of power in the hands of Suharto, commander of the Army Strategic Reserve Command, or Kostrad, who had led the army troops which crushed the coup attempt. Suharto's military accused the PKI of leading the coup and encouraged students and Muslims to join in the army-orchestrated anti-PKI campaign throughout the archipelago.[7] Pressured by the military, which claimed that the political order could not be restored under the current situation, President Sukarno finally authorized Suharto to take any necessary measures to restore law and order in March 1966.[8] The PKI, which had exercised considerable political influence under the Sukarno regime, was quickly eliminated in a spate of military-orchestrated violence. It was in this process that the military gained the dominant power in determining the direction of post-1965 Indonesian politics.

Following the official transfer of the presidency from Sukarno to Suharto in March 1968, Suharto consolidated military rule by emphasizing "stability and order" as the necessary preconditions for economic recovery and development, which had long been sidelined by Sukarno in pursuit of anti-Western foreign policies. Unlike the previous regime led by Sukarno who, as the leader of national independence, favored populist mobilization of political forces to consolidate national integration and pursue his radical domestic and foreign policies, Suharto's Indonesia made economic modernization the primary goal of the government in order to "save" the nation from the disastrous economic situation during the final Sukarno years. The military's political control was justified as necessary to safeguard national stability as the foundation for economic development and modernization. It was the turning point in the history of Indonesia's civil-military relations. Generals were no longer satisfied with their mere "participation" in politics, which was the original projection of their "guardian" self-image, but were highly motivated to dominate the polity. Why did the transformation occur? It was due to the infusion of the idea of "developmentalism" in the minds of the officer corps. Developmentalism, or modernization ideology, provided the military with a rationale that identified political stability as the precondition for development (Honna, 2001).

Since modernization was a decades-long national project, long-term political stability was thought to be necessary. This motivated the military to be totally in control of the political process. Developmentalism was notably encouraged by civilian US-trained economists, whose influence had been severely limited in Sukarno's anti-Western government, and it convinced officers to insist that the nationalistic dream of catch-up industrialization would need a massive inflow of foreign capital from the West, which would, in return, require rigid political stability. Moreover, the US-backed military regime's geopolitical concern that communist infiltration during the Cold War would escalate domestic subversion also hardened officers' belief that the military's total political control and surveillance were required to secure national unity in all fields of national life. Having packed this development theory into its arsenal, the military no longer believed that its self-claimed "guardian" role could be achieved by merely participating in politics. Rather, it was required to dominate the polity. Moreover, such political intervention was not designed as a temporary measure but as a permanent one. These transformations of military thinking and motivation were notable in the transition from the post-independence to the Suharto period.

It was against this background that the doctrine of *dwifungsi*, or dual function, was officially adopted by the military (ABRI) at the beginning of the New Order. *Dwifungsi* claimed ABRI's "permanent" role in the defense and socio-political fields. The doctrine was seen as an embodiment of ABRI's "historical mission" to protect national unity since the war of independence. Since *dwifungsi*'s primary goal in the New Order polity was the maintenance of national stability for economic development, several political programs were introduced to achieve this.

Political repression and ideological surveillance were the major tools used in constructing and maintaining the New Order regime. Soon after the 1965 coup attempt, the army established a security agency, the Operational Command for the Restoration of Security and Order (Kopkamtib), headed by Suharto himself, which conducted a wide range of internal security measures, including the ideological screening of party candidates and government employees, the elimination of communist remnants, and the suppression of campus and labor activists. With this "military within the military" as the core of ABRI's repressive apparatus, everyday politico-ideological surveillance was institutionalized in the country's social life (Tanter 1990). Kopkamtib's activities were backed by the military area commands that controlled political life in each geographic territory.[9] In remote areas of the archipelago, such as Aceh, Irian Jaya, and East Timor (annexed in 1976), anti-separatist security operations became standard practice. In urban areas, military repression targeted the press, students, intellectuals, Islamic groups, and labor and legal activists, who were often labeled as being against the Indonesian state's national ideology, Pancasila.[10] Mass demonstrations were repeatedly suppressed by security forces. As we will see below, the 1974 Malari Affair and the 1984 Tanjung Priok incident were notable cases (Bresnan, 1993). In the name of establishing a stable political system, ABRI relied on repressive political control with the doctrinal backup of *dwifungsi*.

Together with the repression of opposition, social participation in the formal political structure was tightly controlled. To ensure the regime's stability, the influence of the existing political parties was reduced drastically by the establishment of a governmental party, Golkar (Golongan Karya, or Functional Group), which all public servants were forced to join and support. Since the first New Order election in 1971, Golkar has always held a large parliamentary majority, while other political parties were compelled to merge into two—the PPP (Partai Persatuan Pembangunan, or United Development Party) consisting of the old Islamic parties, and the PDI (Partai Demokrasi Indonesia, or Indonesian Democratic Party) which integrated secure nationalist and Christian parties.

ABRI members were also "appointed" to the parliament (DPR) where they sat as members of the ABRI "faction" (F-ABRI) both at national and regional levels as part of the *dwifungsi* mission to ensure political stability in the legislative sector.[11] ABRI members also penetrated non-military administrative bodies, occupying key positions ranging from department ministers to village heads. Sending officers to non-military sectors, called *kekaryaan*, was justified as a necessary measure to secure the smooth implementation of the government's development projects and to overcome alleged civilian incompetence in handling government tasks.[12] The program of *dwifungsi*, namely the backing for Golkar, *kekaryaan* penetration, and military representation in parliament, tightly restricted political participation. In this way, under Suharto's New Order, which called for the country's all-out endeavor to achieve economic development, the military became the backbone of the authoritarian administration.

It should be noted, however, that having wide consensus among top generals regarding the perceived need for establishing an authoritarian political mechanism did not automatically guarantee their agreement on the actual implementation of the *dwifungsi* policies. As the communist sweep was almost complete and a sense of political stability had been produced by the government-manipulated 1971 elections, there was an increasing diversity of opinion regarding the practice of *dwifungsi*. Some elite military officers started to question the political programs directed by Suharto and his close associates under the name of *dwifungsi*. The resulting rivalries between officers frequently undermined cohesion within the military.

In the early 1970s, the antagonism between Ali Moertopo, who had served Suharto as personal adviser since the 1950s, and Soemitro, who had led Kopkamtib, culminated in the so-called Malari Affair in 1974. The largest street demonstration since the establishment of the New Order took place that year. Student activists opposed the government policy of introducing massive foreign investment, which they thought might undermine the opportunity for indigenous businesses and only benefit Chinese Indonesians who had close ties with Suharto. A street demonstration in Jakarta on January 15 during the visit of Japanese Prime Minister Kakuei Tanaka led to a huge riot that was repressed by ABRI. This event was called the Malari Affair and it reflected intra-military rivalries as some officers were sympathetic towards the student movement. They believed that Suharto had relied heavily on a group of personal advisors (Asistan Pribadi, or Aspri) for his early New Order policymaking, including the annexation of East Timor. These Aspri, like Ali Moertopo and Sudjono Humardhani, together with their think-tank, the Center for Strategic and International Studies (CSIS), provided enormous input to Suharto. The dominant role of the Aspri was resented by many officers outside their circle, including Soemitro. Soemitro was unhappy with the Aspri's business links to Chinese and foreign partners and was sympathetic towards student demands in the Malari Affair. Soemitro was replaced just after the incident.[13]

Internal cleavage within the military became more pronounced as the New Order regime started to enjoy a certain degree of political stability. In the early 1980s, several prominent retired officers, including Nasution, to whom the *dwifungsi* concept is often attributed, accused Suharto and ABRI of misleading the nation, and established a critical group consisting of fifty members, including retired officers and civilian intellectuals, who called themselves Petisi 50 (Petition of 50).[14] Suharto's inner circle of officers, such as Sudomo, Yoga Sugomo and Benny Moerdani, labeled these retired officers as *sakit hati* (sick at heart) generals.[15]

Despite the emergence of intra-military cleavages during the early period of the New Order, the subsequent development showed the increasing solidarity within ABRI under the leadership of Moerdani. In tandem with this, Suharto proceeded with his regime consolidation until it was almost complete by the mid-1980s. From 1983 to 1988, Moerdani, as ABRI commander, fortified his power base within the military by establishing the Strategic Intelligence Agency (BAIS), subsuming the role of Pusintelstrat (Strategic Intelligence Center, ABRI's intelligence body) and many of the intelligence functions of Kopkamtib. He now emerged as the most powerful commander in the past decades. It was Moerdani's hardline ABRI that Suharto relied on to perfect his regime's consolidation during 1984–85. In 1984, the government forced all social organizations to accept Pancasila as their sole ideological basis, and in 1985 imposed five political laws to further restrict political participation.

The Pancasila project was resented by Muslim groups who could not accept the idea of placing Pancasila above Allah. It was a big blow for the PPP whose constituency comprised mainly Muslims. ABRI, led by Moerdani, a Catholic, was viewed by many Muslims as being antagonistic towards them. This suspicion was encouraged by the above-mentioned Tanjung Priok incident, which occurred in September 1984 when security troops shot and killed dozens of Muslim demonstrators in Tanjung Priok, north Jakarta.

Muslim groups believed that the repression of Muslims was part of anti-Islam operations led by the Catholic ABRI commander, Benny Moerdani, and the death toll ran into a hundred. Furthermore, radical Islamic groups were imprisoned while others chose self-imposed exile.[16] Overt repression against Muslims represented a symbolic watershed of the New Order polity which, after having actively and ruthlessly mobilized Muslims in the elimination of the Communist party after the coup, now moved against them in the name of political stability.

Suharto's imposition of Pancasila as the state's sole ideology in 1984 was complemented in 1985 by five political laws concerning (1) general elections; (2) composition of the DPR and the People's Consultative Assembly (MPR), the nation's highest legislative body consisting of all DPR members plus additional members appointed by the president, who met once every five years during the New Order to elect the president and vice-president); (3) political parties and Golkar; (4) referendums, and (5) social organizations. Among other things, the laws (1) banned debate over Pancasila and the 1945 Constitution during election campaigns and limited discussion to issues of national development; (2) allocated 100 appointed seats (previously 75) for ABRI in the DPR, while the total number of the DPR rose to 500 (from 460) and 1,000 (from 920) for the MPR; (3) determined Pancasila as the sole fundamental principle for parties and Golkar; (4) set several requirements which made it almost impossible to hold a referendum to revise the authoritarian Constitution; and (5) authorized the government to dissolve any social organization which disturbed law and order or promoted ideas in whatever form that was contrary to Pancasila and the Constitution.

With these measures, Suharto seemed to have completed consolidation of the New Order's regime. From the time of its inception, the New Order had established various political institutions to secure its stability. Now, by introducing the Pancasila project, which could identify any social move as anti-national and subversive, thus becoming a subject of security operation, the state finally established its overwhelming hegemony over society. In other words, the New Order deprived society of both formal and informal channels to politically challenge the government. By these actions, consolidation of the

New Order's power reached a peak, to which Moerdani's ABRI had greatly contributed.

Erosion of Military Dominance (1985–May 1998)

As we have seen, the period between 1966 and 1985 illustrated Suharto's consolidation of power over the regime and domination of politics by the military. From now on, however, the relationship between the president and ABRI began to change as only a threat from within the military could really jeopardize Suharto's position. Suharto probably found that he had become too dependent on ABRI and thus started to widen his power base by relying less on ABRI in non-security affairs. Under Suharto's Fourth Development Cabinet (1983–88), Sudharmono, the head of the State Secretariat, was given increased presidential trust. As secretary of state (Sekneg) he had authority over budget allocations and used much of it to support the business activities of indigenous Indonesians, or *pribumi*, resulting in a decline in budget allocations for ABRI's business activities.[17] Moreover, as the chairman of Golkar during 1983–88, Sudharmono attempted to make it more independent of ABRI by recruiting cadres from the ranks of business who might provide financial support for Golkar, which would, in turn, reduce ABRI's influence in Golkar's administration.[18] ABRI leaders were hostile to Sudharmono's attempts even though they had been approved by Suharto. Against this background, Moerdani moved to block Suharto's attempt to appoint Sudharmono as the vice-president in 1988. Just before the presidential and vice-presidential elections at the MPR, Suharto therefore eased Moerdani out of his central position as ABRI commander by giving him the less important position of defense minister.

The growing disenchantment of Moerdani's officers with the president became evident when Ibrahim Saleh of the F-ABRI interrupted a session in the MPR by openly objecting to the nomination of Sudharmono as vice-president. Ibrahim's unprecedented show of resistance was unsuccessful but not entirely isolated. Try Sutrisno, a close ally of Moerdani and his successor as ABRI commander, also raised questions about Suharto's policies. In this way, the 1998 event exacerbated the cleavage between Suharto and Moerdani. Suharto's decision to abolish Kopkamtib in late 1988 was widely seen as an attempt to weaken ABRI's (and Moerdani's) institutional power base. The period between 1988 and 1993 saw a deepening conflict between Moerdani's group and Suharto's palace circle now led by Sudharmono (Crouch 1992).

The emerging Suharto-ABRI tussle was not the only sign of regime flaccidity. The New Order as a polity faced the need to accommodate historical and social change. Two decades of the Suharto administration from the mid-1960s had ironically produced an environment that delegitimized the authoritarian practices upon which it had been built. Broadly speaking, there were four structural challenges. First, the very success of economic development had created a new middle-class layer that embraced critical intellectuals and legal activists who became the base of the critical sector in political society. Second, in the mid-1980s, Indonesia was required by the World Bank and the International Monetary Fund to implement a series of deregulation policies as its economy moved from resource-export and import-substitution to export-oriented industrialization. This process inevitably demanded that Indonesia implement political transparency in order to attract more foreign investments to promote economic growth. Third, it was ironic that Suharto's "successful" implementation of his political program in 1984–85 undermined the rationale for prioritizing "security" in political life because it now seemed irrelevant to rely on the regime slogan of "threat to Pancasila" in repressing political groups which had already accepted that philosophy. Finally, military officers who had participated in the independence war gradually reached their retirement age in the mid-1980s, and ABRI was inherited by post-revolutionary generation officers like Try Sutrisno, who became ABRI commander in 1988. Since *dwifungsi* had been largely legitimized as ABRI's historical right to participate in national affairs arising from its role in the independence war, the generation change inevitably raised a reasonable question about ABRI's continuous dominance in politics. Why should the younger generation officers who did not participate in the war for independence also enjoy the political "privileges" given to the revolutionary generation officers?

These social changes all contributed to the erosion of the legitimate basis of New Order authoritarianism and, of course, ABRI's political domination. Growing social demands for political democratization resonated with the intra-regime conflict to produce a twin challenge to Suharto. Suharto sought to counter this challenge to his rule by means of the incorporation of political Islam into the regime and the re-establishment of a loyal military. This twofold strategy characterized political developments in the late New Order period but was not able to prevent Suharto's fall from power in 1998.

Suharto's strategic shift from repression to co-optation of Islam was embodied by the creation of the Indonesian Association of Muslim Intellectuals (ICMI) in December 1990. This Suharto-sponsored body was chaired by Suharto's civilian protégé, B. J. Habibie, minister of research and technology. The military leadership led by Moerdani and Sutrisno was very suspicious of the ICMI, partly because of their ideological concern that political mobilization of Islamic forces could undermine the Pancasila-based state system they had built in 1985, but mainly because of their concerns in power politics. Moerdani's circle suspected that Suharto was attempting to counterbalance ABRI by creating ICMI for securing his own political power. They were also concerned that Habibie would consolidate his independent power base outside military control and challenge ABRI in the presidential and vice-presidential elections in 1993.[19]

Suharto's effort to co-opt Islam via the ICMI was also a necessary political strategy aimed at alleviating social criticism directed at the government, which had delivered rapid economic growth but at the cost of a huge economic gap between the rich and the poor. In theory, Suharto's pro-Islamic political reorientation should have worked to shift people's attention away from class conflicts to national unity highlighting religious commonality.

Together with his rapprochement with Islam, Suharto moved to curtail the influence of the military under the Moerdani/Sutrisno leadership. This was apparent in his handling of the Dili Incident, in which ABRI troops fired on thousands of demonstrators in Dili, East Timor, on November 12, 1991. The official Indonesian death toll was nearly fifty, but foreign human rights organizations estimated it to be between one hundred and three hundred. Sutrisno, the ABRI commander, quickly condemned the demonstrators for causing chaos and claimed that the troops were forced to shoot when the mob brutally attacked the soldiers. However, Suharto decided to dismiss two officers, Warouw and Sintong Panjaitan, both of whom were considered formally responsible for violations that took place within their areas of command even though they were not directly involved in the shooting. It was the first time in the New Order history that officers holding the rank of general were held responsible for the shooting of civilians by their troops. In addition, nineteen soldiers directly involved in the killing were court-martialed.

These measures were resented by many officers who believed that the shootings were justified. It was also widely believed in political society that Warouw and Panjaitan were Moerdani's close aides and were thus dismissed to facilitate the purging of the Moerdani circle. Moreover, the Dili killings became the primary factor that pushed Suharto to set up the National Human Rights Commission (Komnas, HAM) in December 1993. It was the first "government" body established to investigate ABRI's human rights abuses. From ABRI's perspective, it constituted another attempt by Suharto to emasculate the military.

Suharto's transformation of ABRI was further accelerated after his presidential re-election in 1993. He tactically received Sutrisno as vice-president to show his respect to the military as an institution but gave no significant authority to the former army commander whose military position could now be given to a more loyal follower. Defense minister Moerdani also lost his strong political influence after the formation of the new Cabinet (1993–98), in which he was assigned no position. Now it was time for the President to fully restructure the ABRI leadership for his own benefit. As the government faced growing social demands for increased democracy, along with the post-Cold War international community's push to liberalize Indonesia's politics and economy, Suharto might have felt that the next five years would be crucial for his political survival. The handling of the succession problem was particularly important for him. Establishing an amenable military was thus vital to successfully cope with difficult times in the late New Order period.

A serious impediment to Suharto in this effort was the generation gap. As a remnant of the revolutionary generation, Suharto seems to have been less adept at judging loyalist officers of the new generation, except for his military aides. Inevitably, Suharto started to accept the advice of trusted cronies in selecting officers who would occupy strategic positions. The role of his family, including Siti Hardijanti Rukmana, his eldest daughter, Prabowo, a military man who, married to Suharto's youngest daughter, Maniek, and even Habibie whom Suharto had known since Habibie was a child, became increasingly apparent in military promotions. In May 1993, Feisal Tanjung, a devout Muslim and long-time friend of Habibie, was appointed as the new ABRI commander on Habibie's strong recommendation. Wismoyo Arismunandar, a brother-in-law of Suharto's wife, was named the new army chief, although he was replaced by Hartono, a close ally of Prabowo, in February 1995.

In contrast to the previous ABRI leadership under Moerdani and Sutrisno, the Feisal/Hartono leadership appealed to Islamic aspirations and the likelihood of extensive cooperation with the ICMI. This new trend was widely seen as the "Islamization" or "greening" (green refers to the Islamic color) of ABRI. In fact, those officers who showed strong personal commitment to Islam were now respected and had good fortune in promotions. Such a trend was remarkable in the history of the New Order military, which had traditionally valued secular nationalist orientations in conducting its *dwifungsi* roles. A dispute soon emerged in society, particularly among retired generals, who criticized the trend as self-destructive for ABRI's manifested principle of playing "politics of the nation."

Above all, Suharto's efforts to reconstruct president-ABRI relations on a new basis, and his search for loyalist officers to this end, were increasingly mediated by Habibie and Feisal as well as Prabowo and Hartono. The transformation of ABRI's high command in the post-Moerdani period was managed through such processes, while the renewed ABRI leadership was highly agreeable to the First Family.

Suharto relied on these key allies to prepare for the smooth handling of both the 1997 general elections, in which he was expected to face a serious opposition movement centered on Megawati Sukarnoputri, the daughter of Sukarno, Indonesia's first president, who chaired the PDI, and the 1998 presidential election. Against this political background, the new ABRI leadership tended to be dogmatically intolerant and repressive towards the widening popular criticism of the government and the growing democratic movements. ABRI soon identified Megawati, the only politician with a chance to challenge Suharto in the next presidential election, as the primary target. ABRI engineered party conflict within the PDI, which led to the toppling of Megawati as the party's chairperson in June 1996. This sparked a physical clash between security troops and Megawati supporters, including NGOs, students, and grassroots people, and resulted in a two-day mass riot in Jakarta on July 27. This was the biggest riot in Jakarta since the Malari Affair in 1974. Nearly 200 people were arrested and some were kidnapped by the elite Army Special Forces (Kopassus) commanded by Prabowo. Many of them remain missing to this day. The ABRI leadership quickly declared that the riot had been instigated by communist-influenced NGOs that were attempting to unconstitutionally topple the government, and called for Islamic unity to combat the anti-government movement.

The removal of Megawati from the political arena and the military crackdown of the popular movement, which was clearly a result of Suharto's instructions, greatly risked the social credibility of ABRI. The military was now widely distrusted by the public as a "dead tool of the government," a criticism that challenged ABRI's self-claim of being the nation's "guardian." Even within the military, voices were emerging that proclaimed that acting as a tool of Suharto would only damage ABRI's corporate interest in the future. A growing number of officers began to see that the direction of the current ABRI leadership was not in line with ABRI's long-term political benefit but was merely serving Suharto's short-term private interests.[20] There was also a serious concern among officers about the high-speed promotion of Prabowo and his allies, which led to confusion about promotion practice and demoralized many officers. The antagonism between those who were linked with Prabowo and those who were not widened, and it resonated with the perceived freefall of ABRI's and *dwifungsi*'s credibility in society in a way that motivated some anti-Prabowo officers into becoming reform-minded. They were convinced that Prabowo's influence should be curtailed and ABRI's response to societal demands for democratization should involve more dialogue rather than traditional repression. The crackdown of the popular movement on July 27, 1996 significantly encouraged such a gap within the military. This gap was important in the transition from the Suharto to the post-Suharto periods.

Suharto's personalization of the military was a notable feature of late New Order politics. By using the amenable ABRI, Suharto succeeded in the 1997 general elections to secure Golkar's victory, his presidential re-election, and Habibie's vice-presidency during the MPR sessions in March 1998. ABRI's subordination to this Suharto-ICMI project well illustrated the erosion of the military's independent power in the political process. However, Suharto's joy did not last long.

Indonesia was badly affected by the currency crisis in Asia that originated in Bangkok in mid-1997. Although Suharto had managed to shift criticism about the nation's worsening economic situation by mobilizing street demonstrations by radical Muslim groups against an invented "Chinese conspiracy," his re-election in 1998 ensured that the public saw him as the principal villain, a sorcerer who had run out of tricks and was clearly unable to cope with the crisis. Ironically, the self-styled father of development now came to be seen as the man responsible for Indonesia's economic implosion. A nationwide student movement demanding his resignation escalated quickly. In dealing with the movement, the gap within the military between pro-Prabowo and anti-Prabowo circles became increasingly obvious. Their antagonism ultimately contributed to Suharto's historic resignation on May 21.

A group of high-ranking officers concerned about Prabowo's growing power within the military believed that Wiranto, commander of the Army Strategic Reserve Command (Kostrad) and later army chief, was the man to support. He was viewed as a non-ICMI general who respected the military's institutional integrity compared with the highly ambitious Prabowo. The seed was sown in Suharto's attempt to let Prabowo and Wiranto compete with each other rather than giving full power to a single person, as this could prevent ABRI as an institution from acting independently from the president. However, such a divide-and-rule strategy backfired when Prabowo perceived that the equilibrium was broken after the presidential re-election. Thus Wiranto, who had succeeded Feisal as ABRI commander in February 1998, was also to occupy the post of Minister of Defense and Security. This provoked the Prabowo circle to take action. It was imperative that the group undermined Wiranto who now held the two top positions in the military hierarchy.[21] He was, in fact, expected by his followers to curtail Prabowo's influence. For Prabowo and his supporters within the military, something had to be done to either gain Suharto's favor or discredit Wiranto. They saw the opportunity for both in the widening anti-Suharto movement in society. If Wiranto was seen as ineffective in handling the political situation, Suharto might be forced to rely on Prabowo to solve the problem. Widespread riots created a potentially attractive opportunity for the Prabowo group.

Triggered by a government decision to cut petrol subsidies and the subsequent rise in petrol prices, mass protests were organized in the North Sumatran city of Medan. They suddenly developed into riots on May 5 and spread to other cities in North Sumatra, destroying many Chinese-owned properties that were not protected by the security forces. A week after the incident, on May 12, four student demonstrators were shot dead by "mysterious" snipers dressed in police uniforms at a peaceful rally against Suharto at Trisakti University in Jakarta. The police troops were under the command of Hamami Nata, commander of the Jakarta Metropolitan Police and a close ally of Prabowo and his friend Sjafrie Sjamsoeddin, Jakarta's military commander. It is widely believed that the snipers were military sharpshooters.

The incident provoked mass protests that quickly developed into large-scale, two-day riots in Jakarta. The rioters burned shopping centers and other commercial buildings, robbed citizens, and raped ethnic Chinese women.[22] Similar violence also erupted in Solo (Central Java), Surabaya (East Java), and Palembang (South Sumatra). Following the incidents, Komnas HAM established a Joint Fact-Finding Team (Tim Gabungan Pencari Fakta, or TGPF) on the May 13 riots and its investigation concluded that in all five places well-trained and organized provocateurs were involved. The TGPF also noted that the patterns of rioting in each case were quite similar, pointing to the involvement of military elements in creating the unrest. The report also recommended further investigation of Prabowo and Sjafrie. Eyewitness accounts also revealed that the riots were orchestrated by Kopassus groups who mobilized gangs (*preman*) to provoke attacks against and looting of Chinese enclaves.[23] Kopassus was led by Muchdi Purwopranjono, a leading ally of Prabowo, who had assumed the position in Kopassus after Prabowo had become Kostrad commander.

In dealing with these riots, Wiranto could not rely on the elite army troops largely under the control of Sjafrie, Muchdi, and Prabowo. Wiranto found troops under these generals too slow in stopping riots, and he thus mobilized the marines in his attempt to restore calm in Jakarta.[24] Only after two days of mass violence could Prabowo and Sjafrie make their presence felt by standing in front of the troops and insisting on the need to restore public order and stability. Prabowo sought to exploit the ineffectiveness of Wiranto's leadership by lobbying Suharto to impose martial law under a revived Kopkamtib under the command of Prabowo or his followers. On May 18, he advised Suharto, via his daughter Siti, to replace Wiranto and to declare a national emergency.[25] It seems probable that the terror in May was engineered by Prabowo and his supporters to advance their interests within the military hierarchy. Suharto's divide-and-rule strategy had failed as internal rivalries within the army had spilled over into the public arena, dangerously fanning ethnic tensions and general unrest.

Wiranto was not silent but weighed in against the moves of military officers aligned with Prabowo. Having confirmed the role played by Prabowo and his allies during the riots, Wiranto, under clear threat of dismissal, immediately reported his findings to Suharto. Suharto's anger and that of his family was directed against Prabowo and thus the plan to reintroduce Kopkamtib was scrapped.[26] Wiranto then followed the advice of his close allies who, after discussion with civilian leaders, finally concluded that Suharto's resignation was the only way to restore stability and order in the nation. Following his meeting with Wiranto on May 20, Suharto announced his resignation the next day. At the presidential palace, Wiranto declared that ABRI would support the new government led by Habibie, who was automatically promoted to the presidency, and would also protect Suharto's security. The fall of Suharto was wildly celebrated nation-wide. Students and anti-government activists who had long voiced support for *reformasi* (political reform) finally saw their dreams come true.

After exerting his leadership in handling the transfer of power from Suharto to Habibie, Wiranto successfully dealt with the new president in settling the problem of Prabowo, a close friend of Habibie.[27] Two days after the inauguration of the new president, Wiranto replaced Prabowo with Johny Lumintang, operational assistant to the ABRI commander, a Christian, and a Wiranto follower, as acting commander of Kostrad. Soon after, rumors of a coup by the Prabowo camp spread in Jakarta.[28] Following Prabowo's transfer, his followers in Kopassus were also removed from their posts.

In retrospect, many factors contributed to the breakdown of the Suharto regime in May 1998 (Aspinall, 2000, ch. 9; Emmerson, 1999). An international factor—the currency crisis that first engulfed Thailand—spread through the region and led to socio-economic catastrophe in Indonesia. This domestic crisis inspired *reformasi* aspirations that developed into a countrywide anti-Suharto movement. It was a crystallization of various civil society forces led by students, intellectuals, and NGOs. Such dynamics not only pushed New Order political elites to distance themselves from Suharto but also prompted them to jump on the anti-Suharto bandwagon, which effectively decreased the president's capacity to survive.

The military also played a crucial role in instigating and managing these developments. As seen above, internal divisions within ABRI intensified after the appointment of Wiranto as both ABRI commander and minister of defense and security. It was in this context that the Prabowo group adopted hardline tactics, for example, supporting the kidnapping of anti-government activists and instigating riots in the face of demands for Suharto's resignation and democratic reforms.[29] These terror tactics by military extremists triggered significant anti-government movements in society. When disorder reached a peak, Wiranto effectively neutralized Prabowo by providing Suharto with intelligence that implicated his son-in-law and exonerated ABRI from responsibility for his unsanctioned, extremist actions. By offering military protection for Suharto if he would agree to step down, Wiranto convinced Suharto that his interests would best be served by accepting Wiranto's implicit recommendation, that is, to resign from the presidential office and distance himself from his rogue relative. Suharto's last days in office demonstrated the desperate brinkmanship and military showdown behind the scenes of domestic political strife, a contest won by Wiranto who finally convinced Suharto, a patron of both factions. Suharto, mindful of the fate of other deposed dictators around the world, finally had to abandon his divide-and-rule tactics in a bid for protection from democratic forces demanding accountability and prosecution.

The Post-Suharto Military: Fragile Civilian Control and Dwifungsi Legacy

Suharto's long-term dictatorship was over and a democratic transition took place in Indonesia. Society was liberated. Participation in politics and the political competition that had been severely restricted during the New Order era soon became the norm. Given the circumstances, the post-Suharto era represented uncharted waters for military leaders in a hostile context of popular resentment of the military as an obstacle to meaningful political reform. Clearly, many people expected a transition to civilian control of the military under the governments of Habibie (May 1998–October 1999), Abdurrahman Wahid (October 1999–July 2001), Megawati Sukarnoputri (July 2001–October 2004), Susilo Bambang Yudhoyono (October 2004–October 2014), and Joko Widodo (October 2014–present). However, twenty years into the post-Suharto period, the military has barely been controlled and it still holds significant political influence. Why is this so? Rather than describing chronological developments after the fall of Suharto, we will examine the dynamics of how the post-Suharto democratic change weakened the military but also produced circumstances negative to the demilitarization of politics.

The early years after Suharto's resignation in 1998 demonstrated that his fall had an impact that went well beyond changes in government form and style. It had shaken the unity of the nation-state. Long-suppressed ethnic, religious, and regional conflicts erupted throughout the archipelago, most notably in East Timor, Aceh, Kalimantan, Irian Jaya and Maluku, plunging some of Indonesia's peripheral regions into chaotic violence. The state seemed to be losing control and demands for autonomy and independence, coupled with religious and ethnic strife, suggested a nation unraveling. The civilian governments seemed ill-prepared to navigate these uncharted and stormy waters of reform, reconciliation, and transformation. Weak leadership had been institutionalized since the 1999 general elections, which resulted in the emergence of various new political parties with no single party holding the majority of seats in the DPR. This forced the ensuing governments into a coalition of several political parties with conflicting interests. Moreover, the legacy of three decades of authoritarian rule had taken a toll on civil society and complicated the process of recovery from the mismanagement, distortions, corruption, institutional atrophy, and political oppression that marked Suharto's Indonesia.

Undoubtedly, the end of the New Order period created democratic change in Indonesia. It was the beginning of the "deconcentration" of political power that had long been personalized by Suharto. His fall was followed by the empowerment of legislatures, reflecting the social demand for broader political participation. The role of parliament both at the national and local levels dramatically increased, thus automatically reducing the relative political power of the executive bodies. During the Suharto period, both central and local politics had been largely dominated by military officers and bureaucrats, but in the post-Suharto Indonesia they lost a considerable degree of their political influence because of the rise of civilian party politicians. These civilian politicians enjoyed a widening political authority in the empowered parliament, and civilian party politics dominated the country's formal political process which in the past had been monopolized by Suharto. The collapse of the New Order thus facilitated the diffusion of state political power, in the process empowering legislatures and strengthening party politics.

Reflecting such changes in power structure, the military lost its political hegemony. The legitimacy of *dwifungsi* was no longer sacrosanct nor, in terms of public opinion and some elements in the armed forces, was it a compelling justification for a pervasive military role in politics. Today's generals claim that the military abandoned *dwifungsi* after the introduction of several reforms under the slogan of "ABRI's New Paradigm" adopted in September 1998. In fact, the New Paradigm's reform projects brought some visible changes (Crouch, 1999). The military eliminated its socio-political section, which had overseen everyday political interventions, from its organizational structure. The military representatives in the parliament were abolished. The military also refrained from interfering with political parties during electoral campaigns. These changes were, to a large extent, promoted by a group of officers who understood the importance of accommodating and responding to pressures for democratic change in order to rejuvenate the ruined image of the military in society and to regain the public trust.

However, these apparent changes in the military did not guarantee its complete withdrawal from politics nor the unqualified acceptance of civilian supremacy. Although the socio-political section was abolished, its political surveillance function was assumed by the territorial section. Moreover, despite the abolition of military representatives in the parliament, the military continued to influence the parliament through back-channel lobbying. Generals no longer automatically sided with Golkar but supported the ruling parties to use their leverage to promote military interests. Thus, it can be said that the military reforms served up old wine in new bottles. The military adapted to the new, emerging political landscape and honed its political skills in accommodating, deflecting, and manipulating pressures for change in ways that enabled it to maintain political influence.

In this way, the post-Suharto military is not the hegemonic political force it once was, but it continues to exercise strong influence on the political process under the civilian government. Why, then, does the military still cast such a long shadow over the emerging Indonesian polity? This is partly by default. After three decades of a repressive New Order regime, the institutions, patterns, and inclinations of the civilian political elite withered to the point that even a weakened military remains a key political actor and *primus inter pares* (first among equals). Twenty years of post-Suharto civilian governments have demonstrated the reality of a weak civilian authority unable to completely depoliticize the military.

Moreover, in the context of political instability, weak political leadership, and threats to national unity, the military has had ample reason and opportunity to avoid a further retreat from political activities. In early post-Suharto years, especially between 1998 and 2004, the meltdown of the authoritarian state exposed many long-suppressed problems in Indonesia and bequeathed a legacy of weak civilian institutions to cope with these festering, if not intractable, problems. The escalating political violence rooted in ethnic and religious animosities clearly indicated that the police were incapable of handling them alone and there was a continuing demand for a strong military presence. It was the powerful logic of preserving national unity and stability that enabled the military to neutralize pressures to return to the barracks. In fact, the number of ABRI's territorial units was increased, rather than decreased, under the civilian governments post-Suharto. It is thus convincingly suspected that the military benefited from the communal violence and that it even had a hand in its continuance.

Three presidents during the early post-Suharto years, namely Habibie, Abdurrahman Wahid (popularly called Gus Dur), and Megawati, enjoyed only ceremonial civilian supremacy over the military. Generals seemingly accepted the principle of "civilian supremacy" but also reserved the right to determine to what extent the writ of civilian supremacy extends into what they consider to be "internal" military affairs. Thus, the notion of civilian supremacy that emerged in Indonesia was circumscribed and incomplete. The military leadership recognized that the era of military supremacy was over in Indonesia and there was no desire to return to that situation. Cognizant of the high costs of political takeover to the institutional integrity of the military and how this could undermine its ability to act decisively with the trust and confidence of the public, there appeared to be wide acceptance among military leaders of the need for civilians to manage politics. This, however, was not to say that the generals were ready to accept civilian initiatives in the "military" field which, in their eyes, included personnel affairs and defense policies. Officers still saw the military field as sacrosanct.

This perception kept providing the military with incentives to oppose civilian governments over national defense-security issues and to sabotage government policies when they were deemed to infringe on military turf. This resistance was easily legitimized, in the eyes of generals, with reference to the military's self-ascribed role as patriotic defenders of the nation and the Constitution. As arbiters of the national interest, they saw a duty to resist or subvert government policies that contradict what they define as the national interest. Thus, the military saw no inconsistency between accepting the principle of civilian supremacy and resisting civilian control of the military. This was clearly a legacy of the *dwifungsi* mindset.

The initial years of post-Suharto Indonesia also revealed that civilian management of the military was fraught with difficulties. Thus, President Habibie experienced a total loss of authority in dealing with Wiranto's military in its conduct of a "dirty war" against East Timor's pro-independence citizens.[30] During the Wahid government, the president's attempts at asserting control over the military backfired in the end. In trying to create a "loyal" military, Wahid intervened extensively in personnel changes in a way that was seen to be arbitrary, unfair, and harmful to the military's organizational cohesion. The politicization of promotions exacerbated military skepticism towards civilian leaders, in effect strengthening the position of hardline elements within the military who resisted reforms and diminished the influence of military reformers.[31] Clumsy civilian interference reinforced existing prejudice within the ranks towards politicians, and thus reduced the incentive to buy into the new arrangements and therefore slowed the pace of reform. Perhaps to avoid the "mistakes" of Wahid, President Megawati gave more of a free hand to the military. This, however, greatly contributed to the decline of pressures calling for military reform. The following government led by Yudhoyono, an ex-military elite, further weakened the reform incentive by widening the military role into the area of counter-terrorism. Yudhoyono's decade was regarded as the period of stagnation in terms of military reform.[32] The current administration under President Joko Widodo has also taken the same approach—providing new roles for the military in areas far from its professional missions.[33]

Of course, reform agendas are complex and involve various short- and long-term projects. They start from short-term organizational streamlining, rethinking doctrines, and redefining roles to long-term educational reform.[34] For civilian democratizers, military reforms are aimed at reigning in the military's political activism by eliminating the legacies of *dwifungsi*'s organizational, doctrinal, and ideological assumptions and implications. It is not terribly hard to juxtapose what is wrong in the military and what should be done to advance reform. Broadly speaking, Indonesia's post-Suharto efforts to democratize civil-military relations appear to have two goals. The first is to depoliticize the military institution which has long engaged in political matters due to the ideology of *dwifungsi*. The second goal is to demilitarize the political process. The two goals are linked and mutually reinforcing, but require different strategies. Depoliticizing the military is aimed at reorienting the professional tasks of the military, while demilitarizing the political process depends on fostering a healthy political system which discourages civilians from seeking military support in their "democratic" competition with rival politicians. These reforms need to proceed simultaneously in order to promote stable and democratic civil-military relations in Indonesia.

Conclusion

As we have examined, the political position of the Indonesian military has changed over time. Prior to the New Order period, the military "participated" in politics as one of several major political forces. Under Suharto's regime, the military "dominated" the Indonesian polity based on the ideology of developmentalism and its doctrinal embodiment of *dwifungsi*. After the fall of Suharto, the military again returned to a participatory position in the political system. Today, after two decades of post-authoritarianism, civil society demands that the military goes back to the barracks. Is it possible to put the military into this uncharted zone? Doing so may require the current civilian leaders to persuade the military that democracy in Indonesia would never fail like in the 1950s.

Apart from such a macro-assessment on the shifting political position of the military in the polity, the history of the Indonesian army reveals that it has always been a promoter of large-scale violence in the country. This is clearly demonstrated in the army crackdown of regional rebellions in the late 1950s; anti-communist mass killings in the mid-1960s; military occupation and subsequent repression in East Timor since the mid-1970s, followed by the escalation of military operations to suppress separatist movements in Aceh, Irian Jaya, and East Timor in the late 1980s; a military crackdown of the popular democratic movement led by Megawati supporters in the mid-1990s; army-orchestrated riots in the last days of Suharto; the systematic destruction of East Timor leading to its independence in 1999; and the lingering conflicts in Aceh, Maluku, Ambon, Papua (Irian Jaya), and other areas where the military has played the role of arsonist rather than fireman of the internal war.

This tradition of political violence in Indonesia not only illustrates the historical role of the army as the agent of terrorizing people despite its claim of being a "people's army," but also reflects the great lack of state capacity in handling social problems in a peaceful manner even after seventy years of independence. Indonesia's current democratic practice is expected to build this capacity both in order to construct viable state-society relations in the post-Suharto period and to wipe out the space for the military to exercise its influence in domestic political affairs.

The prospect is, however, still narrow. The army propaganda of possible national breakup is so far very successful in convincing the civilian political elite to see the situation in Papua as a threat for national unity. Such perception has been significantly encouraged since the 9/11 terrorist attack on New York in September 2001 and the subsequent US-led international campaign for the war on terrorism, which put strong pressure on Indonesia to improve the ability of its security sectors. This was quickly translated by Indonesia's top generals as an opportune time to strengthen its military presence in order to save the country from the threat of "terrorism" rather than weakening the military by conducting reforms aimed at democratizing civil-military relations. When this trend encountered the bloody "10.12" bomb blast in Bali in October 2002, which killed about 200 people, mostly Westerners, the perception of civilian politicians was unconditionally switched to security mode. This has allowed the military to take bigger initiatives in security policymaking which, of course, has significant political implications. Here too, we recognize the history of the US role in conditioning the direction of civil-military relations in Indonesia, which goes back to the late 1950s, as we have seen above.

Notes

1. On the history of Sudirman and his role in leading the army during the revolutionary war, see Said 1991.

2. I use the term "military" as interchangeable with the army because of its dominant power among services and its inclination to speak as if it were the military during the New Order period. The Indonesian military before the New Order consisted of three services—the army, the navy, and the air force. When the Suharto regime was launched in 1966, the police force was integrated into the military and the new four service military forces were named ABRI, an abbreviation of Angkatan Bersenjata Republik Indonesia (Armed Forces of the Republic of Indonesia).

3. For an account of civil-military relations before the New Order, see McVey 1971; Sundhaussen 1982.

4. Regarding the political process during the parliamentary democracy, see Feith 1962; Lev 1966.

5. About the "middle way" concept, see, for example, Sundhaussen 1982.

6. About these military campaigns, see Leifer 1983; Mackie 1974.

7. Besides the official account, there is reasonable suspicion that Suharto himself manipulated or instigated the abortive coup both in order to create a breakthrough for the army to crush the PKI and pave the way for the Kostrad

commander to take control of the army leadership. See, for example, Anderson and McVey 1971.

8. Sukarno's "instruction" to Suharto was conveyed through a letter dated March 11, 1966, which was called Supersemar (Presidential Letter of March 11). The letter authorized Suharto to handle the political situation. However, Supersemar is still a controversial issue because of a suspicion that Sukarno wrote the letter under duress. Regardless of the truth, Suharto banned the PKI the day after the letter was issued. Suspected PKI supporters became political prisoners if they were arrested or victims of military-supervised killings. The most commonly accepted estimate of the death toll was between 250,000 and 500,000. About the coup and the aftermath, see, for example, Anderson and McVey 1971; Cribb 1990; Robinson 1995.

9. There were ten area commands (Kodams) in the ABRI structure and they controlled their respective territories. Under each Kodam there were several Korems (regional commands), except for Kodam Jaya/Jakarta, and each Korem supervised Kodims (district commands) in its own territory. Kodims oversaw Koramils (subdistrict commands). This territorial defense system enabled ABRI's everyday control of political affairs throughout the archipelago. About the New Order military organization, see Sundhaussen 1978.

10. Pancasila is a set of five principles declared by Sukarno in 1945 to oppose the idea that Indonesia should be an Islamic nation. It consists of belief in God, humanitarianism, national unity, Indonesian democracy based on consultation and consensus, and social justice. The first principle refers to God rather than Allah, thus implying that the "Pancasila state" guarantees Indonesia as a multireligious nation. The fourth principle, however, can be exclusionary if the state identifies the opposition as not based on "Indonesian democracy."

11. During the 1970s, F-ABRI occupied 75 seats in the DPR, which consisted of 460 members. When the size of the DPR was extended to 500 in 1987, ABRI's appointed seats were increased to 100.

12. Regarding the *kekaryaan* practice, see MacDougall's empirical studies (1982; 1986). In 1971, for example, among the higher central bureaucracy, 44 percent of cabinet members, 41 percent of secretary generals, and 73 percent of inspector generals were active-duty officers. Regional governments were also

penetrated by military members. In 1977, 78 percent of provincial governors were army men and more than half (155) of Indonesia's 294 *bupati* (regent) and mayors were ABRI men (Jenkins 1984, 47).

13. Soemitro's suspicions of Ali Moertopo and CSIS are described in his biography (Ramadhan 1996, 286, 307–11).

14. Petisi 50 was founded in 1980 in response to Suharto's speech at Pekanbaru in which he said that ABRI would continue to support Golkar in the next election due in 1982. Petisi's members included Ali Sadikin, a retired navy admiral and popular former governor of Jakarta. They openly criticized Suharto's arbitrary use of Pancasila as a tool for repressing anti-regime opinions and demanded that ABRI, as the "national guardian," return to the "original intention" of *dwifungsi*, which was, according to them, to be neutral in conducting its political mission to "stand above all groups" in elections. Petisi 50 called for the "purification of *dwifungsi*." As seen above, Nasution was a former army chief who declared, in 1958, that the Indonesian military would take a middle way (*jalan tengah*) between military rule and an apolitical role. This speech is said to be the origin of the concept of *dwifungsi*. For the emergence of the critical retired officers during this period, see Jenkins 1984, especially pp. 171–87 pertaining to Petisi 50 and ABRI's severe pressure on these retired officers since then.

15. All of these Suharto loyalists served in intelligence security sectors within ABRI. Sudomo had been running Kopkamtib since 1974 after Soemitro, and had been deputy commander of ABRI since 1978. Yoga had been the head of the State Intelligence Coordination Agency (BAKIN) since 1974, which was directly responsible to the president, and he also served as the chief of Kopkamtib from 1978 to 1980. Moerdani had been the head of the Strategic Intelligence Centre (Pusintelstrat), ABRI's intelligence body, since 1977 and deputy head of BAKIN since early 1978.

16. A notable case was that of Abu Bakar Ba'asyir, who escaped to Malaysia with his friends and only returned to Indonesia after Suharto's resignation. Ba'asyir was allegedly the spiritual leader of Jemaah Islamiyah, which was recognized in 2002 by the United Nations as a terrorist organization aiming to create a unitary Islamic state in Southeast Asia. About Ba'asyir and military manipulation during the early 1980s, see International Crisis Group 2002.

Ba'asyir was arrested after the Bali bombing on October 12, 2002 and suspected of masterminding the incident and other bombings.

17. ABRI's business activities go back to the 1950s. The lack of a government budget to finance defense spending had been substituted by business activities conducted by military-owned enterprises. All territorial units had also been engaged in various legal/illegal profit-making activities in order to finance their operations. The official defense budget allegedly covered less than 30 percent of annual expenses. For the involvement of the military in business, see Crouch 1988, ch. 1; Richard Robison 1986, ch. 8.

18. About the rise of Sudharmono, see Pangaribuan 1995, 58–9.

19. About the ICMI, see Hefner 2000. About ABRI's negative response to the creation of ICMI, see Ramage 1995, 132–49.

20. For an account on the cleavage within the military during this period, see Honna 2003.

21. Wiranto's appointment as both ABRI commander and defense and security minister did not mean that Suharto gave his full support to Wiranto in his competition with Prabowo. It was more like a strategy of buying the loyalty of Wiranto, at the same time motivating Prabowo to more effectively defend Suharto's political interests.

22. More than 1,200 people were killed. About the riots, see, for example, Siegel 2001.

23. For details about Kopassus's recruitment and training of hoodlums in organizing the riots, see Anon. "Saksi Saksi Setelah 100 Hari."

24. On May 14, Wiranto asked Sjafrie to obey his order or risk being dismissed. On this account, see Mietzner 1999, 79.

25. For these accounts, see Prabowo's interview in *Asiaweek*, March 3, 2000.

26. Prabowo admitted that Mamiek, Suharto's youngest daughter, called him a "traitor" and requested that he not come to Suharto's palace again. Prabowo accused Wiranto of playing politics against him. See his interview in *Asiaweek*, March 3, 2000.

27. Habibie gave Wiranto approval to remove Prabowo and, in return, Habibie was assured of Wiranto's support for the new government. On this account, see Shiraishi 1999, 82–83.

28. Prabowo tried to lead some of his Kostrad soldiers to an impromptu meeting with Habibie, but the president refused to agree to a meeting. Habibie later revealed that he was informed by Wiranto in advance about Prabowo's attempt to capture him, a claim denied by Wiranto for obvious reasons. According to Prabowo, he wanted to "talk" with Habibie because he had long been promised the post of ABRI commander by Habibie if the latter became president. On this account, see *Asiaweek*, March 3, 2000.

29. From February to May 1998, more than twenty-three activists disappeared. In July 1999, Wiranto admitted that Kopassus was responsible for kidnapping nine of them. The rest are still missing.

30. About East Timor's struggle for independence and the military disturbance under the Habibie government, see, for example, Tanter, Selden, and Shalom 2001. Also see Robinson's (2001) vivid analysis of the military use of militias in provoking violence in East Timor.

31. For the military's internal power struggle during the post-Suharto era, see Honna 2003, ch. 7.

32. See Aspinall, Mietzner, and Tomsa 2015.

33. See, for example, Institute for Policy Analysis of Conflict 2015.

34. Actual reform designs are not analyzed here as they would require a lengthy discussion extending beyond the scope of this chapter. Regarding the reform agendas, see for example, International Crisis Group, 2001. See also Mietzner 2006.

References

Anderson, Benedict, and Ruth T. McVey. 1971. *A Preliminary Analysis of the October 1, 1965 Coup in Indonesia*. Ithaca, NY: Cornell University Modern Indonesia Project.

Anon. 1998. "Saksi Saksi Setelah 100 Hari." *Tajuk* 14 (September): 1–3.

Asiaweek. 2000. "The Scapegoat?" March 3.

Aspinall, Edward. 2000. "Political Opposition and the Transition from Authoritarian Rule: The Case of Indonesia." PhD thesis, Australian National University, Canberra.

Aspinall, Edward, Marcus Mietzner, and Dirk Tomsa, eds. 2015. *The Yudhoyono Presidency: Indonesia's Decade of Stability and Stagnation*. Singapore: Institute of Southeast Asian Studies.

Bresnan, John. 1993. *Managing Indonesia: The Modern Political Economy*. New York, NY: Columbia University Press.

Cribb, Robert, ed. 1990. *The Indonesian Killings, 1965–1966: Studies from Java and Bali*. Victoria: Centre of Southeast Asian Studies, Monash University.

Crouch, Harold. 1988. *The Army and Politics in Indonesia*, revised edition. Ithaca, NY: Cornell University Press.

———. 1992. "An Ageing President, An Ageing Regime." In *Indonesia Assessment 1992: Political Perspectives on the 1990s*, eds. Harold Crouch and Hal Hill, Political and Social Change Monograph 17, 43–62. Canberra: Department of Political and Social Change, Research School of Pacific and Asian Studies, Australian National University.

———. 1999. "Wiranto and Habibie: Civil-Military Relations since May 1998." In *Reformasi: Crisis and Change in Indonesia,* eds. Arief Budiman, Barbara Hatley and Damien Kingsbury, 127–48. Clayton: Monash Asia Institute.

Emmerson, Donald K. 1999. "Exit and Aftermath: The Crisis of 1997–1998". In *Indonesia Beyond Suharto: Polity, Economy, Social Transition,* ed. Donald K. Emmerson, 295–343. New York: M. E. Sharpe.

Feith, Herbert. 1962. *The Decline of Constitutional Democracy in Indonesia*. Ithaca, NY: Cornell University Press.

Hefner, Robert. 2000. *Civil Islam: Muslims and Democratization in Indonesia*. Princeton, NJ: Princeton University Press.

Honna, Jun. 2001. "Military Ideology in Response to Democratic Pressure during the Late Suharto Era: Political and Institutional Contexts." In *Violence and the State in Suharto's Indonesia*, ed. Benedict Anderson, 54–89. Ithaca, NY: Cornell University Southeast Asia Program.

———. 2003. *Military Politics and Democratization in Indonesia*. London: RoutledgeCurzon.

Institute for Policy Analysis of Conflict. 2015. "The Expanding Role of the Indonesian Military." IPAC Report No.19, May 25.

International Crisis Group. 2001. "Indonesia: Next Steps in Military Reform." Jakarta and Brussels, October 11.

———. 2002. "Al-Qaeda in Southeast Asia: The Case of 'Ngruki Network'." Jakarta and Brussels, August 8.

Jenkins, David. 1984. *Suharto and His Generals: Indonesian Military Politics 1975–1983*. Ithaca, NY: Cornell University Modern Indonesian Project no. 47.

Kahin, A. R., and G. M. Kahin. 1995. *Subversion as Foreign Policy: The Secret Eisenhower and Dulles Debacle in Indonesia*. New York: The New Press.

Kahin, George McTurnan. 1952. *Nationalism and Revolution in Indonesia*. Ithaca, NY: Cornell University Press.

Leifer, Michael. 1983. *Indonesia's Foreign Policy*. London: Allen & Unwin.

Lev, Daniel S. 1966. *The Transition to Guided Democracy: Indonesian Politics, 1957–1959*. Ithaca, NY: Cornell University Modern Indonesia Project.

MacDougall, John A. 1982. "Patterns of Military Control in the Indonesian Higher Central Bureaucracy." *Indonesia* 33 (April): 89–121.

———. 1986. "Military Penetration of the Indonesian Government: The Higher Central Bureaucracy." *Indonesia Reports* 14 (March): 2–15.

Mackie, J. A. C. 1974. *Konfrontasi: The Indonesia-Malaysia Dispute, 1963–1966*. Kuala Lumpur: Oxford University Press.

McVey, Ruth T. 1971. "The Post-Revolutionary Transformation of the Indonesian Army." *Indonesia* 11 (April): 131–76.

Mietzner, Marcus. 1999. "From Suharto to Habibie: The Indonesian Armed Forces and Political Islam during the Transition." In *Post-Suharto Indonesia: Renewal or Chaos?* ed. Geoff Forrester, 79. Singapore: Institute of Southeast Asian Studies.

———. 2006. *The Politics of Military Reform in Post-Suharto Indonesia: Elite Conflict, Nationalism, and Institutional Registance*. Policy Studies Series 23. Washington, DC: East-West Center Publications.

Mortimer, Rex. 1974. *Indonesian Communism under Sukarno: Ideology and Politics, 1959–1965*. Ithaca, NY: Cornell University Press.

Pangaribuan, Robinson, trans. Vedi Hadiz. 1995. *The Indonesian State Secretariat 1945–1993*. Perth: Asia Research Centre on Social, Political and Economic Change, Murdoch University.

Ramadhan, K. H. 1996. *Soemitro: Former Commander of Indonesian Security Apparatus*. Jakarta: Pustaka Sinar Harapan.

Ramage, Douglas. 1995. *Politics in Indonesia: Democracy, Islam and the Ideology of Tolerance*. London: Routledge.

Robinson, Geoffrey. 1995. *The Dark Side of Paradise: Political Violence in Bali*. Ithaca, NY: Cornell University Press.

———. 2001. "People's War: Militias in East Timor and Indonesia." *South East Asia Research* 9(3): 271–318.

Robison, Richard. 1986. *Indonesia: The Rise of Capital*. Sydney: Allen & Unwin.

Said, Salim. 1991. *Genesis of Power: General Sudirman and the Indonesian Military in Politics 1945–1949*. Singapore: Institute of Southeast Asian Studies.

Shiraishi, Takashi. 1999. "The Indonesian Military in Politics." In *The Politics of Post-Suharto Indonesia*, eds. Adam Schwarz and Jonathan Paris, 73–86. New York: Council on Foreign Relations Press.

Siegel, James T. 2001. "Thoughts on the Violence of May 13 and 14, 1998, in Jakarta." In *Violence and the State in Suharto's Indonesia*, ed. Benedict Anderson, 90–123. Ithaca, NY: Cornell University Southeast Asia Program Publications.

Sundhaussen, Ulf. 1978. "The Military: Structure, Procedures and Effects on Indonesian Society." In *Political Power and Communications in Indonesia*, ed. Karl D. Jackson and Lucian W. Pye, 45–81. Berkeley: University of California Press.

———. 1982. *The Road to Power: Indonesian Military Politics, 1945–1967*. Kuala Lumpur: Oxford University Press.

Tanter, Richard. 1990. "The Totalitarian Ambition: Intelligence and Security Agencies in Indonesia." In *State and Civil Society in Indonesia*, ed. Arief Budiman, 211–88. Victoria: Monash University Centre of Southeast Asian Studies.

Tanter, Richard, Mark Selden, and Stephen R. Shalom, eds. 2001. *Bitter Flowers, Sweet Flowers: East Timor, Indonesia, and the World Community*. New York, NY: Rowman & Littlefield.

Map 1. The Moluccas in Indonesia

CHAPTER 8

The Consequences of a Failed Demilitarization: Moluccan Soldiers in the Netherlands, 1951–2018

Henk M. A. G. Smeets

From March until July 1951, about 3,500 Moluccan soldiers, who had been part of the Royal Netherlands East-Indies Army (KNIL), were transported with their families to the Netherlands. In all, they numbered 12,500 people. The Dutch government called the arrival of the Moluccan people "the worst conceivable solution." The Moluccans themselves had only accepted the journey to Europe after much hesitation and under threat of immediate dismissal from the army. All those concerned had assumed that their stay in the Netherlands would be a temporary one, about six months at the most (Smeets 1992; Smeets and Steijlen 2006).

Previous History of Maluku's "Black Dutchmen," *c.* 1864–1942

The Moluccas, an archipelago of more than one thousand islands situated in the east of present-day Indonesia, was part of the Dutch East Indies.[1] The archipelago was heavily dependent on export revenues from spices, such as clove and nutmeg. Although the precursor of the Dutch colonial government, the Dutch East India Company, had first taken control of parts of the Amboina islands within the Moluccas in 1605, the story of the locally recruited colonial soldiers and their important military role in the Dutch East Indies starts in about 1864 with the collapse of the world market for spices. From then onwards, Dutch efforts to recruit Moluccans for the colonial army were, for the first time, successful. This does not mean, however, that all Moluccans were equally interested in becoming colonial soldiers because of the geographic, ethnic, religious, and political differences of the archipelago's inhabitants (Enloe 1980; Manuhutu 1995).[2]

The population of the Moluccas was characterized by large, mutual diversity. In their relations with the Dutch authorities, for instance, there were differences between the Christians and Muslims (Chauvel 1980), but differences also ran along geographical lines, notably between the Ambonese from Ambon and its surrounding islands, and the Kaiese from the southeast of the Moluccan Islands. The Moluccans who were recruited as soldiers were almost exclusively Moluccan Christians, who came from Ambon and its surroundings. From them, a military tradition of participation in the KNIL was born and this was then passed from father to son even though most of the Moluccans on the islands remained there as fishermen or farmers. Ambonese KNIL soldiers were given a privileged position in comparison to other native soldiers and they acquired a positive image as soldiers, especially during the Aceh War of 1873–1913 (Joop de Jong 1998, 309–14; Veer 1969), to the extent that they became known as "Black Dutchmen" (Chauvel 1990; Enloe 1980; Manuhutu 1995). In the same period, roughly from the first decade of the twentieth century onwards, the Dutch East Indies was notable for its growing sense of nationalism. However, only a small number of Moluccans participated in that movement. The majority of the population barely displayed any political consciousness (Chauvel 1990; Drooglever 1992).

Fig. 1. Moluccan Soldiers in the Netherlands (Moluccan Museum)

World War II

On December 7, 1941, Japan's destruction of a large part of the American Pacific Fleet in a surprise attack on Pearl Harbor marked the beginning of World War II in Southeast Asia. A day later, following the United States, the Netherlands declared war on Japan.[3] As Japan fought its way into Southeast Asia, it was not until January 10, 1942 that the Japanese army and fleet units launched a massive attack on the Dutch East Indies. Although the fighting would last for almost two months, the outcome was a foregone conclusion as Japanese military force was simply too great for the Dutch colonial forces. The Japanese army was better trained and better equipped than the KNIL, whose primary function had been that of a police force maintaining peace and order among the population. The Royal Dutch Navy and the young air force department of the KNIL were also no match for the enemy. On March 8, 1942, the KNIL surrendered and the Dutch East Indies was occupied by Japan.

Under the adage of "Asia for the Asians," the Japanese occupation authorities tried to win over the population of the Indies. They divested the Dutch of all administrative functions and isolated them from public life by interning them in prison camps, in which the men were separated from the women and children. The Indonesian nationalist elite, under the leadership of Sukarno, seized the opportunity to take over the role of the Dutch in the administrative machinery. The ultimate power, however, remained in the hands of the Japanese.

Apart from the Dutch inhabitants, many indigenous people, among whom were also Christian Moluccans, suffered a great deal during the Japanese occupation. In the eyes of the Japanese, they were a danger to the New Order because of their loyalty to the Dutch authorities. Hence, a number of Moluccan soldiers also ended up in internment camps. There were also Moluccans who played an active role in the resistance. Many of them fell into the hands of the Kempeitai, the Japanese secret police, and were tortured or killed (Chauvel 1985; Immerzeel 1992).

During the Japanese occupation, the Indonesian archipelago was shared out between the Japanese army and the Japanese navy. The areas administered by the army, which included Java and Sumatra, were promised a restricted form of self-government. With that prospect, Sukarno and other nationalist leaders supported Japan. Sukarno even called for Javanese to volunteer as *romusha* (workers). That did not prevent the Japanese army, however, from treating thousands of these "volunteer" workers as forced labor, with the result that many of them perished. The area that was governed by the navy was predestined to remain occupied territory for the Japanese empire. The Moluccan Islands were part of that region.

Fight for Decolonization

In the course of 1944, it became clear that Japan was going to lose the war. Indonesian nationalists wanted to gain independence before the Netherlands could restore their colonial system. With Japanese aid, a committee was established to prepare for independence. However, the sudden end to the war came as a surprise to the leaders. The atomic bombing of Hiroshima and Nagasaki unexpectedly forced the Japanese empire to its knees, and on August 15, 1945, the Japanese surrendered. For a short while, the nationalists were confused but then decided, under pressure from young followers, to declare the Republik Indonesia (RI). On August 17, 1945, two days after the Japanese surrender, Sukarno and Hatta signed the Declaration of Independence.

It was a peculiar deliverance for Indonesia, because almost immediately a new war broke out—the fight between the Netherlands and the Republik Indonesia. It was a period of chaos. The central authorities had largely disappeared and various armed groups were crossing the country. Dutchmen, Moluccans, and Chinese often had to pay the price. Internees who still lived in Japanese prison camps had to be protected by their former Japanese guards against youth groups (*pemuda*) who attacked the camps in the name of the new republic. Moluccan soldiers made themselves useful by spontaneously taking up the defense of the camps. Although the Moluccans were active on both sides,[4] the general public in Holland and Indonesia primarily perceived them as loyal to the Netherlands (Drooglever 1992; Smeets and Steijlen, 2006, 36–37).

Following Japan's surrender, the Netherlands tried to gain a firm foothold as quickly as possible in Indonesia. They were relatively successful in the eastern part of Indonesia, but there were also areas where the RI remained in power. This was due to the fact that the British army, which had advanced into and liberated these areas ahead of the Dutch, believed the RI to be a power to be reckoned with in the postwar period. Moreover, the English army command doubted if its troops, many of whom were recruited from British India, would be prepared to fight in a colonial war against the republic.

After some time, the Dutch troops, both from the KNIL and from the Netherlands, replaced the allied forces. Although they succeeded in gaining control over most parts of the country, the Dutch government quickly realized that in the long run the idea of an independent Indonesia was inevitable and had to be accepted (Groen 1991). In the recently founded United Nations, which was dominated by the anti-colonialist United States, there was little sympathy for a restoration of colonial relations. Besides the many new nations in the Third World, countries like Australia and the United States also believed that no country should be ruling another country in the new postwar world order. The Netherlands government defended its position by referring to the chaotic situation in Indonesia. Peace and order (*rust en orde*) should be restored. Only after that should independence be discussed. Therefore, military actions against the RI were, in veiled language, called "police actions" (Teitler and Groen 1987). World opinion, however, did not accept this justification of Dutch actions, especially the US, which pressed the Netherlands to negotiate with the Indonesian leaders. The matter was settled only after Washington threatened to withdraw help via the Marshall Plan for the postwar reconstruction of the Netherlands (Homan 1997). Following a Round Table Conference (RTC), sovereignty was handed over to the "United States of Indonesia" on December 27, 1949.

The United States of Indonesia: The Period of Federalism Versus Centralism

The formation of the "United States of Indonesia" (Republik Indonesia Serikat, RIS) was a compromise solution by which the transfer of sovereignty was to be managed. The federal model for the newly independent state was a solution that would not last long, however, as it was an unsatisfactory compromise. The Republic of Indonesia itself had wanted to assume complete power to rule Indonesia but, unsurprisingly, the Netherlands would not agree. In fact, the Netherlands had not wanted to negotiate with Sukarno and other nationalist leaders at all because they viewed them not only as dangerous extremists but also as traitors who had collaborated with the Japanese. When foreign pressure forced them to negotiate, the Dutch government tried to curb the power of the RI. In areas under Dutch control, federal states were established, which were then involved in the negotiations. In this way, the RI became one of the federal states that together were going to form the United States of Indonesia (Chauvel 1997; Smeets and Steijlen 2006, 38-39).

After Dutch sovereignty had been transferred to the United States of Indonesia on December 27, 1949, with Sukarno as the first president, it soon became clear that the federal state could not last long. One by one, the parliaments of the component states decided to dissolve themselves and become part of Republik Indonesia. Only the state of East Indonesia (Negara Indonesia Timur, NIT) held out for a while because it considered itself to be politically and economically strong enough to remain largely independent of a Jakarta- and Javanese-dominated Indonesia. Nevertheless, even in East Indonesia a political current was under way, led by the Moluccan politician Urbanus Pupella, which aspired towards the abolition of the federal NIT and a merger with the centralist Indonesian republic (Chauvel 1984).

Other Moluccan politicians, however, including Chris R. S. Soumokil, Joop A. Manusama, and Dolf Metekohy, were concerned about the likelihood of political oppression and economic exploitation of East Indonesia and its inhabitants by the central government in Jakarta. Moreover, the Christian politicians among them were fearful of the Islamic majority in the rest of

Indonesia. They therefore wanted to preserve the federal state and keep possession of their own troops, that is, units with a KNIL background. The central government did not like this last idea at all, and consequently sent units of the federal army, APRIS (Angkatan Perang Republik Indonesia Serikat), to East Indonesia. For the most part, these troops consisted of units that had formerly been part of TNI (Tentara Nasional Indonesia), the army of the RI.

After eastern Indonesian APRIS units (ex-KNIL), led by Andi Abdul Aziz, an army captain, had tried in vain to stop units of the APRIS from leaving Java, the fate of the NIT was sealed. Although the NIT would last until August 15, 1950 before the state of unity was formalized, the die had already been cast. A number of Moluccan leaders who had played a part in the administration of East Indonesia shared this opinion. Led by Manusama and Soumokil, they considered what they now had to do at Ambon. Moluccan KNIL soldiers who were present at Ambon also played a part in these consultations. The leaders of the administration of the district (*daerah*) Maluku Selatan (South Maluku), Joop H. Manuhutu and Albert Wairisal, were put under pressure to declare the South Moluccas independent in protest against the abolition of the federal structure, which was considered a violation of the RTC agreements. Manuhutu and Wairisal did have some doubts, but eventually these two top civil servants decided to declare independence after strong insistence from other Moluccan leaders present at Ambon. On April 25, 1950, the proclamation of the Republic of the South Moluccas (Republik Maluku Selatan, RMS), was solemnly signed. Manuhutu became president of the new republic, Wairisal the prime minister, Soumokil the minister of foreign affairs, and Manusama the minister of education.[5]

Republik Maluku Selatan

The first few days after the proclamation of the Republik Maluku Selatan (RMS), many Moluccans—mostly Christian—on Ambon were jubilant. They had their own state and they believed, on the basis of the RTC agreements, that they would get the support of the Netherlands and the

United Nations.[6] They had anticipated that the government of Indonesia would not accept the proclamation. The central government in Jakarta was quick to send a "brother mission" of RI-minded Moluccans to Ambon. Led by the RI's public health minister, Jo Leimena, the mission was largely in vain. In the meantime, it became clear that nothing would come out of international support for the RMS. The United Nations stayed in the background and was only willing to do something if the Indonesian government agreed, which was not the case. Moreover, before long the United Nations itself became occupied with more serious matters, in particular the Korean War, which had broken out on June 25, 1950. In spite of pressure from people in the Netherlands to help Ambon, the Dutch government did not provide any support.

Fig. 2. RMS President J. Manuhutu inspects his troops at Ambon, 1950

Indonesia blamed the Netherlands for having been involved in the establishment of the RMS, because Moluccan KNIL soldiers were said to have demanded the proclamation of independence. In order to dispel that impression, the Dutch troop commander in East Indonesia, L. Schotborgh, was sent to Ambon to call the soldiers to order, but it was to no avail. On May 9, 1950, Daan J. Samson, commander of the new RMS army, handed over, in front of the troops, a Dutch flag, pistol, and KNIL rank insignia to symbolize that they had left the Dutch army. Not long afterwards, a great number of local Dutch left Ambon for fear of an Indonesian attack. And that attack did come, after Jakarta had briefly tried to force the RMS to its knees with an unsuccessful naval blockade of the Moluccan Islands.

In May 1950, the Indonesian army had already occupied a number of the southern islands. From July 13, onwards, it launched the first attacks on the mid-Moluccan islands, and on September 28, the island of Ambon itself was attacked. The fighting was fierce and casualties were high.[7] At this time, however, the core of the RMS army, the "berets" (commando troops), had mainly been withdrawn from Ambon and been stationed on the island of Seram. Although the Moluccan side showed tough resistance, including the participation of a considerable number of *sukarela* (young volunteers, often schoolchildren), they were ultimately no match for the numerically far superior Indonesian forces (Manusama 1999, 195–202). Nevertheless, the fighting lasted until December 1950 when the RMS government had to flee to its last stronghold, Seram, where it had concentrated its remaining troops. In the jungle of Seram, the war continued, and it was a small guerrilla fight that would last another thirteen years, until December 1963.

The Position of Moluccan KNIL Soldiers

Republic Indonesia's relatively rapid progress against the RMS was in large part due to the fact that most KNIL soldiers of Moluccan origin were stationed far away from the Moluccas and consequently unable to defend their homeland. At the proclamation of the RMS in April 1950, and by the time the Indonesian army captured Ambon in December of the same year, most Moluccan KNIL soldiers were based thousands of kilometers away in barracks (*tangsi*) in other parts of the Indonesian archipelago, still in the service of the Dutch government.

At the formal transfer of sovereignty in late December 1949, it had been decided that the KNIL would be dissolved within six months. The Dutch KNIL soldiers were to be repatriated. The native soldiers were offered a choice. They could either be demobilized or apply to transfer to APRIS, the army of the United States of Indonesia. For many Moluccan soldiers, transfer to APRIS was out of the question as its core was composed of the TNI, the former army of Republik Indonesia, whom they had fought against until recently. Moreover, many Moluccan soldiers feared retaliation for their service in the Dutch KNIL. In particular, members of special forces such as the "berets," who were accused of war crimes, feared revenge (Moor 1999). It was thus little wonder that they hesitated when given the opportunity to join APRIS. However, the idea was not rejected offhand by all Moluccan soldiers as some tried to negotiate favorable and acceptable transfer conditions. Among these conditions was the express wish that they be transferred to APRIS collectively, as units rather than as individuals. They also demanded that they be commanded by their own (subaltern) officers, and that they be stationed in East Indonesia. As discussed above, this was also what the East Indonesian politicians wanted (Smeets 1991a; Smeets and Steijlen 2006, 54–56).

The negotiations over this transfer were in full swing when the RMS was proclaimed on Ambon. Most of the Moluccan soldiers who had not yet been transferred to APRIS chose the side of the RMS. This resulted in demonstrations, for instance in Jakarta, by Moluccan soldiers and civilians and even armed conflicts between Moluccan KNIL soldiers and the APRIS in Makassar on the island of Celebes (now Sulawesi). Transfer to the Indonesian army came to a halt. The Moluccan soldiers, who were concentrated in a few camps on Java after the confrontations in Makassar, now wanted to be demobilized on Ambon (Smeets and Steijlen 2006, 56–58).

The Liquidation of the KNIL

In army regulations, it was stated that demobilization could only take place if the soldiers concerned had arrived "at the place of their choice" within Indonesia. By itself, this was a useful measure. It confirmed that soldiers who had served in an area as vast as Europe could leave the army wherever they wanted to in order to make a new start in life as civilians. However, the Netherlands needed the approval of the Indonesian government for the demobilization, not only because Ambon was part of Indonesia but also because the Moluccans, according to the agreements of the transfer of sovereignty, had become Indonesian citizens. Most Moluccan soldiers wanted to be demobilized in the Moluccas so that they could support the RMS. When it became clear that Jakarta disagreed with demobilization on Ambon, the Moluccan soldiers opted instead for demobilization on neighboring Dutch New Guinea. This choice was driven by relative geographical proximity as well as by the fact that Dutch New Guinea was to remain under Dutch sovereignty.[8] This was reason enough for the Republik Indonesia to disagree a second time.

The government in Jakarta was prepared to let Moluccan KNIL soldiers return to Ambon, however, once the island had been wrested from the RMS. For a very short time, it looked as though the Moluccan soldiers would agree with this provided they were guaranteed they would be left alone by the Indonesian army upon demobilization. As a result of the intervention of the former RMS minister of supply, Piet W. Lokollo, who had arrived in Holland via Australia, this plan was abandoned. The soldiers then repeated their request to be demobilized on either Dutch New Guinea or in Seram where the RMS army was still fighting, but this was rejected once more by Jakarta and The Hague (Smeets 1992; Smeets and Steijlen 2006, 55–56).

The Netherlands was becoming increasingly exasperated. Although the KNIL had been dissolved on July 26, 1950, as agreed by the RTC Agreements of December 1949, nine thousand members of the Dutch army were still based on Java at the beginning of 1951. Among them were four thousand Moluccan soldiers who were still awaiting demobilization and also about five thousand Dutch soldiers who were waiting to return home but who had to act as a buffer between their Moluccan colleagues and the hostile political environment in Indonesia. In order to demobilize the remaining Moluccan soldiers in an orderly fashion, they were temporarily given Royal Army (Koninklijke Landmacht, KL) status (Smeets and Steijlen 2006, 56–57).

At the beginning of December 1950, the Dutch government decided that it could not wait any longer for the demobilization of the Moluccan soldiers. They were concerned about foreign criticism of the slow process of decolonization, in particular from the United States, as well as a deterioration in relations with Indonesia. Moreover, they faced conflict with the Dutch parliament that had called for a speedy homecoming of the remaining Dutch conscripts serving in Indonesia. The Drees/van Schaik coalition government therefore considered demobilizing the Moluccans in Java. This was against the regulations but, so it was argued, this was a case of *force majeure* (Smeets and Steijlen 2006, 60–62).

In the meantime, a delegation of Moluccan soldiers had arrived in the Netherlands to look after the interests of their colleagues. Led by Frederik Aponno, they had instituted proceedings against the Netherlands to prevent this demobilization. With the support of lawyer Karel van Rijckevorsel, the proceedings were won at the highest level. It was decided that the Netherlands was not allowed to abandon its soldiers against their wishes in the territory of the former enemy (Moll 1977; Smeets and Steijlen 2006, 62–64). As the fate of the Moluccan soldiers had become a pressing issue, it was felt that the only remaining solution was the temporary removal of the Moluccan soldiers to the Netherlands. In that way, the Netherlands could buy time in deciding the fate of the Moluccans while the Dutch soldiers could finally return home. These plans were finalized at the beginning of 1951

Fig. 3. A Moluccan soldier and his family board a boat headed for the Netherlands, 1951

when the remaining Dutch troops embarked from Java, some 5,000 Dutch and 3,500 Moluccan soldiers, and about 500 other Moluccans (policemen, civilians). The Moluccans were joined by their wives and children. In total, 12,500 passengers arrived in the Netherlands between March and June 1951. In its desperate quick-fix solution, the Drees/van Schaik government had not considered that the envisaged transitory stay would take on a far more permanent form and, in the process, cause considerable vexation to successive Dutch governments. Now, almost seventy years later, some 40 thousand Moluccans are living in the Netherlands and the fourth generation is now reaching adulthood.

No other ethnic group has ever arrived in the Netherlands so explicitly and collectively sharing the same history, the same profession, and, very importantly, the same employer—the Dutch government. It is the dominant role played by the government in the lives of these Moluccans that makes the history of their immigration so very special. At first, they had to deal with the Dutch government in its role of employer, and then in its capacity as a welfare provider. Eventually, the Moluccans had to deal with a state authority wishing to relinquish these extraordinary roles in order to create a "normal" relationship, of the type common between a government and her citizens. This was a laborious process, partly due to the mistakes made by the Dutch government immediately after the arrival of the Moluccans (Smeets 2001; Smeets and Veenman 2000, 36–63).

Dismissal by Demilitarization Rather than Demobilization

The Dutch government's biggest mistake was that they decided to dismiss the Moluccan soldiers from military service immediately after their disembarkation in the Netherlands. This was a process of "demilitarization" rather than "demobilization," which could only occur at the Moluccans' place of choice in Indonesia.

Why did the government decide on this mass dismissal, which would make a whole community unemployed? The government advanced the following legal reasoning to justify its actions. Because the Moluccan soldiers had automatically acquired Indonesian nationality, they could not, according to the majority of the Dutch Cabinet, serve in the Dutch army.[9] Moreover, the Netherlands had promised the Indonesian government that the Moluccan soldiers would not be deployed operationally.[10] Further, many ministers considered such undeployable soldiers to be rather useless. These formal motives for their dismissal were not correct. In spite of their Indonesian nationality small numbers of Moluccan soldiers did serve in the Royal Dutch Navy and the Dutch commandos. Moluccan commandos were deployed in Asia during the Korean War. The real reason was that the Netherlands did not want to have such a large group of colored people in their army in Europe (Smeets and Steijlen 2006, 79–85).

It was remarkable that the two ministers who were primarily concerned with this matter—s'Jacob, who was responsible for the army, and van Maarseveen, responsible for contacts with Indonesia—opposed the dismissal. They feared that it would be difficult to control the Moluccans once they became unemployed and were ungoverned by military discipline. Dutch civil servants pointed out that there were enough non-operational tasks at hand to provide employment, such as the guarding of military installations, but the rest of the government thought that the maintenance of public order was not a sufficient reason to keep the Moluccans in military service. Public order was the police's prerogative (Smeets 1991b).

The Moluccan soldiers, however, did not accept dismissal. They felt betrayed by their employer whom they had served under particularly difficult circumstances during the decade 1941–51. They took their case to a court of military personnel, and on November 16, 1951 won the case. The government, which then appealed to a higher court, did not have high expectations that the first ruling would be overturned, as indicated by its preparations for re-employing the Moluccans in the army. But, surprisingly, it turned in their favor. On March 4, 1952, the Central Court of Appeal declared that the first court was not competent to pronounce judgement, with the result that the government's first decision concerning the soldiers' dismissal was maintained. This was a setback for the Moluccan soldiers (Moll 1977; Smeets and Steijlen 2006, 79–82).

The consequences of the Central Court of Appeal's ruling were considerable. Relations between the Moluccans and the Dutch government as their ex-employer, already troubled before this verdict, had now completely soured. The aftershocks of the unexpected ruling would be felt for a long time, not least because the Moluccans and their erstwhile employer would still have to regularly face each other after the dismissal. The Dutch government thus remained responsible for the welfare of the Moluccans and was most clearly visible in its provision of housing for the dismissed soldiers and their families. Encampments were used for housing because there still was a severe shortage of regular housing in the Netherlands so soon after World War II. It was hence difficult to find enough accommodation for the 12,500 newly arrived Moluccans. Government housing property, which had previously been used by the government, was the solution. Among the encampments used to accommodate the Moluccans were two former German concentration camps, located in Westerbork and Vught. This encampment housing solution was based on the assumption that the Moluccans would soon return home. Up until 1959, the encampments served the Dutch government's belief that

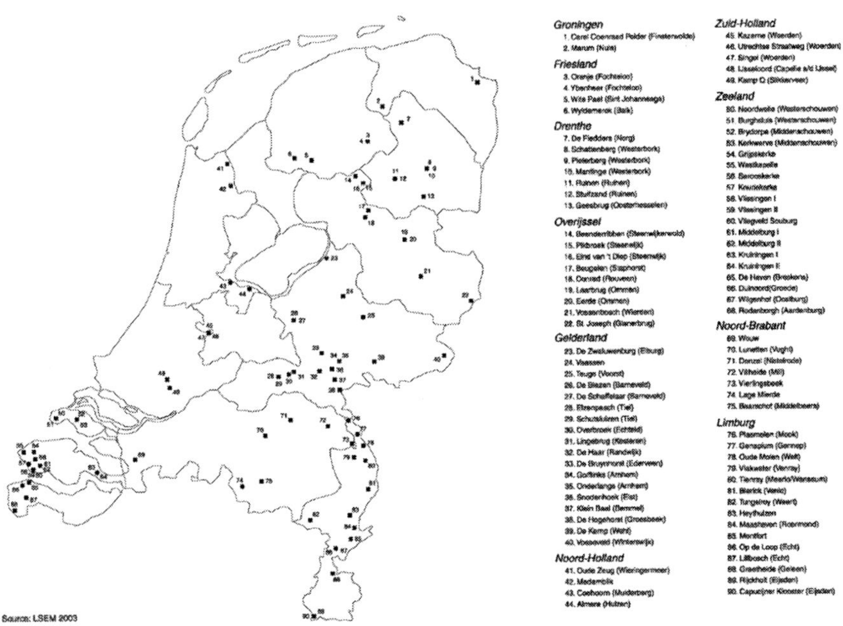

Map 2. Moluccan Camps in the Netherlands (Moluccan Museum)

it was preferable to keep their "temporary" guests away from Dutch society, thereby preventing integration (Akihary 1991).

During the first five years, the living expenses of the dismissed soldiers were paid by the Dutch government. The soldiers and their families were thus not motivated to work. Moreover, the highest official in the ministry of labor did not want "Indonesians" to enter the Dutch job market. The former Moluccan soldiers and their relatives were therefore reduced to idleness and complete dependence on the government. Frustrations over their dismissal still simmered because the soldiers were confronted, day in and day out, by their ex-employer in the form of a special agency, the Commissariaat van Ambonezenzorg (CAZ, or Directorate of Ambonese Care).[11] The CAZ literally took care of the Moluccans from the cradle to the grave. Discontent over this centralistic and bureaucratic organization strengthened existing feelings of unrest (Wittermans 1991; Smeets and Steijlen 2006, 131–41).

Fig. 4. Muster and hoisting the RMS Flag in a Moluccan camp

The situation worsened in 1956 when the government decided, in the name of "self-care", that the Moluccans had to provide for themselves (Smeets 2001; Smeets and Veenman 2000). They had to find work in civilian jobs because service in the army remained closed to them. The Moluccans fiercely criticized this policy. The government had, first of all, dismissed them from military service and now the social welfare accorded to them as a result of the dismissal was also being taken away. The Moluccans emphasized their special relationship with the Dutch government and insisted the state continue taking care of them. In the beginning, there was massive resistance to the "self-care" policy. After a while, Moluccans accepted the new situation, albeit under protest, and most opposition to it gradually subsided. The same happened later when further measures aimed at integrating the Moluccan community were equally unpopular. Resistance was initially fierce but could not be sustained. What was left were deep-seated feelings of frustration that found a voice not only among the first generation of Moluccans but also among their children (Smeets 1991b).

An Ambivalent Policy of Integration

Around 1959, the Dutch government took the decision to gradually close the encampments and to house the Moluccans in regular houses among the Dutch population. They were allowed, however, to be housed in groups (Commissie Verwey-Jonker 1959). Again, there was strong opposition from the Moluccans. Life in the encampments closely resembled life in the barracks (*tangsi*) in Indonesia. Although the Moluccan men had been dismissed as soldiers in 1951, they still had the feeling that they were being housed in a military manner.

Even when the government tried to make up for earlier mistakes, the measures sometimes had the opposite effect. As early as mid-1952, for example, the Cabinet realized that the continued unemployment of Moluccans would lead to undesirable outcomes. It therefore proposed to employ the Moluccans in a corps of civilian guards. This was not, however, an acceptable alternative for the former Moluccan soldiers because it did not restore their military status.

Another example of a government policy that backfired resulted from the fact that the Moluccan soldiers, who were formally Indonesian citizens, had to apply to the Indonesian government for pension claims. But the Indonesian government did not deal with claims from non-residents. In 1959, a Dutch government commission concluded that the Netherlands had dealt with this matter too simplistically. The commission proposed to create a payment scheme to replace the Indonesian pension (Commissie Verwey-Jonker 1959). However, only a part of the Moluccan claims were met. In 1978, following a number of violent actions by radicalized second-generation Moluccan youth, discussed below, the government reconsidered the pensions issue and acknowledged a part of the other claims by giving a one-off payment. But this happened only for a part of the claims, leaving many people dissatisfied (Ministerie van Binnenlandse Zaken 1978; Smeets and Steijlen 2006, 156–59, 162–64).

Disappointment

The already difficult relations between the expatriated Moluccan soldiers and the Dutch government were further soured and rendered more complicated by the former's sympathies for an unilateral Moluccan republic. On Java, Moluccan soldiers had already sympathized with the Republik Maluku Selatan (RMS) movement. In 1951, as mentioned above, RMS leaders had played an explicit part in the decision that Moluccan soldiers stranded on Java should not go back to Ambon, which, in the meantime, had been conquered by Indonesia (Smeets 1991a; 1992).

Soon after their arrival in the Netherlands, the Moluccan soldiers met a number of executives of the RMS movement, as well as a strong Dutch lobby which sympathized with the RMS. From the very beginning, the Dutch government made it clear they could not support an independent Moluccan declaration of independence because it ran counter to the agreements they had concluded with Indonesia. This was a severe blow to the Moluccans who thought they could count on the support of the Netherlands, especially because the RMS wanted close relations with the old mother country. Thus, anger about the lack of support for the RMS was added to frustration over the soldiers' dismissal and displeasure with the welfare policy of the Dutch government. Anger spiked over the years, for instance, in 1966 when Suharto, who had just come to power in Indonesia, had the second president of the RMS, Chris Soumokil, executed; and again in 1970, when President Suharto came to the Netherlands for an official state visit. All these pent-up frustrations would eventually be manifested by the second generation of Moluccans rather than the first. In the 1970s, their violent actions initially targeted Indonesian interests in Holland but were later extended to Indonesian and Dutch citizens (Barker 1980; Steijlen 1996).

Although the idea of the RMS was to remain the symbolic rallying point of these protests, including violent actions, the pursuit of independence was not the only cause of unsatisfactory relations between the Dutch government and the Moluccan population. The essence of the conflict was, and remained, the soldiers' dismissal from military service. If the Moluccan soldiers had been retained in the armed service in 1951 instead of being dismissed, their identification with and support of the RMS may not have dissipated but it would not have reached the same intensity if the Moluccans had been able to lead the "normal" existence of exiles. If they had been occupied with daily activities, their relationship with the Netherlands would have evolved in a completely different way. This is not a hypothesis, but a conclusion reached by comparing the hundred Moluccan soldiers who were part of the Royal Dutch Navy with the expatriated soldiers. Although the majority of Moluccan navy personnel were also sympathetic towards the RMS, they nevertheless remained in service. Their careers did not come to an end in 1951 compared to their colleagues in the land forces, and hence their lives followed a completely different trajectory. Instead of looking back to the past and hoping for a distant future, these Moluccan navy personnel continued working in their own professions and generally their children also did well (Keppy 1994, 71). However, the same did not usually hold true for the children of the dismissed army soldiers, many of whom had been educated towards an eventual return to the Moluccas. Beginning in the 1970s, the most radicalized among them acted out their own and their parents' frustration in a particularly violent fashion.

The 1970s: Years of Confrontation

On December 1, 1963, the RMS president, Chris Soumokil, fell into the hands of the Indonesian army on Seram. He was taken to Java and sentenced to death by a military tribunal on April 24, 1963. The sentence was not carried out immediately, as it is quite usual for the Indonesian authorities to let the timing of an execution be determined by the political situation.

On September 30, 1965, a *coup d'etat* occurred, the exact circumstances of which are still not clear.[12] There is more certainty about the coup's aftermath, however, as the army grasped the opportunity to eliminate the Indonesian Communist Party (Partai Komunis Indonesia, PKI), whose steadily growing influence during Sukarno's Guided Democracy period had been a thorn in the side of many officers. Hundreds of thousands of people lost their lives as a result of army-instigated purges against the communists, as well as other political opponents and the ethnic Chinese community in Indonesia. Many other "suspects" were imprisoned for years without trial. The leader of the coup was Suharto who, on March 11, 1966, formally took over power from Sukarno, thus inaugurating the New Order (Orde Baru) period.

Shortly after, on April 12, 1966, Soumokil was executed on the island of Obi, just off the coast of Jakarta, under the orders of the country's new military regime. His wife and son fled to the Netherlands where, in the meantime, a government in exile had been established under the leadership of Joop A. Manusama, who had been living in the Netherlands since 1953. Soumokil's execution led to radicalization among Moluccan youths. The night Mrs Soumokil arrived in the Netherlands, July 26, 1966, Moluccan youths set fire to the Indonesian embassy in The Hague. In the ensuing years, many actions against Indonesian diplomatic offices were carried out. On August 31, 1970, thirty-three Moluccans occupied the residence of the Indonesian ambassador in Wassenaar, a suburb of The Hague, on the eve of President Suharto's state visit. This event made world news. In the course of the occupation, a Dutch policeman was killed. The Moluccan community generally supported the action.

The 1970s were marked by ever-growing radicalization among sections of Moluccan youth (Steijlen 1996). The causes were complex, but what undoubtedly influenced their radicalization was the knowledge that their parents had not achieved anything by means of peaceful demonstrations. The weak socio-economic position of many Moluccan youths had also increased their willingness to take action. They were also greatly influenced by the international youth culture, and were inspired politically by the Black Panther movement in the United States, and even more by the Palestinians who attracted world attention to their existence in exile and the pursuit of their own state through armed action.

Fig. 5. Occupiers of the residence of the Indonesian ambassador surrender, 1970

Despite the "Action of Wassenaar," the Dutch government continued to underestimate the severity of the problem. Five years later, on December 2, 1975, seven young Moluccans hijacked a passenger train in the northeast of the Netherlands. Two days later, another group of seven Moluccans hit the Indonesian consulate in Amsterdam. The key difference between the trainjacking and the attack on the Indonesian consulate and similar actions in the past was that Moluccan activists had for the first time chosen a Dutch civilian target. This was an indication that the activists blamed the Dutch government for their lack of support for the RMS, and that Dutch civilians had to pay the price for it. The Moluccan youths sent out a statement demanding that the Dutch people and government support their demands "for the peace and faith of the repressed Moluccan people and for peace in the world." Their message ended with a reference to the Dutch colonial past: "If some innocent Dutch got killed for the Moluccan cause, let the Dutch people not forget that in the past thousands and thousands of Moluccans have given their lives for the Dutch cause." For eighteen days, the Netherlands was under the spell of the hijacking drama. In the end, the actions claimed the lives of three Dutchmen and one Indonesian. Eventually, negotiations resulted in the surrender of the Moluccan activists.

Two years later, on May 23, 1977, another train was hijacked at De Punt in the northeastern province of Groningen. At the same time, teachers and pupils of a primary school in Bovensmilde in the northern province of Drenthe were taken hostage. Shortly after the children had been released by the hostage takers, Dutch marines stormed both the school and the train, killing two hostages and six of the hijackers. The 1977 action was followed by a smaller action in 1978 when a provincial government building in the city of Assen in Drenthe province was seized by three young Moluccans and held for a little more than a day before being seized by another contingent of Dutch marines. Two hostages were killed (Barker 1980; Bootsma 2000).[13]

During 1966–77, the actions of disaffected Moluccan youths became not only increasingly violent but were aimed at an ever-widening group of people. In the beginning, the activists had acted against Indonesian interests in the Netherlands. Then the Dutch became targets because of their government's refusal to support the RMS. Finally, the most radical elements within the movement turned against their own community's leader, as the 1977 hijacking was also aimed at the leadership of the RMS, Joop A. Manusama, who was blamed for his lack of determination in achieving independence (Steijlen 1996).

Reorientating Dutch-Moluccan Relations

In 1978, the van Agt/Wiegel Cabinet more or less acknowledged the mistakes made by the Dutch government. It thus wrote that it doubted "whether it had been justifiable socially and psychologically" in taking military status away from the Moluccans. In Indonesia, they had experienced considerable hardship during World War II and the following decolonization period. After their arrival in the Netherlands, the Moluccans had then immediately needed to adjust to an entirely alien environment. It is significant that the government added that "the emptiness that was created in that way had its drawbacks later" (Ministerie van Binnenlandse Zaken 1978).

The hijackings and their dramatic outcomes not only caused much suffering but resulted in a breakthrough as well. While the hijackings did not succeed in moving the Moluccas any closer to independence, they did help bring about fundamental changes in Dutch public policy towards them. The Dutch government started to pay close attention to the obstacles and disadvantages many Moluccans faced in such social and economic fields as education and employment. The government principally opted for a policy of integration and tried their utmost to alleviate the disadvantaged position the Moluccans had occupied for decades. "General policy if possible, specific if necessary," became the adage. It succeeded reasonably well, not in the least because Moluccan individuals and organizations felt jointly responsible for the improvement in the lives of members of their community. For the first time, the stagnation that resulted from the false start of 1951 was being rectified (Smeets and Veenman 2000).

In the 1980s, with the benefit of hindsight, the Moluccan community began heading in the right direction. The level of education was improving; there was a growing differentiation of professions; unemployment was being reduced; the authoritarian "command household" education style in families was, to a large extent, being replaced by a "consultation household style." In short, the process of integration began to develop with great speed,[14] although the Moluccans had still not obtained a position equal to the native Dutch. For example, the percentage of unemployed Moluccans was still twice as high. At that time, it also remained to be seen if the progress that was being made would be lasting if the labor market collapsed again. Ethnic minorities appear to be more vulnerable in such situations. However, it was clear that the Moluccans were successfully making up for lost time as a result of their false start in 1951 (Veenman 1994).

The Joint Declaration of 1986

In 1986, the "Regelen met betrekking" (Joint Declaration) between the Dutch government, led by Prime Minister Ruud Lubbers, and the largest Moluccan organization, Badan Persatuan, under the leadership of the community leader, Samuel Metiarij, represented the changing relationship between government and Moluccans that had occurred since 1978. It was the pinnacle of an important phase in the process of integration. In the declaration, a number of measures were announced with the aim of redeeming some of the frustrations of the past and improving the position of the Moluccans in the coming years (Smeets and Steijlen 2006, 302–20).

For various reasons, the Joint Declaration was a genuine breakthrough as it clearly linked the afore-mentioned measures to things that had gone wrong in the past. The Joint Declaration is sometimes characterized as a "peace treaty." The attitude of the Moluccans on this occasion was different from what it had been in the past. Instead of focusing on the failures of the government and the measures they should have taken to address them, the Moluccans were now concerned with arrangements in which obligations on their side were also explicitly formulated. It was now a question of joint responsibility for the success of any new measures. For the greater part, this give-and-take

Fig. 6. Negotiations for the Joint Declaration of 1986, with representatives from the Dutch Government (*left*) and the Moluccan delegation (*right*)

policy succeeded, exemplified by the evaluation of the "Thousand Jobs Plan," an employment project by which more than 1,200 long-term unemployed people found a job (Dagevos 1993; Smeets 1994). The Joint Declaration was the result of negotiations on an equal footing between partners who kept each other focused on their obligations.

One remarkable point remains. The Joint Declaration did not once refer to the military background of the first-generation Moluccans. Although appreciation for the things the Moluccans did for the Netherlands is expressed in the form of a yearly payment of 900 Euros for the first generation which arrived in the Netherlands in 1951[15] and through the award of a memorial medal, the context in which this happened is not mentioned. References to the KNIL would have caused a minefield of claims, not only from the Moluccan soldiers but also from thousands of non-Moluccan colleagues who had served in the same colonial army.

Although the Joint Declaration seemed to mark a new era of cooperation between the Dutch authorities and the Moluccan organizations, it also appeared to signal the end of such cooperation. From the 1990s onwards, the specific Moluccan policy that had been so successful in the fields of education and the labor market came to an abrupt halt. The idea that the integration of Moluccans was as good as completed, combined with the appearance of new problem groups—the second generations of Turks and Moroccans and asylum seekers—and a general tendency to generalize (and decentralize) government policies, contributed to the disappearance of Moluccans as a specific category of public policy (Smeets and Veenman 2000). Research at the Erasmus University Rotterdam in 2001 revealed the disadvantages of this major policy shift. Justus Veenman (2001) concluded that the integration of third-generation Moluccans had come to a standstill and that the field of education, in particular, had shown disappointing results.

Crisis in the Moluccas and Reactions in the Netherlands

On January 19, 1999, an incident in Ambon City between a taxi driver and his passenger escalated into violence, which quickly spread to other parts of the island of Ambon and subsequently to other islands in the Moluccas (Bubandt 2001; Dijk 2001; Manuhutu et al. 2000). Initially, the violence was attributed to conflict between Christian Moluccans and Muslim immigrants, but soon the clashes extended to Christian and Muslim Moluccans. From its new hotbed in the northern Moluccas, the conflict escalated in mid-2000 as a result of the violent actions of the Laskar Jihad, a paramilitary force partly from Java. Since then, conflicts have subsided only to erupt after a while with even greater ferocity. The Moluccan community in the Netherlands kept a close watch on the events. Peaceful processions were organized with appeals to end the violence and for relief supplies. Although most Moluccans in the Netherlands are Christians, they did not react unilaterally in support of their fellow Christians. Yet, their disquiet grew as the fighting continued and the number of victims increased, some of whom were close relatives.

For most of the Dutch population, the fight was an incomprehensible war in a distant country. The Dutch government provided funds for emergency help, but would not accommodate the wishes of some Moluccans in the Netherlands for a UN-backed armed intervention in the Moluccas. This again led to lack of understanding on the part of the Moluccans. A number of third-generation youngsters who, according to Veenman's research (2001), were already suffering from stagnating integration, lost all confidence in Dutch society. Compounding their feelings was the tepid Dutch reaction to the present crisis in the Moluccas, the old frustrations of the first generation about their dismissal, and the refusal of the Dutch to support the RMS. Following the terrorist assault on Bali on October 12, 2002, the leadership of the Laskar Jihad withdrew their followers from the Moluccas and dissolved. In 2002, two members of President Megawati Sukarnoputri's Cabinet, Yusuf Kalla and Susilo Bambang Yudhoyono, restored peace. In 2004, when the latter was elected president and Kalla vice-president, a reconciliation and reconstruction process was started.

Since the beginning of the century no more research has been done on the position of Moluccans in the Netherlands. One gets the impression that the process of integration shows an upwards tendency and that many Moluccans take up a reasonable position in society. More and more they also appear in noticeable positions: trainer of a top football club, member of parliament, TV actor, lawyer, museum director, medical specialist, etc. The impression, however, that too many young people remain stuck at the bottom of society also exist. Therefore, one thing is sure: for most of them, their future lies in the Netherlands and nowhere else.

Notes

1. The Moluccas consist of more than one thousand islands, most of them small and uninhabited. Some islands, like Halmahera and Seram, however, are very large. Most historical accounts have concentrated on a few small islands, such as Ternate, Ambon, and Banda. See Boelens, van Fraassen, and Straver 2001.

2. According to Enloe (1980), "Colonial military schemes called for local soldiers to be recruited from those communities presumed to pose the least political threat, communities which were fewest in numbers and shortest in financial and organizational resources" (p. 132), and "The Dutch also preferred . . . outerlanders . . ., who were Christians" (p. 138).

3. For the history of the Dutch East Indies during World War II, see L. de Jong 1984–86.

4. Important Moluccans who chose to side with Sukarno and who would rise to prominence in the Indonesian republic included, among others, Jo Leimena, who became minister of public health, and Deputy Prime Minister Johan Latuharihari, who became the first nationalistic governor of Ambon; Martin Putuhena, who became the last prime minister of the federal state of East Indonesia and the Indonesian minister of public works; Joost Muskita, who took part in the recapture of Ambon from the Republik Maluku Selatan, became a general and, among other positions, Indonesian ambassador in Bonn; and Julius Tahya, the highest decorated KNIL officer who later became a successful businessman.

5. For the realization of the RMS and the political and military developments that followed, see Chauvel 1990; Manusama 1999; Smeets and Steijlen 2006, 39–54; van der Meulen 1981.

6. The RMS was not supported by the majority of the Muslim Moluccans at Ambon, nor by all other Moluccans. There were Christian Moluccans who

supported Sukarno and his Unitary State. The Moluccan supporters of Sukarno were organized in Pupella's Partai Indonesia Merdeka (PIM, or Free Indonesia Party).

7. The Australian lieutenant Muir estimated that between four thousand and five thousand Indonesian soldiers were killed, between five thousand and eight thousand civilians, and, on the RMS side, four hundred *sukarela* and one hundred soldiers. The Indonesian general Joost Muskita, who as a captain took part in the conquest of Ambon, pointed out that Muir's estimates of the Indonesian and civilian losses were exaggerated. He estimated that the Indonesian casualties would not have exceeded four hundred to five hundred soldiers. (Chauvel 1990, 391).

8. Dutch New Guinea remained under Dutch sovereignty until 1962.

9. The Indonesian government did not like that RMS Moluccans in the Netherlands had Indonesian nationality. In order to give up its nominal responsibility for them, Indonesia changed its Nationality Act in 1962. Indonesians living abroad subsequently had to confirm their nationality every five years by swearing allegiance to the Pancasila, the five principles of the Indonesian state. Because RMS Moluccans refused to do this, they lost their Indonesian citizenship five years later. The Dutch government did worry about the Moluccans' legal status as they were now effectively stateless, but for a long time failed to find a solution. Some Moluccans opted for Dutch nationality, but many first- and second-generation Moluccans stayed on in the Netherlands without any nationality. On January 1, 1977, a new Dutch law decreed that those Moluccans who had come to the Netherlands in 1951 and had not yet acquired Dutch nationality were to be given the same legal status as Dutch citizens. However, they were subject to two exceptions: they were neither allowed to vote nor to serve in the army. The third generation has Dutch nationality automatically by birth (Smeets and Steijlen 2006, 85–89).

10. This promise was probably intended to prevent operations in Asia, the Netherlands, and New Guinea.

11. The Moluccans were called Ambonese at that time, a reference to the island of Ambon.

12. See Jun Honna's chapter in this volume for a slightly longer exposition of the period.

13. The Moluccan activists were condemned to imprisonment of fourteen to fifteen years. They are free now.

14. Unless otherwise stated, my description of the socio-economic developments in the period 1982–90 is based on Veenman and Martens 1991, and the description of the socio-cultural developments on Bartels 1989.

15. The payments until now have amounted to more than fifty million euros.

References

Akihary, Huib. 1991. "Van Almere tot de Zwaluwenburg. Molukse woonoorden in Nederland" [From Almere to Zwaluwenburg. Moluccan Camps in the Netherlands]. In *Tijdelijk verblijf. De opvang van Molukkers in Nederland, 1951* [Temporary Stay. The Reception of Moluccans in the Netherlands 1951], eds. Wim Manuhutu and Henk Smeets, 40–73. Amsterdam: De Bataafsche Leeuw.

Barker, Ralph. 1980. *Not Here, But in Another Place.* New York: St. Martin's.

Bartels, Dieter. 1989. *Moluccans in Exile: A Struggle for Ethnic Survival.* Leiden/Utrecht: Centrum voor Onderzoek van Maatschappelijke Tegenstellingen/Inspraakorgaan Welzijn Molukkers.

Boelens, Germen, Chris van Fraassen, and Hans Straver. 2001. *Natuur en samenleving van de Molukken* [Nature and Society in the Moluccas]. Utrecht: Landelijk Steunpunt Educatie Molukkers.

Bootsma, Peter. 2000. *De Molukse Acties: Treinkapingen en gijzelingen 1970–1978* [Moluccan Actions: Train Hijackings and Kidnapping 1970–1978]. Amsterdam: Boom.

Bubandt, Nils. 2001. "Themes in the Dynamics of Violence in Eastern Indonesia." In *Violence in Indonesia*, eds. Ingrid Wessel and Georgia Wimhöfer, 228–53. Hamburg: Abera.

Chauvel, Richard. 1980. "Ambon's Other Half: Some Preliminary Observations on Ambonese Moslem Society and History." *Review of Indonesian and Malayan Affairs* 14(1): 40–80.

Chauvel, Richard. 1984. "Indonesia Merdeka! Ambon Merdeka? A Modern Social and Political History of the Ambonese Islands." Ph.D. dissertation, University of Sydney.

———. 1985. *The Rising Sun in the Spice Islands: A History of Ambon during the Japanese Occupation*. Working Paper no. 37, Monash University Centre of Southeast Asian.

———. 1990. *Nationalists, Soldiers and Separatists: The Ambonese Islands from Colonialism to Revolt, 1880–1950*. Leiden: KITLV Press.

———. 1997. "Tarred with the Dutch Brush: The Fate of Federalism in Indonesia." In *De leeuw en de banteng* [The Lion and the Banteng], eds. Pieter J. Drooglever and Marian J. B. Schouten, 201–19. Den Haag: Instituut voor Nederlandse Geschiedenis.

Commissie Verwey-Jonker. 1959. *Ambonezen in Nederland*. Den Haag: Staatsdrukkerij en Uitgeverijbedrijf.

Dagevos, Jaco M. 1993. *Voorkeursbeleid bij de Rijksoverheid* [Preferential Policy of the Dutch Government]. Rotterdam: Erasmus Universiteit.

Dijk, Kees van. 2001. *A Country in Despair: Indonesia between 1997 and 2000*. Leiden: KITLV Press.

Drooglever, Pieter J. 1992. "De vrijheid vanuit Ambons perspectief" [Freedom from the Perspective of Ambon]. In *Sedjarah Maluku: Molukse geschiedenis in Nederlandse bronnen* [Moluccan History in Dutch Sources], eds. Gerrit J. Knaap, Wim Manuhutu and Henk Smeets, 83–108. Amsterdam: Van Soeren.

Enloe, Cynthia H. 1980. *Ethnic Soldiers: State Security in a Divided Society*. Athens: University of Georgia Press and London: Penguin Books.

Groen, Petra M. H. 1991. *Marsroutes en dwaalsporen. Het Nederlands militair-strategisch beleid in Indonesië 1945–1950* [Marching Routes and Sidetracks. The Dutch Military-Strategy Policy in Indonesia 1945–1950]. 's-Gravenhage: Sdu Uitgevers.

Homan, Gerlof D. 1997. "The United States, the Netherlands and the Indonesian Struggle for Independence." In *De leeuw en de banteng* [The Lion and the Banteng], eds. Pieter J. Drooglever and Marian J. B. Schouten, 53–60. Den Haag: Instituut voor Nederlandse Geschiedenis.

Immerzeel, Bert. 1992. *Moluks verzet WO II* [Moluccan Resistance Second World War], Utrecht: Moluks Historisch Museum.

Jong, Joop de. 1998. *De waaier van het fortuin. De Nederlanders in Azië en de Indonesische archipel, 1595–1950* [The Wheel of Fortune. The Dutch in Asia and the Indonesian Archipelago, 1595–1950]. Den Haag: Sdu Uitgevers.

Jong, L. de. 1984–86. *Het Koninkrijk der Nederlanden in de Tweede Wereldoorlog* [The Kingdom of the Netherlands in the Second World War], vol. 11a–c. The Hague: Staatsuitgeverij.

Keppy, Herman. 1994. *De laatste inlandse schepelingen. Molukkers in dienst van de Koninklijke Marine 1915–1965* [The Last Native Crew Members. Moluccans Serving in the Royal Dutch Navy 1915–1965]. Amsterdam: Uitgeverij Focus.

Manuhutu, Wim. 1995. "From Belanda Hitam to Andjing Belanda, From Black Dutchmen to Dogs of the Dutch: The Moluccan Soldiers as a Military Race in the Netherlands-Indies." Paper presented at a seminar on "Ethnic Soldiering and Its Impact." Leiden, January 13–14.

Manuhutu, Wim et al. 2000. *Maluku Manis, Maluku Menangis, De Molukken in Crisis* [The Moluccas in Crisis]. Utrecht: Moluks Historisch Museum/ Moluccan Information and Documentation Center.

Manusama, Joop A. 1999. *Eigenlijk moest ik niet veel hebben van de politiek* [Actually, I didn't really like politics]. Utrecht/Den Haag: Moluks Historisch Museum/Bintang Design & Communicatie.

Meulen, Inge van der. 1981. *Dossier Ambon 1950: De houding van Nederland ten opzichte van Ambon en de RMS* [Ambon File 1950: The Dutch Attitude towards Ambon and the RMS]. Den Haag: Staatsuitgeverij.

Ministerie van Binnenlandse Zaken. 1978. *Problematiek van de Molukse minderheid in Nederland* [Problems of the Moluccan Minority in the Netherlands]. Tweede Kamer, 1977–78, 14 915, nos. 1 & 2.

Moll, L. O. A. 1977. "De Ambonezenarresten" [The Amboinese Decrees], *Rechtsgeleerd magazijn Themis* 3: 237–66.

Moor, Jaap A. de. 1999. *Westerling's Oorlog. Indonesië 1945–1950* [Westerling's War Indonesia 1945–1950]. s.l.: Uitgeverij Balans.

"Regelen met betrekking tot de toekenning van een uitkering en herdenkingspenning" [Rules in relation to the Attribution of an Allowance and Commemoration Medal]. 1988. *Staatsblad* 226.

Smeets, Henk. 1991a. "De plaats van keuze." [The Place of Choice]. In *Tijdelijk verblijf: De opvang van Molukkers in Nederland, 1951* [Temporary Stay. The Reception of Moluccans in the Netherlands, 1951], eds. Wim Manuhutu and Henk Smeets, 7–16. Amsterdam: De Bataafsche Leeuw.

———. 1991b. "De organisatie van de Ambonezenzorg" [The Organization of Ambonese Welfare]. In *Tijdelijk verblijf: De opvang van Molukkers in Nederland, 1951* [Temporary Stay. The Reception of Moluccans in the Netherlands 1951], eds. Wim Manuhutu and Henk Smeets, 17–39. Amsterdam: De Bataafsche Leeuw.

———. 1992. *Moluccans in the Netherlands*. Utrecht: Moluks Historisch Museum.

———. 1994. *Etnische minderheden bij de overheid* [Ethnic Minorities in the Government]. Rotterdam: Erasmus Universiteit.

———. 2001. *Een kwestie van organisatie. Organisatie van het Molukkersbeleid en Molukse zelforganisatie* [A Matter of Organization. Organization of the Policy about Moluccans and Moluccan Self-organization]. Utrecht: Moluks Historisch Museum.

Smeets, Henk and Justus Veenman. 2000. "More and More at Home: Three Generations of Moluccans in the Netherlands." In *Immigrant Integration: The Dutch Case*, eds. Hans Vermeulen and Rinus Penninx, 36–63. Amsterdam: Het Spinhuis.

Smeets, Henk and Fridus Steijlen. 2006. *In Nederland gebleven. De geschiedenis van Molukkers 1951–2016* [Still in the Netherlands. The history of Moluccans 1951–2016]. Amsterdam: Bert Bakker/Utrecht/Moluks Historisch Museum.

Steijlen, Fridus. 1996. *RMS. Van ideaal tot symbool: Moluks nationalisme in Nederland, 1951–1994* [RMS. From Ideal to Symbol: Moluccan Nationalism in the Netherlands, 1951–1994]. Amsterdam: Het Spinhuis.

Teitler, Gerke and Petra M. H. Groen. 1987. *De politionele acties* [The Police Actions]. Amsterdam: De Bataafsche Leeuw.

Veenman, Justus. 1994. *The Social Integration of Moluccans*. Lelystad: Koninklijke Vermande.

———. 2001. *Molukse jongeren in Nederland. Integratie met de rem erop* [Moluccan Youngsters in the Netherlands. Integration with Brakes on] Assen: Van Gorcum.

Veenman, Justus and Edwin P. Martens. 1991. *Een lange weg. Molukkers op de arbeidsmarkt 1990* [A Long Way. Moluccans on the Labour Market 1990]. Rotterdam: Erasmus Universiteit.

Veer, Paul van 't. 1969. *De Atjeh-oorlog* [The Aceh War]. Amsterdam: De Arbeiderspers.

Wittermans, Tamme. [1955] 1991. *Social Organization among Ambonese Refugees in Holland*. London: London School of Economics. Reprint, Amsterdam: Het Spinhuis.

CHAPTER 9

The Expanding Roles of the Vietnam People's Army, 1975–2018

Carlyle A. Thayer

This chapter presents an overview of the expanding roles of the Vietnam People's Army (VPA) since reunification in 1975. The chapter is divided into five parts. The first part provides an overview of the national defense and economic roles of the VPA from unification in 1975 until the adoption of a national reform program known as renovation or *doi moi* in late 1986. During this period, the VPA was assigned to assist in rebuilding infrastructure damaged during the Vietnam war, opening new economic zones and other reconstruction tasks. The VPA's role was also expanded to include participation in economic production, a role that was temporarily curtailed following conflict with Cambodia and China in the late 1970s.

The second part considers the role of the VPA under *doi moi*. During this period, VPA military units were withdrawn from Cambodia and the main force was then subject to massive demobilization. In 1989, military-run enterprises and companies were put on the same legal footing as state-owned enterprises and were granted the authority to sign joint venture agreements with overseas partners. As a consequence, the VPA's role in economic production was expanded to include commercial activities and the number of military-owned enterprises proliferated.

The third part discusses "four waves of reforms" over two decades to consolidate and reduce the number of military-owned enterprises, make them more efficient and competitive, divest them of commercial enterprises, and finally limit their scope in economic activities carried out by civilian enterprises.

The fourth part discusses three major programs designed to increase the capacity of the VPA to contribute to national development and to defend Vietnam: responsibility for creating special economic and defense zones in remote areas of strategic importance, implementation of a legal regime to enhance military professionalization, and force modernization of the navy, air defense-air force and ground forces.

The chapter ends with a concluding fifth part that summarizes the expanding roles of the VPA in civil-military relations in Vietnam.

Two Strategic Tasks, 1975–86

The Vietnam People's Army has been continually engaged in "fighting and economic production" since it was founded in 1944. This was particularly the case during the eight-year war against the French (1946–54). After the 1954 settlement at Geneva, which partitioned Vietnam, the VPA was regrouped to northern Vietnam and reorganized along more conventional lines (Thayer 1985, 234–38).

In this period, the army was assigned a dual role. In addition to its national defense task, it was also assigned economic construction and production responsibilities. For example, the military was put in charge of running state farms that produced industrial crops.

In the period following unification in 1975, the military in the south was primarily involved in maintaining public order and security, including transporting refugees back to their native villages, disposal of unexploded ordnance, and running re-education camps (Thayer 1985, 250–54, 256–62). The VPA's roles were gradually expanded to include building new economic zones and taking part in capital construction projects. VPA units, for example, were given responsibility for building roads, railways, ports, pipelines, industrial plants, civil installations, and airports. The VPA was also assigned to carry out a number of economic construction tasks, such as afforestation projects, engaging in land cultivation, livestock breeding, and producing consumer goods at national defense industries. The People's Navy was tasked with the transportation of merchandise between north and south, repair of commercial freighters, developing a fishing fleet, and participating in the oil and gas exploration program (Le 1976).

In order to accommodate the growing demand for manpower in civilian reconstruction, military conscription was broadened to include service with so-called labor brigades. These developments provoked dissent within the military on the part of middle- and high-ranking officers who objected to the diversion of the VPA from defense tasks. They argued that continued VPA involvement in reconstruction would degrade combat readiness, erode discipline, and delay the process of regularization and modernization. According to Hanoi-based journalist Chris Ray (1979, 24), "some officers point[ed] to the already demonstrated threat to the southern border and argu[ed] that it was dangerous to reduce the military's combat readiness and effectiveness."

In May 1976, in responding to these concerns, the defense minister, General Vo Nguyen Giap, argued in the party journal *Studies* that the tasks of national defense and economic construction were interdependent (Vo 1976). In October, the party's Politburo reaffirmed the military's involvement in economic work by stressing that it was "a fundamental and urgent demand of the revolution" (Ray 1979, 24). One indication of this new priority was the establishment of a General Directorate for Economic Development within the VPA to oversee the efforts of army units in civilian-type economic reconstruction tasks in four main areas: agriculture, industry, communications and transport, and capital construction.

In late 1976, the matter of the VPA's involvement in economic construction was endorsed as a national policy priority by the Vietnam Communist Party's (VCP) fourth national party congress. According to a resolution adopted by this congress, "Our armed forces have two tasks: always to stand ready to fight and to defend the fatherland and to actively participate in economic construction" (Vietnam News Agency, December 24, 1976). In a speech delivered to the congress, Senior General Van Tien Dung elaborated that the VPA would continue to assist in redistributing the workforce throughout Vietnam and consolidate strategic areas that were important for both the economy and national defense. Dung then described the army's educational and socialization roles: "In addition to the aforementioned tasks, the party entrusts the army with the duty to act as one of the great schools to train hundreds of thousands of our youths as new socialist human beings who are resolved to defend the fatherland and are at the same time, skilled laborers enthusiastically engaged in building the fatherland and socialism" (Hanoi Radio Domestic Service, December 16, 1976). Finally, the fourth congress resolution also approved the continuation of military service and importantly called for the development of a national defense industry.

The decision of the fourth congress to intensify the involvement of the VPA in economic tasks resolved a major dilemma facing party leaders: whether to maintain a large yet economically unproductive standing army or to sanction a massive postwar demobilization. The fourth congress chose a middle path. According to Ray (1979, 214): "The case for participation by the armed forces in the economic recovery program was strong. A generation of war had left the army with a near monopoly of resources for certain types of construction and it was by far the largest single source of trained cadres. Disciplined, politicized and often possessing important technical skills, the troops were best equipped to meet reconstruction needs on an emergency basis."

In the months following the fourth party congress, an estimated quarter of all males aged between eighteen and twenty-five were made liable for conscription. Twenty thousand army personnel were given specialized training as district-level economic managers (Vietnam News Agency, October 10, 1977). Army units were assigned a variety of specialized tasks, including the upgrading of the strategic road network along the Ho Chi Minh Trail, running state farms, constructing large-scale irrigation works and hydroelectric power stations, reclaiming land, and other major projects. At the same time, other military units continued to train and maintain their combat proficiency to ensure national defense. Nevertheless, according to the army's newspaper, they too were required "to devote a fixed amount of time to stepping up production and making full use of waste and fallow land . . . to produce grain and food" (*Quan Doi Nhan Dan* [People's Army], December 29, 1977).

Unfortunately, Vietnam's efforts to recover from the devastation of nearly thirty years of war and begin the task reconstruction were cut short by a growing conflict with neighboring Cambodia, where the Khmer Rouge was in power (Thayer 1985, 254–56). Throughout 1977–78, Vietnam was subjected to repeated small-scale attacks and harassing actions by Khmer Rouge military forces. In 1978, large-scale fighting broke out, inaugurating a decade-long conflict known as the Third Indochina War (1978–89). Vietnam invaded Cambodia in December 1978 and China retaliated by attacking Vietnam's northern border in early 1979. During the Third Indochina War, the VPA rapidly expanded in size through national conscription. Main force strength jumped from 615,000 in 1978 to 1.26 million in 1987.

After the Sino-Vietnamese border war of 1979, Vietnam found itself involved in a protracted counter-insurgency operation in Cambodia. The situation along Vietnam's northern frontier remained tense as China kept up military pressure on Hanoi with repeated threats "to teach Vietnam another lesson." Vietnamese leaders characterized this state of affairs as one in which "peace is threatened by the possibility of war" (quoted in Thayer 1985, 257).

Vietnam resolved the potential dilemma of conflict on two fronts by re-emphasizing that the VPA would have to undertake two strategic tasks. According to party secretary, Le Duan, speaking in July 1981: "Our entire party, army and people will have to carry out two strategic tasks simultaneously—successfully building socialism and being constantly ready to fight and firmly defend our socialist fatherland and resolutely defeat every scheme and act of aggression of Chinese expansionism and hegemonism and international reactionary forces.... It is necessary for the people's army to undergo intensive training in order to become a mighty and increasingly modern and regularized revolutionary army... *while at the same time participating in production and economic development in appropriate ways* (emphasis added)" (Hanoi Radio Domestic Service, June 26–30 and July 1, 1981).

In the late 1970s and early 1980s, Vietnam faced an economic crisis of mammoth proportions brought on by a number of factors: repeated natural disasters, the withdrawal of foreign aid and economic isolation, the costs of conflict, and the failure of Soviet-styled central planning that resulted in a grain deficit of nearly three million tons. Shortages of all types—food, medicine, clothing, and consumer goods—became pervasive.

Le Duan informed Vietnam's National Assembly that the country's socio-economic plan for the 1980s would have to be reformulated. Priority was given to emergency measures to overcome the economic crisis. Le Duan outlined three national objectives that had to be achieved (Hanoi Radio Domestic Service, June 26–30, July 1, 1981):

1. To stabilize and take a significant step forward in improving the people's material and cultural life—first and foremost, to definitively solve the grain and food problems and meet the basic clothing needs of the entire society.
2. To overcome the most serious economic imbalances, create considerable sources of accumulation from within the national economy, and establish the key features of the material and technical infrastructure for socialism.
3. To fully meet the needs of national defense and maintain national security.

In March 1982, the fifth national congress of the VCP reviewed Vietnam's domestic and international situation three years after Vietnam's invasion of Cambodia and the imposition of an anti-Vietnam aid and trade embargo by regional countries. The economy was in a perilous state, the VPA was bogged down in a protracted counter-insurgency conflict in Cambodia, and Vietnam's northern provinces were kept in a constant state of tension by Chinese saber rattling. The fifth congress assigned to the VPA two strategic tasks: building socialism and defending the fatherland (Thayer 1983).

The effects of Vietnam's economic crisis were manifest in society at large. "Negative phenomena," such as smuggling, stealing, hoarding, speculation, and draft evasion, became widespread. Food riots occurred in central Vietnam. These conditions only reinforced the VCP's determination to employ the VPA in economic production activities. Under the task of building socialism, the VPA was now expected to contribute to economic development by taking part in a wide range of productive activities in the agricultural and industrial sectors. Specialized economic construction units continued to participate in "productive labor and economic development," and the bulk of these units were stationed between Hanoi and the China border to guard against a second Chinese invasion.

Under the national defense task, which also included internal security duties, the VPA was expected to carry out its internationalist duties in Cambodia and Laos, and stand ready to repel a second Chinese attack in the north. Vietnam's national defense strategy was redrawn to give emphasis to the military's enhanced role in economic development. Individuals who completed their military service were discharged and assigned to their former workplace, a new economic zone, or a vocational school for specialized training. These individuals constituted the core of the ready reserves and were expected to play key leadership roles in local militia and self-defense forces.

In the decade up to 1986, army units of corps (*binh doan*) size were assigned to new economic zones, state farms and forests, hydroelectric and water conservancy projects, road building, and oil and gas exploration (Thayer 2000b, 98). One unit, of roughly twelve thousand men, was given responsibility for completing the Hoa Binh hydroelectric project northwest of Hanoi. Brigades and smaller units planted rubber, tobacco, coffee, and tea.

Doi Moi and Its Impact on the Military

In December 1986, the VCP's sixth national party congress adopted a major reform program known as *doi moi*, or renovation. This had a major impact on the VPA and its roles (*Quan Doi Nhan Dan*, May 12, 1991). Vietnam's priorities now shifted to economic reform and development at a time when the Soviet Union was signaling major changes in its domestic and foreign policies. Vietnam came under heavy pressure from Moscow to improve its economic performance, to seek a negotiated settlement in Cambodia, and to cut military expenditure. It was clear to Hanoi's leaders that Soviet assistance would be cut substantially, and that Vietnam could not afford a large unproductive standing army. In 1987, Vietnam initiated a major "strategic readjustment" of its armed forces (Thayer 1995). VPA units were withdrawn from Cambodia and Laos. The size of the VPA's main forces was cut from 1.26 million (1987) to less than half a million in a demobilization program lasting six years (Thayer 2000a). *Doi moi* also resulted in the VPA becoming involved in commercial activities. This was a marked change from the VPA's previous involvement in economic construction and production tasks.

In March 1989, the Council of Ministers issued Directive 46, a major new policy document regarding the military's role in economic activities. This directive required all VPA units and defense enterprises involved in production and economic construction to conduct their affairs under the "independent economic accounting system" (*Quan Doi Nhan Dan*, August 12, 1991).[1] Nine major VPA economic construction units were converted into legal entities—corporations (*cong ty*) and general corporations (*cong ty tong cuc*)—and subjected to the same state laws as civilian enterprises (*Quan Doi Nhan Dan*, August 13, 1989). By August 1989 so many military enterprises had become involved in economic activities that the table of organization of the Economic General Department had to be changed four times. By the end of the year, even more army units were transformed into corporations, general corporations, or other types of legal entities (Tran Duc Nghia 1990, 67).

Because army enterprises enjoyed tremendous advantages in land-use rights, disciplined labor, and strategic location they quickly expanded their economic and commercial activities. One military commentator revealed that almost all enterprises and factories under the VPA's Technical General Department "produced economic goods which have accounted for 40–50 percent of their production output" (*Quan Doi Nhan Dan*, August 13, 1989). Another source estimated that the army raised 20 percent of its revenue from internal sources (Senior General Le Trong Tan, cited by Hiebert 1991a, 24). The case of Tecapro is instructive. Tecapro was established in 1990 by the Military Technology Institute to specialize in computer science and environmental solutions. It won a number of contracts with Vietsovpetro, the Soviet-Vietnamese petroleum joint venture, and with Petrolimex, Vietnam's national petroleum company. It then set up two joint ventures with overseas partners. In 2000, only 10 percent of Tecapro's business activities were related to contracts with the VPA.

The commercial activities of these diverse military-run enterprises were breathtaking in scope. According to one report, "army factories, which began to produce consumer goods in the 1980s on a small scale, massively broadened their production in 1991 and 1992" (Vietnam News Agency, February 21, 1993). Among the consumer items produced were paper, ready-made garments, raincoats, electric fans, bicycle and motorcycle parts, oil cookers, fluorescent bulbs, televisions, radio-cassette recorders, and computers. Army enterprises also provided services such as running hotels and nightclubs and real estate development. Other army factories manufactured commercial goods such as jute polishers, hydraulic presses, lathes, detonators, electricity meters, transformers, buses, and heavy trucks.

Military enterprises that were given legal status were now able to open foreign currency bank accounts, form legal associations, and enter into joint ventures with Vietnamese or foreign partners. By 1995, there were forty-nine army-run joint enterprises with foreign partners, and this number rose to fifty-six in 1997 (Vietnam News Agency, February 20, 1996)[2] and sixty-seven by 2003 (*Quan Doi Nhan Dan*, January 7, 2003). They were mainly engaged in consumer goods, the garment industry, automobile manufacturing, construction work, ship and plane repair, hotels and real estate, and mechanical engineering (Thayer 1996, 18). In 1993, the VPA set up its first joint stock commercial bank.[3] The VPA also set up a consultancy firm that specialized in international law and accountancy (Cleary 1995).

When military-run enterprises were first established in the late 1980s, they were created from defense industries or existing military units.[4] These corporations originally provided employment to army personnel and their families. It was not anticipated at the time that they would grow so large. According to Lt. General Phan Thu, "Since 1976 the army has assigned a large force to engage in economic construction. A total of 280,000 soldiers in twenty-nine divisions are participating in almost every economic sector." Of this number 70 thousand were employed in 300 army-run commercial enterprises or 12 percent of the entire standing army of 572,000 (Branigin

1993; Hiebert 1991b, 26–27; Hiebert 1993, 40; Phan Thu 1994, 18). The VPA main force alone had nearly sixty organizations legally classified as corporations, general corporations, and scientific and production federations engaged in economic activities. Production on behalf of these organizations was assigned to more than two hundred primary level enterprises (*Quan Doi Nhan Dan*, May 12, 1991). Local militia units were reported to have set up at least 160 enterprises.[5]

Military-run enterprises continued to be involved in economic construction and production during the *doi moi* period. For example, military enterprises continued to be involved in constructing houses, hotels, roads, bridges, and ports; managing coffee, tea, and rubber plantations in the Central Highlands; mining coal, tin, and precious stones; catching and processing seafood; transporting oil workers to offshore rigs by helicopter; producing cement and asphalt; and operating joint ventures with foreign companies (Branigin 1993). Military units were also involved in large-scale construction projects such as the Yali, Pha Lai, and Vinh Son power projects; the Vung Tau oil and gas exploration zone; the Truong Son north–south highway; and the Haiphong export-processing zone (Vietnam News Agency, January 30, 1994).

Four giant military-run general corporations stood out as being especially successful in the new marketplace:

- Truong Son Construction General Corporation (12th Corps) (Tran Duc Nghia 1990, 67–69). This unit once built and maintained the Ho Chi Minh Trail. It was involved in the construction of every major road project in Vietnam, including National Route 1. It has been a successful bidder for major infrastructure projects such as the north–south power line, Hoa Binh hydroelectricity plant, and international construction projects. The corporation has also branched out into such areas as rail repair, exporting coal and marble, coffee growing, goods transport, and general support services (Voice of Vietnam, February 2, 1992). In the early 1990s, the corporation employed seven thousand people, four-fifths of whom were military personnel, in nineteen enterprises (Hiebert 1991b, 26).[6]

- Flight Service Corporation. It is equipped with fighter planes and helicopters. The Corporation provides its services for aerial surveys, tourism, medical emergencies, maintenance of the trans-Vietnam electricity line, and searches for US service personnel missing in action during the Vietnam War. The southern branch of this company runs a helicopter service for eight foreign oil and gas exploration companies.
- Tay Nguyen Corporation (15th Corps). This company manages rubber, coffee, wet rice, and timber production in the central highlands.
- Thanh An Construction and Assembly Corporation (11th Corps). It was formed in 1997 and has eleven affiliates engaged in such key sectors as construction, mineral exploration, coal mining, and training.

In January 1994, the Vietnam Communist Party held its first mid-term conference. This policy meeting decided that Vietnam's main development objectives would be the industrialization and modernization of the economy. This had important implications for national defense industries that came under the direct control of the Ministry of National Defense. They were now tasked with developing and acquiring technology with a dual civil-military application. Army-run enterprises became heavily involved in electronics, computing, and telecommunications.

In May 1994, for example, Prime Minister Vo Van Kiet ended the telecommunications monopoly exercised by the Directorate General of Posts and Telecommunications. The Ministry of National Defense was now permitted to offer services in this sector (Associated Press, *The Nation*, June 1, 1994; Reuters, May 29, 1994; Reuters, July 9, 1995). The Military Electronics Telecommunications Company entered into a joint venture with the American company New Tel to manufacture telephones, fax machines, pagers, and consumer electronic products such as circuit boards for CD players (Huong 1996, 15). In 1998, the army telecommunications company, Viettel, was approved as Vietnam's fifth internet service provider (Reuters, November 3, 1998).

Reforming Military-Owned Enterprises

In 1995–96, the VPA launched the first of several reform efforts to restructure its enterprises and corporations. The pace and scope of these reform efforts were affected by the Asian Financial Crisis that broke out in July 1997 and persisted until early 1998. The National Defense Industry and Economic General Department was charged with responsibility for reorganizing existing enterprises, streamlining top echelons, merging businesses in the same sector, and dissolving a number of loss-making enterprises. Particular attention was paid to merging small and medium enterprises in the same line of business in order to strengthen their domestic competitiveness against local firms, joint ventures, and foreign businesses. By May 1996, the number of military-run enterprises had been reduced from 335 to 193 (Vietnam News Agency, May 12, 1996). As was to be expected, the restructuring program achieved some success but ran into a number of difficulties. On the plus side, a number of army-run enterprises are able to accumulate capital, reduce their workforce, improve competitiveness, and remit increased revenue to the central government coffers. In some cases, restructuring led to the creation of new jobs.

Greatest success was achieved in reforming those industries and trades in which the army already enjoyed an advantage: capital, construction, flight and maritime services, mining, engineering, industrial explosive materials, and garment manufacture. As a result, the already strong role of army businesses in these areas was strengthened. According to the editor of the *Military Industry Magazine*, the following enterprises emerged as the seven largest military-run companies after restructuring: Truong Son Construction General Corporation, Thanh An Construction and Assembly Corporation, Garment Export Company 28 (Le, 1996, 5; *The Saigon Times*, November 17, 1998), Dong Bac (East-North) Coal Company,[7] Military Commercial Joint Stock Bank, Chemical Export Company 21, and Chemical Company 76.

Many military-owned enterprises suffered from the same ills as their civilian-run counterparts in the state sector. In several instances, mergers were merely formalistic paper exercises in which several enterprises were loosely combined under a new management structure. Redundant personnel were still kept on the payroll. Some military-run enterprises maintained a huge stockpile of goods they could not sell. Although these firms faced competition in the market and were economically unviable, they were kept afloat by subsidies from the Ministry of National Defense.

Also, on the negative side, it was discovered that army-run enterprises tended to spend their profits on luxury items rather than reinvesting in capital stock. Luxury items included new automobiles, renovated guesthouses, new conference halls, modern interior equipment, and expensive imported appliances. In June 1997, for example, a commentary in *Quan Doi Nhan Dan* warned that more needed to be done to eliminate wastefulness and corruption. The commentary noted that some army units incurred "big losses" as a result of casual spending, hosting guests, ceremonies, and parties (cited in Thayer 1998, 57). Losses were also due to weak financial management in army construction projects. A thrift campaign was launched to discourage these practices.

A review of the restructuring process revealed that a number of mergers had been mere paper formalities. According to one report, "Worse still, some units have simply combined several enterprises and imposed a newly created corporate apparatus on them, thus only streamlining the top echelon while inflating the indirect apparatuses and making them even more cumbersome and inefficient" (*Quan Doi Nhan Dan*, September 13, 1997, p. 3). The same account also revealed "In addition, when restructuring their productive forces, a number of enterprises have failed to reorganize their redundant personnel, giving rise to negative phenomena."

The restructuring process also did not solve the fundamental problem that many military-run enterprises, like their civilian counterparts, were equipped with old-fashioned machinery, relied on outdated technology, and were short of capital. The Air Defense Cement Company, for example, was reportedly given only 250 million dong in capital, enough to meet only 5.6 percent of its needs. Finally, the restructuring program uncovered another basic problem: many military-run enterprises were owed unrecoverable debts.

In 1997, military-run companies were divided into three main types: defense-economic enterprises (*doanh nghiep kinh te quoc phong*), which produced and repaired weapons and military equipment, undertook special defense duties, and also produced commercial goods as a sideline; national defense economic enterprises (*doanh nghiep quoc phong*), which produced and traded civilian products, provided daily logistics support, or participated in economic development in remote areas; and exclusive economic enterprises (*doanh nghiep chuyen lam kinh te*), which specialized in producing and trading in commercial products. Of the three categories of military enterprise, the exclusive economic enterprises accounted for more than half of the army's business interests. These corporations were involved in the full spectrum of commercial activities from the most basic services (laundry and food processing) to the highly advanced manufacturing sectors (computers and telecommunications).

Vietnam did not release a set of official figures at this time on the contribution of military-owned enterprises to the national economy. The figures that were released were vague and contradictory. But it is clear from comments made by official spokespersons that military-run companies were increasingly successful. In 1996, for example, it was reported that the army's national defense and production enterprises achieved a 25 percent increase over 1995. The following year, it was reported that army-run enterprises had achieved an increase of 30 percent in revenue over 1996. Figures for 2002 also indicated an increase in revenue (*Quan Doi Nhan Dan*, January 7, 2003). Other figures indicated a twenty-four-fold increase in earnings over a nine-year period, from US$25 million in 1990 to US$600 million in 1998, or 0.002 percent and 2 percent of GDP respectively (Thayer 2000b, 108).

Military earnings were reportedly higher than enterprises run by central ministries or other sectors. Military enterprises under the General Logistics Department alone earned record revenues of US$83 million in 1997, while the Truong Son Construction General Corporation increased its earnings 40 percent over 1996. The average wages paid to soldiers working in this sector were seventy dollars per month against the national average of forty dollars.

Vietnam's military enterprises pay taxes like any other legal business. The military is permitted to engage in commercial ventures because it earns funds to support genuine military activities that the state budget cannot afford.

According to Major General Nguyen Van Chinh, head of the Economics Department, "There is a conflict of interest here: defense activities cost a lot of money, while business means profit. So the army is engaged in business not just to make money, but for the sake of national security. If we put the profit motive first, we would be making a big mistake" (cited in Hanh 1999, 23). In 1999, the army had the smallest number of businesses in Vietnam running at a loss.

According to Hanh (1999, 23), the Ministry of National Defense "is structured like a real, if miniature, government." An anonymous foreign economist also stated that it was difficult to conceive of any industry in which the military was not involved as its tentacles reached into every corner of the economy (quoted in Hanh 1999, 23). Of the 164 corporations under the control of the Ministry of National Defense, four were under the direct control of the central ministry while the remaining 160 were under the control of ten subordinate departments, including foreign joint ventures.[8] Over half of the military-run enterprises were small companies that were unable to compete effectively in the market due to limited prescribed capital and outdated equipment (Voice of Vietnam, January 1, 1997).

In May 1998, the Central Military Party Committee issued a directive launching a second wave of reforms for army-run enterprises in order to improve their business efficiency and ability to take on major projects (Thayer 2000b). The Ministry of National Defense was ordered to adopt firm measures to dissolve loss-making military companies. The directive also prohibited army divisions, provincial units, and specialized departments within the defense ministry from setting up and operating commercial enterprises. Late in the year, Prime Minister Phan Van Khai announced that military-run enterprises would be required to rationalize their commercial activities. In order to implement these new reforms, the Economics Division, formerly under the General Department of National Defense Industry and Economics, was upgraded to the status of an independent Economic Department under the direct control of the Ministry of National Defense (Vietnam News Agency, April 28, 1999).

The number of army personnel engaged in economic activities had steadily risen since *doi moi* was adopted. In 1999, it was estimated that the number of regular army personnel employed in military-run enterprises had risen to 100,000 (Watkin 1999). Given the decline in main force numbers, which fell from 1.26 million in 1987 to 480,000 in 1999, this represented an order of magnitude of one-fifth of the standing army.

Most army-run enterprises could not stay solvent by fulfilling their military contracts alone. They had to seek outside work. Army enterprises therefore came under increasing pressure to concentrate on finding a permanent niche in the economy for themselves. At the end of 1999, for example, it was reported that a fourth corps, Binh Doan 16, had been converted into a general corporation with responsibility for fertilizer production in central Vietnam. National Defense Ministry figures showed that up to 80 percent of the army's contracts came from the civilian sector (Hanh 1999, 22). According to Hanh (1999, 22), the second wave of reforms was aimed at "cutting down the number of small-scale enterprises, concentrating on key strengths, promoting co-operation between army enterprises to win state contracts and making their products more competitive."

In the wake of the Asian Financial Crisis the momentum to reform military-owned enterprises slowed as the VPA procrastinated in divesting itself of enterprises that were profitable. It was not until eight years later that a third wave of reform was launched. In January 2007, the VCP Central Committee adopted a resolution at its fourth plenum directing the army to divest itself of all commercial enterprises that they currently owned and operated (Thayer 2000b). Divestiture of these enterprises was an extremely sensitive issue because the VPA would lose an important source of income. The fourth plenum's resolution specified, however, that the VPA could retain ownership and control over companies that were directly related to national defense and security.

The process of handing over ownership was due to begin before the end of 2007 and conclude by 2012.[9] In December 2007, Defense Minister General Phung Quang Thanh stated that his ministry would hand over around 140 military-owned commercial enterprises to the state by 2012 and "focus on training and building up a regular modern army" (*Quan Doi Nhan Dan*, December 19, 2007). Both Viettel and the Military Commercial Joint Stock Bank were slated to be handed over.

The following year, the Global Financial Crisis broke out and led to disruption in global financial markets and banking systems until early 2009. Inflation in Vietnam reached an all-time high. Senior military officers, in a sign of foot-dragging, signaled that the turn-over of military-owned businesses would take many years (*Thanh Nien*, December 20, 2007). Later, a conference that reviewed the activities of army enterprises concluded that the global economic crisis "had a great impact on army businesses" and slowed the pace of divestment. The official defense budget dropped from 2.2 per cent of GDP in 2007 to 1.8 per cent in 2008. Nevertheless, the army-run Viettel Corporation and the Vietnam Service Flight Company both reported profits ("Army businesses grew in 2008 despite economic difficulties," 2009).

In 2008, the National Assembly adopted the Ordinance on Defense Industry that provided the legal basis for the transfer of military-run businesses and set out the principles and legal framework for national defense industries to be retained by the Ministry of National Defense. In April 2008, Prime Minister Nguyen Tan Dung issued instructions for the divestiture of 113 military-owned enterprises (*Viet Nam News*, April 4, 2008). While the initiative led to the divestment, restructuring or breakup of small military businesses, it allowed the VPA and the Defense Ministry to hold on to their most precious asset, Viettel, and nine other major general corporations.

The VPA's Defense Industry General Department reported that despite facing "numerous economic difficulties and negative impacts during the year" it had "surpassed all of 2008's set plans" ("G[D]DI heading for higher objectives despite difficulties," 2009). According to a report in the army's newspaper, "factories and plants under the General Department, in 2008, proactively sought out orders and contracts, extending both domestic and international markets in order to maintain a stable production schedule and pay raises for is workers" ("G[D]DI heading for higher objectives despite difficulties," 2009). In late 2009, Vietnam released a Defense White Paper that listed 10 military-owned general corporations (see Table 1) that confirmed neither

Viettel nor the Military Commercial Joint Stock Bank had been privatized. In addition, the Defense White Paper noted, "there are 98 VPA businesses at present operating in various fields of the economy, such as flight services, seaport services, telecommunications, and ship-building industry ("Song Thu corporation hailed for business achievements," 2014). "Their export commodity and service turnover is ever increasing" (Socialist Republic of Vietnam 2009, 69). The Ministry of National Defense drew up plans to equitize 38 military enterprises during the period 2013–15. It was later announced that 32 had been equitized and that the military had divested all state capital from 10 joint stock companies.

Table 1. Major Military-Owned General Corporations 2009

Name of Corporation	Founding Date	Main Headquarters
Truong Son Construction General Corporation	19.5.59	Hanoi
Military Petrol General Corporation	30.9.65	Cau Giay, Hanoi
General Corporation No. 28	9.5.75	Ho Chi Minh City
Thanh An General Corporation	11.6.82	Dong Da, Hanoi
General Corporation No. 15	20.2.85	Pleiku, Gia Lai province
Tan Cang General Corporation	15.3.89	Ho Chi Minh City
Flight Services General Corporation	1.6.89	Dong Da, Hanoi
Viettel – Military Telecommunications General Corporation	1.6.89	Ba Dinh, Hanoi
Military Bank (Military Commercial Joint Stock Bank)	4.11.94	Ba Dinh, Hanoi
Northeast (Dong Bac) General Corporation	24.12.94	Ha Long, Quang Vinh province

Source: Socialist Republic of Vietnam, *Vietnam National Defence* (Hanoi: Ministry of National Defence, December 2009), 119.

A fourth wave of reform of military enterprises was inaugurated in June 2018 when Vietnam's National Assembly passed an amended Law on National Defense to clarify the economic purposes of military-owned enterprises and ensure equality between civilian and military enterprises. According to Vo Trong Viet, the chairman of the National Assembly's National Defense and Security Commission, "Once the process is completed, there will be no business units that are entirely economic-driven under the defense ministry, and those remaining businesses will be subjected to the same regulations and policies as their civilian counterparts" ("New law to scale down military-own businesses," 2018). The Ministry of National Defense reportedly drew up plans to restructure military enterprises with dual defense and economic objectives and reduce their number from 88 to 17 by 2020, including 29 enterprises that were focused on trade, construction and services sectors (Viet 2018). The amended Law on National Defense came into effect in January 2019.

Professionalization and Modernization

Beginning in the mid- to late-1990s, Vietnam initiated three major programs to increase the capacity of the VPA to contribute to national development and national defense: responsibility for creating special economic and defense zones in remote areas of strategic importance, implementation of a legal regime to enhance military professionalism, and force modernization of the navy, air defense-air force and ground forces. These programs were undertaken after the Cambodian conflict ended when China's rise created new challenges for the VPA, particularly in the South China Sea.

In 1998, the VPA was given responsibility for setting up of special economic-defense zones (*khu kinh te-quoc phong*) in remote strategic areas (Agence France-Presse, November 3, 1998). The program was promulgated by the prime minister's Decision 135/1998/QD-TTG that instructed each military region to establish one or two economic-defense zones to promote economic activity and national defense. By the end of the following year, thirteen economic-defense zones had been set up in strategic areas along borders with China, Laos, and Cambodia at a cost of US$215 million. The VPA was given the responsibility for mobilizing the masses and "building political bases" (Pham 1999a, 20; 1999b, 10–13), thus reinforcing ties between the military and society.

According to the defense minister, Pham Van Tra, "an economic and military combination enhances fighting capacity, improves the defense industries, allocates soldiers in key areas and, perhaps most importantly, balances the budget for all military activities" (quoted in Hanh 1999, 22). The vice minister of defense, Nguyen Van Rinh, stated that the program was aimed at "fewer numbers but greater proficiency" (quoted in Hanh 1999, 22). The objective was to combine economic activities with defense capability in remote and relatively underpopulated areas. Funding for this new initiative came from both the Ministry of National Defense and provincial governments. But because of insufficient revenue, the VPA was given permission to mobilize funds from international organizations as well as domestic sources. In addition, proposals for foreign investment projects were now evaluated for their impact on national defense (Le 2002, 6).

In the new economic-defense zones, the VPA was assigned the task of assisting the relocation of families from highly populated provinces to mountainous areas and islands. The military was also assigned to build the infrastructure for settlers (Ho 2001, 34–36). An estimated 84,000 families were resettled in these areas when the project was completed in 2013.

The Tay Nguyen Corps opened thousands of hectares of new land for the growth and production of rubber, coffee, wet rice, fruit, and industrial crops as well as livestock breeding. Its units constructed industrial processing plants, schools, cultural centers, sports complexes, and amusement facilities. Elsewhere, military units were engaged in dual civilian-military tasks. Naval patrols were involved in offshore fishing, border guard units were assigned afforestation tasks, the Flight Services Corporation combined its commercial operations with pilot training, army hospitals offered services to civilian clients, and military research centers were authorized to sign contracts with non-military bodies. Remarkably, the VPA assumed responsibility for the implementation of social welfare projects that no other ministry wanted to undertake.

Military units were the driving force behind road and dyke construction, the planting of new forests, the relocation of ethnic minorities (Abuza and Nguyen Nhat Anh, 2016, Nguyen Hung Son, 2014 and Thayer, 1997) and the provision of newspapers and television services. The VPA also inaugurated a new program, the Army and People Healthcare Corporation, with the agreement of the Ministry of Public Health. Border troops were involved in an anti-illiteracy campaign. Border guards not only constructed new schools, but also provided the teachers for an estimated 80 thousand pupils. The military worked closely with community elders and religious leaders. The VPA cooperated with state bodies in social welfare activities in remote mountain areas and islands where government officials seldom ventured. As a result of its active involvement, the VPA actively participated in local government decisions and, in effect, acted as an arm of the government in remote economic-defense zones (Tran 1999, 25).

The second major program to affect the VPA was an effort in 1998–99, when the regional security environment was relatively favorable, to further professionalize the VPA officer corps through a web of new laws, regulations, and rules.

For over five and a half decades, military professionalism in the Vietnam People's Army included mastery of three main components: traditional military art, political-ideological affairs, and technological modernization and standardization (Thayer 2001). Because the VPA had been continuously at war for so long, training and education had developed in a more or less ad hoc fashion with emphasis on practical experience over formal instruction.

In December 1999, the sixth session (tenth legislature) of the National Assembly adopted a new Law on Officers of the Vietnam People's Army (Le 2000, 3). This law was the most important development to date in the professionalization of the VPA. The law came into effect on April 1, 2000. For the first time, educational requirements for officer entry into the VPA, further continuing education and training standards, age and time in grade, and requirements for promotion from one rank to another were made compulsory. The curriculum at command and staff colleges was expanded to include a wealth of new subjects in the social sciences, humanities, sciences, and technology.

Officers were now required to attend military schools whose requirements for admission had been raised to reflect a greater stress on formal educational requirements (there were other provisions for promotion from the ranks or during combat). Officers had to attend a military school for each rank they aspired to. Battalion commanders had to attend one of the regional Infantry

Officers' Schools, while regimental commanders had to attend the Da Lat Military Academy. Divisional commanders had to attend the National Military Academy in Son Tay. At senior level, military officers were required to attend the Ho Chi Minh National Political Academy in Hanoi. All officers were also required to obtain a university degree or its equivalent to remain in uniform after the year 2000. Regimental and divisional commanders were required to earn post-graduate degrees in specialized fields, such as politics.

Younger members of the VPA could now expect greater upward mobility and improved prospects for promotion and assignment. In other words, there was now a clear career path for promotion within each service. Officers who failed to meet the selection criteria for promotion to the next rank within a designated time period would be retired. For example, for those pursuing a command and staff career, an officer had to first become a corps commander before qualifying for Military Region deputy commander. Only commanders of Military Regions could become deputy chiefs on the general staff.

As the new law was implemented, it was designed to eliminate the bloated rank structure at senior levels. The number of officers holding the rank of general was limited to 150 (down from a high of four hundred during the Vietnam War). Commanders of Military Regions would hold the rank of lieutenant general, while the highest rank of general (*Dai Tuong*) was reserved for the minister of national defense, the chief of the general staff and the head of the general political department.

The third major program focused on the modernization of the VPA with initial priority given to the navy and air defense-air force, and later the ground force. At the same time, Vietnam developed its national defense industry to support the force modernization of its three armed services.

The first phase of force modernization involved upgrading Vietnam's legacy navy and air fleets and procuring newer naval and air platforms and related weapon systems (Abuza and Nguyen Nhat Anh 2016; Nguyen Hung Son 2014; Thayer, 1997; Vuving 2017). During the latter half of the 1990s, the Russian Federation became Vietnam's major source of "big ticket" military weapons and equipment. Between 1996–2002, Vietnam took delivery of four modified *Tarantul* guided missile fast patrol craft and two *Svetlyak*-class coastal patrol boats from Russia.[10]

In 2006, Vietnam commenced a ten-year naval modernization program that included the acquisition of two *Gepard*-class frigates, Vietnam's first modern surface combatants (Truong Minh Vu and Nguyen The Phuong 2017). During the following decade Vietnam also acquired modern coastal defense systems; restructured its domestic shipbuilding industry and upgraded its technology; and created two new branches – a naval aviation unit and a submarine brigade.

Between 2008–17, Vietnam acquired eight *Tarantul*-5 (*Molniya*-class) guided missile fast attack craft armed with advanced anti-ship missiles. Two were purchased from Russia and six were assembled in Vietnam. Vietnam also took delivery of six additional *Svetlyak*-class coastal patrol boats and commissioned into service six more *Gepard*-class guided missile frigates, two outfitted for anti-submarine warfare.

No development was more significant than Vietnam's acquisition of six Russian *Varshavanyka* or enhanced *Kilo*-class conventional submarines between 2013–17. Crews for these submarines received training in Russia and India. The submarines are armed with heavy torpedoes and anti-ship and land attack cruise missiles (Thayer 2018).

Vietnam modernized its air defense-air force in parallel with naval modernization by upgrading existing inventories and procuring modern multi-role jet aircraft, armed with advanced missiles and capable of missions over the South China Sea (Abuza and Nguyen Nhat Anh 2016; Vuving 2017). Vietnam first procured seven Su-27SK (Flanker B) single-seat air superiority fighters, three Su-27UBK (Flanker C) two-seat trainers, and two additional Su-30Ks between 1995–98. The Su-27s were later upgraded so they could operate advanced air-to-surface missiles.

After having gained experience with the Su-27, Vietnam next acquired thirty-six Su-30MK multi-role all-weather jet fighters. The first four were delivered in 2004, twenty Su-30s were acquired between 2010–12, and the final batch of twelve were delivered in 2014–16. Vietnam also upgraded its Su-30s so they could operate modern air-to-surface missiles.

In the initial phase of defense modernization, the main priority for the army was on refurbishing and upgrading its artillery, infantry fighting vehicles and main battle tanks (MBT). India was contracted to upgrade the thermal sights and fire control systems of Vietnam's stocks of Soviet-era armored vehicles and T-54 and T-55 tanks.

In December 2015, Lieutenant General Vo Van Tuan, deputy chief of the general staff, announced that Vietnam's army had officially commenced a ten-year modernization program. The following year Vietnam made its first "big ticket" arms procurements for the ground force when it took delivery of ten Guardian Armored Personnel Carriers manufactured in the United Arab Republic. More significantly, the VPA announced the purchase of sixty-four modern Russian T-90S/SK main battle tanks (Nguyen The Phuong 2017).

From its founding in 1994, the VPA has always been dominated by the army and its combat arms – the infantry, artillery and armor. The orientation of the VPA was focused on defense of the homeland. In the 1990s, the VPA had to reorient itself to face challenges in the maritime domain to protect its offshore islands and oil and gas production facilities. Force modernization required an officer corps that was professionally educated and technologically savvy; it also resulted in the expansion of the navy and air defense-air force. By 2016, for example, Vietnam's navy had been transformed from an inland and coastal brown water navy to a green water fleet capable of operating in the South China Sea. Vietnam's arms procurements during 2012–16 made it the tenth largest importer of arms globally (Fleurant, P.D. Wezeman, S.T. Wezeman and Nan 2017). Vietnam's main suppliers were Russia (88%), Belarus (3.5%) and the Ukraine (2.8%).

Conclusion

This chapter focused on the expanding roles of the Vietnam People's Army since its founding in 1944, with a particular focus on the period 1975–2018. Since 1944, the VPA experienced a remarkable transformation from a guerrilla force to a conventional army during the Resistance War against the French (1946–54). At this time the VPA was required to carry out two main missions: combat and economic production. These roles were reinforced in the post-1954 period when Vietnam was partitioned. During this period, disparate VPA main, regional, and local forces were converted into a regular army and given the task of defending Vietnam against foreign aggression. The VPA was also tasked with economic production activities such as managing cash crop state farms and growing food to feed itself.

During the 1960s and early 1970s, the VPA was involved in a fifteen-year armed struggle to reunify Vietnam. After reunification in 1975, the VPA entered a period of transformation during which its roles were constantly redefined and expanded. The VPA was given two strategic tasks: national defense and building socialism. The latter took a variety of forms. In the immediate post-reunification years, the VPA was heavily engaged in reconstruction activities as well as economic production. The Third Indochina War curtailed this development.

In the mid-1980s, Vietnam experienced a major economic crisis that led to the adoption of a wholesale reform program called *doi moi*. Vietnam's reform era resulted in the proliferation of military-owned enterprises and their involvement in an ever-expanding net of economic and commercial activities, including joint ventures with foreign partners. Four distinct "waves of reform" were launched. The first wave (1995–96) was aimed at improving the competitiveness of military-owned enterprises by consolidating them through mergers. The second wave (1998–99) sought to make military enterprises more efficient and capable of taking on major projects. The third wave (2007) promoted the divestment of military enterprises that were purely commercial. The fourth wave (2018) is aimed at defining the economic purpose of military-owned enterprises in order to level the playing field between civilian and military enterprises.

In 1998–99, three major programs ushered in a new expansion of the VPA's roles. First, it was assigned essentially nation-building tasks when it was given responsibility for the creation of special economic-defense zones in remote strategic areas. Second, the VPA was subject to a concerted effort to raise its professional standard through a more formal and institutionalized system of education and training and promotion based on clearly defined criteria.

Third, the VPA underwent a concerted program of force modernization that privileged the navy and air defense-air force.

In sum, throughout the period 1975–2018 the VPA saw its roles expand from the two strategic tasks of national defense and building socialism to five main roles: national defense, economic and commercial production, nation-building and regime security, standardization and professionalization, and force modernization.

Developments over the last seven decades have altered the nature of civil-military relations in Vietnam.[11] During its formative years (1944–54) the VPA was led by "political generals" who were party members and revolutionaries first and soldiers second (Turley 1977). In other words, there was a fusion of roles between the civilian elite (party members) and the military. Gradually, Vietnamese civil-military relations were transformed by the expansion of roles assigned to the VPA. Party-military relations were transformed from their initial fused nature to more of a symbiotic relationship.

In the 1990s and subsequently, as the VPA developed distinct corporate interests in the economic sector and modernized into a professional military, the relationship was transformed into what may be called party-army concordance (Schiff 1995). According to Schiff, concordance theory highlights the importance of historical and cultural conditions in shaping civil-military relations. Party-military concordance involves dialogue, accommodation, and shared values and objectives among the political elites, military, and society.

The VPA today has greater autonomy over its affairs than ever before. Its highest ranking member has a seat on the VCP Politburo and the Central Military Party Committee, where he serves as deputy chair to the Party Secretary General. The party committee in the VPA selects delegates to VCP national congresses. The VPA also has block representation on the party Central Committee and in the National Assembly. Military-owned enterprises raise capital to supplement the military's budget. Vietnam has compulsory national conscription and the VPA is charged with conducting nation-wide mandatory defense education courses for high school and university students. In short, the Vietnam People's Army has emerged as a distinct constituency within the Vietnamese political system second in power and influence only to the Vietnam Communist Party.

Notes

1. This system converted accounting methods to reflect profit and loss.

2. Only thirty-four of the forty-nine joint ventures were operational. See Nguyen Nham 1998, 11; Vietnam News Agency, May 12, 1996; and "Vietnamese Army Streamlines Businesses," 1997.

3. "Vietnam Licenses First Military Bank," 1994 and Vietnam News Agency, December 8, 1994.

4. Some units kept their original designation. For example, Binh Doan 15, the 15th Corps that operated in the central highlands (Tay Nguyen), was designated Corporation 15.

5. The local militia, numbering from four to five million, provided a rudimentary defense presence in rural villages and townships as well as urban areas.

6. These included nine corporations, six enterprises, one state farm, one state forest unit, one bridge and road construction unit, and a vocational middle school; see Nguyen Duy Tuyen and Manh Ha Anh, 1991.

7. For details on the operation of the Dong Bac Coal Company, formed after the merger of thirteen coal mining enterprises under the control of various military zones and units, see Vietnam News Agency, February 20, 1996.

8. There was a reduction in the number of foreign partner joint ventures. Some military joint ventures that did not do well were sold to foreign investors.

9. "Decree on reorganization of defense businesses," *Quan Doi Nhan Dan*, December 19, 2007; Tuyet Nhung, 2007.

10. Unless otherwise noted, data on Vietnam's arms acquisitions have been taken from the Stockholm International Peace Research Institute's Arms Transfer Data Base for the period 1990–2016. http://armstrade.sipri.org/armstrade/page/trade_register.php.

11. This argument is presented in greater detail in Thayer and Hervouet, 2004.

References

Abuza, Zachary, and Nguyen Nhat Anh. 2016. "Vietnam's Military Modernization." *The Diplomat*, October 28.

"Army Businesses Grew in 2008 Despite Economic Difficulties." 2009. *Quan Doi Nhan Dan Online,* February 19.

Branigin, William. 1993. "Hanoi's Enterprising Army, Budget Cuts Put Soldiers in Business: From Fish to Hotels." *The Washington Post*, October 17.

Cleary, Paul. 1995. "Plenty of Consultants, but their Quality Varies Widely." *The Australian Financial Review*, May 10.

Fleurant, Aude, Pieter D. Wezeman, Siemon T. Wezeman and Nan Tian. 2017. *Trends in International Arms Transfers, 2016*. SIPRI Fact Sheet, Stockholm International Peace Research Institute, February.

"General Resolution of the Fourth Party Congress." 1976. Vietnam News Agency, December 24.

"G[D]DI heading for Higher Objectives Despite Difficulties." 2009. *Quan Doi Nhan Dan Online,* February 11.

Hanh Dung. 1999. "Military Enterprises." *Vietnam Economic Times*, December, pp. 22–23.

Hiebert, Murray. 1991a. "Defeated by Victory." *Far Eastern Economic Review*, June 13, p. 24.

———. 1991b. "Soldiers of Fortune." *Far Eastern Economic Review*, June 13, pp. 26–27.

———. 1993. "Corps Business." *Far Eastern Economic Review*, December 23, p. 40.

Ho Quoc Toan. 2001. "Xau Dung Khu Kinh Te-Quoc Phong Tren Cac Dia Ban Chien Luoc" (Building Economic-Defense Zones in Strategic Locations). *Tap Chi Quoc Phong Toan Dan*, 7: 34–36.

Huong Lam. 1996. "Defense Ministry Enters Telecom Fray." *Vietnam Investment Review*, July 22–28, p. 15.

Le Van Dung. 1976. "New Important Task of the Viet Nam People's Army." *Vietnam Courier*, 52 (September): 8–9.

———. 1996. "Ministry of Defense Property JV Licensed." *Vietnam Business Journal*, October, p. 5.

Le Van Dung. 2000. "Luat Si Quan Quan Doi Nhan Dan Viet Nam" (Law on Officers Vietnam People's Army). *Quan Doi Nhan Dan*, January 14, p. 3.

———. 2002. "5 Nam Thuc Hien Nghi Dinh 19/CP cua Chinh Phu va Cong Tac Quoc Phong o Cac Bo, Nganh va Cac Dia Phuong—Ket Qua va Phuong Huong" (5 Years Implementing Government Decree 19 on Government and Defense Work in Ministries, Branches and Localities - Results and Directions). *Tap Chi Quoc Phong Toan Dan* 5: 6–9.

"New law to scale down military-owned businesses." 2018. *Viet Nam News*, June 8.

Nguyen Duy Tuyen and Manh Ha Anh. 1991. "About Organizing Party Leadership in an Army Unit Specialized in Economic Construction." *Tap Chi Quoc Phong Toan Dan* 3: 34–36.

Nguyen Hung Son. 2014. "Vietnam: A Case Study in Naval Modernization". In *Naval Modernization in South-East Asia: Nature, Causes and Consequences*, eds. Geoffrey Till and Jane Chan, 127–30. New York: Routledge.

Nguyen Nham. 1998. "Money the New Target for Army." *Vietnam Investment Review*, June 15–21, p. 11.

Nguyen The Phuong. 2017. "What Will New Russian Tanks Mean for Vietnam's Military?" *The Diplomat*, July 27.

Pham Thanh Ngan. 1999a. "Phat Huy Truyen Thong 'Bo Doi Cu Ho' Xay Dung Nguoi Chien Si Quan Doi Nhan Dan Viet Nam Trong Giai Doan Cach Mang Moi" (Promoting the Tradition of 'Uncle Ho's Soldiers' to Build the Vietnam People's Army Soldiers in the New Revolutionary Period). *Tap Chi Quoc Phong Toan Dan* 12: 10–13.

———. 1999b. "Xay Dung Quan Doi Vung Manh Ve Chinh Tri Trong Thoi Ky Phan Trien Moi Cua Dat Nuoc" (Building an Army that is Politically Strong in the New Age of Developing Our Country). *Tap Chi Cong San* 23: 19–22, 27.

Phan Thu. 1994. "The Army Engages in Economic and Productive Labor Activities." *Tap Chi Cong San* 12: 18.

Ray, Chris. 1979. *Vietnam: Reconstruction and the Chinese Invasion: An Eyewitness Account*. Forrest Lodge: Australian Radical Publications.

Schiff, Rebecca. 1995."Civil-Military Relations Reconsidered: A Theory of Concordance." *Armed Forces and Society* 22(1): 7–24.

Socialist Republic of Vietnam. 2009. *Vietnam National Defense*. Hanoi: Ministry of National Defense, December.

"Song Thu Corporation Hailed for Business Achievements." 2014. *People's Army Daily Online*, April 17.

Stockholm International Peace Research Institute. Arms Transfer Data Base for the period 1990–2016. http://armstrade.sipri.org/armstrade/page/trade_register.php.

Thayer, Carlyle A. 1983. "Vietnam's Two Strategic Tasks: Building Socialism and Defending the Fatherland." In *Southeast Asian Affairs 1983*, ed. Pushpa Thambipillai, 299–324. Singapore: Institute of Southeast Asian Studies.

———. 1985. "Vietnam." In *Military-civilian Relations in South-East Asia*, eds. Zakaria bin Haji Ahmad and Harold A. Crouch, 235–66. Singapore: Oxford University Press.

———. 1995. "Vietnam's Strategic Readjustment." In *China as a Great Power: Myths, Realities and Challenges in the Asia-Pacific Region*, eds. Stuart Harris and Gary Klintworth, 185–201. New York: St. Martin's Press.

———. 1996. "People's Army Gets in Step with Era of Friendly Reform." *The Australian* (Special Survey), September 6, p. 18.

———. 1997. "Force Modernization: The Case of the Vietnam People's Army." *Contemporary South East Asia* 19(1): 1–28.

———. 1998. "Marching Orders." *Vietnam Business Journal* 6(4): 57.

———. 2000a. "Demobilization but not Disarmament: Personnel Reduction and Force Modernization in Vietnam." In *War Force to Work Force: Global Perspectives on Demobilization and Reintegration*, ed. Natalie Pauwels, 199–219. Baden-Baden: Nomos Verlagsgesellschaft.

———. 2000b. "The Economic and Commercial Roles of the Vietnam People's Army." *Asian Perspective* 24(2): 87–120.

———. 2001. "Vietnam: The Many Roles of the VPA." In *Military Professionalism in Asia: Conceptual and Empirical Perspectives*, ed. Muthiah Alagappa, 137–49. Honolulu, East-West Center.

———. 2018. "Submarine Acquisition in Vietnam." In *Naval Modernization in Southeast Asia*, Part Two, *Submarine Issues for Small and Medium Navies*, eds. Geoffrey Till and Colin S. L. Koh, 109–18. London: Palgrave Macmillan.

Thayer, Carlyle A., and Gérard Hervouet. 2004. "The Army as a Political and Economic Actor in Vietnam." In *Naissance d'un État-Parti: Le Viet Nam depuis 1945*, eds. Christopher Goscha and Benoît de Tréglodé, 355–81. Paris: Les Indes savantes.

Tran Duc Nghia. 1990. "Truong Son Construction General Corporation: Program to Renew Technical Equipment in the Years 1990–1995." *Tap Chi Quoc Phong Toan Dan* 10: 67–79.

Tran Le Thuy. 1999. "On the Home Front." *Vietnam Economic Times*, December, p. 25.

Truong Minh Vu and Nguyen The Phuong. 2017. "Naval Development in Vietnam." In *Naval Modernization in Southeast Asia: Problems and Prospects for Small and Medium Navies*, eds. Geoffrey Till and Atriandi Supriyanto Ristian, 93–106. London: Palgrave Macmillan.

Turley, William S. 1977. "Origins and Development of Communist Military Leadership in Vietnam." *Armed Forces and Society* 3(2): 218–47.

Tuyet Nhung. 2007. "Vietnam's Army to Hand Over Business Enterprises." *Thanh Nien News*, December 20.

Viet Tuan. 2018. "Defense Ministry Cuts Back on Business Activities." *VNExpress*, October 11.

"Vietnam Licenses First Military Bank." 1994. *Asian Defence Journal*, November, p. 97.

"Vietnamese Army Streamlines Businesses." 1997. *Jane's Defense Weekly*, September 24, p. 13.

Vo Nguyen Giap. 1976. "Xay Dung Nen Quoc Phong Toan Dan Vung Manh, Bao Ve To Quoc Viet Nam Xa Hoi Chu Nghia." (Build a Strong All-People's Defense, Protect the Vietnam Socialist Fatherland). *Hoc Tap* 5: 13–45.

Vuving, Alex. 2017. "Tracking Vietnam's Force Build-Up in the South China Sea." Asia Maritime Transparency Initiative, Center for Strategic and International Studies, November 3. https://amti.csis.org/tracking-vietnams-force-build-south-china-sea/.

Watkin, Huw. 1999. "Proud Military Slips into Decline as Aid Dries Up." *South China Morning Post*, July 7.

CHAPTER 10

From Guerrillas to Guardians: Army and Society in the Lao People's Democratic Republic

Geoffrey C. Gunn

This chapter seeks to present a global picture of army and society in the Lao People's Democratic Republic (LPDR). Consonant with the overall architecture of this book, we are also concerned to establish continuities and discontinuities with the past. While the collapse of the Soviet Union and the LPDR's embrace of market capitalism has ostensibly changed state-society relations, the real and symbolic influence of the military within the state apparatus remains entrenched. We investigate the informal economic activities conducted by the military in a country known to be low on the ladder of economic development. Trajectories of individual military careers and state appointments will further illuminate this problem. Hopefully, such analysis will enable us to read out certain conclusions, such as the role of the military in state-building and in serving or thwarting the full development of civil society in an era when domestic political challenges may well be more significant than external.

Allowing that the army in the post-1975 LPDR is an important arm of the communist state, along with other government organs, it is important to acknowledge the guerrilla origins of the Lao People's Army (LPA) in the thirty-year war waged by the Pathet Lao or Lao revolutionary movement against French and American backers of the Vientiane or Royal Lao Government (RLG). Although there has been significant generational change among the Pathet Lao elite, as age takes its toll, it is also significant that individuals among the founding generation still cling to power. While the Pathet Lao victory over the RLG and its armed forces in 1975 was, arguably, less the result of military force than diplomatic-political preparation, it is also important to acknowledge the political-military role of the LPA in the post-revolutionary period, also described as the period of "building socialism" and "defending the fatherland." Such language is not merely academic or rhetorical but actually defined the "guardian" role of the LPA in a number of tense engagements across the common boundary with Thailand until political rapprochement in the late 1980s, as well as in actions against dissident elements, including ethnic Hmong guerrillas, which is still ongoing.

The Rise of the Lao People's Liberation Army

As in other Southeast Asian countries formerly under Japanese military occupation, the defeat of the colonial power in Laos by the Japanese militarists stimulated a nationalist awakening. The nationalist movement in Laos was known as the Lao Issara (Free Laos). The surrender of the Japanese also created unique opportunities. On October 6, 1945, three weeks after the formation in Vientiane by Prince Phetsarath of a Lao Issara government, a contingent of Viet Minh officers accompanied by the former's half-brother, Prince Souphanouvong, arrived in southern Laos from Vietnam and proclaimed the "Lao Army of Liberation and Defense." Forced into exile in Thailand some six months later by returning French units, this army upheld armed actions against the colonial power and their collaborators for the next four years. They were supported in this enterprise by Viet Minh units and Free Thai and Japanese holdouts. On December 2, 1946, in the montagnard heartland of the central Laos-central Vietnam border region, the Viet Minh-supported Lao Issara-officered "Lao Bao Army of Liberation" was sworn in (Gunn 1988, 133–34).

While acknowledging the general legacy of the various Lao Issara armed actions in the anti-colonial struggle, official Lao communist historians prefer to date the origin of the Lao People's Liberation Army—as of July 1982 known as the Lao People's Army—to the Latsavang unit founded on January 20, 1949 in Sam Neua province by Kaysone Phomvihane, future communist strongman in the LPDR. According to an official publication, "at first it was equipped with outdated weapons, cross-bows and other traditional weapons.

Under a complex situation, they carried out the struggle against the French colonialists in conjunction with the foundation of the revolutionary bases," and, later, with the support of local peoples and the Vietnamese army, they formed companies and battalions ("Lao People's Army" 1989, 6).

While minority peoples did figure, albeit peripherally, in the Chinese revolution, and while the Viet Minh was nurtured in the Viet Bac minority region of northern Vietnam, the outstanding feature of the particular generation of the people's war waged in Laos was that the minority peoples carried the guns for the LPA and that the rear base areas of the guerrillas were the mountain homelands of the minority peoples (Fletcher and Gunn 1981). Undoubtedly the successful recruitment of the ethnic minorities into the LPA was a function of adroit manipulation of strong patriarchal loyalties obtaining among key tribal, clan, and lineage groups. This was over and above the parallel effort undertaken by the US-backed Royal Lao Army (RLA) along with that part of the Hmong community loyal to General Vang Pao (1929–2011), heading up the "secret" CIA-backed Hmong army at least prior to his flight to the United States following the communist victory in 1975. The immense prestige and charisma of Prince Souphanouvong was also consciously exploited to swing allegiance from the majority Lao Buddhist population in the direction of the Patriotic Front.

According to Joseph J. Zasloff (1972), prodigious recruitment efforts enabled the LPA to increase its numbers from twenty thousand in 1964 to forty-five or fifty thousand in 1971. Without question the massive American bombing of Laos during this period also boosted the ability of the Pathet Lao to rally a disaffected population. While we are lacking a breakdown of the LPA by ethnicity, it is reasonable to suggest that a high proportion included ethnic minorities. Zasloff also describes a corollary expansion in Laos of the Vietnam People's Army (VPA) from ten thousand to sixty-seven thousand in this time frame.

We have not sought to trace the vicissitudes of the RLA although it bears noting that, historically, the French and the Americans trained and equipped the royalist forces in line with radically different military doctrines and operational ethos. Lacking the unity of the Pathet Lao forces, the royalist forces were prone to inter-service rivalry and, more particularly, to patron-clientelist arrangements within the military region system which often entrenched localist loyalties around charismatic leaders prone to placing corporativist interests ahead of national vision. Profiteering, corruption, and severe problems of morale always sapped the capacity of the royalist army (Gunn 1985). In backing the Hmong, the American CIA actually played upon this ethnic group's clan loyalties, unleashing a powerful atavistic spirit of armed revolt that continues among a diminishing number of holdouts until the present (UNPO 2018). As bearers of anti-colonial and anti-imperialist nationalism against the French and American presence, and in the full face of the devastating US bombing campaign, the Pathet Lao cultivated, and earned, their image as patriotic, selfless, free from corruption, and in touch with ordinary people.

They were also widely feared. We would go further to suggest that, born out of the crucible of war and revolution, the military in Laos view their role as primordial to the foundation of the state. The state, in turn, mythologizes the role of the army. This can be seen in public ceremonies and displays: witness the function of the Army Museum, the publication of the weekly military newspaper *Kong Thap* (The Army), special events, awards, rewards, and special privileges heaped upon veterans and their families. Even in suffering, the military enjoy the benefits provided by military hospitals. As we will develop in this essay, the privileging of the military elite in post-revolutionary Laos not only conforms to communist practice such as established by the now defunct Soviet Union and as still upheld in the remaining Stalinist outposts of Vietnam and North Korea, but has special Lao characteristics. As a former Buddhist kingdom, culture matters in Laos and well-observed Lao characteristics of patron-client relations, regionalism, clannishness, and less rigid social controls compared to Confucianized Asia also reflect the role of the military in society. In the following pages I seek to demonstrate the tension between socialist rhetoric, especially as it informs military style, and the social and civilizational reality in which this organization operates.

The Party-Army Symbiosis and the Sociology of Elites

The transition of the LPA from being the arm of the insurgent party—the instrument of the dictatorship of revolutionary power, in the official Leninist phraseology—to becoming the instrument of state power, inevitably involved institutional and organizational changes (Gunn 1998, 133). Laos is no exception to the general pattern of communist states where the Party and military have achieved a symbiosis. Even so, throughout the period of armed struggle the Pathet Lao consistently upheld the principle of Party dominance over the military. Consistent with the communist model pioneered in the Soviet Union and more generally adopted in China and Vietnam, the military command in Laos is penetrated and overseen by the Party at all levels through the downward flow of Party commands, through the mechanism of dual Party-military membership, through the watchdog role of the Central Party Military Commission, and through the mediation of the ubiquitous political commissars, the ostensible link which conjoins combatants with cadres. Notionally, civilian control is exercised over the army, but in practice, as demonstrated below, there is a significant overlapping of elites.

But as successors to the old RLG national army, the rump of which was incorporated into the reconstituted LPA, and as inheritors of the former territorial space of the RLG—the heartland of the majority Lao—the minority component of the LPA has been diluted. The death of Sithone Kommadan, symbol of the warrior tradition of the southern montagnards, robbed this minority group of their highest-level representation. The levers of power, therefore, remained with the majority Lao drawn from a combination of aristocratic, mandarinal, bourgeois, and, in some cases, proletarian and peasant backgrounds. Blood or marriage ties with Vietnamese, work or educational experience in Vietnam, and early membership in the Indochinese Communist Party (ICP) were among the various accouterments of the leadership of the LPDR. While the ICP generation and even the Lao Issara generation has passed, an LPA background remains a common element among many of the ruling elite.

A scrutiny of individual roles reveals considerable overlap between army, government, and Party functions. For example, former LPDR president Khamtay Siphandon, a native of Champassak in the south and a former commander-in-chief of the LPA, held concurrent positions as minister of national defense and LPA vice-premier. As of the Fifth Lao People's Revolutionary Party Congress in 1991, Khamtay Siphandon replaced Kaysone Phomvihane as prime minister while Kaysone assumed the presidency. Khamtay eventually won the presidency in 1998 having replaced veteran Nouhak Phoumsavan who took over with Kaysone's death in November 1992, remaining in the LPRP central committee and politburo until 1996 (and surviving until 2008). Sisavath Keobounphanh, a chief of the general staff of the LPA, held concurrent positions as Party Central Committee Secretary, and minister attached to the premier's office and minister of the interior, war veterans, and social affairs, to which the police are accountable. As of the Fifth Party Congress, Sisavath held the office of minister of agriculture and forestry. He subsequently served as prime minister and retained his politburo membership. A native of the southeastern province of Attapue and a Lao Issara/Pathet Lao veteran, General Samane Vignaketh, a member of the Central General Committee, served concurrently as a member of the Central Committee's Military Committee, vice-minister of national defense and director-general of the army's politburo. While not a member of the LPDR cabinet, Samane was appointed minister of education in 1989. From 1993 he served as president of the Lao National Assembly and remained prominent among a second echelon of old guard leaders.

Some observers have tracked the consolidation of the military within the state apparatus, especially since the Sixth Party Congress held in 1996. Not only did the congress signal a shift in the distribution of power to the military network but favored the faction of the Party opposed to too rapid reform, although not the general thrust of reform. Evidence of this shift was signaled by the fact that seven out of nine places in the politburo were then held by military men. Such changes were also reflected in membership in the Party's central committee (Bourdet 2000). Stuart-Fox (1997, 195) has traced this debate back to the Fourth Party Congress held in 1986 where, he speculates, victory by the pro-reform camp over hardliners wishing to preserve state monopolies and patronage was only won with the decisive support of General Sisavath. Importantly, in this arrangement, the army would win access to key timber contracts and trading rights.

Between 1991 and 1996, the Ministry of National Defense was headed by General Choummaly Sayasone, also a southerner. Appointed vice prime minister in 1998, he went on to be named president of the Party at the 2006 Eighth Party Congress in replacement of Khamtay, also adding the state presidency once the National Assembly met (Gunn 1998, 136; Gunn 2007, 183; Stuart-Fox 2008, 58). At the Ninth Party Congress held in March 2011, Choummaly was re-elected Party secretary-general. There was also some generational change as with the retirement of Sisavath Keobounphanh. At the Tenth Party Congress held in January 2016, the former vice president, Bounhyang Vorachit, replaced Choummaly as Party secretary-general. The new eleven-member politburo includes only one serving military figure, but with the military holding three out of nine positions in the central committee, the old guard remain firmly in control. As explained by Bounhyang, himself a former army commander, most of the leadership have been "tested on the battlefield during the struggle for national liberation," and with the rest gaining their laurels in "national development and protection tasks" (Souksakhone Vaenkeo 2016, cited in Gunn 2017, 206). In Laos, it should be emphasized, the Defense Ministry was never placed under civilian leadership as was the case in China in the post-Mao era. This also holds with the appointment at the first Plenary Session of the Eighth National Assembly in April 2016 of the current minister of defense, General Chansamone Chanyalath.

External Patrons and Environment

While a Vietnamese military presence in Laos goes back to the anti-French war, the numbers probably peaked in the late 1970s at around fifty thousand as the regime sought to consolidate its authority in the face of challenges from a spectrum of dissident groups. The hallmark of Laos-Vietnam cooperation was the signing, in July 1977, of the 25-year Treaty of Friendship and Cooperation (Thayer 1982). Additional protocols relate to defense cooperation and the role of Vietnamese advisers. Only in late 1988 were all Vietnamese operational elements withdrawn from Laos.

Commensurate with the development of an air (and river) force, the Soviet Union emerged as the major supplier of such equipment as SAMs and MIG jet fighters, along with technical support and training. Until precipitously withdrawn with the collapse of the Soviet Union, some one thousand five hundred Soviet advisers were based in Laos. The LPA was also supplied with vintage Soviet design PT-76 light tanks, T-54/-55 main battle tanks, and 122 mm and 130 mm artillery. Even so, budget constraints seriously hampered modernization of the armed forces (Savada 1994).

The collapse of communism in the Soviet Union and Eastern Europe also robbed Laos of a strategic ally and supplier of material support. Just as Laos sided with Vietnam in its dispute with China over support of the Pol Pot regime, some thousands of Chinese People's Liberation Army (PLA)-cum-construction workers stationed in northern Laos in accord with an agreement signed between the RLG and China in January 1962, were requested to be withdrawn by the Lao government authorities as of March 7, 1979. But with the settlement of the Cambodia problem in the early 1990s, relations once again warmed with China. Beginning in 1991, military attaché offices opened in both countries. Since then, military exchanges from the highest level have been frequent. In 1995, Laos spent US$6 million of a US$18 million loan from China on defense upgrades, including air defense artillery (*Jane's Defence Weekly*, May 19, 1995), just as ties between the LPA and the PLA have continued to expand over the decades under the general auspices of the China-Laos "comprehensive strategic cooperative partnership" (Xinhua 2017). Even so, Laos still has the luxury of playing off Vietnam with its giant neighbor to the north in winning both economic and military support.

Treaty partners Laos and Vietnam, co-members of ASEAN since Laos joined in 1997, have frequently exchanged high-level military delegations over the years. For example, on February 19, 2002, LPDR defense minister and politburo member Duoangchay Pichit and his entourage were received by counterparts in Hanoi to further consolidate special ties. This visit came just four days after a visit to Laos by Vietnamese defense minister Pham Van Tra. In turn, his visit came just one week after a visit to Laos by his Chinese counterpart, Chi Haotian, suggesting to some a battle for influence in Laos between the two neighboring socialist states (BBC News, February 15, 2001). In some accounts, Vietnamese advisers or troops were retained or invited back to Laos, such as in May 2000, to assist in routing Hmong rebels. While this was denied by the regime, the Treaty allowed Vietnamese troops to re-enter the country when invited.

Ironically, given Laos's revolutionary history, commencing in 1991, the US armed forces began providing humanitarian assistance to Laos, such as school building, hospital renovation, flood control works, disposal of unexploded ordinance, Hmong relocation, among other activities. Working out of the US Embassy and with the cooperation of the Ministry of Foreign Affairs, the program also engaged NGOs and UN agencies. But as with other international agency involvement in Lao civil society, politics was simply off the agenda in a society where the regime maintains strict social controls and sanctions. Undoubtedly, a high point in US-LPDR relations was reached in 2016 with the visit to Laos by US President Barack Obama (Gunn 2017).

Having won international legitimacy from the West, having made up lost time with Thailand, and even having joined the major regional grouping once feared as a stalking horse for imperialist and reactionary interest, Laos today enjoys a relative peace not seen since colonial times. But as demonstrated by a series of "mysterious" bomb blasts in the nation's capital and other towns in 2000, security concerns may well have shifted away from purely external threats to resistance from within. To date, internal challenges to the regime's monopoly on power have been met with a tightening rather than loosening of the screws on surveillance and security. Just as former members of the RLG and its army underwent years of confinement and reeducation in remote locations, we should not lose sight of the fact that the LPA and its auxiliaries oversee a vigilant approach to dissent, much less anti-government demonstrations or acts of civil disobedience.

The Army and Society

Organization of the military command under the LPDR is highly centralized. The LPA headquarters in Vientiane controls four military regions. Military region One is based in Luang Prabang, Two in Phonsavan (Xiang Khouang province), Three in Xeno (Savannakhet province), and Four in Champassak province. Currently at a force strength of thirty thousand, these numbers represent a steep decline relative to even the early 1990s. The LPA were then deployed in five divisions and positioned to meet security threats. The First was deployed in the Vientiane area, the Second along the Laos-Thailand border and north-central Laos, the Third along the Laos-China border, and the Fourth and Fifth in southern Laos (Savada 1994).

This arrangement is to be contrasted with the system of military regions upheld by the RLG whereby separate military clientelist hierarchies within five military regions often aggravated rather than eased relations with civilian administrators and their respective coteries. In the manner of the operative system long existing in the old liberated zones and in the interests of promoting national unity, the LPA instituted a tripartite system of regular forces, regional forces, and guerrilla and self-defense forces that made regions and localities accountable to the center and which, in turn, made all levels accountable to the Party.

Regional armed forces are stationed in all localities, including the plains along the bank of the Mekong River and in the mountainous areas in the north, that is, generally far away from the towns or positions of the regular armed forces. More so than the regulars, the regionals are in close contact with local people, including the minority peoples, as indeed are the local guerrilla forces operating at the canton and village level. As "eternally vigilant guardians" of the villages of which Laos is constituted and by the preparation of "defensive bases," the local forces could be construed as the essential bearers of the general people's war doctrine as it prevailed in Laos. In the manner of a people's militia, self-defense forces have been established in various offices, organizations, factories, hospitals, schools, ministries, departments, and production bases.

During the national liberation struggle, as described, the LPA conformed to the general model of a people's army, albeit a highly dependent exemplar. However, post-1975 a number of changes in military ethos took place, which were not only the structural consequences of maintaining a conscripted standing army, but were also the consequence of doctrinal differences within international communism. After the Sino-Vietnamese conflict intensified into open warfare in February 1979, the LPRP equated Maoism with treason against the Lao state and generally adopted a localized version of Vietnamese-style worker-oriented communism (Gunn 1998, 136–37).

Thus, by 1978 the slogans of the day were "building all-round strong armed forces" and the upholding of a "true people's army and true revolutionary army." While the efficacy of a people's war was in no way repudiated—indeed the role of the guerrilla forces in the people's war was still recognized—the new imperative was expressed in the catch-phrase that asserts the imperative to build a "model modern army." In a move that can be viewed as enhancing the professionalism of the regulars, in the words of a spokesperson, the LPA "has increasingly equipped itself with some modern weapons and techniques... the emphasis is on orderly and systematic military training" (Summary of World Broadcasts, November 11, 1980, cited in Gunn 1998, 137). As a major beneficiary of Soviet weaponry and allowing for the fact that large numbers of Lao officers and students underwent training in Eastern bloc countries, the impulse towards the development of a more professional army was self-evident, all the more so in consideration of the kind of skills required to operate the more sophisticated weapons systems obtained during this period, including MiG-16 aircraft, anti-aircraft installations, and radar systems.

In a further departure from the "pure" people's army model and in a move in the direction of modernizing the army, a system of conferring ranks was instituted in the latter part of 1980. For the first time, the wearing of insignia became mandatory and ranks were designated in echelons all the way down from general to second-class private and cadet (Summary of World Broadcasts, December 20, 1980, cited in Gunn 1998, 137). While this might be viewed as little more than cosmetic change in an institution which had deeply internalized the values of guerrilla egalitarianism over thirty years, the real relevance of a professed modernization of the LPA can only be viewed with reference to the overall pace of economic development and the role of the LPA in that development (Gunn 1998, 138).

In 1982, the armed forces underwent a further consolidation. At the Third Party Congress, then LPA chief of staff, General Sisavath Keobounphanh, stated that "... there must be plans to build the consolidated armed forces with a combined strength composed of the regular army and the people's security forces... so as to turn them into (mobile regrouped forces). We must pay attention to the building of the two types of forces. At the same time, we must not cease efforts to build the regrouped mobile forces into a model modern army" (Summary of World Broadcasts, May 10, 1982, cited in Gunn 1998, 230).

Operational Dynamics

It could be said that the LPA had been well exercised since the advent of the new regime. Confronted by an array of dissident elements, the task of homeland security had never been relaxed and had been sorely tested on a number of occasions. Notable were major clashes involving the LPA and the Royal Thai Army in incidents linked with territorial disputes in Pak Lay in western Xayabuli Province, but also related to the actions of armed resistance groups operating from Thailand, the actions of ethnic rebels, bandits, and smugglers. Reaching international attention in mid-1984 and again in early 1986 and in December 1987, fighting resulted in up to a thousand deaths before a ceasefire was declared in February 1988. Both sides along with civilians took casualties although the LPA was believed to have held its ground well against its adversary in this remote northern location. While Bangkok and Vientiane settled major differences following high-level discussion in 1991–92 aimed at resolving border questions and disarming Lao rebels, the periodic recurrence of resistance activities by Thai-based insurgents frequently poisoned relations between the two countries. For example, in July 2000, Thai-based rebels killed five Lao customs officials in southern Laos and raised the old RLG flag.

While the armed forces are charged with maintaining external security, they also share with the police under the Ministry of Interior certain internal security duties. These range from high-profile counter-insurgency activities to counter-terror measures, especially in the wake of bomb blasts in the capital. But it was their armed confrontation with dissident Hmong that led to credible reports of human rights abuses. The military also upholds a separate system of courts, albeit subject to review by the Supreme Court.

Over the decades, the highest profile clashes involving the LPA have been those against ethnic Hmong rebels especially active in Luang Prabang and Xiang Khouang provinces. The first major operation to destroy Hmong resistance was undertaken after the rainy season in November 1977. LPA and Vietnamese forces using artillery and airstrikes led to thousands of Hmong casualties (Stuart-Fox 1997, 177). While Hmong rebels kept up their low-level insurgency, in a major push launched in January 2000 armed Hmong insurgents attacked provincial towns on and south of the Plain of Jars, inflicting a significant number of casualties upon LPA forces and LPDR officials alike. As mentioned, this alarming breach of security triggered a call from Vientiane to Hanoi to assist in putting down the rebellion. While the majority of the Hmong have since accommodated to the regime, still in 2007 international human rights organizations were alerted to "brutal" military operations mounted against starving bands of Hmong scattered across a number of provinces, including those pushed back from refugee camps in Thailand (Gunn 2008, 66–67).

It would be appropriate to consider the life of the ordinary recruit or conscript in Laos, typically drawn from the rural classes. In line with a long tradition, recruits into the armed forces are poorly paid and, in part, are obliged to subsist on extracurricular income or through participation in agricultural labor. Under a 1994 law revised in 2004, a period of eighteen months of military service is obligatory for eighteen-year old males although in certain circumstances even younger males are pressed into portering and other roles. Even so, evasion is widespread, perhaps matching relatively weak social controls over widely disparate local communities. With its origins as a guerrilla army, the relatively high level of female participation in the

LPA definitely sets it apart from the Royal army and colonial predecessors, although women are not liable for conscription. Invariably, retired soldiers or those wounded in conflict, such as in the border conflicts with Thailand in the 1980s, are thrown back to the support of their communities as social safety nets in impecunious Laos are spread extremely thin.

The Army and Development

While the contingencies of the national liberation struggle in the face of the US bombing onslaught relegated social transformation to low priority, it can be inferred from official statements and verified from eyewitness accounts that at least "several army units assigned to the rear of the old liberated zones also actively participated in building and expanding the economy." Until the late 1970s, at least, the army was still duty-bound to involve itself in economic construction work. As reiterated in an editorial in the party daily *Siang Pasason*: "Our army must hold aloft the spirit of self-sufficiency and self-reliance; actively organize movements to boost production, crop cultivation and livestock raising, guarantee that we must have sufficient and surplus food supply; strive to gradually improve our living conditions, minimize our army's reliance on the people; and pay attention to taking part in the tasks of restoring and developing our economy and culture and building socialism and the foundations for national defense and peace keeping" (Summary of World Broadcasts, January 21, 1978, cited in Gunn 1998, 138).

According to the official account, the achievements of the army in this direction were tangible. Several army units had achieved self-sufficiency in food supplies from between one and three months, other units had helped to organize labor to repair the damage caused by natural disasters, others had planted vegetables, and model army production unit No. 74, for example, had successfully reaped hundreds of tons of rice.

While specialization of military function goes hand in hand with the demands of the new emerging professionalized LPA, it might also be viewed as a diminution of the politically inculcated mission of "fighting will" against seemingly insuperable odds which hitherto had been the LPA's major source of military strength. The Party, however, appeared bent on having it both ways. As expressed by former Party chief, Kaysone Phomvihane in a publication intended for external consumption: "[Our party] has been constantly concerned to elaborate and to consolidate the four categories of relationships involving the army [relations between the army and the people, between cadres and combatants and national and international relations] and the judicious regulation of the relationship between quality and quantity, between organization and ideology, between arms and fighting men, to render operative the politico-moral factor in order to incessantly raise combat efficiency and to resolve material difficulties" (Kaysone 1980, 84, cited in Gunn 1998, 140).

And as echoed in an editorial in the party daily *Siang Pasason* directed towards a domestic audience, Kaysone argued: "[T]he armed forces can become an invincible force only when they are closely related to the masses... quality should be more important than quantity... it is certain that a small unit which is well organized, maintains good relations and discipline, understands how to distinguish friends from foes and maintains a high spirit of sacrifice to fight for the interests of the nation and the people, will be able to defeat the enemy" (Summary of World Broadcasts, October 16, 1980, cited in Gunn 1998, 140).

There is no question that the 1980s debate running in the Party and army or between military figures within the Party over the correct relationship between "quality" and "quantity" was eventually settled, either under Soviet tutelage or through the development needs of the state in line with the slogan that called for "a true people's army advancing step by step towards being a modern well organized army." But, by the 1990s, even the "people's army" doctrine was wearing thin.

The Military in Business

It would not be so surprising that in a state economy where most people live outside a monetized economy and where the macro economy reveals extreme weakness, that the armed forces, individuals or sections, would look to enhancing their own corporate interests through business activities. Indeed, the royalist army notoriously entered the black market in a way which may have sapped their operational capacity. Southeast Asian armies from Indonesia to Myanmar to Cambodia under Hun Sen, are no less prone to crossing the boundary between public duty and private enrichment. But even in the socialist world, China's PLA became notorious in forging business links in the hothouse economic environment opened up by Deng Xiaoping's reforms. With the advent of *doi moi* or renovation in Vietnam, the VPA followed suit.

Similarly, economic reform in Laos led to the emergence of a number of military-backed companies set up with government approval, forming an important element of the state economy. Forestry was one such sector ripe for exploitation. Indeed, there is reason to believe that the LPA was emboldened to make such a radical shift by drawing upon the VPA precedent. As part of the reform in the forestry sector in Laos, foreign logging companies retained the right to process timber, yet they had to do so in agreement with one of three military-based companies operating in north, south, and central Laos (Nette 1998b).

The highest profile military-run enterprise emerging in the mid-1980s was the Mountain Area Development Corporation (MADC). According to Andrew Nette (1998a), since the loss of Soviet support in the early 1990s such enterprises, some in joint venture with foreign partners and with interests ranging from tourism to logging, became crucial sources of government revenue. The experiment also answered ordinary soldiers' needs to forge a living at a time of plunging morale. But also, in this account, the military remained one of the few institutions in the country with the infrastructure and capability of organizing large-scale enterprises. Specifically, MADC owed its origins and prosperity to the logging of the Nakai plateau on the border with Vietnam in a proposed reservoir area. Also engaged in importing cars, manufacturing, and shipping, MADC's operation was then not accountable to civilian control and it published no statistics. Tainted by corruption, and having grown to become a major economic force in the country, in 2003 MADC was brought under the control of the Ministry of Finance (Stuart-Fox 2008, 183). Other initiatives have seen the military enter into joint enterprises with foreign companies. One is the Lao-China Textile and Dyeing Joint Venture Company, a tie-up between the LPA and a Chinese state enterprise designed to cash in on Laos's then newly launched textile export industry.

Such analysis precludes discussion of army involvement in the informal economy which in Laos runs from gemstones to gambling to narcotics. Allegations of narcotics smuggling across the Lao-Thai border by sections of the Lao army cannot entirely be discounted. Illicit timber exports from Cambodia's Stung Treng province entering storage depots and even sawmills in southern Laos could not have transpired without the complicity of the LPA and the Hun Sen army. In any case, as Bourdet (2000, 149) commented almost twenty years ago—and with no less force as it applies today—the limited transparency of the army in political life in general has economic implications and actually encourages forms of rent-seeking activities "and the development of a form of bargaining economy."

Conclusion

Our argument would tend to favor a view of radical discontinuity between the style and practice of the LPA and the colonial armies in Laos and the army they supported, namely the RLG forces. There is no question that the institutionalized communist guerrilla/guardian model such as characterizes the LPA represents a new form of state-society relations in this former Buddhist monarchy. Moreover, contrary to civilianizing trends in remaining socialist states such as China and Vietnam, the military in Laos not only remains an integral part of the state apparatus but, after more than forty years in power, has expanded its dominance in the political and even the economic field.

This is not to say that at a cultural level there are not continuities with the past. Just as conscription remains a reality for many Lao and minorities, so under the colonial regime as well as during the thirty-year civil war forms of corvée labor were also obligatory. Ethnicity still remains a social marker in Laos and it would not be surprising if the less educated, including minorities, did not carry the burden of military service, just as the few elite-level surviving Pathet Lao veterans tend to be drawn from the majority Lao. Moreover, just as the old RLG elite, including the army, notoriously profiteered from misused aid and even narcotics trafficking, so the new LPA business enterprises smack of rent-seeking in ways which hark back to the past.

Up until the mid-1980s it was possible to discern an ongoing debate among the Party-military elite between the adherents of the "true" people's army line and adherents of the modern army line, in turn guided by Party debates over the "correct" application of "proletarian internationalism." Laos's siding with Vietnam over the Cambodia question and its former frontline status versus the ASEAN camp added substance to this debate. However, the needs of a more professional and technically proficient armed forces under Soviet guidance began to vitiate the old guerrilla ethos. Consolidation of the military also brought forth inevitable problems of bureaucracy and hierarchy which the regime readily admitted. Whatever the role of a revolutionary army in the new market economy such as embraced by the regime from the 1980s, it was bound to be controversial. In particular, as this chapter has exposed, the army-business nexus that developed under the aegis of the MADC defies definition within the regime's own socialist rhetoric. Just as Laos (as with China and Vietnam) jettisons Marxism, so in Laos the armed forces as the most powerful institution in the country still positions itself as guardian of the Party-state and even of its corporate interests, a familiar pattern as observed from Indonesia under the generals to Myanmar. As this chapter has demonstrated, the army in Laos, that which spearheaded the thirty-year war of "national liberation" has reverted to a very "traditional" form, albeit in a vastly different conjuncture and setting.

References

BBC News, February 15, 2001.

Bourdet, Yves. 2000. "Laos." In *Southeast Asian Affairs 2000*, 147–52. Singapore: Institute of Southeast Asian Studies.

Fletcher, Don, and Geoffrey C. Gunn. 1981. *Revolution in Laos: The "Fourth Generation" of People's War?*. Southeast Asian Monograph Series No. 8. Townsville: James Cook University of North Queensland.

Gunn, Geoffrey C. 1985. "Laos." In *Military-Civilian Relations in South-East Asia*, eds. Zakaria Haji Ahmad and Harold Crouch, 196–233. Singapore: Oxford University Press.

———. 1988. *Political Struggles in Laos (1930–1954)*. Bangkok: Editions Duang Kamol.

———. 1998. *Theravadins, Colonialists and Commissars in Laos*. Bangkok: White Lotus.

———. 2007. "Laos in 2006: Changing of the Guard." *Asian Survey* 47(1): 183–88.

———. 2008. "Laos in 2007: Regional Integration and International Fallout." *Asian Survey* 48(1): 62–68.

———. 2017. "Laos in 2016: Difficult History. Uncertain Future." *Asian Survey* 57(1): 206–10.

Jane's Defence Weekly, May 19, 1995.

Kaysone Phomvihane. 1980. *La Révolution Lao*. Moscow: Progrès.

"Lao People's Army: 40 Years." 1989. *Laos: A Pictorial Magazine*, 1(2): 6.

Nette, Andrew. 1998a. "Development-Laos: Military Inc Flexes Economic Muscle." Inter Press Service, Vientiane, December 15. http://www.ipsnews.net/1998/12/development-laos-military-inc-flexes-economic-muscle/.

———. 1998b. "Double Jeopardy for Laos: Logging Interests and Hydro Developers Join Forces to Dam Mekong Tributary." *World Rivers Review*, 13(1), February. file:///C:/Users/Owner/Downloads/wrr.v13.n1.pdf

Savada, Andrea Matles, ed. 1994. *Laos: A Country Study*. Area Handbook Series. Washington, DC: Library of Congress.

Souksakhone Vaenkeo. 2016. "Laos' 10th Congress elects new Party leadership." *Vientiane Times*, January 22. http://www.asianews.network/content/laos%E2%80%99-10th-congress-elects-new-party-leadership-8075.

Stuart-Fox, Martin. 1997. *A History of Laos*. Cambridge, UK: Cambridge University Press.

———. 2008. *Historical Dictionary of Laos*. Lanham, MA: Scarecrow Press.

Summary of World Broadcasts. January 21, 1978 for the January 19 editorial in *Siang Pasason*, "The Army and Economic Construction" citing "The Order of the Day" issued by Comrade Khamtai Siphandon to mark the 28th anniversary of the LPLA on January 20, 1980, p. 84, cited in Gunn, 1998, 138.

———. October 16, 1980 for the Vientiane home service broadcast of October 11, 1980 for the editorial in *Siang Pasason*, "Urgently Build, Consolidate and Strengthen Regional Armed Forces in All Respects." cited in Gunn, 1998, 140.

———. November 11, 1980 for the Vientiane home service of November 8, 1980, cited in Gunn, 1998, 137.

———. December 20, 1980 for the Vientiane home service of December 8, 1980.

———. May 10, 1982 for the Vientiane home service of May 6, 1982.

Thayer, Carlyle A. 1982. "Laos and Vietnam: The Anatomy of a 'Special Relationship.'" In *Contemporary Laos*, ed. M. Stuart-Fox, 245–73. St. Lucia: University of Queensland Press.

UNPO (Unrepresented Nations & Peoples Organization). "Alarming Crackdown on a Group of Hmong Individuals in Laos." November 23, 2018 https://unpo.org/article/21243.

Xinhua–"China, Laos to build community of shared future with strategic importance." November 14, 2017 http://www.xinhuanet.com/english/2017-11/14/c_136749706.htm.

Zasloff, Joseph J. 1972. "Leadership and Organization of the Pathet Lao." In *Indochina in Conflict: A Political Assessment*, eds. Joseph J. Zasloff and Allen E. Goodman, 81–97. Lexington, MA: D. C. Heath.

CHAPTER 11

Revolutionary Specialists, Strongmen, and the State in a Philippine Province, 1990s–2001[1]

Rosanne Rutten

The flow of people in and out of a guerrilla movement is an ongoing process, and in the roughly fifty years that the nationwide Communist Party of the Philippines-New People's Army (CPP-NPA)[2] has been active in the Philippines, tens of thousands of women and men from towns, villages, and plantations have successively joined for longer or shorter periods, and then left again, continuing their lives "above ground" in different ways, their activist past leaving its mark on power relations, politics, and personal lives. Since the revolutionary movement began its nationwide decline in the late 1980s, resurging somewhat from the late 1990s onward, this outflow has not been matched by the inflow of new activists. As former cadres rejoined civilian life, they repositioned themselves vis-à-vis the movement, the state, and political elites in ways that affected the movement and poor people's politics in the country.

Hence the questions: where did the former cadres go, what activities did they deploy, and how did their post-movement activities affect local socio-political life? In particular, did they contribute to a new type of contentious politics by applying their convictions, skills, and networks to popular mobilization aimed at reform rather than revolution?[3] Or did they follow other trajectories available to them, for instance, by placing their political talents in the service of the state or traditional power elites; starting a career in banditry and racketeering by capitalizing on skills in "confiscation" and exacting "revolutionary taxes"; or, instead, quietly returning to civilian life, disengaging from the arena of political contention?

I explore these questions for ex-cadres in the province of Negros Occidental, one of the "hotbeds" of the nationwide insurgency in the 1980s-early 1990s.[4] Located on the island of Negros in the central Philippine archipelago, this province epitomizes key processes in Philippine contentious politics: strongman rule, revolutionary insurgency, counter-insurgency militarization, and NGO activism. These four processes were (and still are) interrelated, not only through the contentious interactions between the four parties involved but also, as I will show, by the movement of ex-cadres between these different parties. By passing on their knowledge, networks, and skills to allied or rival groups, these former cadres affected the provincial power balance considerably. At the core of the provincial power configuration is a system of strongman rule: local power holders use electoral positions (mayor, governor, congressman) to expand and defend their control over local resources and populations, aided by a state structure that allows elected officials access to state resources and privilege for private ends. Combining patronage and coercion (McCoy 1991, 142), they may achieve the position of local "bosses"—"predatory power brokers who achieve monopolistic control over both coercive and economic resources within given territorial jurisdictions or bailiwicks" (Sidel 1999, 19; see also Coronel and Lacaba 1995; McCoy 1993).

Marked by a long history of sugarcane plantation agriculture and class polarization, Negros Occidental counted several thousand plantations (*haciendas*) mostly owned by local planter families and cultivated by some 200 thousand resident plantation workers, until a major agrarian reform law of 1988 led to a piecemeal and partial redistribution of plantations among worker families in the decades that followed. Political power has long been dominated by a planter-cum-business elite that controls most of the electoral positions in the province. The CPP-NPA and its recent offshoots contested this power through mass support and membership among plantation workers and their teenage children, upland peasants, and urban students. Moreover, a broad social movement and NGO sector developed, particularly in the 1980s–90s (post-martial law period), through the efforts of Catholic clergy, students, and labor and peasant activists intent on organizing and empowering the local poor and laboring populations. Partly linked to the underground CPP-NPA and partly disengaged from it again, this sector became a new force in the provincial power dynamics.[5]

This exploration of activist careers is based on interviews with former cadres, provincial newspaper reports, and my own long-term research in an upland village (San Juan) and a lowland sugarcane plantation (Hacienda Milagros) where the CPP-NPA had a marked presence in the 1980s until the early 1990s (the names of the two communities are pseudonyms).[6] It focuses particularly on post-movement careers in the 1990s until 2001, the period of my intermittent fieldwork on the topic. In this period a major exodus from the CPP-NPA took place following political democratization since the end of the authoritarian Marcos regime in 1986, an amnesty program for CPP-NPA cadres by the early 1990s, and major splits within the left-wing movement in the 1990s. These nationwide developments, in turn, also influenced the course of cadres' post-movement careers. More recent trends are briefly discussed in the epilogue, and some updates are included in footnotes where relevant and available.

Here, I use the term "cadres" to refer to the women and men who were full-time activists in the CPP-NPA and its offshoots, and community-based, part-time activists who formed the local party branches. Obviously, this chapter covers but a small number of the former cadres in the province, but their life careers suggest some general patterns.

Tracing the Careers of Former Cadres

One can trace the careers of former cadres by considering the cohorts, occupational groups, home communities, or peer groups they belonged to when they entered the movement, and by subsequently following the life paths of their individual activist members.[7] In the next sections, I will concentrate particularly on former cadres from two communities where I did research over recent decades, which allows me to consider the changing personal and structural contexts of their careers, identify variation, and explore local effects. I will also deal with several clusters of people who were cadres together in the movement, of which I personally knew one or more members. In this section, I briefly explore two salient cohorts and occupational groups that supplied revolutionary cadres who would follow divergent (post-movement) careers, namely the cohort of early student activists and the occupational group of Catholic clergy.

Student activists in the province formed the first nucleus of CPP-NPA members in the provincial capital Bacolod City in the early 1970s. By 2000, only a few of these activists were still underground; the others had returned to civilian life. Their post-movement careers diverged widely. How and when they left the movement partly explains this divergence. At least three different career paths can be traced: (1) Among those who left the movement early, some resurfaced in government employment several years after the declaration of martial law in 1972—the populist, reformist period of the Marcos regime when several state agencies were charged, at least nominally, with the uplift and empowerment of the poor. The National Housing Authority in the province, for example, attracted several former activists. Other early leavers in the 1970s became "traditional" politicians and entrepreneurs, who used their sporadic contacts with movement networks to broker mutually beneficial deals. (2) Those who remained in the movement up to the 1980s rose to high positions in the provincial/regional leadership of the CPP-NPA. In the late 1980s, under the newly democratic regime of President Corazon Aquino, a group of these activists left the movement after an internal conflict over policy and strategy. Theirs was a joint exit, with high media and counter-insurgency value. Offered the political space for "above ground" organization, they put up a new labor union (the Democratic and Independent Workers Association, DIWA) and established a network of "rebel returnees," though these initiatives later faded. (3) A third batch of these early student activists left the underground in the early 1990s, individually, through capture or surrender, facilitated by the amnesty policy of the government. They followed very different paths after their surrender, ranging from community activism (see the case of Victoria Justiniani below), to left-wing NGO work, to a career in business.

In contrast to cohorts, a focus on occupational groups suggests the influence of pre-activist occupations on activist careers. In this predominantly Roman Catholic society, several Catholic priests were early entrants into the revolutionary movement, rising to top leadership positions within the province and island.[8] Liberation Theology, the social action work of the Bacolod Diocese, and church support for a peasant organization (the Federation of Free Farmers) and a union of plantation workers (the National Federation of Sugar Workers) facilitated social and emotional links of Catholic clergy with the movement. Those who entered the movement experienced profound changes in their personal lives. They cut their ties with the church hierarchy, turned against the status quo, adopted a new doctrine and party hierarchy, redefined their mission in terms of a struggle for liberation, and accepted the use of defensive violence. Many married within the movement.[9]

By 2001, a majority of the former priests who became movement leaders in Negros were still active in the movement, either above ground or underground. They were holding out for an exceptionally long time compared to those with a student activist background. Given their earlier socialization and experiences as clergymen, they may have possessed a particular sense of duty and mission in life, the ability to function in a hierarchical institution, and familiarity with doctrinal debates, each of which may have helped to keep them in. In 2001, their positions included international spokesman and senior advisor of the National Democratic Front, a CPP-dominated political front organization (Luis Jalandoni, in self-exile in The Netherlands); head of the CPP-NPA on Negros island (Frank Fernandez); and leaders of two competing political groupings in the province formed by cadres who had turned away from the CPP-NPA but later split among themselves.[10] Another prominent "rebel priest," who was chairman of the Regional United Front Committee of the CPP-NPA in Negros, returned to the priesthood after his capture in 1994 and became a parish priest in the province. He separated from his "political wife," a former Augustinian nun. Both embarked on NGO careers. She became the general manager of a large marketing cooperative of small farmers with outlets abroad (Alter Trade, staffed by many former cadres), and he devoted part of his time as executive director of a cooperative supporting poor land-reform beneficiaries.

Former Cadres and (Anti-)elite Politics: Two Trajectories

The careers of former CPP-NPA cadres in Negros Occidental suggest similarities with a previous rural communist-inspired guerrilla movement in the Philippines, the Huk movement in Central Luzon, which saw many of its cadres leave during the 1950s and early 1960s.[11] Former Huks resurfaced as non-violent peasant activists in their home villages, but also as social bandits, plain thieves and racketeers, plantation overseers, and members of paramilitary units led by the Philippine Constabulary.[12] Repositioning themselves within the regional power arena, they followed broadly two conflicting trajectories: contesting elite power through peasant organizations and government cooperatives, or supporting elite power by linking up with established (landed) power holders and segments of the military. The first trajectory was enabled by a state counter-insurgency policy that turned reformist (Kerkvliet 1996, 20; Wurfel 1988, 230–31); the second trajectory by the continuing domination of the region "by wealthy landowners and millionaires [even] after half a century of social upheaval" (Lachica 1971: 212). For Huk veterans who needed protection and a source of income, the established economic and political elite was still an obvious party to which to turn.

Such divergent trajectories were also apparent in the career paths of former CPP-NPA cadres in Negros Occidental in the 1990s. On the one hand, a considerable number linked up to local strongmen and government military, and provided their services in return for economic and physical security. Many of them had operated as "men of violence" in the revolutionary movement, in particular members of assassination squads (*sparrows*) and members of the village-based revolutionary police force (*yunit milisya*). The post-movement activities of these men supported the system of elite rule as they spent their days as bodyguards of politicians, security guards of elite property, and overseers of their plantations, commercial fish ponds, and fighting-cock breeding farms, or as members of paramilitary groups and intelligence sources for the government army. The few I know who turned to robbery and protection rackets after their time in the movement did so under police or strongman protection. Some units of the RPA-ABB in Negros Occidental, the guerrilla section that split off from the NPA in 1992–93, took on a similar role. They became de facto security forces for business tycoon Eduardo "Danding" Cojuangco Jr, to protect his agribusiness projects in the province. Less represented in this broad category are former guerrilla soldiers; most of those I know returned to farming or wage labor and disengaged from the political arena.

On the other hand, a large number of former political cadres, organizers, and administrators of areas under revolutionary control became active in progressive social movements and NGOs in the province, including labor unions, peasant organizations, women's movements, village cooperatives, and a large province-wide agricultural marketing cooperative. These former political cadres engaged in the "legal," "above ground" sphere, using their skills, knowledge, and networks to contest the control of local strongmen. Moreover, they pushed for a new state-citizen relationship. Combatting political clientage, they sought to enlarge poor people's direct access to state resources. Confronting the power of elites to bend the law to serve their own interests, they pressed for the enforcement of laws that supported the interests of poor populations. At the level of village and plantation, in the two communities in which I have done research, several former heads of Communist party branches and other former members of the revolutionary village administrations became active in community organizations that promoted the interests of villagers and plantation workers independent of elite control.

In short, if we look at former cadres in terms of the specialized tasks they had in the movement, it appears that a considerable number of those who had managed violence tended to be co-opted by the elite and the state. In contrast, those skilled in political organization and mobilization tended to use these abilities to contest elite control and to claim, for poor populations, non-particularistic access to state resources.[13] (This oversimplified conclusion will be qualified in sections further below). The following two cases illustrate these different career paths.

Linking up with a Police Chief and a Mayor

"X" was a plantation administrator of rural middle-class background when he joined the CPP-NPA. He became the bodyguard of Nemesio Demafelis, the head of the Negros Regional Party Committee in the 1980s, and head of the mobile armed forces of a district. When he clashed with the regional leadership in 1987 over issues of policy and strategy, he resigned from the movement along with several others. When the CPP-NPA killed several of their group, he opted to join the military and fight the movement by military means.

After his surrender to the military, he became commanding officer of a paramilitary unit of "rebel returnees" in his home area. He also joined the "Eagle Squad," a police team that operated directly under the chief of police of Bacolod City, which consisted of former comrades in the movement. He provided intelligence for the military and participated in military operations. By 2000, he was the bodyguard of the vice-mayor of Bacolod City. Eventually, he became executive secretary of the mayor of Bacolod City after his patron won the mayoral post in the elections of 2001. As one local journalist wrote to me, "One of his many functions is handling what used to be called the 'civil security unit,' that is actually a bunch of rebel returnees he took under his wing when he turned military asset and whom he utilized for a while in his rackets—e.g., providing security for plantations locked in agrarian disputes." Some say that he also worked as a plantation administrator for one of the main political families in the province, and started to lease land for cane farming, turning into a small-time *hacendero* himself.

Contesting the Power of a "Bossist" Mayor

Victoria ("Vicvic") Justiniani, former wife of regional communist party head Demafelis, started her revolutionary career as a student activist from Canlaon City in the mountainous border region of Oriental and Occidental Negros. She became party secretary of the Southwestern Front Committee in

Negros, a member of the Negros-wide executive committee of the CPP-NPA, and eventually headed, in Manila, the External Affairs Commission of the National Democratic Front and the women's organization MAKIBAKA. Captured in 1992 and released the same year, she returned to her hometown in Negros Oriental and started a credit association of widows in the municipality. By the year 2000,

> the innocent association of widows she had formed in the early 90's had been transformed into a political organization that attracted disenfranchised sectors of the town population of forty thousand. These sectors, now politicized and assembled under the banner of CPRM (Canlaon People's Rights Movement, of which Vicvic is president), have suffered physical assault, harassment, murder and militarization. This in response to CPRM's charges of graft, land grabbing, human rights violations, and environmental destruction. (Aguilar 2001)

Justiniani challenged the near monopolistic power of Mayor Jose Cardenas over her home town, including his use of coercion and violence against those who contested his political and economic hold over the place. She became a rallying point for those who were victimized. Townspeople perceived her as a veteran activist, as someone who would fight back. Killings by the mayor's men forced Justiniani into hiding in Manila. In her interview with Delia Aguilar (2001), she deplored the limited opportunities for legal redress by the state given the current distribution of power. Her organization successfully pressed for a congressional inquiry into human rights violations, proof of her organizational skills and vast networks, but with little effect as the mayor succeeded, she said, in influencing local investigators (Aguilar 2001).

Interestingly, Mayor Cardenas had an activist background as well. He was formerly chairman of the left-wing anti-Marcos coalition Bayan (Bagong Alyansang Makabayan, or New Nationalist Alliance) in Canlaon City at the time of the "People Power" uprising that helped to remove President Ferdinand Marcos from power in 1986. Apparently, he also had links with the revolutionary movement. Installed as mayor in 1986, he ruled over the town uninterrupted (as mayor, or vice-mayor, when his three mayoral terms were up) until his death in 2001 (*Philippine Daily Inquirer* [hereafter *PDI*], April 28, 2001). In the process, he developed into a local political "boss." One of the mayor's bodyguards was a former commanding officer of an NPA company in Northern Negros, Santiago Regla. He surrendered in Canlaon City in 1992 and was promptly hired by the city government, initially as a watchman of Canlaon market. "The former NPA commander . . . is now serving the government," the newsletter of the government army in Negros declared (*AFP-Negros News and Features*, July 8, 1992). An NPA-unit ambushed and killed Cardenas in April 2001, together with his sister who was a municipal councilor and four others, as he campaigned for re-election (*PDI*, April 28, 2001). An NPA spokesperson said about the Cardenas siblings, "They were warlords who held absolute control over the economy and politics of Canlaon," and who had propagated a reign of terror in Canlaon "through the use of armed goons, control of the Army and the police, and by arming barangay [village] officials, tanods [auxiliary police] and informers" (*PDI*, May 11, 2001).

This case illustrates how former comrades repositioned themselves in a political configuration that was still marked by strongman politics. The former chairman of the left-wing Bayan municipal chapter moved into the role of political "boss," the ex-NPA commander became the boss's bodyguard, the ex-CPP-NPA organizer and administrator took on the role of municipal activist contesting the power of this local strongman, and those still in the NPA followed their self-imposed policy of countering strongman violence with revolutionary violence.

Besides the two broad categories of ex-cadres outlined above, a third category consisted of leaders of government-funded cooperatives of "rebel returnees," that is, former cadres who took advantage of the government's amnesty program which provided livelihood projects for rebels who had "returned to the folds of the law." The position of these co-op leaders was still indeterminate by 2001. In San Juan village, they kept strictly to their economic role, as the presence of a military detachment in the village severely constrained their maneuvering space. In communities near Hda. Milagros where the government military had no permanent presence, on the other hand, leaders and active members also used their cooperative as a social network for lobbying on their own behalf and for supporting progressive electoral candidates. This suggests that former cadres involved in such "rebel returnees" cooperatives were not necessarily co-opted by the state through government-funded projects, but might use their government-sponsored organization for broader pressure politics provided they had the necessary maneuvering space.

Context

At least three processes formed the context of these divergent trajectories in the 1990s: (1) the continuing centrality of strongman rule and bossism[14] in Philippine provincial politics; (2) the continuing importance of a state counter-insurgency program that sought to attract former "rebels" into its ranks; and (3) a political opportunity structure that facilitated an unprecedented nationwide growth of progressive NGOs and poor people's organizations since the People Power uprising in 1986; at the level of province and town, these organizations contested strongman rule and pressed for the enforcement of laws that would protect the interests of the poor.

The first two processes resulted in a growing demand for specialists in violence on the part of politicians and the state. Political brokers and electoral politicians, particularly those with bossist aspirations, needed coercive means for various reasons: to protect themselves and their following; to defend their turf from encroachment by others, including state agents, elite competitors, or revolutionaries; and to expand their control in the face of resistance. Those who were involved in rackets of various kinds also needed specialists in violence to help run them. For political entrepreneurs, former NPAs were attractive candidates for such positions because of their skills and reputed bravery, as "men without fear." Moreover, by incorporating former NPAs into their network, they possibly sought to ward off extortion claims by the NPA. The government army, for its part, was following the age-old strategy of "using a thief to catch a thief."[15] The success of its counter-insurgency policy depended to a large extent on its vast network of surrendered NPAs who turned informer and military resource.

The expansion of progressive NGOs, social movements, and poor people's organizations since the return to formal democracy in 1986, on the other hand, marked a political opportunity structure that was relatively favorable to contentious politics: progressive "legal" organizations had room to maneuver and their demands had some chance of being met by those in power. This was partly the outcome of the "reformist" solution to the conflict between the state and the CPP-NPA (and its allies) (Hedman 2000, 27–29). Former revolutionary cadres took advantage of these opportunities and helped to staff and shape such organizations.[16]

Using and widening this political space, these progressive organizations were posing a challenge to elite-led clientelist and bossist politics. As Silliman and Noble (1998, 306) stated in the 1990s, "NGOs have increased the capacity of middle-and lower-class Filipinos to act autonomously; consequently, the state is less completely captive of elite interests than previously. Furthermore, . . . [as] advocates of farmers, the urban poor, indigenous peoples, and the environment, they bring pressure to bear on both decision makers and the agencies that implement government policy."[17] At the municipal and provincial level, NGOs and sectoral organizations pushed for the enforcement of laws and for curbing the bossist inclinations of strongman politicians who sought to monopolize local resources and state funds for private gain. The electoral system was crucial here, as NGOs and sectoral organizations could raise popular issues in local election campaigns and mobilize local voters to support candidates who would defend popular interests.[18]

Splits and Realliances: Different Trajectories within the Movement until 2001

Nationwide the revolutionary movement had split, by 2001, into three rival factions at least, partly in response to the widened democratic space since the ouster of President Marcos in 1986. In Negros Occidental, these splits produced a significant repositioning of cadres within the provincial power arena. Since two of these factions eventually abandoned the revolutionary project, their activists may be considered "ex" revolutionary cadres.

In the first split of 1992–93, most of the movement's armed forces in the province disengaged from the CPP-NPA, as did most of the personnel and resources of the NGOs and unions that used to support the CPP-NPA.[19] They regrouped into a nationwide rival faction, the "rejectionists," who rejected the strategic line and leadership of the CPP-NPA. Its guerrilla soldiers formed the RPA-ABB (Revolutionary Proletarian Army-Alex Boncayao Brigade). The split thus resulted in two separate and competing composite networks of guerrilla soldiers, political cadres and supportive personnel, community mass organizations, and legal supportive organizations. In Negros Occidental, the new rival faction far outnumbered the old CPP-NPA.

The second split occurred within the ranks of the "rejectionist" faction in 1998. It pulled apart the functional link between the underground military cadres and above ground political cadres. The conflict initially concerned leadership and participation in the national elections of 1998 (in the party-list section) but ended in a rift between the faction's army (the RPA-ABB) on the one hand, and its political and NGO network on the other. Or, in local perception, "arms" on one side and "funds" on the other, since the NGOs and mass base produced the main funds for the armed wing. Disconnected from a revolutionary army, these NGOs and community organizations no longer encouraged popular support for a revolutionary movement. They still considered coercion necessary, at times, to put pressure on planters and other powerful parties, but they dropped the ultimate goal of an armed takeover of state power.[20]

In the political practice of Negros Occidental, these realignments meant the following: RPA-ABB units lent their coercive powers to organizations and movements sympathetic to their side but frustrated activities of their left-wing rivals. Fielded in the central and southern part of the province, they apparently controlled some 400 high-powered firearms Negros-wide by 1998.[21] In December 2000, a nationwide peace agreement was made between the Estrada government and the RPA-ABB and its political arm, the Rebolusyonaryong Partido ng Manggagawa-Pilipinas (RPM-P). Leaders of the RPA-ABB subsequently reinterpreted their mission by offering their services to provincial strongman Cojuangco.

The rival NPA, with some four hundred cadres on Negros island in 2001, in particular in the north, began to slowly rebuild a mass base and renew its linkages with legal mass movements (*PDI*, January 7, 2001). Its leaders started a nationwide campaign of assassinating provincial and municipal strongmen and "warlords" found guilty of "crimes against the people," with Mayor Cardenas one of the victims in Negros in 2001, as noted above.[22]

Finally, a large array of NGOs, unions, and other "legal" movements within these three factions continued to use the available democratic space to promote the interest of laborers, peasants, fishermen, women, and squatters through legal means. But part of their energies was sapped by competing with their former comrades over turf, following, and funds. After the split in 1992–93 had torn many NGOs and unions apart in two rival factions, the 1998 split again caused bitter conflicts. These conflicts centered on the division of joint NGO property and were sometimes fought out in the courts or through vigilante violence.[23]

The RPA-ABB: Providing Protection Services for Strongmen and the State

The policy change of the RPA-ABB in Negros Occidental at the time of the peace agreement in 2000 deserves closer scrutiny. It illustrates how the rule of local strongmen was still the pivot around which former cadres positioned themselves. Though they were nominally still part of a broad, fragmented "revolutionary movement," these members of the RPA-ABB effectively distanced themselves from the revolutionary project.

How and why did the RPA-ABB develop into a security force for business tycoon Eduardo Cojuangco Jr and, to a lesser extent, for the state? Political expediency, plain survival as armed units, and strategic access to network brokers may provide part of the answer. With the prospect of a guerrilla victory ever more distant, these guerrilla forces created a survival niche by making deals with former enemies: the government, which was keen on making peace arrangements, and Cojuangco, who was keen on forging a network of allies in order to capture political and economic power in Negros Occidental. As one of the richest and most influential Philippine capitalist entrepreneurs and erstwhile "crony" of former Presidents Marcos and Estrada at the time, Cojuangco sought to capture the position of provincial boss in Negros Occidental, the home province of his wife. By forging an alliance with the RPA-ABB, he would gain access to armed force while effectively neutralizing a possible guerrilla competitor and armed irritant in the territory he sought to control. Both Cojuangco and the RPA-ABB used the state to facilitate this link. A local mayor and her husband with activist backgrounds helped to broker the alliance.

The Peace Agreement with the RPA-ABB: Permission to Keep Weapons

A curious rendezvous took place in the cool and remote mountain town of Don Salvador Benedicto in central Negros Occidental on a Sunday in December 2000. Then President Joseph Estrada, his friend Eduardo Cojuangco Jr, and Agriculture Secretary Edgardo Angara joined company with Nilo de la Cruz, representative of the Rebolusyonaryong Partido ng Manggagawa-Pilipinas (RPM-P) and its military arm, the RPA-ABB. Also present were the mayor of Don Salvador Benedicto, Cynthia de la Cruz, and her husband Nehemias, three-time mayor of the same town. Both were movement activists in their youth. Nehemias "Nene" de la Cruz, a former student activist, CPP-NPA organizer, and political detainee, had become an important local ally of Cojuangco.

The occasion was the signing of a nationwide peace agreement between the government and the RPM-P/RPA-ABB, held in Negros Occidental because most of the RPA-ABB forces were located there at the time. Cojuangco and Angara, who headed the two political parties that formed the ruling coalition under Estrada, had helped to forge the peace agreement.[24] The agreement included provisions for amnesty, the release of political prisoners, livelihood funds, and a commitment to provide 500 million Philippine Peso for development projects in areas identified by the RPM-P as its "strongholds," mainly in Negros Occidental.[25]

The agreement also contained an exceptional provision: the granting of permits to carry firearms "for security reasons" to one hundred RPM-P and RPA-ABB members. These "security" matters included permission to do police work, in particular, to "help maintain law and order and arrest wanted persons in areas where its guerrillas are located" and turn them over to the official police (*PDI*, February 1, 2001). The peace agreement, including this specific provision, was honored by the new administration of President Gloria Macapagal-Arroyo in July 2001, pending the decision of a newly formed peace panel charged with reviewing the agreement. This was shortly after the May 2001 elections when Cojuangco's allies won most of the top elective posts in the province (*PDI*, July 27, 2001).[26]

It was a "grand reunion of warlords and gangsters," said the head of the rival CPP-NPA in Negros about the agreement (*PDI*, December 6, 2001). Gangsters, or pacified rebels turned assistants of the state? State agents were not so sure. Some police chiefs thanked the RPA-ABB for handing over wanted criminals and lauded its "continued support in the government's anti-crime drive" (*PDI*, February 1, 2001). But others protested against its privileges. When an RPA-ABB team took the guns of security guards at a plantation in Silay, the provincial police director commented, "This thing should be stopped once and for all because disarming civilians is not a police function anymore and is outside the ambit of law" (*SunStar Bacolod*, March 20, 2001). The issue was settled when RPA-ABB commander Carapali Lualhati (*nom de guerre* of Stephen Paduano) negotiated the return of the weapons. In the campaign period for the May 2001 elections, the Commission on Elections (Comelec) and a regional army chief were alarmed that the RPA-ABB was openly breaching the Comelec gun ban. At the celebrations that marked the RPA-ABBs fourth founding anniversary in the town of Don Salvador Benedicto, the RPA-ABB displayed some thirty high-powered firearms in full view of its political ally, Mayor de la Cruz, and several local vice-mayors (*PDI*, April 3, 2001).

The state's granting of firearm permits and certain police functions to the RPA-ABB, and its apparent acceptance of RPA-ABB territorial control, also aroused protests among organized groups of other factions within the broad left-wing movement, and among Catholic clergy and other sectors. By October 2001, large rallies for and against the peace agreement filled the streets of Bacolod City.

The Cojuangco Factor

After Eduardo Cojuangco Jr returned to the Philippines from exile in 1991[27] and settled in Negros Occidental, he successfully used his vast funds, networks, and business resources to get his local allies elected into office. Already "the province's leading crony capitalist" in the 1980s, with some seven thousand hectares of agricultural land and investments in agribusiness, this "outsider" from Tarlac province was building up a political base in this province as well (McCoy 1991, 121). In the 1990s, the established political clans seemed to be "fast losing their stranglehold on the province" (Parreño 2001).

Moreover, Cojuangco continued to expand his business interests in the province, in particular after he regained control of the beer and food conglomerate San Miguel Corporation in 1998 under the Estrada presidency. San Miguel embarked on a program of vertical integration, engaging in the procurement and processing of raw materials used by its manufacturing plants. In Negros Occidental, Cojuangco started the large-scale production and marketing of corn and cassava to supply other branches of San Miguel's conglomerate.[28] Some seven thousand hectares were to be planted with corn and cassava by contract farmers in two large upland areas, one in the area of Don Salvador Benedicto town, the other in the southern uplands. Cojuangco asked "one of his right-hand men," the former mayor of Don Salvador Benedicto, Nehemias de la Cruz, to organize cooperatives of contract growers (Parreño 2001). By early 2001, several hundred hectares were already under production.

After the peace agreement, units of the RPA-ABB began to protect Cojuangco's two corn-cassava projects in the uplands, located in areas where the revolutionary army used to operate (*Manila Times*, March 3, 2001). Moreover, members of the RPA-ABB apparently acted as armed "goons" in the interest of Cojuangco's candidates in the 2001 elections (*PDI*, February 27, 2001). In contrast, the CPP-NPA defined Cojuangco as a major enemy of the masses, top landgrabber and exploiter, and its allied legal social movements targeted him in public campaigns.[29]

A Replay of "Huk-Coddling"?

In the aftermath of the Huk rebellion in Central Luzon in the 1950s and 1960s, the term "Huk coddling" came to refer to local politicians accommodating to the tenacious presence of armed Huks in their region. As Eduardo Lachica (1971, 209) noted at the time, "the Huks *are* there, whether a politician likes them or not. A politician antagonizes the Huks at the risk of losing his life." Such accommodation occurred when most of the remaining Huks were "no longer interested in a violent seizure of power." Instead, they agreed to a post-rebellion accommodation that was mutually beneficial: they wished to retain an armed presence, some room to maneuver and protection against military repression, whereas politicians sought to neutralize competitors and enlist Huk leaders as vote suppliers. At village and municipal levels, some Huks began to cooperate with the government, operating as "*de facto* police forces in their areas," and sitting in some municipal staffs (ibid., 207–9, 211, 217).

Cojuangco was familiar with such strategies. He had been governor of Tarlac province in the 1960s, then a center of Huk activity, but he declared war on the Huks and had to flee the province to escape possible liquidation. In contrast, his predecessor in Tarlac, Benigno Aquino, apparently made a deal with the Huks out of political expediency: "Aquino had to live with the Huks for they were an ineradicable presence in his constituency" (Lachia 1971, 215). Perhaps Cojuangco chose to follow the model of "Huk-coddling" when he sought, again, to build and maintain a provincial power base in a rebel-influenced area—this time in Negros Occidental.

As the RPA-ABB reached an accommodation with this major strongman and the state in 2000, leaders of the rival CPP-NPA condemned their former comrades for totally renouncing the revolutionary project. They have "long sold out to the state," said Luis Jalandoni (then chairman of the CPP-NPA-NDF panel in its national peace negotiations with the government) as he noted the permission to carry firearms and do police work. He also noted that the government's negotiations with RPA-ABB leaders were "like the government talking to its own shadow" (*Manila Times*, April 11, 2001). "The RPA-ABB is a criminal gang controlled by Estrada through Gen. Lacson[30] and acts as the private army of Eduardo Cojuangco," said Jose Maria Sison, founding chairman of the CPP and chief political consultant of the NDF (NDF Press Statement, February 10, 2001). Units of the RPA-ABB were among several "crime syndicates" in the province that were used as "extensions and tools of the Armed Forces and National Police against the revolutionary movement," said Frank Fernandez, head of the CPP-NPA in Negros at the time (*Manila Times*, March 3, 2001).

Careers of Former Cadres: Opportunities and Constraints

In contrast to the cadres discussed above who remained somehow embedded in underground networks, those who emerged from the underground needed to adjust to civilian life on at least two fronts: finding employment and reconsidering their position vis-à-vis power holders.

The manner in which they surfaced from the underground narrowed their options. When cadres simply decided to "lie low," or to "rest," as they called it, the military remained potential enemies and they had to keep a low profile. Cadres favored this option until roughly 1989, when surrender still risked severe police retaliation. After this period, the state began to attract cadres through amnesty and "clearance" on easy terms, persuading those who had long wanted to return to civilian life.[31] This increased the number of cadres who passed through military headquarters on their way out of the movement. As the military expanded its network of informers, the number of cadres who were captured likewise increased.

After capture or surrender, were they forced to work for the military? The former cadres with whom I talked denied this. According to them, procedures in the 1990s involved a "tactical investigation" by the military without torture, followed by a request to "help the government" as an informer or as an infiltrator in the movement, which would be rewarded financially. A person who refused (usually by arguing that he wanted to live a quiet life now, caring for his family) would be allowed to return home after which he would be monitored for a couple of months. Some, however, felt that these regular military house visits were meant to pressure them to cooperate. Since middle- and higher-ranking cadres were of particular value to the military, these former cadres were offered salaried positions as intelligence and counter-insurgency assets. Apparently, those who accepted such positions were driven, in part, by the need for a dependable source of income, self-preservation in case they had run afoul of the NPA, and/or fascination with arms.

Another constraint for ex-cadres concerned their need for a source of income. As cadres they had survived on food and shelter provided by the "masses" and a meager allowance from the movement, supplemented by small allowances for their children if revolutionary "tax" income permitted. Now they were on their own. Those from elite and middle-class backgrounds, who had also held higher positions in the movement, could fall back on family resources and their network of friends and former comrades. For example, Nemesio Demafelis, the son of middle-class parents and head of the Negros Island Regional Party Committee in the 1980s, became a building contractor, aided by his extensive personal network. Silvino Gallardo, son of the main shareholder in a hospital in Bacolod City and later the commanding officer of the NPA Negros-wide, went into the sugar trade after his surrender, and became a consultant of the marketing cooperative Alter Trade (run by ex-cadres) as well as an active participant in a rural development NGO together with other former cadres. Both organizations partly depended on foreign NGO funding, which former cadres with a middle and upper-class background (college education, strategic networks) were able to obtain.

For the poor, the options were limited, however. Salaried work for the army-supervised paramilitary "Cafgu" (Civilian Armed Forces Geographical Unit) had some attraction, therefore, for those who lacked better alternatives and who, for whatever reason, felt they needed military protection, as will be further discussed below. For ex-cadres with some access to land, farming was a good enough option. In San Juan, most former cadres returned to farming. They were children of farmers at the time they had joined the movement as teenagers, or were children of landless workers who later benefited from a land reform program implemented in the village by the state and, informally, by the CPP-NPA. But in Hda. Milagros, former cadres were not attracted to return to wage labor in the cane fields. Although their underground life had been physically hard because of long treks, lack of food, and sleeping in the open, the physical labor required in their daily activities did not match the backbreaking labor of cane cutting or weeding. Besides, they had apparently lost their right to steady paid labor in the plantation, a right accorded to permanent workers, because of their long absence. Therefore, many moved away to work as factory laborers in Manila or as small farmers on the land of a spouse. Or they tried to eke out a living as drivers of passenger tricycles or in other marginal off-farm occupations.

Being a "surrenderee" with a military record limited the opportunities to engage in contentious politics. In small-scale communities, monitoring by paramilitary and informers could be effective and "surrenderees" took care not to arouse the suspicion of the military anew. In the village of San Juan, ex-cadres felt particularly constrained by the presence of a small military detachment in the village center, with its retinue of fellow villagers who had become informers. They were hesitant to participate in rallies in the city, at least the few who were still interested in participating, and those who were active in government village associations felt they could not forcefully protest against policies that favored the village elite. In Hda. Milagros and surrounding areas, several ex-cadres received a "favor" from those in power on condition they would refrain from "putting up a union." The "favors" concerned a temporary labor contract at a local bottling plant arranged by the mayor, and permission to live on plantation premises granted by a planter. The room to maneuver seemed wider for villagers who had been political cadres in their own communities. As part-time activists in the movement, they were considered less important by the military, and the military were not as well informed about their background.

Finally, a self-imposed constraint was at work in communities with a long history of insurgency. "People are tired of organizing, they're tired of trouble (*gamo*)," a former cadre said in San Juan. And several former cadres and local activists were embittered by previous conflicts with activist fellow-villagers—conflicts about the misuse of power, for example, or petty jealousies. They distanced themselves from new efforts at organization.

Former "Specialists in Violence": Post-Movement Work

Past specialties in the movement shaped to a significant extent the post-movement careers of former cadres, or so it appears from the individual cases studied. In their specific revolutionary work—the management of violence and coercion, political organization, or supportive tasks such as medical, financial, and communication work—these former cadres had developed skills, networks, and a particular identity which affected their future trajectory.[32]

Gender and personality had influenced the selection for these tasks, and so these aspects were interwoven with each specialty and its personal consequences. Men dominated the tasks that called for the use of violence, such as guerrilla fighters, members of liquidation squads, and village militia, although the guerrilla army did count a number of female soldiers. In choosing this line of work within the broad revolutionary project, many men were attracted by the possession and use of firearms. Both women and men were well represented in the ranks of political cadres, in particular as organizers and area administrators, such as secretaries of area party committees. Women numerically dominated the ranks of finance officers and medical personnel in line with Philippine lowland Christian culture in which women hold the purse strings and provide medical care.

Below, I first discuss the paths followed by several types of specialists in violence.

Former Members of Liquidation Squads ("Sparrows")

Many members of liquidation squads, called *sparrows* in local parlance,[33] did not live to experience a life outside the movement. Of the five men from Hda. Milagros who were known to be members of a partisan unit, three were killed by the Philippine Constabulary in 1987–88, as was one of the three men from San Juan. They were the most targeted by the military and the most vulnerable to exposure by informers since they operated from urban safe-houses.

Among those who survived, some became important assets for the police or military, and others withdrew from the power arena. Below are two cases of so-called *sparrows* who turned military assets.

From "Urban Partisan" to Military Intelligence Officer and Bodyguard of Movie Stars

> "A" was the bodyguard of a high-ranking national CPP-NPA leader at the time he was captured by the police in Manila in 1988. After starting his career in the NPA in his home village in the southern Negros uplands, he had risen up the ranks from guerrilla soldier to *sparrow* in Bacolod City, to a member of the Alex Boncayao Brigade in Manila, which counted many members from the Visayan islands, including Negros.[34] In military custody, he became a military intelligence asset and formally married his wife from the movement. As a sideline, he began to work as a bodyguard for movie stars who regularly visited Manila's army headquarters Camp Aguinaldo to choose suitable candidates from among captured NPAs. In his remote home village, his sister had remarkable tales to tell of the time he was the bodyguard of a competitor of the actor Ruben Padilla and was embroiled in an encounter with Padilla's own bodyguard, a colonel. This encounter had a highly ironic tinge. As former antagonists in the insurgency, the colonel and the former *sparrow* were playing their familiar roles but now for a different cause and for different employers.

From Liquidating Policemen to Servicing a Police Racket

"B" was a plantation worker who became a member of the movement's militia in the plantation where he lived, and eventually a full-time member of a liquidation squad that covered his home municipality. He was a *sparrow* from the mid-1980s to about 1988, when he surrendered. Those years were marked by NPA killings of policemen and members of the Philippine Constabulary for perceived misdeeds or simply to capture their arms. Some said that "B" was involved in the killing of a chief of police in his hometown. Different stories circulated about his surrender: he was either caught by the military or he surrendered voluntarily as he feared NPA retribution when he ran off with his lover, taking with him part of the movement's funds. But it was common knowledge that he began to work for the chief of police of Bacolod City after his surrender. He joined a police team charged with tracking down NPAs in the city, became a bodyguard of his new employer, and was sent on missions for the latter's shady businesses, reportedly a protection racket that lived off Bacolod businessmen and weapon sales to civilians. He was also involved in some marijuana trade. Once a killer of policemen, "B" was himself killed by the police in 1991 "because he knew too much," it was said.

Why did these former liquidation-squad members ("A" and "B") use their skills and knowledge to aid their former enemies? They were certainly constrained in their choice by landing up in military hands, either through capture or surrender. With an impressive track record as former *sparrows*, they were valuable potential assets for the military. Possibly, they were presented with attractive conditions, including the waiving of military retribution for their own *sparrow* killings. Besides, they were presented with a secure source of income, a government salary that included social security coverage. Moreover, as former *sparrows* whose identity was known to the state, they were vulnerable to revenge killings by the police or other counter-insurgency forces and vulnerable, too, to possible NPA retaliation in case their former comrades would doubt their military contacts. By joining a branch of the police or military forces, they would receive at least some armed protection. The following cases show a broadly similar pattern.

Former Members of a Liquidation Squad in Bacolod City

Several former *sparrows* who used to be active in Bacolod City in the 1980s as members of one specific liquidation squad linked up with the provincial military or elite as their employees and dependents after they had left the movement. I knew one of its former members well, and in 2000 he related to me what happened with his former comrades.

> "C" became a policeman and intelligence asset. He had started his activist career as a political science student at West Negros College, subsequently became a leader of the movement's youth organization in Negros (Pederasyon sg Kabataan Mamumugon), and eventually a *sparrow* in Bacolod City. After his surrender in the late 1980s, he became an informer for the Philippine Constabulary and acted as a guide in raids on safe houses. He later joined the Philippine National Police (PNP) Scouts in Bacolod City and began working as an intelligence asset for the police. Meanwhile, his wife managed a small grocery store and coffee shop in her hometown, where they settled. He may have been aided in his police career by a relative who served in the police force. In relating his story, his former comrade suggested that his switch to the police was facilitated by his middle-class background as the middle classes were more amenable to the police, and by his love of weapons; with a gun "he felt a bit like Superman," since "women here are attracted by men who have a gun." Possibly, personal grudges were one reason why he turned against the movement. When still a cadre, he was demoted in rank because he carried on a love affair without the proper consent of his superiors. His doubts about the need for armed revolution after the "People Power" uprising of 1986 may have been at play as well.
>
> "D" was killed by the Philippine Constabulary in 1988 after he was picked up at a *welgang bayan* (people's strike) in Bacolod City.

> "E" was killed by the Philippine Constabulary in 1988 during a raid that was apparently led by his former comrade "C." He had a high-powered weapon and was the most wanted member of the group.
>
> "F" became an overseer of a small plantation that was owned by a man who used to be a student activist and CPP-NPA sympathizer in his youth. When this plantation owner entered electoral politics as an active supporter of local candidates in Bacolod City, "F" also served as a bodyguard and vote-mobilizer for his employer's candidates. After successful campaigns, "F" would be rewarded with a temporary post as a casual worker at City Hall. During the campaign of 1998, he recruited several other former *sparrows* among his circle of friends to work as fellow bodyguards for a mayoral candidate. "F" never officially surrendered to the authorities since he left the movement in the 1980s when surrender was still risky. His well-connected employer possibly provided him with the necessary protection.
>
> "G" became a farmer in the Bacolod area. When still a *sparrow*, he was promoted to the position of commander of a liquidation squad in another town. But when he took a "second wife" in the movement, he was subjected to disciplinary action by his superiors. Together with his lover, he quit the movement without permission from his superiors and moved to a neighboring island. They returned years later, were expelled from the movement, but apparently did not surrender to state authorities.

Former *sparrows* had an easier time finding paid work in the city than former guerrilla fighters. The reason was job-related. As the ex-*sparrow* informant explained, members of assassination squads were usually based in urban areas where they developed a vast network of urban contacts for their intelligence work, which included members of the elite. They could tap these networks when looking for a job, for example, as a bodyguard or security guard. In contrast, guerrilla fighters were mostly confined to the upland and mountainous areas, with only temporary sorties to more populated rural areas. This offered little opportunity to develop similar strategic contacts.

A friend of my informant had found a way out of these constraints. A former guerrilla fighter, he approached the old overseer of the plantation where his wife's family lived; he requested if he could succeed him when the plantation owner retired. He knew the plantation well from his days as a movement organizer before he became a guerrilla soldier. The plantation owner agreed as he liked to have a "brave" person manage his property.

Former Guerrilla Soldiers

Of the eight men from Hda. Milagros, or married into Milagros, who were known to have served as guerrilla soldiers, most had taken up "respectable" types of manual work by the mid-1990s. Most had been plantation workers, young and single, when they joined the NPA. After they left the movement, one left for Manila and started a new life as a factory worker, two became small farmers on land of their wives' families, one picked up his pre-NPA work as a taxi driver in Bacolod City, and one became a caretaker of his brother-in-law's fighting cocks. Two men had met violent deaths. One was killed by the military in an NPA encounter. The other, who had tried to make a living as the driver of a passenger motorcycle, was killed a year after his surrender during a drunken brawl.

The eighth former guerrilla soldier had taken up a "disreputable" occupation as a member of a robbery syndicate in another area. His specialized tasks in the movement had partly shaped this twist in his career. In the CPP-NPA he had been one of a team that specialized in "confiscation," including the hold-up of Coca Cola trucks, theft of pigs from a plantation piggery, and cows from cattle ranches. Part of the proceeds went to the movement and the other part to the local poor who supported them. When he was expelled from the movement because of repeated transgressions, which included showing his gun in public, he simply continued to use these skills to make a living, as did several others with the same expertise. He set himself to stealing water buffalo from plantations and farms. Later, he found work as a security guard at the prawn ponds of a politician as a reward for helping out in an election campaign.

In sharp contrast is the career of another former guerrilla soldier from Milagros. He ran for the position of village councilor in the elections of 1995, together with a local organizer from the plantation. In the movement, he had been the main security officer of the party district secretary, who was his plantation mate and friend, and closely followed political developments since then. As a candidate for village councilor, he and his companion were the only ones who campaigned in the village for the implementation of land reform and labor laws, introducing a whole new discourse into the established practice of clientelist election campaigns. But they lost, capturing only a third of the votes. Other former guerrilla soldiers in Hda. Milagros also continued to express left-wing principles, but only in informal conversations. They did not act on these principles by public, collective means. Some were members of the cooperative of rebel returnees in the municipality, but apparently not active in it.

Among guerrilla fighters from San Juan village, one was killed in action and one became a farmer in San Juan after his surrender. By the early 1990s, this farmer served on the board of a cooperative of land-reform beneficiaries in the village, and by 2000 he was a member of the village council, though not very active in village affairs.

Former Members of the Village Militia

In both research communities, the underground village militia (*yunit milisya*) attracted young men who were interested in arms and the use of violence. It formed the recruiting ground for guerrilla soldiers and *sparrows*. At a later stage in the conflict, however, when state counter-insurgency intensified, members of the militia units also formed potential recruits for the state-supported village paramilitary forces. Although it is unclear how widespread this phenomenon has been (it did not take place in Hda. Milagros), the case of San Juan suggests some processes that might have been at work.[35]

The village of San Juan covers a large upland area that was, during the time of CPP-NPA control, divided into three underground administrative units, each with its own party branch, committees, and militia unit. I know of fourteen village men who served some time as members of *yunit milisya* (locally referred to as "YM"), though there were many more. The YMs were mostly poor farmers or wage workers in the cane fields, who operated as a village police force at night. Most were teenagers and young men, recruited through the movement's youth groups in the village, but some were older, with families. Two later became full-timers (a guerrilla soldier and a *sparrow*) while the others remained in the village.

When a military detachment was put up in San Juan, eight of these men began to work for the government military as members of the Civilian Voluntary Organization (CVO), who functioned as village guards and informers. They gained access to some village land as payment for their services. After a period of training, four of them became members of the Civilian Armed Forces Geographical Unit (Cafgu), after which they were armed, received a monthly allowance, and were covered by insurance. They served as guides and aides for the military. By 2000, only one of these former YM-turned-paramilitary was still part of the paramilitary force in the village. One had been killed by the NPA, some had left because of threats by the NPA and/or opportunities elsewhere (they became farmers or laborers in other parts of the province), and others tried to eke out a living as casual laborers or farmers on marginal village land.

Why did these former militia members land up on the side of the government military? The quest for protection was a key motive: protection either vis-à-vis comrades who had turned against them, or vis-à-vis the government military who had put up camp in the village. Both types of motives are briefly explored here. First, some militia members were accused of transgressing movement rules while acting under the banner of the CPP-NPA, and they feared being killed by the very movement they were supposed to serve. They had abused the authority to use violence and other means of coercion. Villagers referred to them as aggressive and self-serving. They hardly conformed to the movement's model of men of *disciplined* violence who had renounced their personal interests. They moved to the military side to save their lives. The following case serves as an example.

"H" was a small farmer who lived in a remote corner of San Juan. "He was a thief—he even stole my pots and pans," recalled a former neighbor about his pre-CPP-NPA status. But he was also one of the first to link up with movement activists who used to pass by the village. Once the movement was firmer in place, he became a militia member together with his younger brother. The brothers then began to take the law into their own hands. With other members of their militia unit, they apparently killed perceived enemies of the movement without permission from their superiors. They murdered a suspected informer and a member of the paramilitary from a neighboring village who was on leave. These so-called "spontaneous" actions, in CPP-NPA jargon, were bad enough, but were possibly not detected and punished by their superiors. What did land "H" with the movement's death sentence was that he turned "confiscation" into plain theft for his personal benefit. He had taken cows from a neighboring cattle ranch in the name of the movement but had pocketed the returns from the sale. When caught by his comrades, he managed to escape. He ran straight to the nearest army detachment for protection.

This was in 1985, several years before the military would put up a detachment in the village itself. He became the first intelligence asset of the military in the area, guiding military patrols. When the detachment was put up in the village, he became a member of the Civilian Voluntary Organization (CVO), and helped the military apprehend several militia members from San Juan who were responsible for the killing of a military man. As a CVO, vested again with coercive powers, he lived up to his reputation. He collected *tong* (protection money) from truck drivers passing by the village, abused his right to some village land as a payment for his CVO services by victimizing others, and, together with another CVO, beat up a drunken fellow villager so severely that the man died shortly afterwards. In line with this career, he later became overseer of a commercial fish pond in another municipality, owned by a local businessman-politician, and left the village.

As these militiamen abused their coercive powers within the movement, their comrades moved against them which, in turn, forced them to seek protection on the government side.

But another motive was also at work for those who had not soured their reputation with the movement. Some militia members, given their violent careers and faced with the inescapable fact that the government military had settled in their midst in 1990, apparently chose to befriend them in order to soften possible retaliation. This, in turn, raised suspicion on the part of the NPA, and moved the former closer to the military for protection.

> "T" was a plantation laborer when he joined the *yunit militia*. The task of his unit was "to catch military men," as his sister recounted. The unit was responsible for the capture and killing of a lone army lieutenant accused of illegal logging who had passed through the village while hitching a ride on top of a truck. When the military detachment was put up in the village, "T" befriended one of its soldiers who used to frequent the coffee shop of "T"'s uncle (apparently, he had already distanced himself from the movement before the military arrived). He became the soldier's helper, hauling water for him and carrying his rifle when he bathed at the village source. He also became a guide for military patrols. When the military started to apprehend the militia members responsible for the lieutenant's murder, including "T," he profited from the support of his protector within the detachment. He got off lightly compared to his former companions and was spared a term in prison. Possibly, a deal to continue cooperation with the military was also involved.
>
> After his release, his soldier-patron advised him to become a CVO. He agreed because he feared retaliation by the NPA. By 2000, he was a casual laborer in the village, with a wife and young children, very poor, and depending on several of the richer village families for work and support. Prominently displayed in his ramshackle house was his Certificate of Amnesty, laminated and framed, and nailed to a bamboo beam. Although he was a member of the cooperative of rebel returnees in the village, he played no active role in the village's power arena. He cut short his

> paramilitary career when his family prevented him from attending Cafgu training ("Why get yourself killed in a fight with the NPA?")

These villagers were invaluable to the military's counter-insurgency campaign. Because of their knowledge of the movement, its of local cadres and village supporters, they helped cut the communication lines between mobile CPP-NPA cadres and villagers, and curtailed the room to maneuver for village-based cadres who were now "lying low" or had surrendered.

Former Specialists in Political Organization and Revolutionary Administration

The CPP-NPA period had offered many sons and daughters of plantation laborers and small farmers a thorough hands-on training in the craft of contentious politics, in managing activist collectives, and in administering populations under CPP-NPA control. This produced a large pool of skilled, committed political activists, specialists in political organization and revolutionary administration, who identified with their political mission. As they left the movement, they formed an unprecedented corps of lower-class political actors in the province, with the capacity to replace traditional elites in positions of authority in the community and beyond.

Many of these former political cadres continued to live by their self-defined mission in life, to uplift and empower their fellow poor, a mission that became part of their political identity forged in the movement. In the communities and surrounding areas in which I did research, those who remained active in the political arena were either involved in progressive, contentious politics or they held positions in government-supported cooperatives and in village and ward councils (or tried to achieve these positions without success). However, some were embittered and discouraged, in part because of the splits and infighting within the movement and its offshoots.

Community Level

Several activist veterans in Hda. Milagros and San Juan village became instrumental in local cooperatives, unions, and government institutions. They included, in particular, former part-time activists who had led the movement's community "mass" organizations and eventually formed the local party branches in the plantation and village. These positions within the revolutionary community structure were often held by local women and men who were interested and able to organize, lead, and administer, as they were partly selected by their activist superiors on those grounds. Before their careers within the CPP-NPA, some had held local leadership positions in union chapters and Catholic community organizations, particularly the progressive Basic Christian Communities influenced by Liberation Theology. Others had developed their skills and commitment within the movement itself. These former community cadres, then, carried on as community activists after the decline of revolutionary politics.

The available means to do so differed markedly, however. In San Juan, villagers were cut off from left-wing activist networks. By 2000, channels for promoting poor villagers' interests were limited to the village council and to state-sponsored cooperatives of land reform beneficiaries and rebel returnees. With constant monitoring from the military detachment in their community, ex-cadres in the village considered involvement in left-wing organizations too risky. Besides, many were tired of it, tired of the personal investment in organization, meetings, and collective action with insecure returns. Class-based organization of rural workers, moreover, ran up against structural constraints. The former sugarcane plantations in the village had been subdivided among the workers in formal and informal (CPP-NPA-instigated) types of land reform, and the land-reform beneficiaries hired casual migrant workers to help them cultivate and harvest their small cane fields. These workers were paid dismal wages but they could hardly claim more from their small-scale employers.

The former party branch secretaries held the following elected positions in San Juan in 2000. One was the president of his village ward and the president of the parent-teacher association of the village school. Another was the vice-chairman of the cooperative of land reform beneficiaries in the village, funded by the state-owned Land Bank, and the chairman of the cooperative of village rebel returnees, which owned and managed a rice mill and a thresher. Notably, these two men, of small farmer background, had reached elected positions of influence hitherto monopolized by the village élite. In contrast, the third and most influential former party branch secretary had withdrawn from all public functions and lived a secluded life as a small farmer.[36]

But as they operated within the available organizations created by the state, some former cadres in San Juan faced painful readjustments. Formerly revolutionary village administrators who held positions of power, they subsequently had to maneuver within the traditional political sphere marked by hierarchy and deference, where they came to depend on others who did not necessarily share their ideas or appreciate their advice. For example, the former party branch secretary who became president of a village ward was disappointed by the limited opportunities to do something tangible for his constituency. When he pushed for relevant government projects, he told me in 2000, he collided with the village head. Used to open and critical debate of policies and plans within his own circle of cadres, he regularly voiced his views on the plans of the village head during council meetings but the latter did not appreciate this. And, he added, "the projects that I proposed for my village ward were not honored." He discussed these problems with two other ex-cadres in the village council but they felt powerless to change the system.

In Hda. Milagros, on the other hand, workers remained involved in left-wing networks through a labor union that was still linked to the CPP-NPA and through the personal ties of some worker families who were connected to a rival faction. In contrast to other *hacenderos* in the area, the owner of Milagros allowed them the space to do so. In the period of counter-insurgency, he did not force his workers to cut their ties with the left-wing union and he continued to honor the union bargaining agreements made at the time of CPP-NPA control in the plantation. Several former members of the party branch and former activists in the movement's youth, women, and workers' groups in the plantation remained active in the local union chapter and continued to participate in rallies and demonstrations of the faction that still sympathized with the CPP-NPA. They kept in touch with union organizers, joined seminars, and just as in earlier years they introduced left-wing discourse into local conversations, such as "globalization" as the source of social ills. They remained well informed of the latest developments in land reform and labor laws and were keen to claim their legal entitlements from the state.

By 2000, they navigated with ease the bureaucratic mazes of the state's departments of labor, agrarian reform, and social welfare and development, as well as the state's social security system. Years of experience in organizing and revolutionary administration in the plantation had diminished their "shame" in approaching government officials. From their ranks, too, came the women and men who pushed for land-reform coverage of Hda. Milagros, though it would still take years before they would succeed. Since several municipal line agencies organized outreach programs for the workers as part of the state's counter-insurgency program in the early 1990s, former cadres from Milagros have sought to use these openings to the full.

But here, too, several experienced and capable former members of the local party branch, embittered or discouraged, eventually withdrew from the arena of power. One reason was the fragmentation of the Left. Those who sided with the "rejectionists" at the time of the split of 1992–93, convinced by one of the high-ranking cadres from the plantation, withdrew from the union and its network and no longer participated in the union's collective actions in the plantation. Another reason was local distrust. Workers of Milagros tended to distrust their activist peers who held leadership positions, and the ensuing conflicts and jealousies discouraged the people who held such positions.

In short, post-movement careers of community-based cadres show divergent trajectories in the two communities. In San Juan, these former cadres operated by 2001 within the confines of state-sponsored organizations that were partly set up for counter-insurgency purposes, and their activities were limited to promoting the immediate socio-economic interests of villagers. In Hda. Milagros, opportunities remained more favorable to collective action and pressure politics, and former local cadres continued to push for the enforcement of laws and for the full realization of their legal entitlements by working through the left-wing union or operating on their own.

In contrast, many ex-cadres from both communities who had served in the movement as fulltime mobile organizers, medical personnel, financial officers, and radio operators, hardly participated in the political arena once they had left the movement. Most had been single youths when they became full-time cadres, both women and men. By 2001, most were married and struggled to support their families. Those from San Juan, for example, included farmers, a truck driver, mothers and housekeepers, and a security guard at a hospital in the city. Some had been embroiled in conflicts with superiors in the movement and turned their backs on it. Moreover, two of the women moved to the side of the government military through their husbands.[37] Only a former officer of the movement's regional bureau of communication and transportation became active in village organizations, as a member of a ward council and an active member of the cooperative of rebel returnees. Among those from Hda. Milagros, several migrated to Manila or Mindanao, either in search of a better livelihood or to escape possible arrest in the 1980s, or, in the case of a former radio operator who surrendered, to escape repeated pressure by the military to become a radio operator for the army. Others returned to the plantation where several participated in the local union. The medical and financial officers from Milagros had all been women, and after they left the movement they concentrated on raising their young families, worked in the cane fields on the side, and some participated in the labor union.

Municipal and Provincial Level

The movement functioned as a political training ground for poor people previously confined to the position of dependent clients of local politicians. They later used these skills not only in their own community but also in the municipal and provincial power arena on both sides of the political spectrum.

Below, I discuss several people from poor backgrounds who reached positions of political influence that would have been unthinkable without their careers in the movement. These were women and men from Hda. Milagros and nearby plantations whose careers as middle-range political cadres propelled them into "above ground" political positions at the municipal or provincial level. Initially, they formed a cluster of youthful organizers of Basic Christian Communities in their home municipality, connected to local clergy inspired by Liberation Theology. They subsequently became union organizers, followed by a switch to full-time work as organizers for the underground CPP-NPA. They all eventually reached the position of secretary (head) of a section party committee or district party committee.[38] As early entrants, their rise in the hierarchy followed the expansion of the movement in the area. From the time they reached their top positions, their careers somewhat diverged, as illustrated by the following examples.

"J," son of plantation workers, was secretary of a section party committee in Central Negros in the 1980s, then demoted for reasons unknown to me. He resurfaced in the 1990s as an organizer for above ground organizations of one of the two "rejectionist" factions. He worked for the union federation BMP (Bukluran ng Manggagawang Pilipino), and during the elections of 2001 he ran for municipal councilor in his hometown under the Partido ng Manggagawa (Workers' Party) but lost.

"K," son of plantation workers, rose to the position of secretary of a district party committee and member of the CPP-NPA Regional United Front Bureau. By 2000, he was vice-chairman of the labor federation BMP on Negros island. Together with "J," he was unsuccessful in running for the municipal council in his hometown in 2001 under the Partido ng Manggagawa.

"L," from the same plantation as the previous cadre, was secretary of a district party committee at the time of his capture and surrender in 1991. He then distanced himself from the CPP-NPA network and began to work for the labor union DIWA set up by rebel returnees in the late 1980s as an alternative to the union NFSW that had links with the CPP-NPA. By 2000, he was on the payroll of the City Engineer's Office of the provincial capital, apparently without having to show up for work. He was "close to some *politico*," as a former friend explained, in particular to the vice-mayor at that time, who cultivated contacts with a network of rebel returnees. The former cadres were known for their good leadership skills and came in handy in election campaigns.

"M," daughter of the overseer of a small plantation, became secretary of a section party committee in the southern part of the province and head of an educational committee at district level. She left the underground in the 1980s by "lying low," without officially surrendering. But she remained active in above ground movement organizations, in particular the "rejectionist" labor union DALO and, after the second split in the movement, in the regional office of the political organization Sanlakas. By 2000 she was "tired" of her work for the movement and discouraged by recent trends in her own faction where, she suggested, leaders were adopting elite behavior, NGOs were recast in a hierarchical and businesslike mold, and the revolutionary spirit of comradeship and the sense of social mission was petering out.

"N," the rebellious daughter of the overseer of another plantation, became head of an organization department at district level, while her husband was secretary of a district party committee. Captured together in 1990, they were released within a year for lack of evidence and moved to Manila. There she became a committed worker for a progressive NGO that assisted internal refugees victimized by counter-insurgency campaigns, and as these campaigns subsided she shifted to the assistance of illegal Philippine migrant workers abroad. Embedded in international NGO networks, she made several trips abroad to help campaign against the illegal trafficking in women.

"O" rose to the influential position of secretary of a district party committee as well, but became a military asset after his capture and surrender in 1988. Son of a plantation foreman and overseer of Hda. Milagros for several years, he followed a path into the movement that was similar to that of the five ex-cadres above. He proved to be a skilled organizer and eventually became a revolutionary administrator of several municipalities that were partly under CPP-NPA control. However, he clashed with his superiors over personal and policy matters and resisted the leaders' decision to prioritize armed struggle over poverty alleviation. When he was captured, he volunteered to work on the government side. At that time, the Aquino administration was changing its counter-insurgency policy to one of attraction rather than repression of movement cadres, and its line agencies offered funds and projects to attract the mass base back to the government fold.

"O" maneuvered within this space. On the payroll of the army, he helped the army's special operation teams in organizing so-called "mass surrenders" in plantations and village communities and sought to convince the population that the current government had more to offer than the movement. At the same time, he used his army network to help former comrades exit safely from the movement and to protect captured cadres from police brutality. Clearly, his good reputation as a former high-ranking cadre and his organizational skills and networks helped to influence community supporters and full-timers to withdraw from the movement. On the side, he began to work again as a plantation overseer. Restyling himself as a reformist, he also entered the electoral arena in the municipal elections of 1992 and tried to mobilize the votes of rebel returnees to support reformist candidates. Most of these candidates lost, however. When the revolutionary movement began to lose much of its following and personnel, and when "O" became embroiled in personal conflicts, the military stopped soliciting his services, his planter-employer fired him, and he was effectively marginalized in the arena of political power. By 2000, he lived a secluded life in poverty.[39]

These women and men had at least one thing in common. From being poor dependents of planter-employers and strongmen-politicians, they became social reformers in the broad sense of the term. Their learning experience in the union and revolutionary movement had changed their self-image and political style. They had learned a new model and ideology of political contestation, separate and in opposition to the established clientelist form. As they developed leadership skills, widened their social networks, increased their sense of efficacy, and expanded their knowledge of the Philippine social and political scene, they gained a potential for autonomous collective action independent of strongman control.

Within the wider category of former political cadres, many realized this potential in the legal sphere of progressive "above ground" work. Even "O," discussed above, perceived his work in the army's employ in this light, as linking poor citizens and state agencies without the self-interested mediation of third parties. Others, however, hitched on to strongmen in clientelist fashion, as the case of "N" illustrates. Still another organized an interest group of former cadres but put the organization at the disposal of clientelist politicians. "He sold his skills to the highest bidder during election time, he organized support for them," one observer remarked derisively. But many put their time and energy into the painstaking work of organizing, mobilizing, lobbying, and project managing in the collective interest of those who had long been denied an active role in the political arena.

Conclusion

This chapter discussed how former revolutionary cadres in the Philippine province of Negros Occidental repositioned themselves in the provincial power arena after they resurfaced from the underground, and how this affected poor people's politics in the province. The period in focus (1990s-2001) covers the time of a major outflow of cadres from the CPP-NPA nationwide, in which former cadres redefined their position vis-à-vis the revolutionary movement, the state, and political elites. The following patterns can be discerned.

First, among the cases discussed, many former "specialists in violence" and former political cadres landed up on opposite sides of the provincial power spectrum. "Specialists in violence" placed their coercive skills and strategic knowledge at the service of provincial strongmen and the military. Former political cadres, on their part, used their political skills, tactical knowledge, and convictions to contest the power of local strongmen by working through NGOs, social movements, cooperatives, and the like. Strikingly, past specialties in the underground partly shaped post-underground careers. The cadres developed skills, networks, and a particular identity that affected their future trajectories.

Second, the rule of local strongmen remained the pivot around which former cadres positioned themselves as contestants, allies, or dependents. Despite decades of left-wing contention in the province, above and underground, the system of strongman rule still figured as both the core model and the reality of politics in Negros Occidental. Fueled by a district-based, winner-take-all electoral system that provides elected officials privileged access to state resources for private ends, entrepreneurs continued to compete for electoral positions as a means to expand and defend their business interests and political clout through state patronage and privilege. This contest persistently fed their demand for armed guards to protect their turf from encroachment by others, be they state agents, elite competitors, or revolutionaries, and to expand their control in the face of resistance. Here, strongmen and former cadres specialized in violence linked up, as employer and employee, in a shared quest for protection and, in the case of ex-cadres, for a source of income as well. Although the presence of private armed personnel was nothing new in the provincial power arena, the influx of large numbers of skilled ex-revolutionaries into this job market allowed local strongmen with the right connections to ex-cadre networks to gain an edge over their competitors. The apparent deal between Eduardo Cojuangco Jr and units of the armed rival of the NPA, the RPA-ABB, in the context of a peace agreement is a special variant on such an arrangement. It likely enhanced Cojuangco's control over local populations and resources considerably.

Third, strongman rule prompted, in turn, counteractions by numerous local NGOs and social movements based in villages, towns, and cities that were staffed to a large extent by former political cadres of the CPP-NPA. With varying success, they sought concessions from planters and other economic power holders for the benefit of laboring populations, functioned as their substitutes in providing access to resources, and tried to curb the bossist inclinations of strongmen-politicians who sought to monopolize local resources and state funds for private gain.

In doing so, these former political cadres contributed to a significant change in the configuration of state, citizens, and strongmen. Greatly expanding the ranks of skilled progressive activists in the legal sphere of collective action, they pushed for an impartial, non-clientelist access to state resources. They organized and mobilized poor populations hitherto excluded from the arena of power, except as clientelist voters. Moreover, they pressed for the enforcement of laws that benefit these populations. As they contested the entwinement of interests of strongmen and state officials, an entwinement that had long been taken for granted, they contributed to a redefinition of citizen rights and state responsibilities, and so to a change in Philippine political culture.

The discussion of post-movement careers also suggests another point. It shows how revolutionary movement(s), strongmen-politicians, the various arms of the state (police, army, line agencies), and new social movements in the legal "above ground" sphere, may be intimately connected through the histories of their "personnel." In studies on contentious politics the various actors, whether social movement activists, state, strongmen, or citizens, are treated as distinct entities, with distinct interests, goals, and strategies. Connections are analyzed in terms of strategic alliances and contentious interactions. This perspective is certainly useful. But if we take seriously the call to relate "social movements to all forms of contentious politics" and contentious politics to politics in general (Tarrow 1996, 874), then we should also consider how political actors are making such connections in the course of their life careers, how they possibly move through these institutions, linking them by passing on their knowledge, networks, beliefs, and skills.[40]

We may add this specific angle to analyses that explore changes in Philippine power configurations. For example, Abinales (1998) argues that provincial strongmen whose access to the means of violence, economic capital, and the state was severely curtailed in the period of martial law (1972–91) under President Marcos, nevertheless did manage to regain power in the last years of martial law by forging tactical alliances with local units of the CPP-NPA. Such alliances provided local strongmen with access to legal "above ground" organizations of the movement and allowed them to campaign in CPP-NPA controlled territory during election time. These pacts, then, "managed to offset [their] loss of 'guns, goons and gold' by allowing them access to the public arena" (Abinales 1998, 154). If one would observe this process of strongmen resurrection from the angle of cadres' careers, one may find that an actual shift of armed personnel from the CPP-NPA to local strongmen (by way of a state-managed surrender or otherwise) may have accompanied and intensified this process in later years.

Hedman (2000, 28–29) shows that the "reformist" anti-Marcos mobilization of 1986, which culminated in the "People Power" revolt, was a campaign to restore formal democracy and undercut "more radical demands for social change and democratization." One might add that, eventually, the more radical (revolutionary) demands were also undercut by the exodus of political cadres from the CPP-NPA underground since the late 1980s. Conversely, this shift of political cadres from the underground to the newly expanded sphere of progressive NGOs and social movements promoted radical (non-revolutionary) collective action across the country, and so partly frustrated the conservative aims of major actors in the "People Power" revolt.

Epilogue

Key developments highlighted above (products of the mass exodus from the revolutionary underground in the 1990s) still reverberate in the provincial power arena in 2019. Nationwide, the CPP-NPA, its various offshoots, the state, provincial strongmen, and left-wing reformist organizations staffed in part by former revolutionary cadres are still locked in a struggle marked by contestation, coalition formation, and crossovers by individuals and groups. In the process, these various actors continue to press for their specific versions of poor people's politics: revolutionary, elite-led clientelist, or left-wing reformist. The CPP-NPA (which still pursues armed struggle) and its allied legal, above-ground labor unions and other sectoral organizations have continued their steady resurgence after the major 1992–93 split in the movement, with several thousand armed fighters across the country (Quimpo 2018; see also Caouette 2015). Though the CPP-NPA no longer poses as serious a threat to the Philippine state as in the 1980s, the state still uses its familiar repertoire of military counter-insurgency, repression, amnesty programs, community-based mass surrenders, intermittent peace negotiations, and periodic invitations to the left to participate in government in order to neutralize the radical flank, secure support from the poor, and reward left-wing electoral support. The latter process has allowed, for instance, factions of the reformist left that include former revolutionary cadres to take up cabinet positions under President Macapagal-Arroyo (2001–8) and in particular under President Benigno Aquino II (2009–15), pushing a pro-poor and anti-clientelist agenda with mixed results (Reid 2018).[41] President Rodrigo Duterte (2016–), in an exceptional move, invited prominent persons associated with the revolutionary left to lead several government departments, including agrarian reform, but this coalition was short-lived, as Duterte turned against the revolutionary movement and its allied above-ground organizations by 2017, supposedly because the CPP-NPA had not honored a ceasefire.[42]

The government's peace agreement with the RPA-ABB and its political party RPM-P, made in 2000, still awaits the government's signing of a "closure agreement" that would finally regulate the disposition of its arms, among other things (Stinus-Cabugon 2017). Government-funded livelihood projects for its hundreds of former members, mainly in Negros Occidental, are implemented only piecemeal. These include several upland settlement areas where former RPA-ABB members were granted access to state land and a job as forest guard in 2018 (*SunStar Bacolod*, December 12, 2018).

In the meantime, the RPA-ABB continues its policy of close alliances with local strongmen. These alliances are currently meant to protect RPA-ABB units from CPP-NPA attacks and to support its ventures into electoral politics. Former RPA-ABB commander Stephen Paduano, based in Negros Occidental, became a successful congressional candidate for the party Abang Lingkod (Humble Servant) in the congressional party-list system; he was elected into Congress in 2013.[43] Though the party claims to represent the poor and marginalized, Paduano has made close alliances with local politicians of established clans, in particular with Congressman Benitez of one of the Negros districts, a wealthy and influential businessman and politician who apparently offers Paduano access to his ample campaign and patronage resources in return for access to his grassroots networks. Moreover, the alliance of the RPA-ABB with the mayor of Don Salvador Benedicto town (where the peace agreement was signed in 2000) apparently helped to establish the mayor's family as a local political clan, with two sons in the positions of mayor and vice-mayor by 2017, and their father a "known ringleader of the paramilitary group RPA-ABB," according to critical left-wing observers (Uma Pilipinas 2017).[44]

Local strongman rule has further expanded and solidified, primarily through electoral politics, government decentralization, and ample state patronage funds to feed clientelist practices. The various factions of the left are unable to present a meaningful challenge—in the electoral sphere and beyond (Quimpo 2018). In Negros Occidental, four different left-wing labor groups that are the product of the various splits in the revolutionary movement have not been able to join forces as yet, and they still reflect the fragmented field of left-wing mass movements and NGOs in the province and the country at large. Nevertheless, these activists and other former cadres have been instrumental in successful struggles for the implementation of the redistributive land reform law in their own plantation communities, and almost half of the former sugarcane plantation area of the province is now officially in the hands of former plantation workers. The prime sugar land of established planter clans with political clout, however, is mostly beyond their reach.

Notes

1. This article is a slightly revised and updated version of an article published in *South East Asia Research*, 9(3), 2001. I thank Eva-Lotta Hedman, Paul Hutchcroft, Charles Tilly, John Wiersma, and Frank de Zwart for their comments on the first version of this paper.

2. The CPP-NPA was founded in the Manila region as a Maoist guerrilla movement in 1968–69. By 1988, it counted some 24 thousand cadres nationwide and controlled or influenced an estimated 20 percent of the country's villages and urban neighborhoods. Decline of the movement set in as the Aquino government (1986–92) launched a concerted counter-insurgency drive coupled to an amnesty program; as the restoration of electoral democracy won middle-class support for the government and strengthened the position of provincial elites; and as the movement split over issues of strategy and leadership. By 1993, territorial control and influence had dwindled to roughly 3 percent of

the country's villages and urban neighborhoods, and by 1997 the estimated number of guerrilla fighters had dropped to 6,800. In recent years, however, the movement is regaining influence and manpower. By 2003, the NPA reportedly had about 13,500 full-time fighters deployed nationwide. See McBeth 1993; *Philippine Daily Inquirer*, March 29, 2001; *SunStar Bacolod*, July19, 2003. On the CPP-NPA, see also Abinales 1996; Chapman 1987; Rocamora 1994; Rutten 2008; Thompson 1998; Weekley 2001.

3. Doug McAdam (1988), for example, shows how the experience of activism may resocialize individuals so thoroughly that they become activists for life. In his study of American students who worked as civil rights volunteers in the conflict-ridden registration of African-American voters in the US south in the 1960s, McAdam (1988, 5) concludes that the experiences "effectively resocialized and radicalized the volunteers while the ties they established with other volunteers laid the groundwork for a nationwide activist network out of which the other major movements in the era—women's, antiwar, student—were to emerge." See also the call for more research on "the role of social movements or revolutions as a force for aggregate level shifts in life course patterns" (Goldstone and McAdam 2001, 216–17).

4. In Negros Occidental (with a population of 2.5 million in 2015), student activists established the first rural base in the southern peasant uplands in the early 1970s. In the late 1970s and 1980s, local CPP-NPA organizers expanded into the plantation lowlands. By 1986, some 100 thousand peasants and plantation workers across Negros island had joined the CPP-NPA's community-based mass organizations, and some 450 guerrilla fighters recruited from the local population who were fielded across the island, backed up by several thousand community militias (see Coronel 1991). After a decline in the late 1980s and 1990s, the number of guerrilla soldiers and political cadres has since risen again. In 2017, the government estimated some 200 NPA fighters were active on Negros island as a whole, though the CPP-NPA stated this figure was too low (Bayoran 2017).

5. Relevant studies of the plantation society of Negros Occidental include Aguilar 1998; Berlow 1996; Billig 2003; Duñgo 1993; Larkin 1993; McCoy 1984; 1991; Rutten 1996). See also Da-anoy Satake 2001.

6. For a discussion of the rise and decline of the CPP-NPA in Negros Occidental as experienced in the two communities in which I undertook research, see Rutten 1996; 2000b. For Negros Occidental at large, see Rutten 2008.

7. Jiang and Ashley (2000), for example, followed the life careers of former Red Guards who were all born in Shanghai in the same period.

8. Several Catholic nuns also joined but, parallel to the gender hierarchy in the church and society at large, they did not reach similarly high positions.

9. Marriages between former priests and nuns were not uncommon in the movement.

10. In 2018, Luis Jalandoni was still based in the Netherlands as an international spokesperson and senior advisor of the National Democratic Front (NDF), and Frank Fernandez is a spokesperson of the NDF in Negros Occidental. See also Gomez 2016.

11. The Huk movement (Hukbong Mapagpalaya ng Bayan) was officially led by the Partido Komunista ng Pilipinas (PKP).

12. On the careers of former Huk cadres see, in particular, Kerkvliet 1974, 1977; Lachica 1971; van den Muijzenberg 1973.

13. Literature on former cadres elsewhere in the Philippines suggests similar trajectories. For instance, the impressive family memoir of the activist Quimpo siblings from Manila who became political cadres in the CPP-NPA since their student days relates that, after they left the movement, one became a political scientist who aims to "help mold a new generation of more upright and progressive political actors who could bring about substantive political and social change," another sibling became an art therapist for human rights workers among others, with many former cadres among her colleagues and among the staff members of her partner organizations, and a third sibling who had been based in Paris for international work chose to stay in Paris and continued to be active in Philippine migrant organizations there whereas many other former cadres in Europe "opted to return to the Philippines and work for nongovernmental organizations" after the split of the CPP-NPA in 1992–93 (Quimpo and Quimpo 2012, 460, 462).

14. "Bossism" refers to "the interlocking, multitiered directorate of bosses who use their control over the state apparatus to exploit the archipelago's human and natural resources" (Sidel 1999, 19).

15. As John S. Koliopoulos (1987, 294) phrased it, with reference to the somewhat different process of the incorporation of bandits into paramilitary units in Greece.

16. Vincent Boudreau (1996) explains the nationwide expansion, since 1986, of progressive NGOs and of sectoral coalitions that campaign for concrete rights and issues as the outcome of the strategic efforts of social movements to retain mass support. Given a widened democratic space and an increased flow of international funds for NGOs, social movements "began acting upon their members' need for material relief by delivering livelihood resources directly to mass constituencies through NGO-administered programs" and by initiating collective actions "most likely to yield concrete reforms" (Boudreau 1996, 73). See also Boudreau 2001.

17. James Putzel (1998, 83–84) notes that rural communities and people's organizations "have seen NGOs as a vehicle to promote their interests at the level of the state, through lobbying state agencies, central and local elected officials, and the national-level political alliances during election time. NGOs have promoted participatory models of development in contrast to the top-heavy state-centered models of the past." He defines "people's organizations" as "membership-based organizations, like farmer organizations, trade unions, women's organizations, community organizations, and cooperatives, which are set up primarily to promote the interests of their members" (ibid.).

18. See, for example, Franco 2000.

19. The nationwide split within the CPP-NPA in 1992–93 concerned issues of strategy and leadership. As CPP founder Jose Maria Sison and his followers "reaffirmed" the strategy of a rural-based protracted people's war, his opponents, the "rejectionists," placed more emphasis on the legal struggle using the expanded democratic space of the post-Marcos era and/or more emphasis on urban insurrectionist activities, and deplored Sison's stifling of party debates. See, for example, Rocamora 1994; Weekley 1996.

20. By 2000, the two "rejectionist" factions had crystallized into Negros-wide parts of nationwide networks.

21. Philippine News Agency (PNA) e-mail news list *Balita News*, December 27, 1998.

22. These killings took place, in particular, during the peace negotiations between the government and the CPP-NPA-NDF from April to June 2001. Killed in that period were Congressman Rodolfo Aguinaldo of Cagayan province because of "his long list of heinous crimes against the people" as a torturer under Marcos and a provincial warlord, according to the CPP-NPA (*PDI*, June 14, 2001), Congressman Marcial Punzalan of Quezon province, Mayor Cesar Platon of Tanauan, Batangas, and Davao councilor Jun Pala (*PDI*, June 17, 2001). The government suspended the peace talks in June 2001 following the Aguinaldo killing.

23. The more spectacular examples include the following: the two factions literally fought over the control of the office and funds of the union DALO in Bacolod City in late 1998, with one faction starting a criminal case against the other for "grave coercion" in the forcible takeover of the office. In a separate incident in the first half of 1999, units of the RPA-ABB burned two trucks of the marketing cooperative Alter Trade, apparently to push their demand for a monthly share of the profits. The cooperative had been sympathetic to the RPA-ABB until the split of 1998. See, for example, Guanzon 1999.

24. PNA, e-mail news list *Balita News*, December 27, 2000.

25. Amnesty for RPA-ABB members and the allocation of Peso 20 million to facilitate their re-entry into society. *PDI*, July 25, 2001. In December 2000, 1 US dollar = Peso 50.

26. The local party formed around Cojuangco allies (United Negros Alliance) captured five of the seven congressional seats in the province as well as the positions of provincial governor and vice-governor.

27. As a close friend and ally of Ferdinand Marcos, Cojuangco had fled the country in 1986 when President Marcos was ousted from power.

28. Corn for its animal feeds sector, and cassava for its processing plants that produce starch for the manufacture of alcohol and biodegradable materials.

29. They campaigned explicitly against him during the elections of 2001 (*Manila Times*, March 5, 2001). On October 29, 2001, some 1,500 peasants and plantation workers from northern and southern Negros linked to the peasant organization Kilusang Magbubukid ng Pilipinas (KMP) and the National Federation of Sugar Workers (NFSW) started a two-day "People's March" to demand the immediate distribution of Cojuangco's landed properties to the tillers (*SunStar Bacolod*, October 30, 2001).

30. General Panfilo Lacson, a senator in 2001, was, during the brief Estrada regime, the Philippine National Police chief and head of the Presidential Anti-Organized Crime Task Force (PAOCTF). It has been alleged that he was involved in drug trafficking and in a kidnap-for-ransom racket.

31. This was part of a nationwide counter-insurgency strategy that consisted of community-based counter-mobilization coupled with the granting of amnesty. So-called Special Operations Teams (SOT) were trained in psychological warfare and approached the CPP-NPA's civilian mass base with a mixture of persuasion and tacit coercion. The SOTs combined forced community "mass surrenders" with civic action, a strong military presence, recruitment of a local paramilitary force, and funding of livelihood projects for rebel returnees. The army combined this relatively non-violent approach towards civilians with violent offensives against suspected guerrilla fighters.

32. Despite the explicit policy of the movement to have cadres combine military and political "mass" work, specialties did develop, in particular as the movement shifted by the mid-1980s towards larger military operations. Similar continuities in individual specialties within and outside a movement can be found among former leaders of the Partido Komunista ng Pilipinas (PKP), linked to the Huk movement. "Intellectuals" among top PKP leaders continued their intellectual pursuits after their release from prison in the 1960s and 1970s. Jesus Lava worked in Prague for almost two decades as the PKP's "representative of the council of the English-language *World Marxist Review*, sponsored by the Soviet Union" (Dalisay 1999, 158). William Pomeroy became a correspondent for British left-wing newspapers in London. His wife and ex-cadre, Celia Mariano, found work as a teacher in London but she also became active in a teachers' union and a British women's organization (Lanzona 2000, 264–67).

33. From SPARU, Special Partisan Unit.

34. The Alex Boncayao Brigade was formed in 1984 as the first NPA guerrilla unit in Metro Manila. By 1987, it counted fifty members and was responsible for the killing of some 120 soldiers and policemen as well as several government officials, factory owners, and US servicemen (Jones 1989, 247–48).

35. Participation in state-supported paramilitary groups by former supporters or members of the CPP-NPA was not uncommon in Negros (see, for example, Task Force Detainees of the Philippines (TFDP)-Negros 1988). Conditions preceding their incorporation may explain why, including state coercion, guerrilla oppression, or the state's policy of attraction. For a discussion of such processes elsewhere, see Starn 1998.

36. He had started a promising career as the head of an NGO project for land reform beneficiaries in the village after disengaging from the movement. When his successor accused him of trying to undermine CPP-NPA control in the community by means of the (non-left-wing) NGO, he received death threats from his former comrades, and took refuge in the city. Returning to the village years later, he avoided former cadres and refrained from any type of organizational activity.

37. The husband of one, himself a former organizer, became a paramilitary (Cafgu) after his arrest. The other young woman, who had long left the movement, became the lover of the military intelligence officer who accompanied the first batch of government soldiers in the village, and eventually married him.

38. A section covers one municipality, a district three to five municipalities, in CPP-NPA underground governance .

39. For an extensive discussion of this case, see Rutten 2000a.

40. The very existence of such flows of people from, say, a revolutionary movement to police or paramilitary forces of a non-revolutionary state, or to the ranks of elected politicians, or to new social movements in the legal sphere, may appear anomalous to political scientists who have come to believe in their own reifications. But for people "on the ground" it may appear quite a natural process. This is certainly so in the Philippines, where the political culture is characterized by boundary-crossing rather than boundary-marking and maintenance. Fegan's biography (2000) tells of a village elder in the province

of Bulacan whose oppositionist stance "led him to support everything from millenarian nationalist conspiracies to peasant unions and radical minority parties . . . His account makes linkages between a number of organizations that have been dealt with in the dominant histories as if they were discrete and even distinct: millenarian movements, peasant unions, nationalist movements, and electoral parties" (Fegan 2000, 337).

41. Among the positive achievements is a nationwide conditional cash transfer program for poor families whose implementation is designed to bypass local (clientelist) politicians.

42. Duterte has a history of strategic alliances with the CPP-NPA during the time he was mayor of Davao City on the southern island of Mindanao, where the revolutionary movement was particularly strong. The CPP-NPA and allied above-ground organizations were supportive of his presidential election campaign in 2016 for his initially "socialist" electoral program. When Duterte proclaimed an all-out war against the CPP-NPA in 2017 and a cessation of peace negotiations, this was followed by intensified counter-insurgency activities but also by a new government amnesty program for CPP-NPA cadres (Ebreo 2018, Gonzales 2019).

43. Since 1998, twenty percent of the seats in the Philippine House of Representatives are reserved for so-called party-list representatives who initially were meant to represent the marginalized and unrepresented sectors in Philippine society (this criterion was abandoned in 2002). They are elected nationwide on the basis of proportional representation, in contrast to the other representatives who are elected on a district-based, winner-take-all principle.

44. In another case, several former RPA-ABB members in northern Negros Occidental were accused by radical left-wing activists of participating in the private army of a local landed political clan implicated in the 2018 murder of plantation workers who were claiming land under the land reform program (Gamil 2018).

References

Abinales, Patricio N. 1998. "State Building, Communist Insurgency and Cacique Politics in the Philippines." In *Images of State Power: Essays on Philippine*

Politics from the Margins, ed. Patricio N. Abinales, 137–65. Quezon City: University of the Philippines Press.

Abinales, Patricio N., ed. 1996. *The Revolution Falters: The Left in Philippine Politics After 1986*. Ithaca, NY: Cornell University Southeast Asia Program.

AFP-Negros News and Features (published by the Armed Forces of the Philippines, Bacolod City), July 8, 1992.

Aguilar, Delia D. 2001. "Revisiting Vicvic: Of Widows and Revolution." *Against the Current*. www.igc.org/solidarity/atc/91Delia.html.

Aguilar, Filomeno V., Jr. 1998. *Clash of Spirits: The History of Power and Sugar Planter Hegemony on a Visayan Island*. Honolulu: University of Hawai'i Press.

Bayoran, Gilbert. 2017. "Army Hopes Peace in NIR to Last Long." *The Visayan Daily Star*, 9 January. http://www.visayandailystar.com/2017/January/09/topstory6.htm.

Berlow, Alan. 1996. *Dead Season: A Story of Murder and Revenge on the Philippine Island of Negros*. New York: Pantheon.

Billig, Michael S. 2003. *Barono, Brokers and Buyers: The Institutions and Cultures of Philippine Sugar*. Quezon City: Ateneo de Manila University Press.

Boudreau, Vincent G. 1996. "Of Motorcades and Masses: Mobilization and Innovation in Philippine Protest." In *The Revolution Falters: The Left in Philippine Politics After 1986*, ed. Patricio N. Abinales, 60–82. Ithaca, NY: Cornell University Southeast Asia Program.

———. 2001. *Grass Roots and Cadre in the Protest Movement*. Quezon City: Ateneo de Manila University Press.

Caouette, Dominique. 2015. "Ups and Downs of a Contemporary Maoist Movement: Shifting Tactics, Moving Targets and (Un)Orthodox Strategy, the Philippine Revolution in Perspective." In *Emancipatory Politics: A Critique*, eds. Stephan Feuchtwang and Alpa Shah, 133–67. Open Anthropology Cooperative Press. http://openanthcoop.net/press/emancipatory-politics-a-critique/.

Chapman, William. 1987. *Inside the Philippine Revolution*. New York: W. W. Norton.

Coronel, Miguel G. 1991. *Pro-Democracy People's War*. Quezon City: Vanmarc Ventures.

Coronel, Sheila S., and Jose F. Lacaba, eds. 1995. *Boss: 5 Case Studies of Local Politics in the Philippines*. Manila: Philippine Center for Investigative Journalism.

Da-anoy Satake, Mary Angeline. 2001. *Sugar Industry Workers and Insurgency: The Case of Victorias-Manapla*. Bacolod City: Southeast Asia Centre for Resource Studies Consultancy and Training (SEACREST).

Dalisay, Jose Y. 1999. *The Lavas: A Filipino Family*. Pasig: Anvil Publishing.

Duñgo, Nanette G. 1993. "Changing Social Relations in the Negros Sugar Plantation." PhD thesis, University of the Philippines.

Ebreo, Benjamin Moses E. 2018. "Army Eyes More Rebels Joining Govt. Amnesty Program." *Philippine Information Agency*, August 9, 2018. https://pia.gov.ph/news/articles/1011365.

Fegan, Brian. 2000. "Dionisio Macapagal: A Rebel Matures." In *Lives at the Margin*, ed. Alfred W. Mc Coy, 337–88. Quezon City: Ateneo de Manila University Press.

Franco, Jennifer Conroy. 2000. *Campaigning for Democracy: Grassroots Citizenship Movements, Less-Than-Democratic Elections, and Regime Transitions in the Philippines*. Quezon City: Institute for Popular Democracy.

Gamil, Jaymee T. 2018. "Massacre Blamed on Private Army." *Philippine Daily Inquirer*, October 27. https://newsinfo.inquirer.net/1047277/massacre-blamed-on-private-army

Goldstone, Jack A., and Doug McAdam. 2001. "Contention in Demographic and Life-Course Context." In *Silence and Voice in the Study of Contentious Politics*, eds. Ronald R. Aminzade et al., 195–221. Cambridge: Cambridge University Press.

Gomez, Carla. 2016. "Negros Rebel Priest Surfaces After 30 Years." *Philippine Daily Inquirer*, 24 December. http://newsinfo.inquirer.net/856131/negros-rebel-priest-surfaces-after-30-yrs#ixzz4Thj5ZEqN.

Gonzales, Cathrine. 2019. "DILG: More Than 1,000 Red Surrenderees Given Financial Aid." *Philippine Daily Inquirer*, January 11. https://newsinfo.inquirer.net/1071998/dilg-more-than-1000-red-surrenderees-given-financial-aid.

Guanzon, Zyra Joy. 1999. "Altered Alter Trade of the Visayas." *The Visayan Free Press* 1(1): 17, 22.

Hedman, Eva-Lotta E. 2000. "*Trasformismo* and Philippine Democracy." In *Philippine Politics and Society in the Twentieth Century: Colonial Legacies, Post-Colonial Trajectories*, eds. Eva-Lotta E. Hedman, and John T. Sidel, 13–35. London: Routledge.

Jiang, Yarong, and David Ashley. 2000. *Mao's Children in the New China: Voices from the Red Guards*. New York: Routledge.

Jones, Gregg R. 1989. *Red Revolution: Inside the Philippine Guerrilla Movement*. Boulder, CO: Westview Press.

Kerkvliet, Benedict J. 1974. "Agrarian Conditions Since the Huk Rebellion: A Barrio in Central Luzon." In *Political Change in the Philippines: Studies of Local Politics Preceding Martial Law*, ed. Benedict J. Kerkvliet, 1–76. Honolulu: University of Hawai'i Press.

———. 1977. *The Huk Rebellion: A Study of Peasant Revolt in the Philippines*. Berkeley, CA: University of California Press.

———. 1990. *Everyday Politics in the Philippines: Class and Status Relations in a Central Luzon Village*. Berkeley, CA: University of California Press.

———. 1996. "Contemporary Philippine Leftist Politics in Historical Perspective." In *The Revolution Falters: The Left in Philippine Politics After 1986*, ed. Patricio N. Abinales, 9–27. Ithaca, NY: Cornell University Southeast Asia Program.

Koliopoulos, John S. 1987. *Brigands with a Cause: Brigandage and Irredentism in Modern Greece 1821–1912*. Oxford: Clarendon Press.

Lachica, Eduardo. 1971. *Huk: Philippine Agrarian Society in Revolt*. Manila: Solidaridad Publishing House.

Lanzona, Vina A. 2000. "Romancing a Revolutionary: The Life of Celia Mariano-Pomeroy." In *Lives at the Margin: Biography of Filipinos Obscure, Ordinary, and Heroic*, ed. Alfred W. McCoy, 229–78. Quezon City: Ateneo de Manila University Press.

Larkin, John A. 1993. *Sugar and the Origins of Modern Philippine Society*. Berkeley, CA: University of California Press.

Manila Times, March 3, 2001; March 5, 2001; April 11, 2001.

McAdam, Doug. 1988. *Freedom Summer.* New York: Oxford University Press.

McBeth, John. 1993. "Internal Contradictions: Support for Communists Wanes as Party Splits." *Far Eastern Economic Review*, August 26.

McCoy, Alfred W. 1984. *Priests on Trial.* Ringwood, Victoria: Penguin Books Australia.

———. 1991. "The Restoration of Planter Power in La Carlota City." In *From Marcos to Aquino: Local Perspectives on Political Transition in the Philippines*, eds. Benedict J. Kerkvliet and Resil B. Mojares, 105–42. Quezon City: Ateneo de Manila University Press.

McCoy, Alfred W., ed. 1993. *An Anarchy of Families: State and Family in the Philippines.* Madison: University of Wisconsin Center for Southeast Asian Studies.

McCoy, Alfred W. 2000. *Lives at the Margin: Biography of Filipinos Obscure, Ordinary, and Heroic.* Quezon City: Ateneo de Manila University Press.

Parreño, Earl G. 2001. "Negros and the Cojuangcos." *Philippine Daily Inquirer*, May 3.

Philippine Daily Inquirer (PDI), January 7, 2001; February 1, 2001; February 27, 2001; March 29, 2001; April 3, 2001; April 28, 2001; May 3, 2001; May 11, 2001; June 14, 2001; June 17, 2001; July 25, 2001; December 6, 2001.

Philippine News Agency (PNA) e-mail news list *Balita News*, December 27, 1998.

Putzel, James. 1998. "Non-Governmental Organizations and Rural Poverty." In *Organizing for Democracy: NGOs, Civil Society and the Philippine State*, eds. Sidney G. Silliman and Lela Garner Noble, 77–112. Honolulu: University of Hawai'i Press and Quezon City: Ateneo de Manila University Press.

Quimpo, Nathan Gilbert. 2018. "The Left: Struggling to Make a Comeback." In *Routledge Handbook of the Contemporary Philippines*, eds. Mark R. Thompson and Eric Vincent C. Batalla, 396–404. Routledge.

Quimpo, Susan F. and Nathan Gilbert Quimpo. 2012. *Subversive Lives: A Family Memoir of the Marcos Years.* Manila: Anvil Publishing.

Reid, Ben. 2018. "Crossovers Double-Crossed: NGOs, Semi-clientelism and Political Reform." In *Routledge Handbook of the Contemporary Philippines*, eds. Mark R. Thompson and Eric Vincent C. Batalla, 386–95. New York: Routledge.

Rocamora, Joel. 1994. *Breaking Through: The Struggle Within the Communist Party of the Philippines.* Manila: Anvil Publishing.

Rutten, Rosanne. 1996. "Popular Support for the Revolutionary Movement CPP-NPA: Experiences in a Plantation in Negros Occidental, 1978–1995." In *The Revolution Falters: The Left in Philippine Politics After 1986*, ed. Patricio N. Abinales, 110–53. Ithaca, NY: Cornell University Southeast Asia Program.

———. 2000a. "Changing Sides in Revolutionary Times: The Career of a Lower-Class CPPNPA Leader in Negros Occidental." In *Lives at the Margin: Biography of Filipinos Obscure, Ordinary, and Heroic*, ed. Alfred W. McCoy, 423–68. Quezon City: Ateneo de Manila University Press.

Rutten, Rosanne. 2000b. "High-Cost Activism and the Worker Household: Interests, Commitment, and the Costs of Revolutionary Activism in a Philippine Plantation Region." *Theory and Society* 29: 215–52.

———. 2008. "Regional Dynamics: Rise and Decline of the CPP-NPA in Negros Occidental." In *Brokering a Revolution: Cadres in a Philippine Insurgency*, ed. Rosanne Rutten, 280–347. Quezon City: Ateneo de Manila University Press.

Sidel, John T. 1999. *Capital, Coercion, and Crime: Bossism in the Philippines.* Stanford, CA: Stanford University Press.

Silliman, Sidney, and Lela Garner Noble, eds. 1998. *Organizing for Democracy: NGOs, Civil Society, and the Philippine State.* Honolulu: University of Hawai'i Press.

Starn, Orin. 1998. "Villagers at Arms: War and Counterrevolution in the Central-South Andes." In *Shining and Other Paths: War and Society in Peru, 1980–1995*, ed. Steve J. Stern, 224–57. Dunham: Duke University Press.

Stinus-Cabugon, Marit. 2017. "The RPA-ABB: Whatever Happened to the 2000 Peace Agreement?" *Manila Times*, October 9. https://www.manilatimes.net/rpa-abb-whatever-happened-2000-peace-agreement/355371/.

SunStar Bacolod, March 20, 2001; October 30, 2001; July 19, 2003; December 12, 2018.

Tarrow, Sidney. 1996. "Social Movements in Contentious Politics: A Review Article." *American Political Science Review* 90: 874–83.

Task Force Detainees of the Philippines (TFDP)-Negros. 1988. *Vigilantism in Negros.* Bacolod City: TFDP-Negros.

Thompson, Mark P. 1998. "The Decline of Philippine Communism: A Review Essay." *South East Asia Research* 6: 105–29.

Uma Pilipinas. 2017. "More Peasant Killings Surface as Slain Farmworkers' Leader Buried in Negros." February 2, 2017. https://umapilipinas.wordpress.com/tag/negros-occidental/.

van den Muijzenberg, Otto D. 1973. "Political Mobilization and Violence in Central Luzon (Philippines)." *Modern Asian Studies* 7: 691–705.

Weekley, Kathleen. 1996. "From Vanguard to Rearguard: The Theoretical Roots of the Crisis in the Communist Party of the Philippines." In *The Revolution Falters: The Left in Philippine Politics After 1986*, ed. Patricio N. Abinales, 28–59. Ithaca, NY: Cornell University Southeast Asia Program.

———. 2001. *The Communist Party of the Philippines 1968–1993: A Story of Its Theory and Practice.* Quezon City: University of the Philippines Press.

Wurfel, David. 1988. *Filipino Politics: Development and Decay.* Quezon City: Ateneo de Manila University Press.

CHAPTER 12

From Cassette to Video CD: A Shan Army Musical Band in the Transnational Space of the Thailand-Burma Border

Amporn Jirattikorn

The Shan armed struggle against the Burmese government has been waged for more than seven decades, from the time the country gained independence from the United Kingdom in 1948 to the present. It is one of the longest ethno-nationalist movements in the history of Burma. Armed insurgency by the Shan, at independence among the largest ethnic groups in Burma, and other minorities stemmed largely from their dissatisfaction at being unfairly excluded from the newly formed post-independence government. Failing to receive the promised option of splitting from Burma a decade after independence if they were dissatisfied with the central government, an armed resistance movement was started in Shan State in 1958. Since then, the Shan armed struggle has attracted considerable attention because of the serious nature of Shan ethnic grievances, the multiplicity of Shan armed groups, and the political economy of a war involving the narcotic trade that has sustained the insurgency for many decades. However, the history of Shan armed resistance from the perspective of those who fought the war, many out of deep ideological conviction, others motivated by pragmatic reasons, and those who were affected by it, has received little scholarly attention.

This chapter sketches the lives of several individuals who formed Jerng Laew (Freedom Way), a Shan army music band, and the roles the members played in serving Shan ethno-nationalist sentiments with their songs. It covers the period from the mid-1980s, when Freedom Way was formed, to about 2006 when the Shan armed organization which the band members joined was relocated to the Thailand-Burma border. Throughout several decades of fighting, these individuals joined multiple armed forces and produced many musical albums. Not only do their rich personal experiences offer a rare insight into the nature of the Shan armed revolt and the social dynamics of Thailand-Burma border areas where the conflict was focused, but their songs also reflect the evolution of the Shan-Burmese relationship and the socio-political changes within the period. Their stories as well as their music have played out within, between, and across two national boundaries and against the backdrop of the rapidly changing political, technological, and demographic situation in Burma.

This chapter has two main purposes. First, an examination of the lives of Freedom Way members sheds light on the emergence of Shan nationalism "from below." Literature on nationalism claims that elites commonly create popular nationalism (Whitmayer 2002). Like any rise in nationalism, the question of how ordinary Shan soldiers came to imagine a Shan "nation" goes hand in hand with the question of whether "nation" is a way for certain elites to manipulate mass sentiments for their own ends. In many cases, ethno-nationalist movements emerge not out of mere manipulation but also the ability of revolutionary elites to connect with the concrete aspirations of the local populations in whose culture these elites are firmly embedded. In other cases, alliances between elites and the subordinate sector also stem from grievances the elites and the populace share. The concept of the Shan nation from the followers' perspective cannot be understood in isolation from leaders' efforts to unite people on economic and ideological grounds. My aim in analyzing these stories is to shed light on the formation of Shan nationalist consciousness in relation to the notion of youth and the idea of the revolutionary.

Second, the chapter examines a new phase of the Shan armed struggle in relation to the shift in Shan demography. Since the mid-1990s, the mass migration of Shans into northern Thailand has resulted in a demographic shift in the Shan population. This, in turn, has influenced the politics of the Shan armed struggle. From the 2000s onwards, there have been attempts by Shan armed organizations to reach out to the Shan migrant population in Thailand through various means, including the use of mass media and the deployment of cross-border insurgency networks. These have, in effect, transformed the Shan armed struggle from a local movement confined to fighting with the Burmese army to a larger movement with a Thai and Shan migrant audience. In trying to understand the role of transnational insurgency networks, the chapter also highlights the difference between the Shan diaspora and economic migrants. In contrast to economic migrants, whose reason for migration is indeed purely economic, the Shan diaspora is comprised of current or former militants, exiled activists, and other intellectuals who feel obliged to maintain links with their homeland's politics. Freedom Way's members who work in tandem with the Shan insurgency in order to draw support from the migrant population exemplify a particular segment of the Shan diaspora.

An examination of the lives of Freedom Way band members also reveals the ways in which popular music has been employed as an effective medium to sustain the insurgency movement as well as to provide a channel for expression of ethnic discontent. Popular music, unlike "print capitalism," offers a different kind of mediator that utilizes both old and new technologies and involves a wide range of communicative means. It conveys both language and sound and utilizes audio cassettes, CDs, DVDs (or VCDs in this case), radio broadcasts, and live performances. These media each involve different levels of technology and also impose different social relations. In situating the lives of the Freedom Way band members within the mass movement of Shan peoples and rapidly changing technology, the Shan ethno-nationalist project, seen through the lens of Freedom Way, must be understood beyond the confines of Anderson's (1991) territorially bounded nationalism. It is through examining the way in which Freedom Way's members operate across the border that the chapter seeks to understand what effect the media and the border have when neither the insurgency nor the audience fits within the boundaries of the nation-state.

This chapter draws on my ethnographic research among both the Shan armed organization and the Shan migrant community in Chiang Mai, Thailand. Ethnographical data was collected during 2005–6 using textual analysis and participant observation in the process of media production and consumption. Observations took place in a variety of settings as I chatted, ate, drank, worked, and participated in festivities with my informants. I also made two short trips in February and July 2006 to the Shan State Army's headquarters where I interviewed Shan soldiers and participated in festivities with them.

The Rise of Shan Nationalism: The Politicization of Ethnicity

The year 1958 opened a new chapter in the turbulent modern history of Burma when the first Shan armed group was founded. In the decades to follow, a plethora of armed groups claiming to represent Shan nationalism emerged. Details of the development of Shan armed resistance spanning three decades of fighting since the first Shan armed group emerged in the mid-1980s when the Shan armed forces rivaled each other to dominate cross-border trade in the opium business, provide a background for the narratives of the Freedom Way's members in the following section.

Historically, the area that we call Shan State[1] today was divided into several principalities ruled by hereditary chiefs called *sawbwa* (Lord of Heaven). The Shan came under Burmese rule during the sixteenth to nineteenth centuries. After 1888, they transferred their allegiance to the British. Under British rule, Shan State remained relatively autonomous as a protectorate while "Burma proper" was incorporated into British India under direct rule (Silverstein 1958, 45–46). Taylor (1982, 8) has argued that the ways in which the British governed Shan State by allowing greater autonomy helped to separate the interests of the Shan chiefs from those of the rest of Burma, and thus contributed to the historic separatism between Shan State and Burma proper.

While it can be argued that the British practice of divide-and-rule had infused the idea of separate ethnic identity, it was only in the post-independece period that the idea of a Shan nation was fully formed. On the one hand, the idea of Shan nationhood was rooted in a "primordial" claim based on ethnic and cultural traits as well as in a political claim on an existing, well-defined autonomous territory given to the Shan States during British rule. Thus, when the Shan *sawbwa* agreed to join the Union of Burma in 1948, but gave up their rights to rule and collect taxes, ethnic grievances emerged (Silverstein 1958, 43–47). On the other hand, the very idea and consciousness of a nation was mobilized towards the end of ten years of the Panglong Agreement. The agreement signed between the Burmese leader General Aung San and other ethnic leaders in 1947 during the struggle for independence in theory granted the Shan States a secessionist right after ten years of joining the Union of Burma. The right of secession, while in principle a genuine right, is hardly exercisable in practice due to the demand for an extraordinary majority requirement of two-thirds in the State Council and a majority vote in a plebiscite (Silverstein 1958, 43–57). Towards the end of ten years of the signing of the Panglong Agreement, when many Shan felt that their right had never been recognized by the Burmese government, the first Shan armed group emerged.

Bertil Lintner (1994, 185–89) notes another factor that triggered separatist intentions. The beginning of the 1950s was the first time the Shan populace experienced the arrival of two newcomers, both of them armed. Following the victory of the People's Liberation Army of China—Mao would proclaim the People's Republic of China in October 1949—units of the retreating Kuomintang Army (KMT) started to enter northern Shan State in 1949. To counter this, the Burmese government sent troops into Shan State, extending direct central government control into many areas of the state for the first time. While the KMT invasion had brought opium business into the area, the presence of the Burmese Army (Tatmadaw) provoked resentment among people everywhere in Shan State.

Fredholm (1993, 156) mentions a third factor in the formation of the first Shan resistance group, the young university students who fled Rangoon and Mandalay for the jungle in pursuit of a nationalist ideal. Not only did these students, mobilized during the anti-Japanese resistance, try to end the Shan princes' feudal control and bring about democratic reforms, they also took up arms to fight against both the KMT and the Tatmadaw. While the Shan students were the ones who were sensitive to the cause, no Shan armed force existed at this time, and the initiative to form one did not come from the student activists in Rangoon. The first Shan armed movement was, in fact, founded by Sao Noi, an illegitimate son of a Yunnan Shan prince.

He founded Noom Suk Harn (Young Brave Warriors) on May 21, 1958 at the Thailand-Burma border with a group of thirty-one young men. A year later, the group of students mentioned above who walked down from the city to the border of Thailand-Burma joined the movement (Chao Tzang Yawnghwe 1987, 7).

The decade following the launch of the first Shan armed group saw the emergence of various other armed groups claiming to represent Shan nationalism. While it is not possible to cover the many decades of fighting in detail within the scope of this chapter, discussion about resources, internal factionalism, and external forces will be highlighted in order to shed light on the nature of the Shan armed struggle. Shan resistance during the period between the 1960s and the 1980s can be characterized by three important aspects.

First, factionalism is one of the major characteristics in the history of the Shan armed struggle. Split and merger was a common feature. For example, in 1960 Shan students had broken away from Noom Suk Harn to set up the Shan State Independence Army (SSIA). In 1961, the Shan National United Front (SNUF) was set up by a former Noom Suk Harn commander and SSIA leader. The same year saw the merger of the Shan National Army (SNA), which operated in eastern Shan State, with money from opium sold to Laos (Lintner 1994, 182). In 1964, the Shan State Army (SSA) was launched by the merging of SSIA, SNUF, and the Kokang Revolutionary Army. By the end of the twentieth century there were an estimated forty different armed forces in Shan State (McCoy 1999, 135).

Second, the narcotics trade has always been a major factor influencing the Shan struggle for independence. The reliance on the drug trade to finance Shan ethnic armies arose for several reasons. While peripheral and mountainous regions of Shan State provided good conditions for the production of opium, it was the KMT troops retreating to Shan State after their defeat to the communists in China who introduced the opium business into Shan State. Prior to the arrival of the KMT, opium had been traded as a local economy product under British colonial rule. Having gained control over the northern and eastern sections of Shan State, the major opium-producing regions, the KMT expanded their control over the opium trade. They exacted heavy taxes from opium farmers in Shan State and sold the opium in Thailand in exchange for guns and military supplies (McCoy 1991, 172–75).

The emergence of counter-insurgency also contributed to the increasing use of opium to support the armed forces. With the emergence of ethnic armed forces throughout Burma at the beginning of the 1960s, in 1962 the Rangoon government set up counter-insurgency operations in the form of independent militia units in remote areas that could not be defended by regular troops. These units were called Ka Kwe Ye, or home guard militias. Ka Kwe Ye became one of the major forces in the politics of ethnic armed struggle in Shan State for several decades. Under this counter-insurgency, any guerrilla unit which chose to become a Ka Kwe Ye on the government side would be allowed by the Burmese government to retain its arms and concessions. The survival and increased strength of these groups often depended on the transnational narcotic trade. By 1972, over 90 percent of the opium trade was in the hands of the militias on the Burmese government side (Cowell 2005, 5). The most notorious example of a Ka Kwe Ye unit was Khun Sa's militia force. Khun Sa, also known as Chang Chi-fu (1934–2007), a Chinese-Shan, eventually emerged as the most powerful of the local militia commanders. During the 1970s his unit was well equipped with modern weapons bought with opium profits on the black arms market in Thailand (Lintner 1994, 207).

The third important aspect of the Shan armed struggle for independence between the 1960s and 1980s was the multiplicity of external forces that came to influence the politics of Shan State. The Communist Party of Burma (CPB) emerged in the 1970s with the support of guns and ammunition from China. There was also the Kuomintang (KMT), backed by the CIA due to the American fear of communism, with support from Taiwan and Thailand. These external forces added complexity to the conflicts already in existence in Shan State. Within a single decade, while competing over resources in order to buy arms and ammunition, many of these groups shifted from revolutionary to home guard militia, and from negotiating with the Americans to communism (Cowell 2005, 6).

The 1970s in Shan State saw the three Shan armed forces playing different roles in relation to different external forces in the politics of the Shan struggle. The Shan State Army (SSA), founded in 1964, a seemingly true Shan nationalist force yet with little money and no foreign backing, became an ally of the Communist Party of Burma (CPB). Khun Sa, after being released from jail in Rangoon in the early 1970s, set up a new armed force in 1974, the Shan United Army (SUA). The SUA force was, in fact, dominated by ethnic Chinese opium merchants, but by adding "Shan" to the name of their army they hoped to gain favor from the closely related Thai. In the 1970s, Khun Sa's new base at Ban Hin Taek in Chiang Rai province in Thailand was developing fast. Lintner (1994, 244) notes that during that period heroin refineries were established in the mountains north of Ban Hin Taek, where uniformed SUA soldiers mingled with Thai border patrol policemen and Thai paramilitary forces. Colonel Gon Jerng, who broke with the SSA, of which he was the co-founder, set up a new force in 1969, the Shan United Revolution Army (SURA). Joining forces with General Li's third army of the KMT for protection, SURA was established at Piang Luang, a small market town on the Thai border (Smith 1999, 334). While Khun Sa's SUA dominated cross-border trade in opium, Gon Jerng's SURA allied with the KMT rivaled Khun Sa in the opium business.

In the 1980s, the Shan armed struggle shifted towards a new direction. Khun Sa's booming town at Ban Hin Taek on Thai soil began to cause the Thai government anxiety. In 1982, it was attacked before Khun Sa retreated across the border to Burma. One year later, he set up a new camp in Homong, opposite Mae Hong Son province in northwestern Thailand. SURA came under pressure from Khun Sa's SUA, which by then had overrun all the areas surrounding SURA's headquarters. In 1985, SURA agreed to merge forces with SUA. The joint force under the name Tailand Revolutionary Council/Tailand Revolutionary Army (TRC/TRA)[2] was renamed the Mong Tai Army (MTA) in 1987. Since then, it has remained entirely under the control of Khun Sa. The MTA was not only numerically strong but also heavily armed with a variety of modern arms financed by the narcotic trade (Lintner 1994, 259–64; Smith 1999, 339–44). By merging SURA and some of the SSA into the MTA, Khun Sa was able to project a pan-Shan image and foster the hope that one day he might bring independence to the Shan people.

The history of the Shan armed struggle from the mid-1980s to the mid-1990s—a decade that saw Khun Sa leading the strongest Shan insurgent group in the history of the Shan resistance—is well represented in the story of the Shan musical band Jerng Laew (Freedom Way), whose members were part of Khun Sa's MTA. Below is an account of life stories of the band members in relation to broader politics inside Burma as well as to the particularities of the struggle itself.

Freedom Way: Writing History through Music

Sai Mu[3] was born at Moeng Pan, a small town in central Shan State, in 1960. Like most Shan children growing up during that time, Sai Mu was exposed not only to small, disunited armed groups claiming to represent Shan nationalism but also "in virtually every valley and on every mountain top a different ethnic army, militia or local warlord force was fighting to gain control" (Smith 1999, 251). Sai Mu was educated in Mandalay and worked as a school teacher before going to Piang Luang in 1983 to join SURA.

At Piang Luang, Sai Mu met Sa Ka Ha, a former SSA soldier, who also joined SURA that year. Sa Ka Ha was born in 1952 in Tangyan, once a storage town for opium before it was transported to Thailand. Having run away from school to pursue his nationalist ideals, Sa Ka Ha became part of the SSA in 1973. A few years later, when the SSA force allied with the Communist Party of Burma (CPB), Sa Ka Ha, who was not convinced that he should join the communists, decided to join the right-wing SSA, which merged with SURA in 1983. Sai Lek, a Shan-Chinese, had been there for quite some time because his father was part of the KMT's third army, which had been allied with SURA since 1969. Sai Han, a son of SURA founder Gon Jerng, who left the SSA to form SURA in 1969, was sent to Chiang Mai for education, only to return to Piang Luang the same year.

When these young, educated Shans met at Piang Luang, they agreed to set up an insurgent music band, Jerng Laew (Freedom Way). Initially, the band consisted of four members: Sai Mu, lead singer and songwriter, Sai Lek, lead guitar, Sai Han, drummer, and Sa Ka Ha, bass. Other members, such as Sai Mon and San Loi, joined later. All of them were Shan except for Sai Lek who was of mixed Shan and Chinese parentage. Their role was to entertain soldiers and, in the process, foster Shan nationalist sentiment among them. With financial support from the army, Freedom Way released its first album, *Wan Tai Hao Te Lodlaew*[4] (The Day Shans are Free), in 1984. The title song, written by Sai Mu, reflects the problem which had been deeply rooted in the history of the Shan armed struggle—unity or the lack of it.

Wan Tai Hao Te Lodlaew (The Day Shans are Free)

If you wish to be rich,
If you want to reach nirvana, what will you do?
Longing for the day Shans embrace each other,
Yearning for the day Shans join hands with each other.
We live in the same house, eating from the same rice bowl,
the Shan motherland is now imprisoned,
Brothers still fight each other, it's a shame.
Brothers make war, others are happy.
The day Shans join together, we shall be independent.
The day we are united, the day we are free.
Let the Salween River be our proof, we shall make history.
So that the next generation will know we turned the page of history.
Our Shan motherland is now being imprisoned,
I am longing for the day Shans are united.
The day Shans join together, we shall be independent.
The day we are united, we shall be free.

(written by Sai Mu, 1984; my translation)

Wan Tai Hao Te Lodlaew metaphorically refers to several armed groups claiming to represent Shan nationalism and calls for unity among them. In the following year, after the first album came out, the SURA force merged with Khun Sa's SUA. It seemed then that the band's call for unity had been realized. The reason behind this merger was not only for the sake of unity but, rather, that SURA found itself overrun by Khun Sa's troops and blocked from bringing in supplies to their headquarters. While the insurgent politics along the border seemed to be moving in a new direction as the two strongest forces agreed to merge and fight together, inside Burma Ne Win and his socialist government plunged the whole country into chaos. In 1985, the government announced the demonetization of fifty and hundred kyat banknotes. Each family was given compensation up to five thousand kyat regardless of how many fifty and hundred kyat banknotes they had. Jerng Laew then released its second album, *Ne Win Jone Kap Joy* (Ne Win is Stealing People's Money). While condemning Ne Win as evil, *Ne Win Jone Kap Joy* tells how the demonetization policy had a crucial impact on every level of Burmese society.

Ne Win Jone Kap Joy (Ne Win is Stealing People's Money)

Because of the hundred kyat banknotes, people's tears drop
Ne Win just cancelled them, with little compensation
Oh Dear, Ne Win is so evil
Who would dare to argue with this devil?
No full compensation, except five thousand kyat
Even the rich cried,
The poor were broken, laborers suffered
Socialist is in fact *sot-sat-lit*[5](corruption).

(written by Sai Mu, 1985, my translation)

Although Freedom Way's albums were not produced for commercial purposes, a thousand copies of each album were sold due to the demand for political songs inside Burma. The fact that the members of the band lived along the border area and were under the umbrella of the insurgency enabled them to produce songs that served as an expression of socio-political discontent which was otherwise almost non-existent inside Burma because of governmental censorship. And while Shan retailers inside Burma had to sell the albums secretly due to the political content of the songs, this secret business also allowed them to freely copy the albums. Thus, even though their albums were produced in small numbers, the songs were disseminated widely through illicit channels.

In 1987, while power politics inside the group took a new turn as the combined forces (Gon Jerng's SURA and Khun Sa's SUA) were renamed the Mong Tai Army and came under the complete control of Khun Sa, Freedom Way released its third album titled *Khao San Ka Ik Kap 75* (Expensive Rice and the 75 Kyat Banknote). This, of course, referred to events in the year the Ne Win government demonetized the 25, 35, and 75 kyat banknotes with no prior warning. This time, no compensation was offered to banknote holders, rendering some 75 percent of the country's currency worthless. *Khao San Ka Ik Kap 75* condemned the demonetization that caused everything to increase in price until people could not afford to even buy rice. A further sudden demonetization of all large denomination notes in 1987 caused widespread dissatisfaction, which turned into unrest and contributed to the political upheaval in 1988 which ended Ne Win's 25-year single-party rule. After mass protests against Ne Win's regime ended in bloodshed, the student activists fled Burma's interior for the border areas where ethnic insurgents were encamped. A spokesman for Khun Sa then came out to say that "Khun Sa was against an armed struggle with the Rangoon regime and that students should drop their campaign" (*Bangkok Post,* December 18, 1988). Suspicions that Khun Sa had a tacit agreement with the military authorities in Rangoon grew stronger (Lintner 1990, 159).

Inside the MTA itself, Freedom Way faced a similar dilemma when Khun Sa criticized the band for being too political and too critical. Freedom Way produced its fourth album, *Kang Jai Kor Luk Fuen* (The Hearts of Revolutionaries) in 1989 before Khun Sa withdrew his financial support and the band members dispersed. Sai Lek was assigned a position as a military trainer, which took him to Homong, Khun Sa's new camp on the Burmese side of the border opposite Mae Hong Son province, where the MTA's headquarters were located. Remaining at Piang Luang, Sai Mu took up a position as headmaster for the Shan middle school in the village. Sa Ka Ha, since joining SURA, had been assigned the task of public relations for the army. He was relocated to Homong to work closely with Khun Sa. The printing house, which initially was set up under the SURA fund, located at SURA's headquarters at Piang Luang, was also moved there. Sai Han remained at Piang Luang attending to his sick father, Gon Jerng, who had lost all his power to Khun Sa only to die two years later.

"The Hearts of Revolutionaries," the title track of Freedom Way's fourth album, tells of a Shan soldier who endures hardship in the jungle, only wishing that when he comes back from the battle his lover will still be waiting for him. For young revolutionaries like members of the Freedom Way band, first and foremost in their hearts and minds was the fight for national liberation, for Shan autonomy. They looked outward, confronting the Burmese regime wholeheartedly. They may or may not have known that what was dominating their leader's mind was his lucrative business. They were willing, however, to fight for the army since they believed that Khun Sa could eventually liberate Shan State.

Yet, it is just as difficult to maintain a single political objective within a band as it is within a larger organization. In 1992, Sai Mu left the MTA to join the SSA-Northern Command, which had signed a ceasefire agreement with the Burmese government in 1989. Between 1991 and 1994 Sai Mu financed and released another four albums under the Freedom Way name. While Khun Sa's MTA was enjoying a heyday with the narcotic trade, the rest of Freedom Way's members who remained with the MTA did not produce another album until several years later.

It was not until 1995 that Sai Lek, Sai Han, Sa Ka Ha, Sai Mon, and San Loi, another singer, released a new album. This ninth album, entitled *Haw Luang Kengtung* (Kengtung Palace), voiced resentment at the destruction of the symbolically important Kengtung Palace. The palace had served as the administrative center of the Kengtung *sawbwa*, one of thirty-three former

Shan principalities, until Shan *sawbwa* relinquished their powers in 1959. The palace then became the property of the Rangoon government. In 1991, the Burmese government had announced a plan to demolish Kengtung palace and to build a major hotel for tourism on the site. Despite local protest, the palace was demolished the same year.

Haw Luang Kengtung (Kengtung Palace)

Hundreds of years ago, it was built by our ancestors.
We never imagined, it would be gone forever.
Kengtung Palace, it's a shame!
Where have all the owners gone?
Aren't they humiliated that their history is being erased?
We, the people, feel ashamed for them.
We are furious!
Where are all the guardians who used to protect this city?
Hopeless! Monks and people who try to stop them [the regime].
We must fight with guns and swords, only then will we gain it back.
An earthquake might take only one person.
But when people devour other people, the whole race is wiped out.
Our grief shall never be forgotten, and we shall make our history.

(written by San Loi, 1995; my translation)

Soon after this album came out, in December 1995, Sai Mu died at the age of thirty-five.[6] Less than two weeks later, in January 1996, Khun Sa shocked his army by surrendering his arms and men to the Burmese regime in exchange for the Burmese government's guarantee of protection while living a life of luxury in Rangoon. Sai Lek insisted on continuing the fight, and walked through the jungle to find his new leader, Yawd Surk, who at that time was operating his battalion inside Shan State. Sai Han remained at Piang Luang, waiting for the new Shan armed group to come. Sa Ka Ha decided to settle down in Chiang Mai and to establish an independent Shan news agency which, in his view, should not be associated with any armed force.

The members of Freedom Way, as well as the Shan insurgency movement, were taking a break before proceeding to a new phase in the decade ahead.

In tracing the lives of Freedom Way's members, we can see that it was a guerrilla unit, which university students fled the town to join in the fight for national self-determination and Shan independence. They became cultural units, taking on the task of feeding those Shan guerrillas a pinch of nationalist sentiment with their songs. But what they themselves had experienced were the realities of warfare, their dependence on narcotic taxes, and their loyalty to leaders. The ambiguous, not clearly defined nationalism in which profits and personal power were much more important than Shan independence drove some of them away while others remained with their revolutionary dreams. In a single decade, the group they joined had passed from militia, to revolutionaries, to traitors negotiating with the Rangoon government. Shans may find it hard to accept this ugly history, and from outside observation we may begin to criticize the Shan as too unpredictable to take seriously. Yet, what this history of warfare reveals is the reality of opportunistic, personal power whose sacrifices have always been young, pure-hearted revolutionaries.

The Shan State Army: Relocating the Insurgency

If January 1996 marked a turning point in the history of the Shan armed struggle when Khun Sa, whose powerful forces had fostered hope of Shan independence, decided to surrender to the Burmese army, January 2006 was significant for a rather different reason. It marked the tenth anniversary of the Shan State Army-South (SSA-S)'s refusal to accept Khun Sa's surrender to the Burmese regime. The SSA-S was, in fact, a 1996 creation of splinter groups of Khun Sa's MTA. They immediately declared their intention to continue fighting against the central government after their leader's surrender (International Crisis Group [hereafter ICG] 2003). A year before Khun Sa surrendered, the Shan State National Army (SSNA), led by Gan Yod, left the MTA. The SSNA, formed in 1995, immediately signed a ceasefire agreement with Rangoon (Ball and Lang 2001, 8). Another group operating in northern

Shan State, the Shan State Army-North (SSA-N, sometime referred to as the SSA), also signed a ceasefire agreement in 1989 (Tucker 2001, 177).

Fig. 1. After relocating to near the Thai border, the SSA-S began to organize events to celebrate the long-standing fight for Shan autonomy. These have drawn a large number of attendants from both sides of the border

Colonel Yawd Surk, once a lieutenant of Khun Sa, wrote in his diary, which was published in January 2006 to mark the tenth anniversary of non-submission to Burmese rule, gave as a reason the proliferation of Shan armed organizations after Khun Sa surrendered. It was well known, in fact, that Khun Sa had given up his ten thousand-strong army in exchange for a luxurious life under the protection of the Rangoon government. Yawd Surk and the three hundred men in his battalion vowed they would never give up fighting for Shan independence. In March 1996, Yawd Surk held a meeting with the other two ceasefire groups, the SSA-N and the SSNA, in which they agreed to combine forces under the common designation of the Shan State Army. This combined force appealed to Rangoon for official recognition and proposed a ceasefire agreement for Yawd Surk's newly formed group, which had yet to make contact with the junta. It was turned down by the military, which then resumed its offensive against the group. After failed negotiations, Yawd Surk was left with no choice but to continue fighting against the government. He then adopted the name Shan State Army-South (SSA-North) for his group. "South" was added to avoid confusion with SSA-North, the group which had agreed to a ceasefire (Yawd Surk 2006).

In 1999, after it became clear that the SSA-S would have to fight the Burmese Armed Forces (Tatmadaw) alone, it relocated close to the Thai border, establishing a stronghold on top of Loi Tailang. Although this mountain is situated in Burmese territory, the SSA-S built an unpaved road connecting it with Thailand. This move was a geopolitical one. In his diary, Yawd Surk outlined three important factors that led him to locate close to the Thai border. First, he anticipated that his insurgency group would increasingly have to make contact with the international community, and thus he required a location that was easily accessible to the outside world. Second, over the past few years, many Shan orphans and displaced villagers had been displaced under the Burmese army's forced relocation program and the SSA wanted to help them find shelter. Third, the Shan insurgency was often wrongly accused of being a drug army but, in fact, it wanted to move to a new phase of ethnic insurgency that waged war against drugs. In addition, Thailand was seen by the group as a gateway to international media and public awareness (Yawd Surk 2006). Beside these three official reasons, proximity to the Thai border provided unofficial benefits to the Shan insurgency, facilitating support from Thai military commanders and units, having access to markets inside Thailand, and, in particular, receiving revenue from taxed goods crossing the border from insurgent-controlled areas. As Yawd Surk stated in an interview when asked how his army got financial support: "We survive on taxes levied on the cross-border trade in contraband from Thailand to Burma and vice-versa" (*Salween Post*, 2005, p. 10).

The relocation of the group was followed by the creation of the Restoration Council of the Shan State (RCSS), a civilian organization charged with overseeing non-military and political operations on behalf of the SSA-S. The RCSS, which is still in operation, is in charge of all non-military activities, including (1) setting up a refugee camp for Shan orphans and displaced villagers who were affected by the forced relocation program; (2) producing an SSA-S newsletter and website www.taifreedom.com; and (3) conducting public relations and maintaining contact with the international community (Yawd Surk 2006). This meant that international politics could play a leading role in the Shan struggle. In this spirit, close association with Thai society was considered important in order to facilitate the SSA-S's goal to fight the Burmese army.

While Thailand's national security has shifted in a new direction, the Burmese regime, in its attempts to wage war on drugs, has resorted to its old tactics. On the one hand, the regime has taken to naturalizing one group in order to have it fight against another. Since 1997, it is known that the Burmese government is using the UWSA, which has signed a ceasefire agreement with Burma and has agreed to become a government militia force to counterbalance the Shan rebels (ICG 2003). Hence, instead of waging war with Burmese troops, the SSA-S has fought with the UWSA. The offensives that occurred in 2002 and 2005 along the border area appeared to be Shan insurgents fighting with the UWSA, whereas the Burmese troops were not directly involved in the battle (Black and Fields 2006). On the other hand, the Burmese regime deployed the tactic of making support for insurgents too heavy a burden for its population by introducing a forced relocation program and a "four-cut policy"[7] (Coster 2007; Shan Human Rights Foundation [SHRF] and Shan Woman's Action Network [SWAN] 2002).

The four-cut policy and the forced relocation program have had a tremendous impact on the movement of Shan migration. Since March 1996, when the Burmese military regime began to forcibly relocate over 1,400 villages throughout central Shan State, thousands of Shan people have fled to Thailand. During 1996 and 1997 it is estimated that over 80 thousand Shan people arrived in Thailand as a result of forced relocation. The more the relocation intensified, the greater the number of Shans arriving in Thailand. Statistics indicate that a large number of the new arrivals were under eighteen years of age (SWAN 2003, 6). These are Shan children who have grown up in Thailand in the last twenty years, and hence have supplemented Thailand's labor force. The above contexts provide the background against which the lives of Freedom Way's members reconnected. This time, however, their paths crossed under the context of a new insurgency, a transnational one.

Sai Lek, who remained with the Shan State Army, the SSA-S, has been in charge of training new recruits since 1996 and most of the time is based in Loi Tailang, SSA-S's headquarters. After Khun Sa's surrender, Sai Han settled down in Chiang Mai, only to rejoin the army again after the SSA-S had moved to Loi Tailang. From his base in Chiang Mai, he has been assigned a job in public relations along with Sai Mon, whose task is to open lines of communication with the Thai. As times changed, the new generation of armed insurgents changed as well, with revolutionaries suddenly appearing in the city.

While his fellow band members remained attached to the insurgency, Sa Ka Ha, in contrast, settled down in Chiang Mai and decided to become independent. In seeking his own way to establish Shan media in exile, he and his senior colleague, Khuensai, once a spokesman and political advisor for Khun Sa, set up a news agency with the same name as the one they both used to work for under Khun Sa's sponsorship, the Shan Herald Agency for News (SHAN). No longer a propaganda agency whose task was supporting and cheerleading for its military leader, they sought international funding and aimed to be independent. This is, however, not a clear-cut business, as individual nationalist objectives often coincide with group ideology. While Sa Ka Ha intended to distance himself from any political or armed group, he has always been an active supporter of the SSA-S in terms of both giving advice to SSA-S leaders and reporting news in the SHAN newsletter about the Shan State Army's activities. SHAN, which has its own website (www.shanland.org) and circulates news in Shan and English concerning Shan issues via e-mail, has become the site where all official SSA statements, memoranda, and proclamations are circulated. In 2000, after the SSA-S relocated to Loi Tailang, Yawd Surk formed an SSA advisory board whose members included Sa Ka Ha and Khuensai. These two individuals served both as members of the advisory board for the SSA-S while also working for the Shan news agency in Chiang Mai, and have become the chief architects of SSA-S publicity and propaganda.

The Migrants, the Diasporas, and the Insurgency

With the increasing porosity of the borders and the attempt to construct a new phase of Shan insurgency, since the mid-1990s Thailand began to experience a massive flow of Shans coming from Burma to perform migrant labor. These migrants provide low-paying services for everything from construction work to serving as housemaids, and from food vendors to market sellers. What emerged from this new influx are the two newly formed categories of Shan living in Thailand—the diaspora and the migrants.

The Shan diaspora is defined as those who will continue to dwell in a host nation but for whom the mythical homeland is more important than the host nation or the current homeland (Kearney 1995; Safran 1991; Sheffer 1986). They differ from the recent migrant population who were forced to leave their homeland because of political conflict rather than economic need. They had been in Thailand for quite some time before the influx of large numbers of Shan migrants began to arrive. Some managed to acquire Thai citizenship and married Thais. Some ran their own businesses. By definition, they already possessed factors necessary for mobilization: a shared identity, common grievances, and symbolic resources. They had left home for good, yet they nurtured a common desire to create a sovereign state, a nation-state yet to be. Freedom Way's members exemplify this type of Shan diaspora.

In contrast, Shan migrants who arrived in Thailand from the mid-1990s are young, struggling to survive, and driven by economic need. Most of the money they earn is sent to family members back home. As the mass migration of Shans across the border is increasing every year, this demographic change, in turn, influences insurgency politics in the homeland. Only a few years earlier, the SSA-S was still looking for new recruits from Shan State. As the 1999 SSA-S annual meeting report stated, one of the SSA-S's plans was to seek new recruits among young Shan men inside Burma (Yawd Surk 2006). In 2007, the SSA-S commander had come to terms with the fact that perhaps half of the young Shan population was now living in Thailand. He had stated that he wanted "his people [now living in Thailand] to come back to Burma to help him fight for independence" (Coster 2007).

It can be argued that the Shan insurgency today has strived to cross the border in response to the shift in population. This is a peculiar cross-border exchange, whereby the insurgency and the Shan diaspora work in tandem, on the one hand drawing support from the Thai and on the other winning the hearts and minds of the migrant population. In what follows, I attempt to show that not only does the diaspora sustain the insurgency campaign but it has also brought the insurgency into closer contact with migrant populations.

Along with self-representation as anti-drug fighters, cultural productions play an important part in SSA-S politics. Moving away from drug resources which had previously empowered the insurgency, the Shan insurgency began to rely heavily on media and cultural products as a new resource to propagate the new imaginative idea. Again, there is nothing new about insurgencies making use of media. Most insurgencies operate their organizations in a way that resembles a nation-state. In other words, they form a "shadow state" with military and political wings as well as public relations and media departments. While the Shan insurgency utilized mass media to draw attention to the plight of Shan people for decades, what is new about the Shan insurgency's involvement in mass media from the mid-2000s are the transnational characteristics of the movement, as they target both the Shan migrant community and the Thai, both of whom are located beyond their immediate territory.

SSA-S's public relations with the Thai media cover a wide range of forms and practitioners, from print media to pop music and film and from singers to journalists and film producers. Of the many Shan sympathizers, "Ad" Carabao provides an extreme version of support for the movement. "Ad," or Yuenyong Ophakul, is lead singer of the Thai folk-rock band Carabao. Because of his involvement with social justice and his role as social critic, SSA-S found a perfect supporter. In May 2001, Yawd Surk invited Ad Carabao to visit Loi Tailang. Ad was inspired to write music about the Shan after his visit. He said he started researching the long history of the Shans' fight after returning to Thailand. He found that the Shan and the Thai share the same origins (Yuenyong 2002). A year later, he came up with an album called *Mai Tong Rong Hai* (Don't Cry), devoted to the Shan struggle for independence. Ad Carabao uses Bob Marley's reggae rhythms with his own lyrics to justify the struggle because he himself believes that the Shan have been wrongfully treated by the Burmese regime.

Fig. 2. Ad Carabao's album *Mai Tong Rong Hai* (*Don't Cry*), devoted to the Shan struggle for independence, was released in 2002

After Ad Carabao, in 2001 the SSA invited Thai TV producer Noppon Komarachoon to visit Loi Tailang for the Shan National Day celebrations (Barnes 2001). Noppon's success with *Pai Kep Phaen Din . . . Thi Sin Chat* (Fight for the Promised Land), a TV series based on the story of the Karen struggle for independence which came out after the God's Army's storming of Ratchaburi hospital in early 2000,[8] attracted the attention of the Shan insurgency. They hoped that Noppon could produce a new TV series based on the "heroic" struggle of a Yawd Surk-like character. The project, however, did not make it to the TV screen because of budget considerations.

After this involvement of pop singers and a TV producer in the Shan cause, came a movie, *Phrangchomphu* (Saving Private Tootsie, 2002), inspired by Hollywood's *Saving Private Ryan* (1998) and *Blackhawk Down* (2001). It tells the story of six lady-boys from Thailand who find themselves trapped in the middle of an armed conflict on the Thai-Burmese border and fall under the protection of a leader of the Shan struggle for independence, played by Ad Carabao. The movie portrays Ad Carabao as a Yawd Surk-like character. A few of the songs in the soundtrack were written by Ad. The soundtrack also includes a Shan song, *Ler Hue Lod Lai Pen Kan Jai* (It is My Duty to Fight) sung by one of the soldiers from Loi Tailang.

Thai print media has also written about the struggles of the SSA-S. Yawd Surk often appeared in Thai newspapers and weekly magazine articles. In 2006, a book by Nipatporn and Nuankaew, *Tai Rop Phama* [Shan Fight the Burmese], was published. The book outlines the background history of Shan State, the lives of the people under Burmese military rule, and the SSA-S. It also features an interview with Colonel Yawd Surk in which he shares an account of his life and struggle. Nipatporn Pengkaew, co-author of the book, says this book was written to promote better understanding and sympathy for long-suffering minorities of Burma.

Since the mid-2000s Loi Tailang has become a popular "tourist" destination for Thai media and some entertainers. The SSA holds celebrations and military gatherings as often as four to five times a year. The celebrations are organized according to significant dates on the Shan calendar, such as Shan Resistance Day, Shan National Day, and Shan New Year. Occasionally, Loi Tailang also organizes celebrations according to significant dates of the Thai calendar. In July 2006, when Thailand celebrated the sixtieth anniversary of the Thai king's succession to the throne, the SSA organized a large-scale celebration at its headquarters. Thai newspapers published the story, stating that even the Shan State Army located on Burmese soil worships the Thai king and considers him to be the only remaining Shan prince (Nipatporn 2006).

Various media may have actively participated in this movement for their own purposes, and the SSA-S, drawing upon the support of select groups within the Thai media, has been able to present their struggle to a wider audience. What Thai media have offered to the audience is a picture of a hero who is, in fact, the Thais' "forgotten brother." The message that Thai media have sent to readers can be read as stating that the Shan and the Thai share the same origin. "While these people are suffering," the message goes, "we should sympathize with and support them." Besides, the Burmese are old enemies who, whether or not Thailand is faced with a drug problem, are still bitterly blamed in Thai history books for destroying the Ayutthaya kingdom in 1767. The perception of the Burmese as Thailand's worst enemy is deeply rooted in the Thai psyche. While the Shan and Thai are believed to be ethnic cousins with a similar language and culture, it is comparatively easy for them to take the same side in confronting the Burmese. From the Shan insurgency side, celebrations and building a network with the Thai media create a sense of ethnic solidarity across the border which, in turn, encourages the Thai to take a friendly stance toward the Shan struggle for self-determination.

It would be a mistake, however, to view these networks as constructed by the SSA-S alone. Networks, of course, need to be created, and members of the Shan diaspora in Chiang Mai and Bangkok have played an important role in bringing the Shan insurgency into close contact with Thai media. These networks provide a site of busy traffic and linkages bridged by both Thai sympathizers and the Shan diaspora. It was Sai Mon, a member of Freedom Way and now public relations official for the SSA-S, who made initial contact with Ad Carabao. It was a Thai woman, a girlfriend of Sai Han (son of the SURA founder), another Freedom Way member and now an SSA-S lieutenant, who invited the Thai writer Nipatporn to visit Loi Tailang and to write a book about the Shan struggle. It was a Thai man married to a Shan woman who helped raise funds for the SSA-S from his base in Bangkok and who once in a while comes to Loi Tailang to give donated money to Yawd Surk. The transnational aspect of the Shan insurgency introduces actors who are not permanently embedded in the locality of the struggle. Sai Mon, who mobilizes Shan youths in Chiang Mai to support the movement and also builds a network with the Thai media, is an excellent example of how individuals can operate within several opportunity structures simultaneously. These networks reap the benefit of transnational openings and the porosity of the border. Not only do they mobilize financial, diplomatic, and social capital in the service of an insurgency in the homeland, they find ways to draw support from their host country. The insurgency and its diaspora are intimately tied to one another.

To this end, it is worth considering whether or not the public relations efforts mobilized by the SSA-S and their transnational ethnic networks have made any impact on Thai readership. On a pragmatic level, we can speculate that the Thai will never be like many radical Islamists who view Iraq as a battlefield against the US and have traveled to the country to join the fight (Staniland 2006). On the moral level, I have heard many Shan migrants complain how ordinary Thais cannot distinguish them from ethnic Burman Burmese and refer to them as *khon phama* (Burmese people) or sometimes *ai phuak phama* (the damned Burmese) without being sensitive to the differences between the Burman Burmese and the Shan Burmese. While the representations of the Shan struggle remain positive, the penetration of the alien "others" threatens a mythical national identity and local Thais feel anything but kinship with the poor and displaced Shans struggling to survive within the country's underground migrant economy. On the flip side of the coin, the positive representation of the Shan in Thai media has given rise to a newfound sense of pride among Shan migrants. My Shan migrant informants often say that they are proud that Ad Carabao supports the Shan and they wish there were more people like him. They buy his albums, wear T-shirts bearing his image, and sing "Don't Cry! Shan" in a melody resembling Bob Marley's "No Woman, No Cry." Of all the ironies, the images and ideas that are produced for Thai readership with intent to draw support from them for the Shan have instead come to generate a sense of ethnic pride among the Shan migrants themselves, the other side of the target.

The Insurgency and the New Technology

The Shan insurgency's attempt to reach out to the Shan migrant population in Thailand from the 2000s onwards began with the advent of video CDs as a new domestic movie-making technology. When Freedom Way began producing music to foster nationalist sentiments among its fighters, it was in the era of audio cassettes. With this new mode of movie-making technology, which allows visual images to be presented alongside music, the Shan State Army can now present moving images of its fighters to its target audience. While Freedom Way's music was able to sneak across the border to Shan listeners inside Burma through the illicit channels of piracy and copying, the shift in population, however, has reversed the flow as the Shan insurgency today is aiming at winning the hearts and minds of its migrant population who are now living across the border in Thailand. Since the early 2000s, several VCDs have been produced by members of the SSA-S and others associated with the insurgency under the name of the SSA-S as well as a joint project between SSA-S soldiers and their transnational insurgent counterparts.

The first VCD was produced in 2003 by a group called the Young Turks whose leader is Sai Han, a former Freedom Way member. Sai Han, like many transnational insurgents, wears many hats. Besides being a PR person for the SSA-S and a leader of a music band, he runs Tiger Studio in Chiang Mai where the album was recorded. The band members consist of seven Shan youths living in Chiang Mai. The album *Pun Phon Lae Khon Noom* (Young Shans and Their Duties) is a collection of thirteen songs sung in the Shan language, except for one song recorded in Thai. While the first song celebrates Aung San Suu Kyi's struggle, the remaining songs talk about the Shan struggle for independence and the hardships of being Shan soldiers. There are songs such as "Suk Wan Tai Muea Nai" (The Shan Fight Today), "Wan Koet Moeng Non" (Our Shan Motherland), "Sai Te Ok Tang" (I am Going to War), "Thin Kamnoet" (Our Motherland), and one song sung by a female singer, "Thaew Lang Yang Pai' (To You, My Shan Fighters). The nationalist lyrics of the entire album send out a call for young Shan men and women to participate in national emancipation. For example, the title song of the album, "Young Shans and Their Duties," calls for young Shan men and women to maintain their obligation to their Shan homeland. "Slow but Sure" sends the message that, under tenuous circumstances, we should not give up. Victory may come late but it will come. In "To You, My Shan Fighters," the female singer sings "I will always be there for you, do your best in battle." Another song, "Thin Kamnoet" (Our Motherland), calls for Shan unity to free the motherland. Along with strong nationalist lyrics, the visual component on the VCD comprises images of SSA-S fighters and their military training, footages of war as well as images of rice fields and the beautiful countryside in Shan State. It is noteworthy that images of war scenes in the VCD are taken from existing war movies such as Hollywood's *Hamburger Hill* (1987) and a Thai movie, *Bang Rajan* (2000),[9] mixed with original clips taken within the SSA-S headquarters.

Another VCD, *Wan Luk Fuen* (Revolutionary Day), was produced in 2004 by the Shan State Army band. The band members consisted of seven Shan soldiers and two female singers who were family members of SSA-S soldiers. It was recorded at Loi Tailang studio run by Sai Lao who, in 2000, came down to Chiang Mai with a small team of Shan soldiers to acquire skills in the operation of a mini-DV video camera and basic video editing. The VCD is a collection of thirteen songs sung in the Shan language, except for one song sung in Burmese. The lyrics are a mixture of love songs and nationalist ballads. While the love songs sung by female singers give moral support to Shan soldiers on the front, the nationalist songs talk about fighting and war, and call for Shans to join hands to fight for the revolutionary day. The visual images portrayed in this VCD are similar to the first one mentioned above, including images of SSA-S fighters, military marches, and life at the SSA-S headquarters.

The last and very interesting example is a VCD portraying a special event—when the Shan State National Army (SSNA), a ceasefire group led by Colonel Sai Yi, closed down his camp in Burma and brought one thousand men to join the SSA-S. I have yet to mention that in May 2005, the SSNA, which had been a ceasefire army since 1995, decided to end the ceasefire agreement with the Burmese regime and join the SSA-S to fight against the government (Black and Fields 2006; Chann 2005). The reasons behind this were twofold: (1) The detention of Khun Htoon Oo and other prominent leaders of the Shan Nationalities League for Democracy (SNLD, allied with Aung San Suu Kyi's NLD) in February 2005. These nine leaders were arrested and sentenced to an extreme and unreasonable length of time (79–106 years) in prison; (2) Despite the ceasefire agreement, which granted the group the right to remain armed and to enjoy special autonomy, including business concessions, in early 2005 the SSNA was forced to disarm under the pretext of "Exchanging Arms for Peace" (Maung Chan 2007). The SSNA, left with the choice of either turning in their arms or turning to fight the Burmese Army, chose the latter and merged their forces with the SSA-S. The addition of one thousand SSNA soldiers in 2005 made the SSA-S the strongest ethnic force remaining in combat against the Burmese government.

This VCD features the activities of SSNA from a journey begun at their camp in northern Shan State until they joined hands with the SSA at Loi Tailang. In the beginning, it shows scenes of the camp being demolished, with a bonfire consuming all vehicles and buildings. This is followed by footage of the insurgents' journey through the jungle. The middle of the VCD shows the soldiers trying to cross the Salween River while being attacked by a small group of Burmese soldiers. They manage to cross the river, arrive at Loi Tailang, and join Colonel Yawd Surk of the SSA-S. In actual fact, the SSNA filmed all the above activities for their own records. When the group arrived at Loi Tailang, a technician who worked in the recording studio saw the footage and went on to edit it by adding some Shan songs written by both Shan songwriters inside Burma as well as Freedom Way songs as a soundtrack.

Most of the songs included were political songs written and sung by Sai Mu, the late member of Freedom Way. After adding songs and captions in order to provide details of dates, places, and activities, they made copies and circulated them among SSA-S members. It was only later, when the VCD was given to one of the Shan Youth Group's members in Chiang Mai, that it was copied for sale in the market. As is common, retailers in Chiang Mai copy freely from any original copy. The VCD was then widely circulated and bought by members of the Shan migrant community in Chiang Mai. Visiting Loi Tailang for the second time in 2006, I took along the VCD, which had just been released, with me. After a man who had been involved in the making of the original VCD saw the copied version of his VCD, he said: "If I had known that it would sell, I would have made it better." Of all the ironies, it is hard to deny the power of VCD technology. Not only does footage of the insurgents abandoning their camp constitute a "movie," but, once treated as a movie it comes to be mass-produced and distributed through the same illicit channels as Hollywood films. Along these lines, VCD technology, which allows images to be copied easily on a personal computer disc drive, helps blur the line between media makers and media distributors.

Regarding visual representation, we can place the images in these VCDs into five categories: (1) Images of sorrow and tragedy of people affected by war, which are taken from outside sources); (2) Images of the military marching and training, intended to instill in viewers a sense of solidarity and the notion of physical strength and discipline; (3) Images of singers in a recording studio or performing on stage during military festivals; (4) Images of military leaders, in particular, a portrait of Yawd Surk; and (5) Images of ritual or spectacular events, such as when two Shan armed groups united. In addition to the images related to the military, this last category presents Shan women wearing traditional Shan costumes against beautiful landscapes in Shan State.

From these observations, two points can be made. First, these VCDs can be seen as an effort on the part of the SSA-S and members of the diaspora to cultivate support from the migrant audience. The messages conveyed through these visual images and lyrics can be called "insurgent morality" for they not only transport the audience to "be there" as a witness to the events, but also invite them to join in the fighting; in other words, to join the "feeling" of fighting. Video technology can produce "virtual reality" to the extent to which movie images allow one to observe ongoing life in another place. Regardless of whether real fighting is taking place or not, the audience is invited to participate in this "virtual" national emancipation. Second, coupled with the transnational flows of objects, media, and ideas, VCD technology that allows for the compilation and mixing of forms and genres as well as copying have come to facilitate a new connection between the insurgency and its migrant population, bringing them into closer contact with one another in a way that audio technology of the former era was never able to do.

The question remains, however, can we assume that the insurgency's attempt to reach out to the Shan migrant population has been successful? In general, Shan migrant audiences can purchase these VCDs at a local store, from festival bootleggers, or from motorbike vendors and pick-up truck drivers who carry a small collection of pirated Shan VCDs along with Shan food to sell at construction sites around the city. Even if people do not purchase them, these VCDs can be heard and seen at Shan festivals held six or seven times a year in the city of Chiang Mai. At the fairs, bootleggers will play Shan VCDs on a TV set with speakers all day long. The VCDs produced by the SSA-S are often played repeatedly by the music bootleggers. During the festivals, I observed that the audience, especially males, always formed a big crowd to watch these images. When a Shan audience gathers in front of a TV set to watch these images in a mass public viewing, can we then assume they are attracted to the message being transmitted by the insurgency movement?

Many of the audience members with whom I spoke say they like to watch these images along with listening to lyrics expressing strong nationalist sentiments because it makes them "feel good" that the Shans are still fighting. The VCDs were designed to inspire patriotic pride among the audience by representing masculinist, militarized notions of a "nation." They therefore feed into the imagination of the audience that Shans have not yet given up. Some Shan men say that these VCDs expose them to the "reality" and hardships of the battlefield. When asked if exposure to the images and emotive cultural symbols motivated them to join the army, many Shan migrant audiences commented that they were only interested in watching, not taking part in the action or joining the army. Some added that they did not want to be killed by the enemy. Others said they had responsibility for their families back home. They liked the fact that someone had made these videos because through them they came to know about Shan fighting with the Burmese and they could see images they had never seen or never had a chance to see if they were still living in Burma.

Further contradictions arise in this field of audience reception. During two visits to Loi Tailang in 2006, I had informal conversations with many low-ranking soldiers. This included asking them how they came to know about the SSA-S and Loi Tailang, and what made them decide to quit their jobs and join the army. Many of them said they had actually migrated to work in Thailand years before joining the army, and while working in Thailand they came to know about the SSA-S through media consumption, both Thai and Shan media, though they did not specifically mention the VCDs I have discussed here. Thus, we have a complex situation where, on the one hand, the media exposes migrants to knowledge and information that would be absent in the homeland. Acquiring a new understanding of the wider world from exposure to broader currents and imagery about the struggle has made some quit their jobs to join the fight. On the other hand, I often heard that one of the reasons Shan men migrate to work in Thailand is precisely because their parents do not want them to be recruited as Shan soldiers.

There is a Shan expression, *jap suek* (lit., captive soldier), which is often used when Shan male migrants express their fear of being taken from their villages to be Shan soldiers for the Shan insurgency. Many Shans say they would rather be a migrant than a recruit. "Being a migrant, I work for myself. I can spend money I earn or send it to my family back home, whereas being a soldier, I can die any time. And if I do not die, I only earn one hundred baht (US$2.5) a month," one Shan man said. Another complained that "In the Shan State, every time we harvest, the first portion is to feed the Burmese army, the second is for the Shan army, the third is for the Wa, and only the fourth portion is for our family." This factor has not only driven them to seek their fortune in Thailand, it also contributes to our understanding of why they do not share the sentiments the insurgency tries to foster in them. They feel they have enough involvement with the army already.

Conclusion

In situating Freedom Way both in the broader context of Burmese politics and within the particularity of the Shan insurgency movement, we come to understand the dynamics and complexity of ethnic insurgency in the period from the mid-1980s to 2006. As far as their music is concerned, Freedom Way offers a fascinating history of politics inside Burma, much of which has been devoted to the politics within and outside Shan armed organizations and the government policy which has affected people's lives. As far as technology is concerned, Freedom Way's history reveals a period of technological shift from the cassette era to the video CD as the new domestic movie-making technology. The inexpensive and accessible new communication technology of VCD has also helped transform Shan pop music from literacy into visual culture and allowed images of the Shan "nation" to be constructed.

What is new here is that not only does new technology offer a powerful tool to communicate with its dispersed population not predicated on the singularity of the nation, but we are also moving to a more democratic process in which media is no longer solely the product of elites and institutions. As for the members of the group, examining their lives offers a rare insight into the nature of Shan armed resistance that evolved from dependence on narcotic trade and rivalry over personal power to symbolic and transnational insurgency. Seeing their lives woven together through a mixture of songs, migrants, and transnational space, we come to realize the important role they played in feeding the Shan populace a dose of nationalist sentiment with their songs.

On a different note we may ask, what is it the Shan insurgency is fighting for today? As I have attempted to show, the Shan insurgency today is fighting against drugs in a bid for legitimacy and international support. It is also busy building networks with the Thai as well as making itself visible to the Shan migrant population with the aim of winning their hearts and minds. We can perhaps characterize contemporary Shan insurgency as a "symbolic insurgency," whose strategies are employed through the cultural and political realm and whose fighting is mediated by mediascapes. In suggesting that the Shan insurgency today has become a symbolic insurgency to the point that the real fighting is hardly taking place, I am, however, not arguing that the struggle has ended. The insurgency has not died. It lives on in the minds of many Shan migrants. It may not be a real struggle but it is virtually being rediscovered within the spirit of many Shan migrants who today no longer deal with Burma on a day-to-day basis but come to identify with the struggle even more than before through the means of insurgent media. In the age of virtual insurgency, we may conclude that what these migrants are being recruited for is to "join the feeling." "A revolutionary never dies," Che Guevara would say, but the concept of revolutionary has to be refashioned so that the seeds of it, now dispersed outside the land, can be rediscovered within the Shans' own hearts and minds.

Notes

1. Burma is divided into seven states and seven divisions. While "divisions" are predominantly Burman, "states" are home to particular ethnic minorities. The seven states are Arakan (Rakhine), Chin, Kachin, Karen (Kayin), Karenni (Kayah), Mon, and Shan. I use "Shan State" here to refer to the present geographical area of Shan State. However, the terms "Shan States" is also used when discussing several states ruled by Shan chiefs which existed before and during the British annexation, when the Shan States remained autonomous as a protectorate.

2. The Shan call themselves "Tai" while the Thai call them "Thai Yai" and the Burman call them "Shan." Here. "Tailand" symbolically refers to "Shanland" as an independent nation.

3. The Shan use Sai, literally "man," in front of male names to indicate male identity whereas Nang is used in front of female names.

4. The transcription of Shan words in this chapter is slightly adapted from the *Shan-English Dictionary* by Sao Tern Moeng (1995). However, I have made changes in the transcription of some sounds. In some Shan words that have Thai equivalents, I follow the Thai transcription system. My intention is to give non-Shan speaking readers a general sense of the way the word is pronounced.

5. The lyrics of the song provide a play on two terms with similar pronunciation, Socialist and *sod-sad-lid* (corruption). During the Socialist government led by Ne Win from 1962 to 1988, many people felt that the Burmese Way to Socialism was, in fact, equivalent to corruption. The song therefore plays with these two words by saying that Socialism is *sod-sad-lid.*

6. The cause of his death is unknown to Sai Mu's family. His daughter told me she believed he was poisoned. His friends said he had been drinking a lot over

the years before he died which might be the cause of his death. Some suspected that his death might have been due to a drug overdose.

7. The four-cut policy aims to suppress the support for rebel groups by cutting off four main links to them: food, funds, information, and recruits. These links are currently seen as existing between the insurgents and their families and local villagers. The policy is implemented by terrorizing, controlling, and impoverishing the civilian population in resistance areas so that they have neither the opportunity nor the means to provide any form of support to the opposition. In practice, as SHRF (Shan Human Rights Foundation) and SWAN (Shan Women Action Network) note, many villages in the resistance areas have become targets of forced relocation, crop destruction, ethnic terror tactics which include rape, beating, and intimidation, and the depopulation of the central Shan State area to isolate the insurgencies. Deprived of their lands and livelihood, forced to work without pay by the military, and constantly fearful of torture or execution on suspicion of supporting the Shan resistance, many of these villagers have ended up fleeing to Thailand. See SHRF 1998; SHRF 2003; Smith 1999.

8. God's Army, formed in 1997, was an armed revolutionary Christian insurgent group that opposed the then military junta of Burma. It was led by twin brothers, Johnny and Luther Htoo, who were estimated to be only ten years of age at the time. They were a breakaway group from the main ethnic rebel army along the border, the Karen National Union (KNU). In January 2000, ten members of God's Army seized a hospital in Ratchaburi, Thailand. The group held 700–800 patients and staff members hostage for 22 hours. They demanded the Thai government open its borders to the Karen refugees and provide treatment for their wounded. Thai security forces stormed the hospital, killing all ten of the gunmen. See BBC News "Profile: God's Army," 24 January 2000, http://news.bbc.co.uk/2/hi/asia-pacific/616772.stm.

9. *Bang Rajan* is a 2000 Thai historical drama film depicting the battles of the Siamese village of Bang Rajan against the Burmese invaders in 1767. The village is remembered in Thai history for its alleged resistance against the Burmese invaders in the war that ended the kingdom of Ayutthaya.

References

Anderson, Benedict. 1991. *Imagined Communities: Reflections on the Origin and Spread of Nationalism*. London: Verso.

Ball, Desmond and Hazel Lang. 2001. *Factionalism and the Ethnic Insurgent Organizations*. Canberra: Australia National University.

Bangkok Post. 1988. "Burma Students Should Return, Says Khun Sa." December 18.

Barnes, William. 2001. "Fighting on a New Front in a Forgotten War." *Asiaweek* 27(2), January 19.

Black, Mihchael, and Roland Fields. 2006. "On Patrol with the Shan State Army." *Irrawaddy* 14(7): 12–13.

Chann, Nandar. 2005. "Shan Group Denies Regime Allegation." *Irrawaddy Online*, June 14. http://www2.irrawaddy.com/article.php?art_id=4711.

Chao Tzang Yawnghwe. 1987. *The Shan of Burma: Memoirs of a Shan Exile*. Singapore: Institute of Southeast Asian Studies.

Coster, Alice. 2007. "Shan State Army: Fight for Peace." *The Nation*, February 20.

Cowell, Adrian. 2005. "Opium Anarchy in the Shan State of Burma." In *Trouble in the Triangle: Opium and Conflict in Burma*, eds. Martin Jelsma, Tom Kramer, and Pietje Vervest, 1–23. Chiang Mai: Silkworm Books.

Fredholm, Michael. 1993. *Burma: Ethnicity and Insurgency*. Westport: Praeger.

International Crisis Group (ICG). 2003. *Myanmar Backgrounder: Ethnic Minority Politics*. ICG Asia Report no. 52. https://www.crisisgroup.org/asia/south-east-asia/myanmar/myanmar-backgrounder-ethnic-minority-politics.

Jelsma, Martin, Tom Kramer, and Pietje Vervest, eds. 2005. *Trouble in the Triangle: Opium and Conflict in Burma*. Chiang Mai: Silkworm Books.

Kearney, Michael. 1995. "The Local and the Global: The Anthropology of Globalization and Transnationalism." *Annual Review of Anthropology* 24: 547–66.

Lintner, Bertil. 1990. *Outrage: Burma's Struggle for Democracy*. Bangkok: White Lotus.

———. 1994. *Burma in Revolt: Opium and Insurgency Since 1948*. Bangkok: White Lotus.

Maung Chan. 2007. "Discussion on Contemporary Situation in Shan State with Sai Wansai of SDU." http://www.peacehall.com/news/gb/english/2005/11/200511300029.shtml.

McCoy, Alfred W. 1991. *The Politics of Heroin: CIS Complicity in the Global Drug Trade*. New York: Lawrence Hill Books.

———. 1999. "Requiem for a Drug Lord: State and Commodity in the Career of Khun Sa." In *States and Illegal Practices*, ed. Josiah McC. Heyman, 129–67. Oxford: Berg.

Nipatporn Pengkaew. 2006. *Hoksip pi nai luang bon dòi tai lang* [Sixty Years Anniversary of the Thai King's Succession to the Throne at Loi Tailang], *Krungthep Thurakit*, June 16.

Nipatporn Pengkaew and Nuankaew Burapawat. 2006. *Tai rop phama* [Shan Fight the Burmese]. Bangkok: Openbooks.

Safran, William. 1991. "Diasporas in Modern Societies: Myths of Homeland and Return." *Diaspora* 1(1): 83–93.

Salween Post. 2005. Interview with Yawd Surk, vol. 20, January 7–12, February 1–15.

Sao Tern Moeng. 1995. *Shan-English Dictionary*. Kensington, MD: Dunwood Press.

Shan Human Rights Foundation (SHRF). 1998. *Dispossessed: Forced Relocation and Extrajudicial Killings in Shan State*. Chiang Mai: SHRF.

———. 2003. *Charting the Exodus from Shan State: Patterns of Refugee Flows into Northern Chiang Mai Province of Thailand, 1997–2002*. Chiang Mai: SHRF. http://shanhumanrights.org/old_version/images/stories/report/Reports/chartingtheexdous_final.pdf.

Shan Human Rights Foundation (SHRF) and Shan Women's Action Network (SWAN). 2002. *License to Rape: The Burmese Military Regime's Use of Sexual Violence in the Ongoing War in Shan State, Burma*. Chiang Mai: SHRF and SWAN.

Shan Women's Action Network (SWAN). 2003. *Shan Refugees: Dispelling the Myth*. Chiang Mai: SWAN.

Sheffer, Gabriel. 1986. *Modern Diasporas in International Politics*. London: Croom Helm.

Silverstein, Josef. 1958. "Politics in the Shan State: The Question of Secession from the Union of Burma." *The Journal of Asian Studies* 18(1): 43–57.

Smith, Martin. 1999. *Burma: Insurgency and the Politics of Ethnicity*. London: Zed Books.

Staniland, Paul. 2006. "Defeating Transnational Insurgencies: The Best Offense is a Good Fence." *The Washington Quarterly* 29(1): 21–40.

Taylor, Robert. 1982. "Perceptions of Ethnicity in the Politics of Burma." *Southeast Asian Journal of Social Science* 10(1): 7–22.

Tucker, Shelby. 2001. *Burma: The Curse of Independence*. London: Pluto Press.

Whitmayer, Joseph. 2002. "Elites and Popular Nationalism." *The British Journal of Sociology* 53(3): 321–41.

Yawd Surk. 2006. *Kuk khop sip pi òm wang kueng* [Tenth Year Anniversary of Non-submission] (no publication details).

Yuenyong Opakul. 2002. *Mai tong rong hai* [Don't Cry]. Bangkok: Mingmit.

Contributors

AMPORN JIRATTIKORN is an assistant professor at the Department of Social Science and Development at Chiang Mai University, Thailand. She received her PhD in anthropology from the University of Texas at Austin in 2008. Amporn's research interests are in the areas of media flows and mobility of people across national boundaries, with particular focus on the movement of Shan migrants from Myanmar into Thailand. Amporn's recent publication has centered on the construction of migrant identities through media consumption, cross-border religious movement along the Thailand-Myanmar border, and the formation of Shan nationalist consciousness.

MARIE-EVE BLANC is a research coordinator at the University of Montreal, Quebec (Canada). She holds a PhD in sociology from the Université de Provence, Aix-en-Provence (France) and is a specialist in Vietnamese Overseas Communities with a focus on health prevention behaviors and pharmaceutical drug uses. She worked on civil society and HIV prevention in Vietnam. Her research was included in *Rethinking Vietnam*, edited by Duncan McCargo (Routledge, 2004). She was also co-editor of *Sociétés Asiatiques face au Sida* (L'Harmattan, 2000).

KEES VAN DIJK is emeritus professor of the history of modern Islam in Indonesia at Leiden University and a former senior researcher of the KITLV/ Royal Institute of Southeast Asian and Caribbean Studies (Leiden). The title of his PhD thesis was *Rebellion under the banner of Islam: The Darul Islam in Indonesia* (KITLV, 1981). Among his other publications are

The Netherlands Indies and the Great War, 1914–1918 (KITLV, 2007) and *Pacific Strife: The Great Powers and Their Political and Economic Rivalries in Asia and the Western Pacific, 1870–1914* (Amsterdam University Press, 2015).

VOLKER GRABOWSKY is professor of Thai studies at the Asia-Africa-Institute, University of Hamburg. He is (co-)author of several books on the history and culture of Tai ethnic groups, including the translations and analyses of Tai Lue chroncicles, such as *Chronicles of Chiang Khaeng* (2008) and *Chronicles of Sipsòng Panna* (2012). Since 2011 he had directed various projects pertaining to the manuscript cultures of the Tai peoples in the Upper Mekong valley. Among his most recent publications is *Ethnic and Religious Identities and Integration in Southeast Asia* (co-edited with Ooi Keat Gin, SEATIDE-Silkworm Books Series, 2017).

GEOFFREY C. GUNN is emeritus professor, Nagasaki University. He is a graduate of Australian universities and the author of several books on Indochina, including *Rebellion in Laos: Peasant and Politics in a Colonial Backwater* (Westview, 1990); *Rice Wars in Colonial Vietnam: The Great Famine and the Viet Minh Road to Power* (Rowman & Littlefield, 2014); and *Monarchical Manipulation in Cambodia: France, Japan, and the Sihanouk Crusade for Independence* (NIAS Press, 2018).

JUN HONNA is professor at the College of International Relations, Ritsumeikan University. His current research focuses on politics in Indonesia and regional security in Southeast Asia. His book *Military Politics and Democratization in Indonesia* was published by Routledge in 2003.

JOYCE CHAPMAN LEBRA holds a PhD in Japanese history from Harvard and an Honorary Doctor of Humane Letters from the University of Minnesota. She was professor of the history of Japan and India at the University of Colorado. She is author or editor of fifteen books, including *The Indian National Army and Japan*, and *Japanese-trained Armies in Southeast Asia*. She has lectured extensively at universities around the world.

FREDERIK RETTIG is co-editor of *Colonial Armies in Southeast Asia* (Routledge, 2005) and has published in the *Journal of Vietnamese Studies* and *South East Asia Research*, including a special issue in the latter on the Nghe-Tinh Soviets (1930–31) in central-north Vietnam. His research interests include Vietnamese colonial soldiers and workers during the interwar period, and women warriors and revolutionaries in Southeast Asia.

FELICE NOELLE RODRIGUEZ has a doctorate in history from the University of the Philippines. Her published work includes Philippine warfare, urban history, nationalism, the social impact of religion, and selected aspects of Southeast Asian history, as well as a translation from Spanish of a nineteenth-century book.

ROSANNE RUTTEN is a researcher in anthropology and sociology of non-Western societies at the University of Amsterdam. Her interests include social movements and collective action, land rights, rural change, and livelihood strategies of peasants and workers, and her research and publications have focused on issues in the Philippines and Indonesia.

HENK SMEETS (1943) is a historian who, among other things, has been coordinator of the Advisory Board for the Welfare of Moluccans; advisor for Moluccan affairs of the minister of Education, Culture and Sciences; member of the board of directors of the Moluccan Historical Museum and of the National Centre for Moluccan Education in Utrecht; and business director of the Institute for Sociological and Economic Research (Erasmus University Rotterdam). Since 2010 he has been chairman of the Vught Museum and as such has been involved in the restoration of Barrack 1B (Camp Vught) and the DePetrus meeting space in Vught. Together with Fridus Steijlen he published the study *In Nederland gebleven: De geschiedenis van Molukkers 1951–2006* [Still in the Netherlands: The history of Moluccans 1951–2006] (Bakker, 2006).

CARLYLE A. THAYER is Emeritus Professor, The University of New South Wales at the Australian Defence Force Academy, Canberra. He is a Vietnam country specialist and the author of *Vietnam People's Army: Development and Modernization* (Institute of Defence and Strategic Studies, 2009) and *The Vietnam People's Army Under Doi Moi* (Institute of Southeast Asian Studies, 1994).

Index

D

T

Y

Z